WRITING AFTER WAR

WRITING AFTER WAR

American War Fiction from Realism to Postmodernism

JOHN LIMON

New York   Oxford
OXFORD UNIVERSITY PRESS
1994

Oxford University Press

Oxford   New York   Toronto
Delhi   Bombay   Calcutta   Madras   Karachi
Kuala Lumpur   Singapore   Hong Kong   Tokyo
Nairobi   Dar es Salaam   Cape Town
Melbourne   Auckland   Madrid

and associated companies in
Berlin   Ibadan

Published by Oxford University Press, Inc.
200 Madison Avenue, New York, New York 10016

Oxford is a registered trademark of Oxford University Press

Library of Congress Cataloging-in-Publication Data
Limon, John.
Writing after war : American war fiction from realism to postmodernism /
John Limon.
p.   cm.   Includes index.
ISBN 0-19-508758-5 — ISBN 0-19-508759-3 (pbk.)
1. War stories, American—History and criticism.
2. American fiction—20th century—History and criticism.
3. American fiction—19th century—History and criticism.
4. Postmodernism (Literature)—United States.
5. Realism—In literature.
I. Title.   PS374.W35L56   1994
813.009'358—dc20   93-33717

2 4 6 8 9 7 5 3 1
Printed in the United States of America
on acid-free paper

For Frances and Emma

Acknowledgments

I am very grateful to Williams College and the American Council of Learned Societies for their support of the writing of this book. I am also grateful to the Arizona Board of Regents for permission to use material adapted from an article published in the *Arizona Quarterly*. I would like to express my deep appreciation to four people who made it possible for me to reproduce the etchings on the cover: to the artist himself, Günter Grass; to Grace Budd; to Gerhard Steidl; and especially to Helmut Frielinghaus, whose kindness was essential. I could not have worked on the book without the strategic endorsements of Robert Ferguson and Frederick Crews. Michael Bell and Warner Berthoff read the entire manuscript with humbling precision; I have occasionally wondered, and now wonder again with more anxiety, about the presumption of expressing public gratitude for help in the production of a very faulty work. Not only are the faults mine; many of them have been detected, and I have retained them only because I prefer them to yawning gaps. I could not have gotten anywhere on this project without the generosity and advice of Frances Restuccia; the same cannot be said about Emma Limon; but without the existence of both of them, I would hardly have had any interest in writing this book at all.

Contents

WRITING AFTER WAR

The Emperor, surrounded by his suite of officers and courtiers, was mounted on a bob-tailed chestnut mare, a different horse from the one he had ridden at the review. Leaning over and gracefully holding a gold lorgnette to his eye, he was looking at a soldier lying on his face with blood on his bare head.

Tolstoy, *War and Peace*

Introduction

Is war beautiful? I have not seen combat, and reading books about war has not had the effect of putting me on intimate terms with it. I agree with Socrates who disputes the paralogism that if the rhapsodes are expert in Homer, and if Homer wrote *The Iliad*, then the rhapsodes must be expert in war. This book is premised on the faint hope that something may be made of the ignorance and naïveté I have managed to retain in the presence of war literature. Why—if the history of literature began with war and has never forsworn it—do I nonetheless feel that literature is a failure in capturing the experience of war for beauty? This book will either justify that judgment or prove that my naïveté is congenitally adamant.

It is, at any rate, naïveté of a certain kind, and an equal and opposite innocence is also possible on the same subject. The most universal way to put the competing version of radical ingenuousness is that war is perfectly available to literature because what, to a man anyway, is more beautiful?[1] This dovetails conveniently with another challenge, apparently from a different region of the intellectual map: must not power and domination inhere in any form of discourse, even one apparently quite nonviolent? (The latter point is occasionally feminist. The former is apt to be age-of-feminism masculinist: how lupine we cannot help being!) These two questions, both rhetorical, together produce an unexpected synthesis: representation if anything is closer to war than to, for instance, peace, since what is representation but aesthetic violence done to reality? War may sometimes be beautiful, but beauty is always bellicose. Writing *is* war.[2]

The latter naïveté appears to have almost all of the history of culture on its side. You might be inclined to wonder how literature could proceed without war; if Western literature begins with an account of the Akhaian expedition, then the yearning of neophyte male writers for combat material is a literary version of ontogeny craving phylogeny. Writers who miss the available or most pertinent war—for example, Henry James or Fitzgerald or Faulkner or Pynchon—will wonder not what the failure means for their manhood (if they are men) so much as for their art. The most reasonable assumption is not that writing and war are skewed enterprises, but that they have a perdurable affinity.

You have to get over, apparently, these simplicities: that literature is a mode of beauty but war is the perfection of squalid disarray; that the experience of literature is private and peaceful but war is, to quote William Tecumseh Sherman precisely, war. These antitheses have the distinction of seeming both obvious and obtuse. I cling to them for the pragmatic reason that I believe I have noticed that the literature of war perennially concerns itself with this odd self-challenge: why, since war is ugly, does writing beautify it? (What would be sacrificed by literature in not beautifying it?) I believe I can trace this question to Homer; it is as if literature cannot help modeling a beautiful object out of raw material acknowledged to be unpromising. What is the relationship—what is the meaning of the courtship—of war and beauty? If the first literary war was *for* beauty, why should literature reward combatants with exactly what they require, a Helen for every Greek, rather than deprive them, like Lysistrata, of the thing that makes them fight? Why should it not congratulate itself when it so deprives them?

I want to suggest that the answer is at least partly historical: war makes possible, or helps make possible, literary history. I am taken with the idea that what determines literary history (war or, for another example, science) is uncontainable by literature. My concern is with what authors do not know, what contexts they cannot textualize, despite all the ways of ruling the subject illegitimate, for example, the New Historical (Walter Michaels: "the only relation literature as such has to culture as such is that it is a part of it"),[3] the deconstructive (Paul de Man: "the bases for historical knowledge are not empirical facts but written texts, even if these masquerade in the guise of wars or revolutions"),[4] the writerly (Norman Mailer: "the one mind a novelist cannot enter is the mind of a novelist superior to himself").[5] *Il n'y a pas de hors*: something. This is, despite our taste for fragmentation and marginalization, the essential form of all postmodernist doctrine, itself an effect, I shall claim, of World War II. But literature, as I argued elsewhere,[6] has no peculiar history—it is the thing that has no peculiar history, since if it had one, it would be classifiably something else, for example, science, myth, religion, or fashion. Literature is intellectual endeavor that cannot produce a coherent account of time; thus it is intellectual history that can only have faithless relations with all genres of monolithic history.

Assume that war is the most vivid of historical markers and, along with science and technology, the most definitive sign of modernity for a discipline that is historically in search of exterior demarcations, but which cannot incorporate any such unitary and unilateral historical reductions. The first corollary would be that novelties of literary technique designed to internalize the modernity of the newest war must exhibit their own recalcitrance or failure. A story from Michael Herr comes painfully but usefully close to refuting this point, but I think it supports my argument after all. A brutally mad soldier tells Herr a brief parable: "Patrol went up the mountain. One man came back. He died before he could tell us what happened."

At first glance, this anecdote, which I have re-related in its entirety, is a fine example of something new in literary technique perfectly correlative with a novelty of war. The tale goes a long way toward identifying post-modernism, as a technical or stylistic denomination, with Vietnam: in the deadpan madness of the tale is a taste of lowbrow, American, punk post-modernism; in its self-reference (it reads like a John Barth exercise: write the story of a story that fails to be told) is a précis of highbrow, international, post-structuralist postmodernism. Like *Gravity's Rainbow*, like *Dispatches* as a whole, it brings these two discrete versions of postmodernism impossibly together. Vietnam, it could be argued, is the source of a unified post-modern sensibility that has two faces (American postmodernism following French, as America followed France to Vietnam): where reality at its most demented met fabulation at *its* most demented.

But something odd happens when the story is framed. Herr's comment on it is a quiet usurpation: "what a resonant story he told me, as one-pointed and resonant as any war story I ever heard, it took me a year to understand it." Note of course that Herr's laconicism mimics the soldier's though it is placed in advance; but register also the inversion, since the soldier's tale is about a premature foreclosing of explanation and Herr's is about an almost open-ended maturation of it. Another way to put this is that the story is, precisely, deadened and pointless. Nevertheless, the story is, to Herr, superlatively resonant and one-pointed.

The negative relationship of the soldier's tale and Herr's—though they are the same tale—comes out best in Herr's anticipatory unriddling of the parable, by means of a dizzyingly simple résumé of the sociopathic soldier's career. "In 1965 he'd been the only survivor in a platoon of the Cav wiped out going into the Ia Drang Valley. In '66 he'd come back with the Special Forces and one morning after an ambush he'd hidden under the bodies of his team while the VC walked all around them with knives, making sure."[7] The inference is that the teller of the tale is the tale's protagonist: it is a story about his own death prior to any possible communication, including his own parable, a story about his own madness disguised as a subtle form of enlightenment just as his death has been disguised as madness. If the soldier evaded the Cong by faking death, he evades Herr by feigning life. We have a sense of unlocking the parable here, which is, by the circular logic of parables, equal to joining a community of initiates, defined as those who know how to understand such parables, so that you cannot join the interpretive community if you are not already in it. This is basically a meta-parable, but it has the peculiar feature that to be admitted to the interpretive clique, you have to recognize (so long as you are not the soldier himself) your exclusion from it, by two criteria.

First, the soldier's position is exclusive because he knows, in a sense I wish to honor without knowing myself what I am talking about, something of what it means to die. (Herr says elsewhere that the death of a friend is the closest you come to your own death.) Knowledge of war is faulty insofar as only survivors write memoirs, yet war is war only if it generates nonsurvivors. The most daring war writers—for example, Herr and Pynchon and Tolstoy—act on the necessity of representing the point of view of the dead by representing the afterlives of casualties who feel, approximately, like fatalities. The approximation, atrophied descendant of classical visits to the underworld, is inevitably the operative fact.

Second, the soldier's position is exclusive because he is not merely the teller and protagonist of his tale—he is its sole audience. The complete set of all potential cognoscenti of the story has been wiped out by the terms of the story itself. War for this soldier is a way no one else will ever be, to adapt Hemingway's phrase adopted by Herr. If war uniquely resists discourse because language is denied to the dead who are war's single necessary element, it is also the case that the survivors' discourse is peculiarly self-referential: they tell stories to themselves about themselves, as if to survive is as different from mere living as death—since their community is with the dead—while the rest of us look on stupidly. "We were the survivors [writes Siegfried Sassoon]; few among us would ever tell the truth to our friends and relatives in England. We were carrying something in our heads which belonged to us alone, and to those we had left behind in battle."[8] Herr's elliptical story has two foci: is it a victim's or a survivor's tale?

The final question—the fact that it can be asked—attests to the tale's hermetic aspect: we cannot communicate even with veterans if their interpretive society welcomes the dead rather than the living. On the other hand, Herr's invitation to understand the story, even the story's introversion, has induced me to universalize it: it is, on my elaboration, neither a particularly postmodern story nor an artifact uniquely of Vietnam. By giving the story "resonance," I have trespassed on its solitude; it no longer belongs to the soldier alone, though the story is about his exclusive ownership of it. This seems an impregnable paradox, yet the anecdote already has a tradition of commentaries, and the usual assumption is that Herr simply equals the mad soldier insofar as he has untransmissible knowledge. The charge is that this sacerdotal privacy is the essence of war's mysterious beauty for men.[9] My own opinion is that Herr's reticence subsumes but compromises the soldier's. *Dispatches*, after all, aims toward this climactic revelation: "Vietnam, Vietnam, Vietnam, we've all been there." (If we are estranged from the truth of Vietnam—if we are estranged from the craziness and danger of our home-front lives—then we are not far distant from the experience of the Vietnam grunt.) Just as Herr tenders this opaque anecdote as an illumination of Vietnam, he bombards us with unsorted information (technical terms, slang, acronyms) in imitation, perhaps, of the unmeaning bombardment of Khe Sanh.[10] You had to be there—you are.

Dispatches, in short, is the most convincing contemporary attempt to establish an analogy of war and literature. The book endeavors, by metaphoric virtuosity, by metaphors that brilliantly succeed in sensationally failing, to bring Vietnam, still undomesticated, home. It is, however, only in terms of such radically oxymoronic tours de force (here, declares the book about its own picture of Vietnam, is an unlike likeness) that we can begin to imagine a metaphoric leap to modern war in literature. It is by way of what the text says it cannot say that we infer the presence of Vietnam. Conversely, though the soldier's story may serve as an emblem of war's masculine allure, still we have to notice that war is most fascinating, thus, where least narratable; and that even a minimal narration of it (instead of darkness we get a parable about darkness with an illuminating frame) is tantamount to replacing one object of fascination with another, guarded secrecy with a mystified eloquence. To get from war to literature, even in this case, requires a mistranslation; my ambition is to expose, describe, diagnose, and taxonomize, as exactly as I can, all such transfigurations.

They are, first of all, nearly always metonymic. The substitutions that lead from war to literature do not, as a rule, pretend like Herr's even to be paradoxically metaphoric. I shall use, primarily, Elaine Scarry's war theorizing to dissect the metonymic strategies that make possible the various itineraries from war to peace. I will consider such phenomena as these: William Dean Howells, to produce realism in *A Hazard of New Fortunes*, replaces the Civil War with the labor wars of the 80s, and the labor wars with controversies within labor reporting, and journalistic infighting with the war for realism itself, so that, at long last, war evasion becomes the moral and aesthetic equivalent of war; Fitzgerald moves us, as the basis of his modernism, from the Great War to *The Great Gatsby*, with football, cheating at golf, and the manufacturing of a fictitious World Series as increments; Hemingway rejects the metaphoric closure of the bullfight (in an early draft at the beginning as well as the end of *The Sun Also Rises*) and the metaphoric connection of war and writing by means of a bullfight aesthetic, in favor of starting the book with Cohn's boxing, then his football, then his tennis, then his bridge, then his career as a novelist, and ending the book with his absence altogether (fetishistic metonymy is the basis of *Hemingway's* modernism); metafictionists of the 60s generate their own version of international high postmodernism by avoiding direct contact with Vietnam but using verbal playfulness, at its most programmatic an unpleasantly belligerent playfulness, as a kind of homeopathy.

It is close to the truth to say that literary history progresses by inverting, rather than internalizing, the lessons (formal, narratologicial, technical) of contemporaneous warfare. Only the old conflicts can be beautifully narrated; *The Iliad* begins literary history by demonstrating this. (The fall from duel war is the fall into literature.) The theme is not, of course, exclusively American. Nevertheless it seems accurate to say, approximately, that America is "a country made by war," in which method of construction it is unique among modern nations. For an American novelist to miss war is to miss, apparently, America. But American novelists, or rather those who define or represent literary periods, *keep* missing war, which is a first approximation of how war determines American literary history. I therefore begin with "Rip Van Winkle," ancestor of *Hazard* and *Gatsby* and *The Sun Also Rises*, and progenitor of *Beloved* (whose eighteen missing years elide the Civil War), *The Natural* (whose absent fifteen years include the duration of World War II), and *Lolita* (the three years of "Dolorès Disparue" are nearly concomitant with Korea). "Rip Van Winkle" is the American inauguration of fiction as the absence of an epic, an inaugural, war.

1

The Art of War:
The Contest and the Duel

Toward the beginning of our anthologies, Rip Van Winkle flees his wife—
the shrew, the termagant, the virago—to go hunting in the Catskills.[1] Rip's
henpeckedness is no particular credit to his gender, and his hunting is not
on a heroic scale (he stalks squirrels and pigeons); nevertheless, even men
with a somewhat stronger title to the attributes of traditional masculinity,
such as the hardboiled friends of Jake Barnes, know enough to flee women
and go fishing rather than confront a superior female ruthlessness. So off in
Irving's tale goes a man with man's best friend—a henpecked dog with the
nostalgic name "Wolf"—to indulge at least a poor man's fantasy of a return
to the better days of undomesticated hunting and killing.

   This is one way to begin to retell the story; I would guess that in
the American mythic imagination, if the American imagination still makes
reference to literature, this is the beginning of the story as everyone remembers it. But the story also contains a rather different flight. Rip, of course,
manages by his comatose twenty years to evade service in the Revolutionary
War, from which at least one of his friends, Brom Dutcher, never returned.
Is it not likely that this is the true flight of the story? Writing his *Sketch
Book* still (perhaps) under the spell of his lost love, Matilda Hoffman,
Irving had no historical grudge against matrimony.[2] On the other hand, he
was born in 1783 in the near shadow of the Revolutionary War, traveled
to Europe during the Napoleonic Wars which he largely ignored (Stendhal
was also born in 1783), was an officer in the War of 1812 but did not get
into combat, and treated war in *The Sketch Book* (against the Indians) as a
brutal disgrace.

   If on one level these two evasions are complementary acts of cowardice,

9

on another they are contradictory: one is a flight from women and marriage, one from masculinity and homosocial bonds. In one case, Rip is supposed to inspire a ready male compassion; in the other, he merits men's scorn. (The two flights might have been assimilated if there had been anything shrill in American pre-Revolutionary life besides Dame Van Winkle, but Irving makes no such point; the two liberations might have been aligned if Rip saw as much in his post-colonial as in his post-connubial emancipation, but his instincts are entirely nostalgic for colonial days.) Jake Barnes and some of his friends are at any rate veterans: they can blame the necessities of masculinity for their emasculation. One might have thought that Rip, had he really been intended to earn the support and sympathy of men, should have been allowed to flee from marital to martial strife. That is the echt masculine way of being scared of women. His hunting is not an ancestral form of the masculine warrior mentality; it is the atrophy of it.

Nevertheless, Rip comes off as a lovable scamp, and the best hypothesis is that he has been assigned an honorable cowardice in order to disguise a disreputable one. It is true that Irving acknowledges Rip's deficiencies of valor and virtue, in contrast to his ancestors, "the Van Winkles who figured so gallantly in the chivalrous days of Peter Stuyvesant, and accompanied him to the siege of Fort Christine" (*SB*, 39). (Irving's "earliest recorded ancestor was the armour bearer of Robert Bruce" at the battle of Bannockburn — another heroic predecessor from the heroic age.)[3] But to assume that the days of chivalry are over is to exculpate Rip in the process of indicting him. It is the age, not the man, that is at fault: Irving generates affection for Rip as a living "chronicle of the old times 'before the war.'" The complement of Irving, who was born too late for the Revolution, Rip is always too early for it. It is not that the Revolutionary War was ignoble; for blessed souls, it has not occurred. Dame Van Winkle's shrillness informs contemporary life such that escaping *her* to the future (Rip) equals escaping *it* to the past (Irving).

Why does Rip sleep for exactly twenty years? His literary descendant, Malamud's "Natural" Roy Hobbs, only sleeps fifteen, long enough to miss World War II. The answer begins to materialize when we notice that after the preface, the seventh word of *The Sketch Book* proper is "Homer": Crayon's "account of himself" begins with the implication that he is a latter-day Odysseus in his capacity for protracted exile. The twenty years of Rip's sleep are the score of years of *The Iliad* and *The Odyssey*. The American short tale has as one of its inaugural motives the determination *not* to write an epic of war and return: Rip's journey home after twenty years is an unarduous hike; Rip conceals his identity not to bring death to his wife's suitors but to make sure his wife is herself suitably dead.

One of the nagging questions of American literature — where is our Homer? — is answered self-interestedly by Irving. The Homeric epic of American history is what puts Rip to sleep:

> Triumphant Washington, with brow serene,
> Regards unmoved the exhilarating scene,
> Weighs in his balanced thought the silent grief
> That sinks the bosom of the fallen chief,
> With all the joy that laurel crowns bestow,
> A world reconquer'd and a vanquish'd foe.

Who would not doze in the presence of lines that make Washington ("unmoved," "balanced") exactly as heroic as a heroic couplet?[4] In place of this sort of metaphoric connection of war and writing, American fiction, eschewing epic prestige, likes to metonymize *from* war *to* writing: hunting makes possible an evasion of war by means of an apparently masculine flight, and the hunt leads to the game of ninepins. Ninepins is of course the fantastic alternative to thunder, but it is also an alternative to acknowledgment of the distanced war. (Margaret Mitchell compares the sound of a distant cannonade to thunder; Edith Wharton compares the sound of a distant cannonade to bowling.)[5] And ninepins dissolves into pacifism and passivity on an epic scale. Rip enjoys not only hunting: he "assisted [the children of the village] at their sports, made their playthings, taught them to fly kites and shoot marbles [games that maintain linguistic traces of a descent from hunting by predator or projectile], and told them long stories of ghosts, witches, and Indians" (*SB*, 39). War has a border with hunting, which has a border with sport, which has a border with play, which has a border with fabulation.

That Rip likes to tell stories of ghosts and witches gives us the clue to conceive his twenty-year absence as an escape; the story of where he had been is imaginative, but from the beginning we are assured that Rip had sufficient imagination to invent it. So his flight of fancy allows him to evade without persecution both the Revolution and (when his imagination begins to dominate the town's) the "busy, bustling, disputatious" place that the town and America had become in its wake. (America becomes this sort of place after the Revolutionary War, the War of 1812, the Civil War, World War I, World War II, and Vietnam. Every post-war degradation is pre-war innocence. Every American war is a Miltonic or Melvillean descent into business and bustle.) The single misfortune is that the triumph of Rip's imagination implies a threat to his identity. Rip seems to believe, upon his return, that he no longer exists. "The man in the cocked hat demanded who he was, and what was his name." "'God knows,' exclaimed Rip at his wit's end. 'I'm not myself—I'm somebody else—that's me yonder'" (*SB*, 50). "That's me yonder" indicates his son, who looks exactly as Rip had looked, and is called "Rip Van Winkle." "I'm changed," says Rip Senior, "and I can't tell what's my name, or who I am!"

Who is he? There is a second "Rip," there is even a third "Rip." The first one does not look as much like himself as the second one does. The second one also acts like the first, suggesting that, from the literal point of view, patrilineage is everything, and from the literary point of view, patronymics are. What is the relationship of the second Rip to the first? It is more than filial; the second Rip may as well have been cloned. ("Rip" Junior is said to be the "ditto" of his father, as if to stress that the duplication is a typographical matter, enabled by writing. Escaping time into language entails difficulties.) If the Revolutionary War is in traditional terminology a fathering, is it a triumph or a disaster of patriarchy when fathers and sons on two sides of the Revolution collapse into typographical twins? Instead of Revolution, we get redundancy. The mirroring is felt by Rip as bewildering and uncanny—he does not take it as a happy item of genetic revenge against Dame Van Winkle's domination.

On the sign in front of Rip's favorite pre-Revolutionary inn had been a "rubicund portrait of His Majesty George the Third." When Rip returns after twenty years, the inn is sadly aged; the apparently sudden disrepair puzzles Rip, though the portrait is still familiar. "He recognized on the sign . . . the ruby face of King George, under which he had smoked so many a peaceful pipe; but even this was singularly metamorphosed. The red coat was changed for one of blue and buff, a sword was held in the hand instead of a scepter, the head was decorated with a cocked hat, and underneath was painted in large characters, GENERAL WASHINGTON" (*SB*, 48). It would take a semiotician to analyze the fluctuations of signifiers and signifieds on this sign. Though the peace pipe no longer seems appropriate under this military figure, nevertheless it is almost the same signified (same face but different costume) that appears over a different signifier. If it had been precisely the same signified, the situation would reduce to the Lacanian example of two identical doors, one of which says "Ladies" and one of which says "Gentlemen." Irving proposes the awkward case of a *slightly* different signified, or rather, he represents a signified that is itself composed of revolutionized signifiers plus something else unchanged and apparently insignificant. What if the sign had formerly said, merely, "GEORGE"? "George" is the name of the undamaged vestige, neither signifier nor signified nor referent, within the fluctuating sign. "George" is what can be dittoed.

At issue is whether Washington is George the First or George the Fourth, whether or not the Georges are merely duplicates and the revolution a reflection, whether anything has begun. But if American history always looks to wars for our narratives of endlessly threatened independence, American literature may choose to avert its glance rather than face its own historical dependency. As the antebellum George is still not the original George, the post-bellum Rip is not the last of the Rips—Rips do violence to the pages of history. Posit, as a final semiotic exercise, that the new sign over the inn, under whose paternal authority the men had once told tales, did not say GEORGE, but rather, to mark a cleaner independence from England, said only WASHINGTON. Then Washington Irving, born into precisely the world Rip returns to and refuses, would forfeit exactly the independence that America gained. He would merely be a belated Washington, a generic Washington, a weak and filial namesake not of George IV but of Washington I.[6] Irving is ready to undermine the possibility of identity at all rather than inherit an identity (if all Rips and Georges are the same, so are all Washingtons), which involves sacrificing history if American history is an inheritance from the Revolutionary War; and in the sacrificial rite he builds the loss of an inaugural epic into his own preference for the tale and the sketch.

"Rip Van Winkle" is the exemplary American demonstration of how not to bring literature into contact with its pertinent war.[7] That is not to deny, of course, that emergency tactics had to be improvised—Irving's trick is to evade the long-lived association of combat and literature, from Ion to Mailer. He does so, in effect, by ignoring the metaphoric connection of (epic) art and (duel) warfare implicit in the work of his contemporary, Carl von Clausewitz (born three years before), and by adumbrating the metonymic (prophetic) defusing of war to the violence-displacements of contests (on the model of the musical or dramatic competition) as theorized in the work of Elaine Scarry.[8]

First Clausewitz. And first Clausewitz's famous definition of war as "nothing but the continuation of policy with other means," which he expands as follows: "war is not merely an act of policy but a true political instrument, a continuation of political intercourse, carried on with other means" (W, 69, 87). This implies that of war and peace, peace is the inclusive category: unlike Hobbes (or Mailer, who writes a book on a peace march that he calls *Armies of the Night*), Clausewitz takes war to be the special case. "We must always consider," Clausewitz says, "that with the conclusion of peace the purpose of the war has been achieved and its business is at an end" (W, 90–91).

Clausewitz does not stop with conceiving of war as the local condition and peace as its environment; he also insists that war is permeated with the negotiations of peace. "Do political relations between peoples and between their governments stop when diplomatic notes are exchanged? Is war not another expression of their thoughts, another form of speech or writing? Its grammar, indeed, may be its own, but not its logic" (W, 605). We should not imagine war to be the frustration or the demise of communication, or the consequence of failed communication; it communicates. The language of peace includes the dialect of war. Clausewitz believes that this definition of war would be correct "even if war were total war, the pure element of enmity unleashed" (W, 605). War is in every actual instance a function of policy. It is never dumb amok destructiveness.

Yet though war is in every case political, it is of course not utterly political; war possesses an apolitical "element of enmity." This fact does not belie Clausewitz's expanded definition of war as policy but does belie his pithier assertion that war is "nothing but" policy. Clausewitz is paradoxical, and here the paradox—war is wholly one thing but partly something else—is a perversion of the first paradox of Christian theology. This is not, I confess, my own aperçu. "As a total phenomenon," Clausewitz theorizes, war's "dominant tendencies always make [it] a paradoxical trinity—composed of primordial violence, hatred, and enmity, which are to be regarded as a blind natural force; of the play of chance and probability within which the creative spirit is free to roam; and of its element of subordination, as an instrument of policy, which makes it subject to reason alone" (W, 89). The first aspect of war belongs properly to the people, the second to generals, and the third to governments.

The essence of war seems to have slipped in this last formulation to another person of the trinity, to the person of the people: war is primordially its violence and hatred—these are its "pure element"—which are always subordinated to policy. Unless, that is, the enmity is produced—or rather, at least, provoked—by the policy. The result of the antinomy is that war has the natural capacity for both expansion and deflation. It always, on the one hand, tends to get bigger, it tends to be all that it can be, because violence is a blind force (it cannot oversee itself), and because blind force is precisely what is most susceptible to simple laws. If one side proceeds with more blindness to policy, with less compunction, "undeterred by the bloodshed" it produces (W, 75), its enemy will be obliged to retaliate with more force and less compunction until it gains the advantage, then the first side will re-reciprocate, until both sides reach extremes of fury. The clarity of the logic is threatened by the empirical fact that almost never are extremes of fury arrived at. Why? "Once this influence of the political objective on war is admitted, as it must be, there is no stopping it; consequently one must also be willing to wage such minimal wars, which consist in *merely threatening the enemy*, with *negotiations held in reserve*" (W, 604). The two opposing persons of war's trinity (pure passion and pure reason) make it possible for wars to have "all degrees of importance and intensity, ranging from a war of extermination down to a simple armed observation" (W, 81).

The third element of real war—the third person of the trinity—is chance, which evokes the general's genius; this is the aspect of war that Clausewitz desires to elucidate, the realm of strategy and tactics. We are not, however, to think of the general as perfectly efficacious even in his own sphere, because there is also, between reason and fury, the effect of "friction," which leads to Clausewitz's almost Tolstoyan dictum that "everything in war is very simple, but the simplest thing is difficult" (W, 119). Finally we have a graph of real war as a vector produced by the forces of fury, reason, genius (Father, Son, Holy Ghost) and a recalcitrantly secular world (friction), each in every possible intensity. That is the messiness of real war; on the other hand is the enchanting lucidity of absolute war.

The difference between them might be put this way: real war occurs in time and space, absolute war only in space. Friction and chance are aspects of the temporal (we might say, entropic) dimension of real war, which play on fury and on which reason and genius must themselves play. Absolute war is perfected war; both reason and fury may be abstracted from it (it pursues its own disinterested, dispassionate objects); the only procedure of genius with respect to it would be to find its logic and submit, since there is no realm of chance to play in. Clausewitz puts it this way: "In the absolute form of war, where everything results from necessary causes and one action rapidly effects another, there is, if we may use the phrase, no intervening neutral void" (*W*, 582). This rapidity must be extremely rapid, if there are *no* causal or temporal gaps — no opportunities for randomness or attrition. Clausewitz is straining to say, or rather, I believe, straining against saying, that absolute war does not occur in time at all: war would achieve perfection if it "were a wholly isolated act, occurring suddenly," and if it "consisted of a single decisive act or a set of simultaneous ones," and if the decision were "complete and perfect in itself, uninfluenced by any previous estimate of the political situation it would bring about" (*W*, 78). So absolute war — war left to its own devices — usurps "the policy the moment policy had brought it into being; it would then drive policy out of office and rule by the laws of its own nature, very much like a mine that can explode only in the manner or direction predetermined by its setting" (*W*, 87). The metaphor is advisedly a synecdoche as well (absolute war is only comparable to war); the explosion may occur in time, but nothing that continues in time — for example, the continuation of policy — affects it. The explosion is momentary.

Why define war as continued policy, then assert that absolute war discontinues policy? The answer is that all real wars can only be considered as such against a purified measure; war may further policy but Clausewitz is a war theorist, not a political scientist. You might similarly say, for example, that dance is a modification of the gestures of work or a channeling of ecstatic rites, though formal dance criticism need only concern itself with the affective qualities of the human motion before it. A point that is necessary to my argument swims into view: absolute war is war considered in the manner that a formalist, though not a historicist, considers a work of art. (Real war is a communication, but absolute war transcends communication as its *donnée*.) Clausewitz briefly wonders whether the absolute war he is at pains to define is a mere theorist's chimera — but with his own eyes he has "seen warfare achieve this state of absolute perfection" (*W*, 580). He is thinking of Napoleon, the great advocate of complex integrity in war. "Nothing," says Napoleon in Maxim 64, "is more important in war than unity of command. Thus, when war is waged against a single power there must be but one army, acting on one line and led by one chief."[9] A century later, the god of formalists, Henry James, would confuse himself in his last moments with Clausewitz's god of war.

Add that Clausewitz also conceives of absolute war as a duel ("nothing but a duel on a larger scale" [*W*, 75]), and we begin to see how literature — to which war might have been thought to present an insuperable challenge — might nevertheless have found in war the condition for coming into existence. In Homer, war is always in relation to the duel: how it varies from the duel is one of Homer's great worries. This is because it is primarily at the concept of the duel — which in (pre-Tolstoyan) representations leaves friction and chance behind once it begins, in which policy is irrelevant ("creative or foundational war is that in which the natural restlessness and love of contest are disciplined, by consent, into modes of beautiful—though it may be fatal—play"),[10] which concludes with the entire annihilation of one side (a closure available to absolute war though not to real)—that war is aestheticized. For Clausewitz, real war is not a mechanical art, since it is not "an exercise of the will directed at inanimate matter," nor is it a fine art directed "at matter which is animate but passive and yielding." Since war is a part of man's social existence, directed at animate matter that *"reacts"* (Clausewitz's emphasis), it is best compared to commerce (*W*, 149). Yet absolute war—the explosion, the duel—is removed by definition from social existence; in the duel's closure, reactive matter on one side yields utterly, stops reacting, so that commerce arrives at the fine arts. We might as well rechristen absolute war "aesthetic war." This is one way of bringing war into contact with art: by metaphor.

The metonymic method is similarly implicit in the work of Elaine Scarry. Scarry is a war theorist very much in the school of Clausewitz, to whom she bows. I mean that she is concerned to find the formal essence of war. She is uninterested in its psychology except insofar as a psychology may be deduced from the persistence of its form; in this she is usefully contrasted with Klaus Theweleit, for whom war is an aspect of male psychology, which in turn may be traced to the origin of humanity and is therefore more or less inalienable.[11] Men are not all fascists to Theweleit, but we cannot, on the other hand, survey a boundary between manhood and fascism. His emblem of male behavior is the German Freikorps, for whom World War I never ended. But Scarry wishes to argue, in the Clausewitzian fashion, that peace is the larger concept, the thing that continues; in order to do this, also in the Clausewitzian fashion, she prefers ontology to psychology.

As in Clausewitz, in Scarry war is ontologically double: "war is injuring," "war is contest." This looks like the distinction of "absolute war" (whose aim is devastation) and "real war" (whose aim is the settling of a political dispute, in adaptation to which violence must always be restrained). The oddity is the way that "war as contest" begins to migrate in Scarry to the position of Clausewitz's "absolute war," as if war, by an absolute purification of its own logic, could do without the homicide.

You might have thought that the author of *The Body in Pain* would insist that war is essentially murderous. So she does, with a peculiar spin. "The object of war is to kill people." "The main purpose and outcome of war is injuring." Injuring is "the central content of war's activity" (*BP*, 61, 63, 64). Nevertheless, Scarry writes that a person "who believes (perhaps quite rightly) that the *outcome* [her emphasis] of a particular war will be greater political freedom for a given population may wrongly think of the interior act as 'freeing.' But the 'immediate activity' is not 'freeing' but 'reciprocal injuring'" (*BP*, 68). The outcome in one formulation (though not in another) breaks free from the central content. A first take on the complexity is that in trying to sort out war's immediate activity from its purpose, Scarry is involved in the paradoxes of Clausewitz's ("real war") trinity: war is policy (its outcome in one sense) that is consubstantial with unleashed violence (its outcome in another). The categories get even more entangled (and Scarry diverges from Clausewitz) when the connection of injuring to the (political) outcome is revealed to be so conventionally reinforced that you begin to wonder if the injuring is essential after all, and begin to suspect that "contest" is the essence of war from which real, bloody wars inevitably lapse.

This is not precise: contest and injuring are both aspects of real war; one aspect is not more real—or more absolute—than the other. The analogy is useful nonetheless. If the question is what element of war is conceptually primary, Scarry's answer would be contest (though no war has ever been a nonviolent contest), and Clausewitz's answer would be violence (though no war has ever been purely violent). Clausewitz's ultimate recourse is to injury because injury seems to guarantee that disputes stay settled. Scarry replies that this logic would make absolute war not only a paradigm but also a historical commonplace, since anything short of an annihilated enemy cannot ensure that a dispute will not be appealed and reopened. What is the advantage of war over any other contest for producing uncontestable solutions to critical, non-negotiable problems? The losing side of any armed conflict can in fact go on fighting, implying that the purpose of wars unlike duels is not only to kill people but to make the survivors swoon à la mort. Scarry's insistence, despite this analysis, on the centrality of injuring results from a "real war"-"absolute war" distinction with the terms reversed. Every real war involves the maiming and killing of humans, but any other reciprocal contest that produces an unreciprocal result may be substituted, if one can be imagined that has the same quality (perhaps it would require the killing of animals) of fictional, conventional decisiveness.

Wars are, in Scarry, fictional through and through: battles are predicated on fictions (surprise tactics, camouflage); the relationship between the injuring and the cause is fictional (injuring is symmetrical even if righteousness is not); most important, injuring only produces an outcome through the intervention of a fiction. The losing side agrees that it cannot continue to fight though it can, and that the winners get their way without further right of appeal. It is not that the memory of the dead or the visibility of invalids determines defeat, for the victorious side bears witness to the same absences and presences. The losing side acts *as if* (in Scarry's language) that sort of evidence is evidence of having been defeated. To read Scarry sympathetically is progressively to grant that what is most real about war (its injuring) is without significance except in a structure of fictions; our sense of the extensiveness of the fictions grows, so that eventually we lose track, or almost lose track, of what is necessary besides the fictions. (You may need, as I noted Scarry notes, *some* injuring as substantiation, but it need not be, she suggests, *human* injuring; and in any case, the relationship of the injuring to the outcome will be conventional.) In Clausewitz, you can do without conventions altogether: war is self-substantiating by reason of its massive injuring. In Scarry, you can do without the human injuring altogether, with a good enough substantiating convention, just as you can do without human sacrifice once you have invented animal sacrifice.

One way to summarize the mirror relationship of Clausewitz and Scarry is that Clausewitz idealizes war by leaving out its politics (though in policy is its definition and purpose), and Scarry by leaving out its human injuring (though injuring is its central content and at least its *immediate* purpose). Both Scarry and Clausewitz make possible the assimilation of war and art by extinguishing the temporal dimension of war, but Clausewitz does so by making absolute war an instantaneous achievement of what was predetermined by its conditions (pushing its inception immediately to its decisive climax), Scarry by arguing back from the fictional, indecisive climax until we wonder why the injuring needed to *begin*. (This would make Rip Van Winkle, both as procrastinator and fabricator, the ideal Revolutionary soldier.) Clausewitz implicitly compares war and art by metaphor (an absolute war is like an art object), Scarry by metonym (war is a member of the class of all contests, including, as she often specifies, artistic contests). The metaphoric pose is available to post-war writers who demand for literature all the intensity and authority and facticity of war; the metonymic method is available to all writers who need to assimilate war to their own fictional but not ahistorical projects.

Both of these elaborations of the art of war have a pertinence to *The Iliad*, the epic removed from "Rip Van Winkle" that is so incomparable with "Rip Van Winkle" as to suggest an operation in which the surrounding body is removed, leaving a single, vulnerable, delicate organ. *The Iliad* is premised on the metaphoric connection of war and poetry, both formalized by the duel, though at a critical moment the duel fails and Homer needs the contest to maintain a backchannel negotiation of war and art. I shall posit that this occurs because, between the Trojan War and *The Iliad*, war itself failed, became less like a duel and more like a contest. Between the Revolutionary War and Vietnam, between Irving and Pynchon, war failed again, and similarly; so I call attention to the fact that Clausewitz is Irving's contemporary and Scarry is ours, with the divide of the Civil War between. Irving had to justify his own minor, nostalgic, piecemeal oeuvre by denying the necessity of an analogy with originary war (such as the Revolution) or absolute war (such as Napoleon's), by defining his work in terms of their absence from it, by contradicting, in effect, Clausewitz's epic aestheticism. Modern American writing (from realism to postmodernism), on the other hand, justifies its own failure to produce a war epic by means that Irving anticipates but that Scarry explicitly theorizes: if war by the implications of its logic aspires to the status of the creative contest, then literary self-consciousness—at its extreme, metaliterary "play"—can both refuse to represent anaesthetic war and at the same time exploit all possible metonymic connections (temporal but not archaeological, historical but not formal, by category but not similitude) for the sake of replacing, technique by technique, belligerency with belles lettres.

Even if the Old Testament is almost as occupied as *The Iliad* with protracted combat, nevertheless it is not the Israelite aggressions that are pointedly left out of American post-war (post-any-war) literature, for example "Rip Van Winkle." I need to dispute, therefore, Eric A. Havelock's likening of the two paradigms. Havelock believes that the Trojan War is not so much recorded in Homer as fitted to the necessities of oral poetry. He notices a passage in *The Odyssey* indicating that at some stage of the delivery of *The Iliad*, the internal Akhaian division is Akhilleus against not Agamémnon but Odysseus. Both versions, he argues, indifferently

> illustrate what seems to be one of the laws controlling the composition of myths for oral commemoration. The action has to take the form of confrontation between two or more parties. It is stories of confrontation and struggle which are most seductive to the memory and which give most pleasure to recall. War is a subject preferred to peace. . . . Agents who have to dominate the action are placed in adversary relationships. . . . The tale best remembered is the tale of a duel. The characters become wrestlers, battlers, fighters.

Havelock adds that the "fighting [of *The Iliad*] is carefully structured as a series of duels and confrontations." He finds the same epic necessities in *Joshua* and *Judges*: an *Odyssey* and then an *Iliad* in a struggle for home.[12] This analysis seems to me wrong in three important ways. First, when Havelock refers to the *Iliad* system of confrontations, he refers to "duels," but illustrates it casually in terms of duels or contests ("wrestlers, battlers, fighters"). This ignores the crucial point, to both Homer and war theory, that a contest never has the finality of a duel. Second, *The Iliad* is *not* "carefully structured as a series of duels." Duels are supplemented by contests at all points but the final one. Third: if an epic necessity produces duels, then it is crucial to notice that there are almost none of these in *Joshua* and *Judges*.

The Greeks, in short, cannot have their ratios; the Jews abhor them. Not only does war in the Old Testament almost never reduce to a 1 : 1 confrontation; war is almost never put in terms of ratios at all. For example, the Philistines "gathered together to fight with Israel, thirty thousand chariots, and six thousand horsemen, and people as the sand which is on the seashore in multitude" (1 Samuel 13:5). The hyperbole gains credibility from the initial impulse to make a count. That gesture is not always felt to be necessary: the "Midianites and the Amalekites and all the children of the east lay along in the valley like grasshoppers for multitude; and their camels were without number, as the sand by the sea for multitude" (Judges 7: 12). There seems to be an interval—known as multitude—between infinity (God) and finitude (the Israelites) that the enemies of Israel always fill. Against this overwhelming power, God insists that Gideon bring only three hundred men into battle. Why? "Lest Israel vaunt themselves against me, saying, Mine own hand hath saved me" (Judges 7:2). The Israelites have to be inferior in numbers to rest assured that their one God is supreme. They discover themselves to be inferior to their enemies technologically as well, for example, to the Canaanites and their "nine hundred chariots of iron," though this enemy too would be defeated by the Israelites, beaten on the battlefield by the Jews under the generalship of Barak but in spiritual fact "delivered" into Barak's hands by God (Judges 4: 3, 11:14). Chariots were invented around 1800 B.C. by the steppe people of Southern Central Asia and introduced into the Israelite neighborhood by the Hittites, Assyrians, and others. "Chariot aristocracies" dominated the world, since only the richest of potentates could afford the manufacturing process; naturally the Jews were aghast.[13] The spiritual component of their terror was that the weapon threatened to substitute measurable and progressive for eternal and incomparable power.

The exception to the arational bias of the Old Testament is the duel of David and Goliath—no wonder that this seems the most "literary" of all the Old Testament battle scenes. But even here, it is ratio as much as Goliath that is defeated. David is small, smaller than all the other sons of Samuel, including Eliab, "the height of [whose] stature" does not impress God. Goliath, on the other hand, measures "six cubits and a span." A cubit is around 20 inches; a span is around half a cubit; with some allowance for variable measures here, Goliath must be 10 or 12 feet tall. But David of course brings him down, or rather, of course, God does: "for the battle is the Lord's" (1 Samuel 17:47).

On the other hand, the Greeks were in love with the ratio. There is a continuity from Homer to Pythagoras in their precarious faith in the appropriateness of measure to a description of the world; did Homer discover the irrational lurking in the ratio a few centuries before Pythagoras? Was he not similarly bemused? If so, then Plato was both right and wrong in asserting that art is irrational in its unwillingness to declare that some things are "larger or that some are smaller than the others or equal"; Homer is full of "measurement and reckoning"—except that the gods keep ruining the ratios.[14]

Homer seems intermittently, in various ways, troubled by the irrational disorganization of war. The obvious question he has to address is why a war epic whose origin is a dispute of Meneláos and Paris should be centered on a dispute of Akhilleus and Agamémnon, both of the Akhaian camp. Even if Homer is indifferent to who is dueling, as Havelock asserts, he cannot be aloof from the scandal that the duel has become, as if on the Hebraic model, internecine. So Paris replies to Hektor's taunting: "Let Meneláos alone/ and me, between the lines, in single combat,/ duel for Helen and the Spartan gold."[15] The duel would have come to a satisfactory conclusion if Aphrodítê had not saved her favorite from death at Meneláos's hands. Nevertheless, of course, Meneláos performs more successfully in the duel—call it a contest now, since thanks to Aphrodítê the outcome is not self-enforcing. Helen might therefore have been returned to Meneláos—but Athêna and Hêra are not satisfied with so sanguine and unsanguinary a resolution. Gods not infrequently save their favorites in duels, reducing duels to contests of moot fairness. It is different from Old Testament protocol: God gives victory to the weaker warriors; gods only temporarily prevent their defeat. Still, you might conclude that "divinity" is both the Hellenic and the Hebraic answer to the question, "why aren't wars duels?" Gods are the frustration of ratio in tests of power.

We can infer that *The Iliad* is about, or partly about, the evolution of *bellum* out of *duellum*, to rehumanize Thoreau's etymology-obsessed, entomology-obsessed, *Iliad*-obsessed, formal, formic distinction. We see the melee—war deprived of ratio is melee to Homer—unfold out of rationality. In Book 5, Aineías and Pándaros combine against Diomêdês; they use a chariot, which seems to magnify the unfairness of their advantage. Yet later when Antílokhos supports Meneláos *against* Aineías, it seems a worthy precaution. (Meneláos is fighting for the bodies of two compatriots, and he has been falsely encouraged by Arês.) We begin with a sense that only a duel of Paris and Meneláos would decide the war fairly; in time the logic of the duel is forgotten, or repressed.

It seems to be an allegory of the birth of *bellum* out of *duellum* when Arês "wielding a gigantic spear/ by turns led Hektor on or backed him up" (*I*, 128)—in an advance against Diomêdês. It is as if two warriors— Pythagorean units—may be commensurable when face-to-face; but when joined only in a triangle with the god of war as hypotenuse, they produce irrationality out of the ratio. Despite the gods, however, men continue to look for the possibility of a single fair fight to end the war, as when Hélenos urges Hektor to "defy/ whoever may be the greatest of Akhaians/ to face you in a duel to the death" (*I*, 163). Aías wins the lottery to answer the challenge; he would have won the duel decisively, had not Apollo saved Hektor. Once it is established that the outcome of the duel is not the violent subtraction of one from two—as soon as the duel is vitiated to the status of a contest—it does not matter who gets the advantage, and the war does not end. Thereafter the war seems increasingly anarchic, with duels only occasionally crystallizing in the bloodbath.

In the middle chapters, war almost entirely loses touch with the ratio (it returns to the ratio at the end). In Book 11, the battle is abjectly summarized this way: "Infantry killed infantry/ . . . chariot fighters/ killed chariot fighters." A single warrior only by a miracle can escape the formlessness: "Zeus mysteriously guided Hektor/ out of the spears and dust, out of the slaughter,/ out of the blood and tumult" (*I*, 256). In Book 12, the war begins to exceed poetry's ability to contain it in human measures: "Now there was fighting at the various gates—/ a difficult thing for me to tell it all/ as though I were a god!" (*I*, 286). In Book 13, we witness the slow-motion unraveling of ratio into irrational melee. First, the simplest ratio: Idómeneus challenges Dêíphobos. Then, as if by a Pythagorean harmonic sequence, the battle continues as follows: "Challenged so, Dêíphobos/

weighed the choice before him: should he pair/ with some brave Trojan
. . . or take Idómeneus on alone?" Prudence rules that he should pair with
Aineías. Aineías charges Idómeneus; but Idómeneus calls for help from five
of his friends. The series of ratios has gone: 1 : 1, 2 : 1, 1 : 1, 6 : 1. Aineías
then calls on Dêíphobos and two others: 6:4. Then "troops moved up/
behind him [Aineías] now," and then "both masses came together" (*I*, 313–
314). This is the production of troops out of warriors and "mass" war out
of the duel, in diagram.

   It is no surprise that the epic cannot—*contra* Havelock—maintain an
organization based on the duel; the epic begins with the disarray of the
Akhaians, which is to say that the war cannot itself be imaged as a dualism,
with duelists as synecdoches. The war itself, therefore, cannot be a closed
aesthetic object: whatever shape the poem has will not be based on a war
with a pleasing shape (the epic ends with a duel that does not end the war).
If even a war fought for beauty is not beautiful ("We cannot rage at her, it
is no wonder/ that Trojans and Akhaians under arms/ should for so long
have borne the pains of war/ for one like this" [*I*, 72]), we need to understand why.

   We arrive at the mystery of why wars are fought; we might have assumed that by eliminating a political continuity for the Trojan War (cf.
Thucydides, who traces the war at least on the "Greek" side to the defeat
of pirates and thus the accumulation of wealth and thus power by the
"dwellers of the sea-coast," so that Agamémnon could intimidate other
principalities into fighting his commercial war with him, which is to say
that politics and war are more than continuous in Thucydides, they are a
single ruthlessness),[16] Homer would be free to aestheticize an absolute, not
a real, war. Somehow he is not—the explanation is that a war for beauty
turns out to be precisely the species that cannot be beautiful, which is the
paradox that generates, sustains, and justifies the epic. Helen's rare beauty
makes her as valuable as gold but harder to own; the hoarding of beauty as
a precious object means that beauty is what must be fought over without
end.

   Compare the duel/war of Aeneas and Turnus over Lavinia in *The
Aeneid*. Lavinia's position, not her beauty, is at issue: Virgil seems to be
making the canny point that if the exchange of women is to be the basis of
civilization (the Roman civilization as paradigm), then civilization will be
dogged by war, civilization will in fact imply war, since women are always
contested objects. Homer goes further: if women are not merely tokens of
power but prized possessions for their own physical qualities, then wars
are fated to internalize, civil wars will be inevitable. Female beauty, unlike
position, is not durable: the king's daughter will remain the king's daughter
when she is married to the king's ally, but she will lose her beauty. And just
as female beauty keeps disappearing where once it had been, it keeps emerg-
ing where it had never been before, so that the newest beauty is not apt to
belong to the aging king, and may belong to the king's friend. The ownership of the most prized possession of power by the most powerful would

be, otherwise, a tautology—and a stabilizing one. War, if its object is beauty, must follow beauty's aleatory rhythms rather than either policy or its its own absolute logic.

We begin with a potential duel over Helen: this should involve Paris and Meneláos, or Paris and Trojans vs. Meneláos and Akhaians. Yet this is not arranged, and the war goes on and on. Thucydides, keeping women out of it, traces its protraction to the insufficiency of Akhaian wealth. The invaders could not support the war themselves, so had to live off the land, farming and pillaging, never able to commit all their soldiers to a battle against an otherwise outnumbered Trojan force.[17] But Homer only refers the problem, when we arrive at it, to the replicability of female beauty. A war over Helen becomes derailed in a conflict over the daughter of the priest, Khrysês. Agamémnon lets her go (though her beauty is greater than Klytaimnestra's), but takes Brisêis ("flower of young girls") from Akhilleus as compensation. Apollo is appeased (Khrysêis is returned to his priest), and Agamémnon is appeased (he gets Brisêis), but Akhilleus is enraged. This is the eternally transitive nature of wars fought over a limited resource (beauty) that nevertheless cannot be safely hoarded (it depends upon publicity for its always fading value) and, despite its rarity, is not unique. A war, even one nine years from its beginning, can be returned to its starting point as a contest for beauty at any moment. It can never be secure in its possession of a beginning, middle, and end; it may always only have beginnings; it can never close; but the work whose aesthetic object is a war for an aesthetic object must itself close.

Perhaps this is why, from Homer's point of view, the desire for war may be insatiable: "All [other] things/ have surfeit—even sleep, and love, and song,/ and noble dancing—things a man may wish/ to take his fill of, and far more than war" (*I*, 318–319). This is Meneláos denouncing, it is true, the insatiable taste for war of his enemy; it is a more reasonable question why his own allies should consent to go on fighting. There may be a ratio of the vehemence of combat to the possibility of winning and owning its object that goes out of orbit if the object approaches infinite unpossessibility. This eventuality would obviate on a global scale the aestheticizing of war by the ratio. The inverse of this is the lesson drawn by Aristophanes: if the valued object is plentiful, then the vehemence of war diminishes. If there is a limitlessly bountiful yet at the same time supreme value, then war passion reduces to zero.

Policy seems closer to the essence of war in *Lysistrata* than in *The Iliad*: Lysistrata seizes the gold and silver of Athens in order to end the war, leading the magistrate to wonder whether she means to suggest that gold is "the cause of war."[18] She answers that it is, and sounds convincing. Yet the closing of the sacred treasury to the men of Athens, and their approach with sticks to smoke out the women, and the women's throwing water on them in self-defense make it clear enough that the withholding of money is really a forewarning of the withholding of sex. Why, to understand the relation of sex and war, should sex be metaphorized satirically as money?

The point of the experiment is to turn sex into something hoardable and rare; in peacetime, apparently, it is as abundant as Juliet's always sufficient love as opposed to Helen's always insufficient attentions. Withholding it does to men what they already have done to themselves by going to fight: it inflates the value of what they want. Apply Aristophanes to Homer: the lesson is that the drive of war, if there is any motive for it deeper than policy, deeper than the merely functional desire for gold or silver, must be aesthetic—its object being whatever is as brilliantly rare as gold or silver—rather than erotic.

Homer is perfectly aware of how complicitous is the love of poetry with the love of Helen that causes the fiasco and tragedy of the war, so that the Homeric situation may be diagrammed: the aesthetic object takes as its object an ugly (i.e., irrational) war that takes as its object a beautiful woman who, by the way, completes the cycle by weaving a robe on which she re-beautifies the irrational melee. The war for Helen is a war for Homer. The perplexity that needs appreciating here is the close association of the beauty that Homer would like to refer to the ratio and the irrational melee itself. Beauty is the source of the war's irrationality; and the irrationality of the war needs to be restored to beauty.

This is Homer's job, but Homer foists it on the gods. The most telling moment of the whole *Iliad*, for my fundamental question of how war comes to be taken as a mode of beauty, is when, after a meeting at which the divided and discouraged Akhaians are whipped into a renewed frenzy for war, Athêna descends to fulfill the last craving of warriors (the appeal to their pride, their greed, and their loyalty is not enough): the hunger for their own work to be beautiful. "For at her passage war itself became lovelier than return, lovelier than sailing in the decked ships to their own native land" (*I*, 50). Lovelier, that is, than peace; lovelier than Penélopê. Lovelier than Helen. This is a lovely *Homeric* passage. The Akhaians require and receive the identical assurance in Book 11, just as the war dissolves into disarray.

At the very beginning of war literature, the epic poet admits that war is not beautiful, that its beauty is a divine illusion. Men fight wars not because they are beautiful but because they are made beautiful; wars are not beautiful but they may be, deeply, *for* beauty. I am struggling to make another point as well, to find a way of understanding the paradox that if the answer to the question "why is war not a duel?" is "the gods," then the answer to the question "why is war beautiful?" is also "the gods." But these are complementary assertions: gods, for their own sakes denying men the capacity to make their wars as aesthetically pleasing as a duel, since the measure of that beauty would be human (this is the sacred rationalization of the fall of war from rational duel), are forced to beautify the melee by way of compensatory illusion (this is the sacerdotal rationale of the poem). If war is not as beautiful as a duel, it has to be made beautiful by other means. War in the process becomes not finitely (rationally) but divinely (irrationally) beautiful, not beautiful per se but immortally beautified, emblematized as a struggle for the infinitely rare object, the object of which there can be no adequate terrestrial measure, the object that Aristophanes knew was an inflated figure, and poetry can hardly turn its dazzled admiration from the figment it has created. For war thus serves art. Art has war offer art this bargain: make me beautiful, and I will make you historical. Or: grant me immortality of form, and I will lend you, as the supreme source of this content, death and time.

To make this analysis more pertinent to American literature, make it more pointed: where I said "gods" in the last paragraph, read "goddesses." In return for the loss of the masculine beauty of war as rational duel— usually prohibited by a goddess in *The Iliad*—Athêna condescends to the battleground to offer the soldiers the illusion of beauty, war as if it were feminine irrational divinity itself.[19] Emasculating war is cloaked as masculating war: the divine femininity that interferes in duels reappears to arouse men by a compensatory, better say hallucinatory, aesthetics. Wounds are beautiful to goddesses, to whom envagination (which Mailer and James Jones will eventually see explicitly in wounding) is remasculation. Assume that we are talking about one event from two perspectives. There are no more beautiful wars; a war, instead, *for* beauty must be unbeautiful and unmanning; the same event that fosters the illusion of masculinity emasculates. Then poets may arrive for the remasculation.

Between the Trojan War and *The Iliad*, war changed, a fact I would not mention if it were not that between the Revolutionary War and the Civil War, between the war whose literary disappearance I have described in this preamble and the wars that will disappear in my book proper, there occurred a similar disjunction. The question is always what literature can make of an aesthetically diminished warfare. Keegan and Holmes tell us that

> the onset of mass-produced weapons, something approaching which was made possible by the introduction of iron about 1200 B.C., confronted the champion of single combat with a threat he had not previously had to face. It was that of a body of enemies who, because they could match him both in quantity and quality of weapons, did not need to equal him in skill in order to beat him. Not, at least, if they were prepared to undergo collective training and to conform vigorously to drill and to orders during the course of action.

Organized armies began to appear around 1000 B.C., so that a warrior began to be transformed into a soldier. Previously,

> Hector and Achilles [had fought] as individuals, indeed, as the poet tells us, almost as performers under the eye of their assembled supporters. The object of each is to outwit the other in the skill with which he handles sword and shield; their encounter is certainly a duel, even a variation on a sporting contest, despite the grim and bloody outcome it will have for whoever proves the loser.[20]

The diction is evocative: war for Homer's heroes is a "duel"—perhaps a "contest"—like a "performance." Around halfway from Homer's war to Homer, the nature of combat changed so that it was no longer possible to consider it according to a continuum that connects war, by means of its relation to the duel, by means of the duel's relation to the sporting contest, almost naturally to performance (such as the heroic mnemonic and improvisatory feats of an oral poet, performing under the eye of assembled supporters). Is it possible that the revolutionary inscription of Homer's epic has something to do with the interruption of this continuum, the opening of a gap (at the place of the duel) between tenor and vehicle?[21]

Just before *The Iliad* was written (c. 750 B.C.), the Olympic Games were invented, according to legend (776 B.C.).[22] And toward the end of *The Iliad* itself, games are held in honor of the death of Patróklos. The games seem to be designed to facilitate conceptual motion in two directions between duels and contests: we can see exhibited in the games the need for a new measure of male prowess now that wars have lost contact with duels; we can also observe the inferiority of the games to the duel of Akhilleus and Hektor that does not typify the war. The games of the Patróklos festival are: (1) chariot racing—a war skill; (2) boxing and wrestling—belligerent activities but not war skills; (3) running—a peacetime and ludic skill useful in war; (4) spear fighting—a war skill and a belligerent contest even in the games, so that it is referred to as a "duel" and has to be broken off before Aías is injured by Diomédês; (5) shotputting—like boulder heaving, a war skill but not in the games injurious; (6) archery—a war skill, and a bird is injured in the games; (7) javelin throwing.

The continuum between war and play is filled in at every interval: one event involves real human injuring, another involves sacrificing a bird as a substitute for human injuring, several involve war activities deprived of death, two involve combat but of an agonistic rather than a truly murderous nature, one involves a peacetime skill that is useful in war. When war begins to be replaced as a sacred institution by metonyms that lead conceptually to play (musical competition accompanied some athletic festivals, as if to arrive at Scarry's own outcome), when war begins to lose its character as a duel (to invoke the Clausewitzian metaphor), and contests with codifiable rules seem preferable as a means of adjudicating questions of valor and skill, there we might feel the appropriateness of the passing over of oral literature into written literature.

One of the shortcomings that Homer has noticed in the results of a contest, however, which keeps him from joining the new era wholeheartedly, is that they can be contested—unlike the outcome of a duel. A duel, as in the case of Aías's competition with Diomédês in the Patróklos games, will end in death unless it is broken off. The discrepancy makes contests seem ludicrous—even grave, sacred ones.[23] In the chariot racing, Antílokhos challenges the awarding of the second prize to Eumêlos, who is the best charioteer but who finishes last because of the intervention of Athêna. Antílokhos has only managed to finish second himself by a maneuver against Meneláos located ambiguously between skill and cheating, closer to cheating, but Akhilleus, who is amused by Antílokhos, returns the second prize to him anyway and offers another valuable prize to Eumêlos. Now Meneláos is upset, and challenges Antílokhos to swear that he did not cheat. Antílokhos, no fool, allows the second prize to go to Meneláos, now the *third* charioteer to be awarded second prize. It is a farcical replaying of the open-ended dispute over women (all second prizes, given the pre-eminence of Helen) that begins the poem — the dispute that causes war-as-duel to turn into a fiasco in the first place. Women are like prizes in a competition (women of course may *be* prizes in a competition, as in the chariot race itself) because ownership can always be disputed, if all is fair in love and contest. Then how does one get from contests to closure — one seems to be returned by contests to the pseudo-origin of the whole regrettable loop.

Perhaps as homage to Homer, perhaps as a way of obscuring the issue of his own secondariness, Virgil also is interested in the fact that contests can be contested. In one of his "Contests for Trojans" — in honor of Anchises — there is a running race and a foul: Nisus trips Salius to help Euryalus win. Then there is the same post-event dispute over prizes.[24] Take it for granted that in a contest- as opposed to a duel-society, rules and refereeing will have to be perfected. In the meantime, Virgil and, to even a greater extent, Homer will look upon the necessity of sacred games as marking a decline from the days when wars were duels. The epic poem can make use of contests to allude to duels if only as what has been lost to warfare: Akhilleus, who allows the games to formalize his reconciliation with the Akhaians, is himself divinely superior to the contests he organizes, as marked by the conclusive duel with Hektor.

But the war itself, though not *The Iliad*, ends with a strategem that in a refereed contest would be disallowed; the war is as unsatisfactory as the chariot race. Homer's epic looks two ways, between two types of war as between two types of poetry: losing the duel is losing exactly the dualism that orality prefers. At the point that games began to represent the ideal of sacred strife as the best way of measuring, or rationalizing, or beautifying male aggression, writing replaced orality.[25] Eventually, Irving and Fitzgerald, not to mention Twain and all the postmodern sports novelists of the Vietnam era, will discover that leading war to writing by means of a metonymic (not a metaphoric) chain in which sport (not the duel) mediates is the best way to absorb the historical specificity of war without beautifying it. But Homer's epic concludes with the duel as an act of sacred nostalgia for the lost beauty of war. Homer ends by refusing to aestheticize war by the only extant rationalization; only the ancient wars are beautiful.

"In the middle of the nineteenth century," write Keegan and Holmes,

> the technological equilibrium which had endowed the European infantryman with his battle-winning capacity was suddenly upset. New firearms, rifled to

enhance accuracy at unprecedented ranges and then furnished with a magazine to decuple firepower, rendered close-order infantry tactics not merely ineffective but dangerous and self-defeating. The character of the battles of the American Civil War, 1861–65, had issued that warning in stark terms. . . . By the end of the first decade of the twentieth century it was clear to any dispassionate observer that the era of the primacy of man in warfare was drawing to a close and that the era of the primacy of the machine was at hand.[26]

Add the consideration that the train and the telegraph, the major technological innovations of the first half of the nineteenth century, were instrumental in the North's victory, and the Civil War is a plausible candidate for the title of first modern war.

The first modern war was followed by what we take to be the first modern American literary movement: realism. Not that realism was a simple attempt to adapt to a new military reality. What we generally nominate as the great texts of high realism (any list would begin with *Huck Finn*, *Connecticut Yankee*, *A Hazard of New Fortunes*, and *The Bostonians*) have in common elaborate apologies (as opposed to Irving's simple neglect) for *not* making an epic of the epoch-making war. This is one way to avoid the fallacy that the realists were realistic, without losing track of referentiality altogether. Realism was the first modern literary movement partly because it was self-consciously located at the representational crisis that the Civil War announced.

Subsequent names for watersheds in the dehumanization of war include World War I and Vietnam. The Civil War's rifled musket—which favored the defense and so invited trench warfare—was ancestor of the machine gun and all the other World War I inventions (poison gas, flame throwers, the tank, the submarine) for killing anonymously. The invisibility of enemy to enemy in Vietnam (in bombers, in the undergrowth) brought the horror and terror of faceless, duel-less war to a new, vivid realization. The devolution from warfare-as-duel that was Homer's preoccupation has come to a nadir in our own century. The change in warfare before Homer wrote adumbrates the change in warfare marked by the Civil War. Every moment of the decline is accompanied by a new form of art that seems to make a revolution in the history of literary self-consciousness out of a (refashioning of) nostalgia for an earlier, less inhuman and more easily describable time, before the war, whichever war.

I do not mean to imply that the writing of literature is merely a function, even an inverse function, of the history of combat. The history of a society is not unitary; a modern society is an arena of competitive histories. The history of war in America is so driven by technology that if the current generation of stealth bombers and smart bombs could write its own history, it would be very Whiggish, but this would not be the literary view. To say why not, I should consult Geoffrey Perret's *A Country Made by War*, which does not quite argue that our national history is a history of belligerency,

concept of literary "play" to associate writing with "war-as-contest," though the concept makes representation itself seem anachronistic. A second estimate: war is where the world is lost to literature but regained in the experience of privation. The Homeric tradition is a home-front tradition, as available to women as to men; at the American foundation of it is Alcott. To lose the world in writing may function as an emblem of what it means to lose everything, even life, in combat. Literary history is born and survives as the first casualty of modernizing war.

2

Swords to Words:
Realism and the Civil War

In 1880, at the beginning of the decade of the "realism war," William Tecumseh Sherman almost said, "War is Hell." What he in fact told a reunion of veterans in Columbus is that "there is many a boy here today who looks on war as all glory, but, boys, it is all hell."[1] The remark seems not to be prescriptive. Sherman does not say or mean: "Make war Hell." He is not arguing that war should be palliated either. ("War is Hell, but we do what we can.") "War is Hell" means that combat—as such—is unbounded destructiveness. Sherman is restating Clausewitz's theorem that armed conflict, freed of political, that is, external restrictions, tends toward maximized intensity.

But Sherman's famous remark, perfectly or imperfectly quoted, is not merely theoretical; since Sherman argued unflaggingly for less political interference in war, once it is declared, the apparently declarative "War is Hell" implies the hortatory, "Let war be Hell." (Let war be itself.) Michael Walzer is right to find in the apothegm not so much a condemnation of war as a defense of any outrage convenient to its prosecution.[2] Sherman had, on a notable occasion during the Civil War, almost said "War is Hell" already. In a letter to the city fathers of Atlanta, defending his decision to depopulate the city, Sherman wrote that "war is cruelty, and you cannot refine it" (*MG*, 600). Of course you can refine it, but not without doing violence to the nature of violence. Sherman admitted that his policies would cause deep distress, but "they were not designed to meet the humanities of the case" (*MG*, 600). He warned that he would "ever conduct war with a view to perfect and early success" (*MG*, 602). Sherman is a special case of what Walzer takes to be the "realist" opposition to the very possibility of war ethics: "Realism is the issue. . . . War strips away our civilized adornments and reveals our nakedness."[3] If, in science, reality is a veiled woman, in war theory, it is a uniformed beast.

It turns out that there has been a second avatar of combat "realism": in the 1950s there was a self-styled "realist" school of war philosophy whose realism consisted chiefly in the argument that war ought to be waged on behalf of a calculus of interests rather than an ideal. The premise, which Walzer demolishes, is that idealistic wars tend to be bloodier. Sherman qualifies for the title of "realist" on these terms also, though, in anticipation of Walzer, he disproves the proposition by his own example. Sherman had no keen position on slavery. He was characteristically uninterested in justifying the Civil War at all, since in his view the South had begun it before the necessity of justification arose: "secession was treason, was *war*" (*MG*, 171). Because of his indifference to the moral stakes, Sherman was well liked in the South so long as he was not devastating it. Immediately after the war (in autumn 1865), he was on a steamer with his very recent antagonist, Joseph Johnston. "We were, of course, on the most friendly terms," Sherman writes, "and on our way up we talked over our battles again, played cards, and questioned each other as to particular parts of our mutual conduct in the game of war" (*MG*, 507). Hell is a game, like cards. One tries to win, so long as the game lasts; then one moves on to other games. It is not only by means of his clarity in war but also by his unromantic moderation in the subsequent peace that Sherman earns the middle epithet in the title of Liddell Hart's military biography: *Sherman: Soldier, Realist, American.*[4]

Both aspects of Sherman's realism derive from the same tautology (a fondness for tautologies is at the heart of Sherman's non-strategic thinking): "generally war is destruction and nothing else" (*MG*, 301); "if the people raise a howl against my barbarity and cruelty, I will answer that war is war" (*MG*, 585). That war is war entails the cruelty of his combat tactics. That (therefore) peace is peace entails the moderate pragmatism of his post-combat dismissal of Reconstruction.

I mentioned that Sherman's war philosophy is a special case of Walzer's realist tradition; his "war is war" implies that reality becomes a uniformed beast only by exceptional historical provocation. (Sherman in peacetime was a painter, a reader of novels, an addicted play- and concert-goer.) There is, however, a deeper tradition of the realism school, taking inspiration from Thucydides, that finds in everything that varies from war a kind of Maya. Because of the power and longevity of this idea, Walzer is obliged to begin his discussion of war ethics by contradicting the assumption that ethics is just talk while war is mute reality itself. The equation of combat and reality might be termed the synecdochic fallacy of war theory. It tempts literal minds by its apocalyptic mysticism; it tempts literary minds with its promise of freedom from words.

If it seems doubtful that a writer, say one as voluminous as Tolstoy, would respond to that promise, the key to the enigma is the will to divine, amid prolix and prolific life, the proximity of death. Tolstoy's soldiers feel their mortality—a premise of Tolstoyan realism—the way a saint does; but in case that seems to give soldiery an exalted (not just an emblematic) status, Tolstoy makes life as death-threatened for his soldiers' wives as for his soldiers. Two fictionally prominent men die in Tolstoy's war, but two prominent women die in Tolstoy's peace. His literary descendant Michael Herr finds in war a uniquely glamorous Hell. Nevertheless, he thinks of the drug deaths of rock stars as untabulated Vietnam casualties, and he ends his book with a vatic inclusiveness: "Vietnam, Vietnam, Vietnam, we've all been there."[5] There are Biblical echoes in Herr's rhythms: "They have healed also the hurt of the daughter of my people slightly, saying, peace, peace; when there is no peace" (Jeremiah 6:14).

The oddity is that for a non-militarist writer such as Tolstoy—or such as, for another example, Siegfried Sassoon—the assimilation of peace and war is all to the advantage of peace. "We were moving steadily nearer to the Spring Offensive," Sassoon writes; "for those who thought about it the days had an ever intensifying significance. For me, the idea of death made everything seem vivid and valuable."[6] This is typically ingenuous, but the straightforwardness of Sassoon's remark does not disguise how quickly and quirkily the idea that war may serve as a synecdoche of life arrives (even for incipient pacifists) at the oxymoron that life is most lifelike—"vivid"—where death rules. Characters in *War and Peace* as unlike as Pierre, Nikolai, and Prince Andrei feel this identically. What justifies the sentiment is always that society is a (female, verbose, therefore for writers dangerous) simulacrum; this makes mute war a revelation.

> As he mounted the steps to the knoll Pierre glanced at the scene spread beneath his eyes and was spell-bound at the beauty of it. It was the same panorama which he had admired from the mound the day before, but now the whole prospect swarmed with troops, smoke-clouds from the guns hung overhead and the slanting rays of the bright sun, rising slightly to the left behind Pierre, filled the clear morning air with rosy golden light and long shadows. . . . Over the Kolocha, over Borodino and on both sides of it . . . a mist had spread, melting, parting, shimmering with light in the brilliant sunshine, magically colouring and outlining everything. The smoke of guns mingled with this mist, and over the whole landscape, through the mist and smoke, sparkled the morning sun, gleaming on the water, on the dew, on the bayonets of the infantry congregated along the river banks and in Borodino. . . . [The] puffs of smoke and the reports that accompanied them were, strange to say, what gave the chief beauty to the spectacle.[7]

War is the direct ancestor of environmental art. The distant cannonade can sound like the bass incitement of an outdoor symphony; the distant file of enemy troops brings out the contours of the landscape like Christo's fence.

War is Hell; war is beauty; what the two predicates have in common is mother death. Still, speaking both propositions in one breath is a difficult enunciation. Tolstoy only manages to do it—only desires to do it—at the margins of battle: before combat (when the shimmering smoke is not yet infernal and the heat of battle only warms the exposed flesh to life) and after (when the almost fatally wounded soldier again sees nature as if just born into it). The beauty of war is a diabolical temptation once it has alienated you from the allures of society. It is perhaps not until Michael Herr that the Hellishness itself of war, not merely its liberation from "refinement" (to return to one of Sherman's formulations) but also its inhumanity, is located as the source of its aesthetic appeal. War is Hell but the chthonic divinity is a goddess. A colleague of Herr's is invited to write a book to "take the glamour out of war."

> "Take the glamour out of war!" [the colleague exclaims]. "I mean, how the bloody hell can you do *that*? Go and take the glamour out of a Huey, go take the glamour out of a Sheridan. . . . Can *you* take the glamour out of a Cobra or getting stoned at China Beach? . . . Ohhhh, war is *good* for you, you can't take the glamour out of that. . . . Ohhh, what a laugh! Take the bloody *glamour* out of bloody *war!*" (*D*, 268)

The friend thus raving is in recovery from a shrapnel wound to the brain that should have left him paralyzed for life, but his dithyramb reveals the continuing influence of the mechanical goddess. "Glamour," the perfect word for the intersection of Hell and beauty, means, etymologically, enchantment or witchcraft. (It is also the pacifist Vera Brittain's word: "the glamour [of war] may be the mere delirium of fever, . . . but while it lasts no emotion known to man seems yet to have quite the compelling power of this enlarged vitality.")[8] In the correspondent's paralysis and resurrection, in Brittain's vital illness, we feel the presence of the emasculating and remasculating goddess. She has been depersonified and mechanized, throughout Herr, as the Vietnam helicopter: "In the months after I got back the hundreds of helicopters I'd flown in began to draw together until they'd formed a collective meta-chopper, and in my mind it was the sexiest thing going" (*D*, 7). The helicopter is the sacred and erotic cynosure of the war, the glamour of its glamour, because she drops you into the terror of battle and plucks you out: "saver-destroyer, provider-waster . . . vitality and death." The helicopter, condescending from the sky for such antithetical purposes, is Athena's or Siva's technological disguise, machina ex dea.

I have swept by the realists in this unfairly foreshortened introduction. The purpose has been to sidestep those critics who with good cause have reduced realism to various intersections in a reticulated culture.[9] But an abiding question of the realist tradition, from Homer through Stendhal to Herr, is how to represent mass war; and insofar as artificial intercourse in society is the foil of realism, for example, Howells's, war has always had a high function, as in Howells's own Tolstoy. What if we follow Michael Bell in taking the realistic claim seriously as a claim: if the façade of realism is transparent, if the term cannot be given aesthetic or epistemological credence, why did intelligent men pretend? Bell's answer, in short, is that they were men, assuring themselves.[10] I add as codicil that they were men with a particular representational crisis to finesse. The problem of how to represent reality is not entirely unrelated to the issue of realism. The realist lineage, from Homer through Tolstoy, had crossed the Civil War; to evade the war (in writing) was simultaneously to evade Sherman's reality and to repudiate *the* literary tradition. But the realist participation in the Civil War amounted to Twain's two weeks.

The realistically brutal war, in Sherman's sense, had to be acknowledged realistically, in some sense. The modernity of the war (another attribute that made it inevitable as a realist concern) ruled out traditional aesthetic glamorization: the war was a melee (to observers raised on Homer) until, from the point of view of the twentieth century, it could be revised as a necessary stage in the revelation of total war. What beauty could art— true art—offer as compensation for history and time? Not the beauty of romance: the Civil War romance, in which war is always glamorized by the presence on the battlefield of a new incarnation of the one emasculating and remasculating goddess, the omnipresent Woman on a Horse, was the literary province of veterans. (See Chapter 3.) The strategy of realism was necessarily to find a way of defining itself as post-bellum, post-*Sherman*, while depreciating the importance of the war; it had to turn its incapacity for making more than allusions to the war into the condition of its newly achieved techniques for describing peace. The solution was a version of the Scarrian metonymic method (the Civil War becomes, by substitutions, a crusade to free the scribes): deployed brazenly by Howells, with considerable symmetrical unease by James in *The Bostonians* and Twain in *Huck Finn*, brought to its logical limit in *Connecticut Yankee*. For Stephen Crane, heir of the realists but not a war-evader, modernism consisted in the discovery that the best literary substitute for the Civil War was the Civil War.

Of the three paradigmatic realists, Howells apparently had the least tortured response to the Civil War which he shirked: he does not give us much reason to suspect more in his evasion than his blank inability to imagine what the war could contribute to his literary prospects. Even in *Years of My Youth*, which might have confessed to more than a half century of remorse, Howells puts the matter with boggling complacency. He feels the sublimity of the soldiers' common ideal at the outbreak of war; he writes an elegy for a boy thought mistakenly to have been killed at Manassas; then: "It was a question now whether I could get the appointment of a consulate which I had already applied for."[11] The sinecure eventually came through at Venice, and Howells used the Civil War period to study literature, Italian, and the prospects of laying siege to enclaves of Boston culture.

At some point around the time of the war, it is true, Howells transformed himself as an artist. Prior to the Civil War, he had valued life insofar as it resembled art; after the war, he says, he reversed his preference.[12] We might expect that as a realist his regret about avoiding the most vivid and consequential reality of his time would be as conversely wholehearted as his previous determination to avoid it. This inference can be supported: De Forest's *Miss Ravenel's Conversion from Secession to Loyalty* was apt to inspire regret in Howells that he had missed the chance to be his own model realist. De Forest is "distinctly a man's novelist" on the rougher wing of realism (opposite to Henry James on the refined wing); his novel is of "an advanced realism, before realism was known by name."[13] Why not agree with Kenneth Lynn and many others that Howells's evasion of the war would "adversely affect his performance as a chronicler of American reality"?[14]

The difficulty is that "realism"—as an American literary phenomenon—is more or less what Howells said it was: he defined it, wrote it, theorized it, advertised it. Unless we install ourselves in Howells's chair as arbiter of all pretensions to realism—what would be our authority?—there is no alternative to acknowledging that American realism followed from noncombatant biographies more readily and successfully than from combatant biographies. Otherwise, bathos is inevitable: one standard book on realism spends seven pages on how De Forest, Tourgée, and Cable prepared the way for realism as a Northern victory over Southern sentimentality, a simplification of these authors that I dispute in the next chapter, until we arrive at Howells, the hero of the study, who "had no experience with the problem of slavery, or with the South. Since he was convinced that he should write about that which he knew, he was compelled for twenty years to treat these problems only indirectly." Here is the short version of this bathos: "the Civil War marked the real end of American innocence and the tentative beginnings of a complex new American fiction. Henry James, Mark Twain, and Howells had difficulty converting the war into imaginative literature, but they were acutely aware of its effects."[15] Convert this "but" into an "and" so as to weigh the two halves of this statement equally, and you have a synopsis of my case. The only hypothesis to proceed on is that Howells's missing the war did not hinder his career as a chronicler of American reality: it made it.[16]

The crucial fact is that realism as a movement began in the 1880s, not the 1860s, so that De Forest could only be a protorealist. The central novel by Howells of the realism war—*A Hazard of New Fortunes*—exists to make good on the delay.[17] The book is praised for its diversity of characters—but if most of them agree on one thing, it is that only by the 1880s has the entire complicity of the Civil War in the ascension of American capitalism been finally charted. Colonel Woodburn, the Southern ideologue, is appalled by the New South, whose commercialism is consecrated by the marriage of his daughter to Fulkerson, homo sapiens evolved into Advertising Man. Lindau, the German-born radical who lost his hand fighting the war to save the Union, has withdrawn his loyalty from the country he kept intact: "What gountry hass a poor man got . . . ?" (*HF*, 94). Conrad, the son of the parvenu Dryfoos, tacitly agrees with Lindau that the Civil War was a struggle to unify a country safe for capital.

In reading the Civil War this way, Howells is not alone; what is typically Howellsian is that he moralizes the transformation of capitalist culture. In a famous anecdote from *Years of My Youth*, Howells is home in

Ohio, visiting James Garfield, veteran and future President, and Garfield's family. Howells has begun reminiscing about the literati he has known when Garfield interrupts him to run from neighbor to neighbor: "He's telling about Holmes, and Longfellow, and Lowell, and Whittier!" Howells is not allowed to continue until all the neighbors have gathered. Then the talk swerves: Garfield remembers once during the Civil War when he came upon some men apparently sleeping; they were dead. It caused him to doubt the "sacredness of life." Garfield

> went on to say how the sense of the sacredness of other things of peace had gone out of some soldiers and never come back again. What was not their own could be made their own by the act of taking it; and he said we would all be surprised to know how often the property of others had been treated after the war as if it were the property of public enemies by the simple-hearted fellows who had carried the use of the war in the enemy's country back into their own.[18]

What is remarkable in this modulating anecdote is not that Howells passes along Garfield's attribution of the growth of greed to the temptations of soldiers (Sherman's would be the model) rather than to government economic policies (or to the maneuvers of big-time war speculators like Jay Cooke)—this is a token of Howells's axiom that a socially engaged realism will always be congruent with an ethical realism. More revealing is that the Civil War has been inserted into *literary* history. Somehow the quaint Midwestern awe of Eastern high culture still lingers not as a foil for, but simply as the atmosphere of, Garfield's etiology of post-war acquisitive brutality. One might well ask how that could happen, how Garfield had had his faith in the sacredness of life assaulted without any threat to his faith in the sacredness of Holmes and Longfellow. The answer begins with a literary history of the spirit in which the war was waged in the first place. The two veterans in *A Hazard of New Fortunes* fought the war under the influence of high romanticism. Colonel Woodburn admires, in the Southern fashion, Scott (and Addison), Lindau venerates Victor Hugo and Schiller (*HF*, 334). Howells did not avoid the war for the sake of literature (the implicit claim runs): he avoided the romanticization of brutalizing reality on behalf of his realistic aspirations. The Civil War was fought under the aegis of a literary mode that was not appropriate to it; Howells's war evasion was the condition of a rapprochement of social and literary history.

By the 1880s, the consequences of the Civil War for a new, predatory phase of capitalism could be analyzed, and on this analysis Howells wished to found his realism. This is not to say that he thought the realists could wrest the war from the very spirit of capitalism the war had fostered. In 1885, four years before *Hazard*, when *Huck Finn* and *The Bostonians* (and *Silas Lapham*) were running in the *Century Magazine*, so was the series *Battles and Leaders of the Civil War*, not to mention Grant's *Personal Memoirs*, the posthumous best-sellerdom of which was beneficently prophesied and promoted by Twain.[19] This is the world of literary speculation that Howells wished to describe in the inevitably meta-realistic aspect of his realism. Thus the central character of *Hazard*, Basil March, unable to get beyond a jokey retrospect on slavery (*HF*, 46, 48), is nevertheless clear-minded enough to realize that one of his jobs as literary editor of *Every Other Week* is to sentimentalize the Civil War so as to distract New York and the country from the labor exploitation of its own day. March offers to print Colonel Woodburn's article in defense of slavery, on the grounds that no one would be as offended by it as by a story from Lindau on "the slavery which Lindau claims still exists" (*HF*, 357).

The most caustic conceit of the book is that sentimentality about the Civil War is perfectly emoted by the literary entrepreneur Fulkerson. Though he detests Lindau's radicalism, he always forgives him: "I don't like that dynamite talk of his; but any man that's given his hand to the country has got mine in his grip for good" (*HF*, 320). The lost hand is fictionally restored so that Fulkerson can shake it—the Gothic sentimentality of the apparition is what allows Howells simultaneously to allude to the war and dismiss it from his realistic project. By the 1880s, the Civil War is, according to *Hazard*, the emblem of the sentimental capitalistic imagination; it was fought on behalf of a tardy romantic aspiration, conjured in print like the ghostly hand to prevent a realistic appraisal of the current social tragedy. The strategy is to diminish the war from both sides.

There is a Gothic excess in Howells's disillusion with the war, in the devices he is willing to indulge to make the war negligible. In a labor strike, Lindau loses his whole arm, as if to say that the hand would have gone anyway, and rather more goes in these *new* wars in which Howells (to move from inside to outside the fiction) is playing an honorable part. Howells risks melodrama to protect his fiction's claim to realism in the face of its failure to deal with the Civil War. The disarming is disarming, however, insofar as we can believe in the labor movement not as a grander struggle but as a truer one—as an attempt to make real what the Civil War falsely, romantically promised. In the fragmentary "Autobiographical" supplement to *Hazard*, therefore, Howells addresses the "slavery implicated by our liberty" in reference to the "bombs and scaffolds of Chicago"—meaning, of course, the Haymarket terrorism and counter-terrorism (*HF*, 506). These obscure phrases are explicated in *Years of My Youth*: the Civil War was fought "for freedom; such freedom, lame and halt, as we have been able to keep for the negroes; . . . for democracy, such democracy as we shall not have for ourselves until we have an economic democracy."[20]

Lindau is disarmed to make invisible what he had sacrificed for the Union's sake; the Civil War has to be made invisible in a realism that would take the labor wars as a preferably realistic cause. Still, the Civil War sacrifice could have been transcended this way: Lindau loses his hand (or why not his leg?) in the Civil War, his life in labor combat.[21] Why must the devastation spread incrementally from hand to arm to person? Edmund Wilson assumes that the ghost in Henry James's "The Jolly Corner" served in the Civil War because he is missing two fingers.[22] The point in both cases is not merely that the Civil War preserved a literature inappropriate to it, but also that the Civil War prevented a literature adequate to it. The disabled combatants cannot write; only war-evaders can be artists. It was not lost on Howells that William and Henry James, but not Wilky or Robertson, were succeeding in literary endeavors, along with Twain, Henry Adams, and himself. It was a common question in Howells's circle why the Civil War had not yet had its Tolstoy.[23] The answer emerges from the fact that the only person in *Hazard* who, as a victim of both combat and capitalism, is inclined to falsify the rampant war nostalgia is in that position for the same reason that he cannot take pen to hand. The engaged realism that Howells implicitly championed in *Hazard* would therefore assume as its first commitment a literary enlistment in the labor struggle, a more realistic war than the Civil War by definition, since its opponent was the very source of current literary sentimentality — mawkish capitalism.

The Howellsian project from *Hazard* to the late short story "Editha" was more ambitious yet: the thesis seems to have been not merely that realism was in the service of a more realistic war than the Civil War; realism *was* a more realistic war. *Hazard*, which occasionally displays the militarization of everyday life in capitalism as a tightening of Fulkerson's sentimental handshake ("Some one always has you by the throat, unless you have some one else in *your* grip" [*HF*, 436]), insinuates the moral equivalent of the labor movement into the literary affairs of *Every Other Week*. When March refuses to follow Dryfoos's demand to have Lindau fired from the staff of the journal, March risks sacrificing the journal altogether. "Well, it's a good thing it's a holy war," he says to his wife not about the labor struggle itself but about the journalistic in-fighting that displaces it (*HF*, 361). This is a double displacement: the Civil War is displaced by labor violence which is displaced by a literary controversy *about* labor violence. The metonymic method translates the authority of war into entirely bloodless occupations, as if belletrists were belligerents. War is Hell; Hell is Purgatory; writing is war.

The displacement has in fact been implicitly tripled. The literary struggle not on behalf of labor but on behalf of realism itself is always described in combative terms, as Cady iterates and reiterates in the second volume of his biography not of Sherman but of Howells: *The Realist at War*. The editor of the *Boston Transcript* delays introducing Hamlin Garland to Howells while "war is being made upon him." The next realist in the succession, Stephen Crane, who would have his own preoccupation with the Civil War, acknowledges that his early "creed was identical with one of Howells and Garland and in this way I became involved in the beautiful war between those who say that art is man's substitute for nature and we are the most successful in art when we approach the nearest to nature and truth, and those who say — well, I don't know what they say."[24]

The beautiful and holy war does not have much in the way of an articulate enemy. But the enemy's language manages to infect Crane's own (no wonder he cannot imagine the antithetical doctrine): should we say of the realists, not the romancers, that they *substitute* art for nature? Yes: the first point about realism is that its bad conscience is the result of missing the real war and substituting for it a beautiful war. We can justify Crane's diction more precisely by observing that the way to avoid the Civil War draft was by substitution. Dryfoos the speculator had paid for a substitute (who was killed), which prompts the artist Beaton to suggest acidly to Fulkerson that he "might get a series of sketches by substitutes; the substitutes [meaning the actual combatants] haven't been much heard from in the war literature" (*HF*, 336). (They are either dead or dead to writing.) Howells himself, guilty that in setting sail for the Venetian consulate he had left his parents precariously reliant on his brother Joe, offered to buy a substitute for him if he were drafted.[25] Which simply says that if all versions of American realism are as haunted as Crane's manifesto by the apparition of romance, the reason is not far to seek. Realism cannot avoid invoking the Civil War but only as the first occasion of its series of substitutions, the missing origin of its fetishistic metonymy.

In "Editha" (published in *Between the Dark and the Daylight*, 1907), a young man has no enthusiasm for yet another war—in this case the Spanish-American. The conflict, however, is never named: it is merely referred to by the heroine Editha as a "glorious" war "for the liberation of people who have been struggling against the cruelest oppression."[26] It might as well be the Civil War as far as her vague sentiment is concerned. The hero, Gearson, however, knows all about *that* war. His father lost his arm in it, and somehow, like Lindau, goes on to lose his life in an elusive, postponed, two-step martyrdom. Like Lindau, also, his misgivings about the war "grew on him" (*E*, 586; grotesque image in this light), and he willed his skepticism to his wife, who passed it on to Gearson. Editha, nevertheless, pressures Gearson to volunteer; he does, and is killed; Editha, blamed for the death by Gearson's mother, ends the story reconciled to his death and her self-fulfilling viduity and begins "to live again in the ideal" (*E*, 589).

Editha's name attaches her to the editorial opinions that sell the war to increase sales: "she was conscious of parroting the current phrases of the newspapers, but it was no time to pick and choose her words" (*E*, 581). The triple alliance of war, yellow journalism, and Editha serves to dissociate combat from masculine realism. Meanwhile, Howells gets the noncombatant position subliminally associated with manliness and his own compulsion to write. "My father was in the Civil War," says Gearson, "all through it; lost his arm in it." Thereupon Editha "thrilled with the sense of the arm round her; what if that should be lost?" The thrill results as much from the fancy as from the horror of Gearson's anticipated dismemberment; Gearson is in a struggle to maintain his manhood, though Editha is a modern Athena for making of castration a remasculating loveliness, and the struggle quickly takes another guise. The recollection of his father's injury makes Gearson remember that he must inform his mother of his intention to enlist: "I shall have to write and tell her." Editha interrupts his thought: "Would you like me to write, too, George?" "I don't believe that would do," Gearson replies. "No, I'll do the writing." When they both get up, Gearson keeps "his arm still round her" (*E*, 585–586).

Gearson has two arms to hold one woman and write to another; only shirking the war would have preserved that status. The ad absurdum of Howells's reductio of realism has been gained: fighting a war dismembers and emasculates and finally dispatches the soldiers who could have depicted it realistically; avoiding wars is the only hope for rescuing a militantly masculine literary art from the alliance of capitalism with a hawkish, mawkish feminine sensibility; the struggle to avoid all literal wars is the essence of the substitute literary war for a realism that can only sing of disarming and unmanning.

Both Mark Twain and Henry James made stronger attempts than Howells to deal with the war more or less per se. In *The Bostonians*, James approximated a Howellsian attempt to win the war for writing—but in the outrage he transcended Howells by daring to allude respectfully to the war whose moral force he wished to usurp. The interest of the case is that he did so by techniques used by Twain; if these antithetical artists are realists, then realism is a method of discovering in the Civil War a romance that cannot be alienated, but must be branded.

We begin James's case (like Twain's) with an apology for evading the war: James no more than Twain could *assume* the evident absurdity—on which realism would be based—that the war was personally and artistically negligible. We return inevitably to the famous and enigmatic back injury that kept James out of the war, by means of which, paradoxically, James tried to absorb the Civil War rather than repudiate it. The physician made no diagnosis and gave no prognostic warning; "but I [James writes] have little forgotten how I felt myself, the warning absent, treated but to a comparative pooh-pooh—an impression I long looked back to as a sharp parting of the ways, with an adoption of the wrong one distinctly determined."[27] How not, in the wake of Edel, to interpret the parting of the ways as a turning off the warpath, away from the more obvious forms of manhood and—adding the retrospect of "The Jolly Corner"—away from business and, finally, America? Nevertheless, all this is exactly not what James intended by the "parting of the ways." The conscious point of James's referring to the participation of his back injury in a "vast visitation" is not that he has repeated his father's "vastation," but rather that his injury neutralizes the "marked disparities" of the combatant and noncombatant conditions (*N*, 297). At an army hospital, which James visited on an outing as a hotel of invalids, he feels a "common Americanism" bridging "gulfs of dissociation" (*N*, 315).

In short, the back problem, far from confirming or excusing James's civilian status and therefore his un-American, emasculated, private, artistic exile, is James's closest approach to common Americanness by way of the vast visitation, the Civil War. This is the biographical premise of James's three Civil War tales, taken by all critics determined to psychologize James, such as Wilson, Edel, and Aaron, as symptoms of what James cannot quite repress: "what makes them interesting are the clues they contain to the author's state of mind during the War years. . . . [T]he characters with whom James most closely identifies are invalids or noncombatants who do not have to fight and who betray the men who do."[28] This is misleading. In "Poor Richard," James may or may not identify with the pathetic title character, but it is the soldiers who do the betraying. In the other two Civil War stories, "The Story of a Year" and "A Most Extraordinary Case," the invalids *are* the combatants. The Civil War conjoins combatants and noncombatants in a common infirmity.

Then what is the "parting of the ways"? The answer appears to be not a disjunction of James and America, but a disjunction, a deeper Civil War, of two Americas. One is an America of invalids, of Henry James, noncombatant, but also of Wilky and Robertson and, on the fictional level, of James's Colonel Mason, hero of "A Most Extraordinary Case," and Howells's Lindau and the father of Gearson in "Editha." The other America, perhaps epitomized by the betraying sharper of "Poor Richard," Major Luttrell, or by the practical landlord that Brydon might have been in "The Jolly Corner," will make its fortune. It is in a shared woundedness—in the possibility of merging his "inward" war with the "outward" war his brothers fought (*N*, 243–244)—that James hopes to find an access to public life that is not commercial life. Woundedness is the "negative" in negative capability, a kind of inverse "experience," which James defines as "an immense sensibility, a kind of huge spider-web of the finest silken threads suspended in the chamber of consciousness." We might have thought that this was an apt description of the mechanism for capturing and imprisoning experience, not experience itself, until we realize that James is trying to abrogate the distinction.[29] The vast visitation seems to be the event—imagined as an experience of the flesh not of the mind, and as a casualty rather than a capturing—in which that eventuality comes closest in biography and history to occurring.

Only closest: the trip to the injured soldiers is at best, James says, his "nearest approach to a 'contact' with the active drama," a drama described as "what was most publicly, most heroically, most wastefully, tragically, terribly going on" (*N*, 311). If it is a drama, a tragedy, then the Civil War has met James and his hope for a connection with the war halfway. But there is always, even after the ultimate attempt at contact, an alternation of communication and reserve between each wounded soldier and the wounded visitor that keeps the former exalted as "the most attaching and affecting and withal the most amusing figure of romance conceivable" (*N*, 313). Here the imposition of the literary term paradoxically indicates distance from the writer: the Civil War insofar as James cannot assimilate it is romantic. In the Civil War hospital, let us say, the subjective romance almost gets attached to public reality to make nonsense of the distinction. (The romance of the soldiers is in their objective remoteness from James but only as the distance is registered in *his* amused consciousness.) It is the place where a common Americanness verges on making moot the division of the aesthete James and prosaic America. His visit is the event, therefore, on which James might almost have based his desire in the 1880s to make reality (as Howells urges) his romance.[30] The logic of the case leads to the visit to Memorial Hall in *The Bostonians*—conceivably on the Hegelian idea that in death if not in injury, subjects go completely over into objects. If we can believe in that synthesis, we can believe in James's realism as what does not permit romance its reserve.

Making this transition from the Civil War stories and the memoirs to *The Bostonians* is an obvious move that, strangely, Edmund Wilson overlooks, despite the fact that once Wilson fixes on an author's relation to the Civil War, he will not relent until he judges the author's whole oeuvre. Wilson goes so far as to assert that after the three Civil War tales of 1865–1868, "James does not, I think, revert to the war in any serious way in his fiction, though in one of his late short stories we find what I take to be a significant reference to it," that is, the ghost with two missing fingers of "The Jolly Corner."[31] Wilson is blind to *The Bostonians* for a reason: if the hypothesis is that James's evasion of the Civil War was responsible for the evasiveness of his late style,[32] then evading the Civil War could not have been the impetus of James's best contribution to the realism campaign.

Why is the ghost of "The Jolly Corner" missing precisely two fingers? It would be foolish to have confidence about it, but two is, noticeably, the repeated number of the story. Brydon owns two houses in New York, one for money and one for memory. The bifurcation is key to the story and represents an internal division mimicking the Civil War: "He has been dodging, retreating, hiding, but now, worked up to anger, he'll fight!" thinks Brydon of the ghost;[33] the confrontation is a "combat" leading either to "liberation or . . . supreme defeat" (*JC*, 624, 633). None of this is suggestive of the two fingers until we realize that the two houses "come wholly into [Brydon's] hands" as the result of the deaths of his two brothers (*JC*, 604). Two of James's brothers had fought in the Civil War; two of James's cousins had died in the Civil War;[34] and in the war, Wilky "received," as James puts it, "two grave wounds" (*N*, 241). James had already fantasized yet graver wounds for Wilky and Robertson: noting it allows Wilson's own intuition to bring us back to the Civil War book he ignored. Olive Chancellor lost two brothers in the war, a fact that should add another dimension of horror to our enjoyment of her moral destruction by a Southerner.[35]

It is as if we are reminded of Olive's grief precisely so that we may fail to recall it—and fail to grieve—later on. The visit of Basil Ransom and Verena Tarrant to Memorial Hall at Harvard is similarly a way of remembering to endorse various forms of forgetting: in a building named for the obligation to recollect, one reads tenderly "each name and place—names often without other history, and forgotten Southern battles," with the effect on Ransom that he "forgot, now, the whole question of sides and parties," recalling instead the simple combat emotions that united Southerners and

Northerners. The regional détente (as Verena forgets her own regional loyalty) is the basis of the "sentiment of beauty" experienced by Ransom (*B*, 210). This is a sentiment that Howells might mock. The war turns into romance in Basil's half-forgetfulness. But only his half-forgetfulness allows him to remember the war at all: its reality is restored to him on condition that it come romanticized. Only in the presence of a half-remembered and half-romanticized war is realism a possibility for James; it is produced by remembering the war to forget it; this might be the unspoken slogan of American realism.

Another reason Wilson does not see *The Bostonians* as a serious attempt to consider the war, I think, is that its hero is not merely not an invalid but not a Northerner — doubly distant from James and the project of biographical criticism. But both James in *The Bostonians* and Twain in *Huck Finn* — not quite ready to subsume the Civil War into Howells's holier war for realism, and not bold or guiltless enough to pretend along with Crane that they are capable of portraying it — restage their simultaneous preoccupation with and remoteness from the war by moving as best they can to the other side of it. James's hero is Ransom, whose triumphant reconciliation with the North as represented by Verena is superimposed on his triumphant humiliation of the North as represented by Olive. Both conquests are described in war diction, especially during the siege of Cape Cod, as if to confuse the desire for reunion with the desire for secession. At almost the same moment, Twain produced, as his own hero, Grant, but *Huck Finn* was already in existence to establish Twain's abolitionist sympathies as an antebellum fact. Playing out this symmetry — James as a belated Southerner, Twain as a proleptic Northerner — produces our ultimate idea of how Twain and James can be momentarily and jointly enlisted in the realism campaign.

First of all: realism is not natural for them; it is earned by tergiversation. The impediment to Twain's realism is the Southern romance heritage, traced to Scott, exemplified in the pointless feud of Grangerfords and Shepherdsons. The impediment to James's realism is Northern Transcendentalism, culminating in women's conflation of a war against slavery and a war against men. In each instance, the national Civil War is displaced by an intra-regional conflict — in one case, a source of Civil War passion, in the other, a prolongation of it — that allows Twain and James to look for peace on the other side of the war. The literary name of that distant peace is "realism" — in this manner, the "realist" tradition of war theory is exactly inverted. The Civil War, not peace, was Maya; the Civil War was the imperialistic moment of a regional romance.

Second: realism is therefore escapist, and escape is the apolitical, ahistorical, fabulistic version — as in Irving — of independence. The two modes of freedom in *Huck Finn* are flight and manumission, symmetrical acts of individual will. Freedom through political activity is laughable in *The Bostonians* — only private freedom is a value. The cause of liberty (but not emancipation of the slaves or suffrage for women) is protected from the

Civil War in both cases: the war is preempted evasively in *Huck Finn*, attenuated slyly in *The Bostonians*.

Third: since emancipation or its offspring, enfranchisement, is the repressed political content of freedom, rescuing in the symmetrical realisms of Twain and James must appear as a species of kidnapping. Huck leads Jim further South until he is captured; Basil carries off Verena southward with an éclat that overwhelms the issue of whether she is willing or not, since the subservience of her own will is what she is persuaded to consent to.

But fourth: we are meant to conceive of both kidnapped characters as eventually, unexpectedly, liberated: a slave-owner needs to possess or capture a slave to free him, and we note that Basil, as the only character in *The Bostonians* who does not want to buy or sell or lease Verena, is by virtue of not being a Northern capitalist the only nonparticipant in the (white) slave trade. That the liberating in *The Bostonians* is done by Basil— a character to please a Grangerford, his "magnificent eyes . . . dark, deep, and glowing," his forehead "high and broad, and his thick black hair, perfectly straight and glossy" (*B*, 6)—means that if history is repressed to produce realism, then romance cannot be. It returns as burlesque: the rescue of the maiden Verena from her monster lover; Tom's farcically medieval rescue of Jim. To be free means to be kidnapped, to be modern means to be pre-modern, to be realistic means inviting melodrama (*Hazard*), farce (*Huck Finn*), or the two combined (*The Bostonians*), so long as it is the absent Civil War that defines emancipation, modernity, and reality.

Why try to imagine freedom at all, in a realistic work? What postpones the step to deterministic naturalism? The twin obligations are (1) to allude to the Civil War, and (2) to substitute the idea of personal freedom, in the abstract, and one's freedom as a writer, in particular, for its emancipatory promise. Eric Sundquist excellently says that *Huck Finn* has to end with the absurdity of freeing a free man because the book, completed in the 1880s, is Twain's attempt to free the slaves already legally free since the war.[36] I merely add that Tom Sawyer replicates the absurdity not only of Twain's society but also of his personal and professional situation: Tom is trying to effect emancipation by literary means. The real war to free the slaves is metonymically displaced by a mock literary struggle to free *a* slave on behalf of a meta-literary campaign to free a writer *from* slaves.

Verena's freedom is similarly subordinated to Basil's, and Basil is trying to redeem James's whole American failure: Basil, unlike James, fights in the war and completes his law education, but his ambition is to become a man of letters, since only in this last endeavor is final masculinity attained. (Publishing is public presence and public presence is masculinity; Ransom only seeks a decisive battle at Cape Cod when his first article has been accepted for publication.) The historical struggle for political freedom— Jim's, Verena's—is sublated in a latent and surrogate struggle for a freedom from politics and history—Huck's and Basil's—on behalf of their authors, one of whom thought he lost his boyhood and the other of whom thought he lost his manhood in the Civil War. Realism is historical tragedy wittingly repeated as farce (the re-enslavement of Jim to free him, the enthralldom of Verena to free her).

I want to spend one moment longer on how James accomplishes his own liberation by means of realism, on the stages of his metonymic method, because the mechanism has ramifications for the gendering of literature by means of the gendering of war. Recall that *The Bostonians*, written in the 1880s, takes place in the 1870s: it is, in effect, a Northern Reconstruction novel, or rather an end of Reconstruction novel. Reconstruction was the Civil War continued by other means; partly because carpetbaggers were reviled in the North as well as the South, Reconstruction failed and the verdict of the Civil War was reversed. James's novel plays a willing role in this outcome. There are no carpetbaggers in *The Bostonians*, but there is a carpetbagger proxy. When Ransom first sees Verena, he falls in love with her but decidedly not with her father:

> Ransom simply loathed him, from the moment he opened his mouth; he was intensely familiar—that is, his type was; he was simply the detested carpet-bagger. He was false, cunning, vulgar, ignoble; the cheapest kind of human product. . . . [Tarrant is a] varlet, Ransom said to himself, making use, as he did generally, of terms of opprobrium extracted from the older English literature. He had seen Tarrant or his equivalent, often before; he had 'whipped' him, as he believed, controversially, again and again, at political meetings in blighted Southern towns, during the horrible period of reconstruction. (*B*, 51)

I find this passage peculiar: assume (incorrectly, as Albion Tourgée urges) that the description of carpetbaggers is accurate; but what makes this pathetic charlatan a carpetbagger? Clearly not all hapless charlatans can be accused of ruthlessly capitalizing on the the the misery and degradation of fellow Americans. James allows Ransom a skewed disgust, and much strategic work is done thereby. Realism is rendered inseparable from romance, a necessary condition of this book; Ransom's skepticism calls up the diction of Malory. Second, "whipping" has been safely surrounded with quotation marks: Southern violence (the term unites slavery and war) is now only a matter of controversies, of secondary acts of violence, of words, like James's. Thus third, James finds a rhetoric for becoming a publicist of the Southern conception that the defeat of the Confederacy was a tragedy, a loss of homeland, a colonization.

If James had stopped there, he would perhaps have managed to justify, at least to himself, his own nonparticipation in the Civil War as a prerequisite of his own noncombatant, romantic realism. But James also wanted, like Howells, to redeem his evasion as an exercise of superior war-making masculinity. So the carpetbagger's crime gets sexualized: Ransom is impatient with "Tarrant's grotesque manipulations, which he resented as much as if he himself had felt their touch, and which seemed a dishonour to the passive maiden. They made him nervous, they made him angry, and it was only afterwards that he asked himself wherein they concerned him, and whether even a carpet-bagger hadn't a right to do what he pleased with his daughter" (*B*, 52–53). The "carpetbagger" theme had been momentarily dropped until this lucubration; it is revived at the point that the scene is sexualized. "To do what he pleased with his daughter" sounds like a euphemism for child abuse; at the same moment that Ransom excuses the bodily manipulation, he tacitly recondemns it. This is how we are to imagine the Northern penetration of the South—Ransom seems to feel Tarrant's touch himself. It seems, before he recovers and identifies with the patriarch, to turn Ransom into a passive maiden. Did the North have a right to do with the defeated South as it pleased? Was that equal to the right to sodomize it?

I have described the beginning of a novel in which the Southerner ought to spend several hundred pages winning the carpetbagger's daughter from the carpetbagger, winning back his own heterosexuality in the process. That this novel does not happen to be *The Bostonians* indicates James's stated intention: the book is not a tardy contribution to the war against Reconstruction, it is a book intended to wage war on feminism. But this further regression of the metonymic method entails an ascending difficulty: if a war against a man as unmanly as Tarrant is infectious, what can be said for a war against Olive? As Ransom prosecutes that war, he notices, as he must, that his chivalry is at risk: he is ungallant toward Mrs. Luna at one key moment of the campaign, toward Olive at many others; nor does he always treat Verena with sufficient courtesy. Yet it must be a war *for* chivalry.

There is no possible circumvention of this impasse; for feminism to be defeated, women must be defeated; the only possible resolution of the double bind is a joke. Ransom tells Verena:

> I am of the opinion of that historical character—wasn't he some king?—who thought there was a lady behind everything. Whatever it was, he held, you have only to look for her; she is the explanation. . . . Now, you don't mean to deny that power, the power of setting men in motion. You are at the bottom of all the wars. . . . What do you say to Helen of Troy and the fearful carnage she excited? . . . And as for our four fearful years of slaughter, of course you won't deny that the ladies were the greatest motive power. The Abolitionists brought it on, and were not the Abolitionists principally females? . . . I regard Eliza [P. Moseley] as the cause of the biggest war of which history preserves the record. (*B*, 80–81)

This completes Ransom's picture of a passive and aggressed-against Southern masculinity. I do not feel encouraged to put pressure on these words; Ransom is on a characteristic flight of aggrieved humor, and his humor always protects him. Still, the illogic of the peroration is clarifying: Helen inspired a war by her pregnable femininity, Eliza by her pseudo-masculine, advanced verbal assault. When Ransom and James need a woman warrior-figure elsewhere, they name Joan of Arc, but we may assume that the image James is sketching merges Eliza and Joan. Ransom's remark about Eliza ("the cause of the biggest war . . . ") is an echo of what Lincoln may have said to Harriet Beecher Stowe: "So this is the little lady who made this big war." The woman warrior must be somewhere between a verbal duelist and an actual combatant, if realism is to be redeemed as the appropriately bellicose, masculine response.

Only by raising the ghost of Joan of Arc, I suppose, can the war against women seem like a worthy adventure of chivalry. We might wonder what the triumph of even such a compromised chivalry is doing in a work ostensibly of realism, but that has a ready rationale, as in Howells: (noncombatant) realism exposes the alliance of capitalism with hawkish-mawkish femininity. The Civil War is a product akin, on this analysis, to the woman's novel; capitalism has its own interest in keeping the war sentimentalized; when, in New York City, Verena is brought into contact with gilded philanthropy, we see that feminism is the most delightful of all the possible revolutions for capitalism to coopt. Ransom can be, as a medievalist and thus as the only character in the book who does not wish to capitalize on Verena, the book's realist if he is thereby usefully distanced from the phenomenon under realism's consideration.

To be, according to Twain and James, a realist is to be, with various but always detectible self-mockery, a medievalist. The flight, as in Rip Van Winkle, is to the early side of the war when masculinity was intact, so that war can be revised as the place where manhood is not earned but martyred. The ultimate realist text—where the logic of realism is overthrown only by being scrupulously obeyed—is *A Connecticut Yankee in King Arthur's Court.*

Twain's most direct approach to the Civil War was *The Private History of a Campaign that Failed*, a rejoinder to the heroic memoirs of the 1880s. Partly, the piece is an explanation of his abandoning the war, though the explanation divides into half confession, half apology. "My campaign was spoiled," says Twain concerning the shooting of the unarmed man. "It seemed to me that I was not rightly equipped for this awful business, that war was intended for men and I for a child's nurse. I resolved to retire from this avocation of sham soldiership while I could save some remnant of my self-respect."[37] Is the remnant of self-respect conserved by not proving, repeatedly, that you are meant for a child's nurse, or rather by not consenting to kill "strangers against whom you feel no personal animosity" (*PH*, 139)? The hedging takes another form further on: as Grant approaches, Twain exits westward before the small-scale campaign becomes mass war. Twain's departure precedes the metamorphosis of his confederates "from rabbits into soldiers" (*PH*, 135). Or is it before they learned "to obey like machines" (*PH*, 135)? He either maintains his boyhood by deserting—while everyone who remains is masculinized—or he preserves his manhood—while everyone who remains is mechanized.

The ambiguity implies a tension of historical senses; the Civil War seems to define the issue of history as whether humanity (or call it mankind

or manhood, to see it from Twain's persepective) must be deposed by
machines. The Civil War is the first modern American war, ancestor of
World War I, partly because it first exhibited modern warfare as a triumph
of technique (the telegraph and train, the great technological advances of
the first half of the nineteenth century, were instrumental to the North's
victory), and because the current ballistic technology, especially the development of the rifled musket, favored the defense, favored, that is, trench
warfare.[38]

Yet the point of *A Connecticut Yankee in King Arthur's Court* is to
minimize the importance of the Civil War in focusing the historical crisis. If
the Civil War raised the question of whether man or machine was to prevail, *A Connecticut Yankee* exists to set the question ahistorically in the
Middle Ages and suggest a trans-historical answer to it. Man *is* a machine.[39]
The South had resisted the modernity of the Civil War. It had eschewed
defensive, entrenched warfare as long as it could: defensive war was feminine, and trench-building was for slaves. But in 1889, halfway from the
Civil War to World War I, Twain realizes that for a Connecticut Yankee,
the technological defense of an entrenched position might appeal both to
manhood (since science and technology were gendered that way) and to
boyhood (all Hank's children die in defense of their uterine retreat, to use
Nathanael West's technical term, after the Battle of the Sand Belt, namesake
of Hank's medieval wife, Sandy). In this pre-Oedipal identity not of a
mother and child but of an enwombed father and fifty-three sons, Twain
finds the justification of removing Yankee modernity to what he always
conceives of as the infancy of humanity, as if the Civil War, setting of the
mechanization and the mechanized decimation of man, were a timeless
potentiality, preserved in an unconscious and perdurable desire. The first
commandment of the Howellsian literary ethic—bring literary history up
to date with social history—is honored in *A Connecticut Yankee* only by
pushing back social history as far as it would go.

This ends the metonymic hope of literature that war, no longer *like* art
since the decline of the duel, can be led to art by a series of defusing
approximations at some stage of which the violence drops out. That was
the program of Hank Morgan; or rather, that was Twain's scheme that
Hank Morgan, baseball fan, allows him to float. What did baseball have
to do with the Civil War? Historians differ: either the Civil War spread
baseball throughout the nation from its origins in the Northeast (Union
prisoners taught the game to their captors) or the Civil War slowed the
growth of baseball, and post-war prosperity caused the boom (baseball was
largely professionalized within a few years of the war, an organized, nearly
monopolistic business with the founding of the National League in 1876,
a centerpiece of the American entertainment industry by the time of *A
Connecticut Yankee*).[40] Twain has a larger inquiry concerning the relation
of war and games in mind. If *The Iliad*, perhaps, is inscribed as a tribute to
an outmoded style of warfare in the first era of the Olympic Games, then *A*

Connecticut Yankee is a tribute to a passé form of warfare in the first era of the National League.

Baseball metaphors come quite naturally to Hank Morgan, almost always as a joke on Sandy. "She had somehow failed to get the first innings" in her conversation with hostile knights (CY, 90); "Go to the bat," Hank orders her when he wants her to begin informing him about it (CY, 91); when she does not understand him she "couldn't fetch the home plate" (CY, 151). The routinization of the routine makes it possible to intuit that the first philosophical question posed by baseball to Victorian America was whether sports were manly or boyish.[41] Near the end of the book, the metaphor literalizes when Morgan creates a league, with two teams of knights and Clarence as umpire. The description of knights at play seems like one of Twain's interludes of pure silliness; yet the interlude is carefully placed. It occurs in Chapter 40, "Three Years Later." What had occurred three years before was Morgan's demoralization of knighthood by means of the dragoon revolver, so that the baseball chapter begins: "When I broke the back of knight-errantry that time, I no longer felt obliged to work in secret" (CY, 283); he exposes his schools, mines, and factories, and his next project is team sports. The chapter ends happily: "The first public game would certainly draw fifty thousand people; and for solid fun would be worth going around the world to see. Everything would be favorable; it was balmy and beautiful spring weather, now, and Nature was all tailored out in her new clothes" (CY, 290).

But the next chapter is entitled "The Interdict." Just after the book's civil war between the Yankee and the cavaliers that apparently puts an end to the South forever, thirteen hundred years before its secession, and just before the millenarian spring when nature puts on its new baseball uniform, all of Morgan's revolution falls apart. This is the refutation of the metonymic hope, the dream of a "revolution without bloodshed" (CY, 285) that Morgan had put this way: "It was a project of mine to replace the tournament with something which might furnish an escape for the extra steam of the chivalry, keep those bucks entertained and out of mischief, and at the same time preserve the best thing in them, which was, their hardy spirit of emulation" (CY, 288).[42] When, in Chapter 42 (entitled "War!"), Morgan is informed of the devastation that began while he was away, he thinks of it exclusively as the apocalypse of baseball. Hearing about the death of Sir Gillimer, he exclaims, "What a handy right fielder he was!"; informed of Sir Kay's demise, he laments, "My peerless shortstop!" (CY, 296). What has gone wrong, so that instead of sports, instead of perfectly refereed contests, instead of grand theatrical competition with Morgan as impressario (the metonymic hope turns epic war almost into Greek competitive drama), instead of peace, we get World War I?

Twain's prescience is not merely that he saw in technology the opportunity for a new advance in the impersonal and efficient murderousness of war; he recognized that the advent of war in such a rationalized setting would inevitably look perfectly contingent. Rationality, that is, would both enable war and render its approach invisible. As John Keegan has re-marked, the hopeless task of identifying the *cause* of World War I ought to be replaced by the attempt to identify its *conditions*: what buried network of fears and resentments, enflamed by the techniques of diplomacy, and what combination of scientific and political techniques, made possible the development of local pan-Serbian aspirations into a world war that would kill eight and a half million soldiers?

Compare the Armageddon of *A Connecticut Yankee*: no reader who has finished the book more than two years in the past can remember the precise chain of events that leads to the war. Morgan, trying to insult a knightly humorist, insults a more ferocious knight by accident; this entails at long last the tournament in which Morgan neutralizes, so he thinks, the power of knighthood; but soon thereafter Launcelot ruins Mordred in a stock deal (capitalism and baseball grow *pari passu* after this civil war as well as the later one, both institutions appropriate to their era as zero-sum competitions statistically and democratically representable in newspa-pers),[43] and Mordred vengefully reveals Launcelot's affair with Guenever to Arthur; Launcelot and Arthur arrange a truce, but Mordred, while Ar-thur is away because of circumstances too irrelevant to review, tries to marry Guenever and usurp the throne; this calls down the interdict of the Church on Mordred.

At this point the linking of events is broken before it arrives at Morgan; but as if there were a connection of some kind, an interdict is also put on the Connecticut Yankee. Why? — simply because the Church had been out to eliminate him, and the time seemed opportune. Two interdicts are as easy as one, apparently. (So did we need all this machinery?) Revived by the Church, all the once humiliated knights, still alive to contest the historical decision against them, make war on Morgan, joined by the common people of England, whose loyalty returns to their betters. The mechanism is so Rube Goldbergian that one thinks, momentarily, that the only purpose is somehow to assimilate Malory's version of the holocaust to the incidents of this novel.

But something is working itself out: Mordred and Morgan (to return to the missing link) have been associated not merely by the interdict but also in name (Mordred is a traitor in Malory, but what Twain sees in his name, in naming Morgan partly after him, is perhaps the "mort" of "Morte Darthur"), and accordingly as the only two characters who entertain the treacherous notion of succeeding Arthur, Morgan of course by running for President. Mordred is first referred to as the King's nephew (*CY*, 295); as if that does not make his crime sufficiently patricidal, when he finally kills Arthur the newspaper refers to the King as "his father Arthur" (*CY*, 298). (He is, in Malory, the king's bastard.) And Mordred is not the only one who has been pursuing Guenever, pursuing, that is, if Arthur is the national father ex officio, the nation's matriarch. So has, of course, Launcelot, with the apparent enigma now understandable that Morgan and Launcelot have been weirdly identified as well: not only is Launcelot, after his defeat by Morgan, the best Yankee speculator in the country, but he also acts as if he is the father of Morgan's baby, in advance of our knowing that the sick baby in question *is* Morgan's, so that all first-time readers are confused as to the issue of paternity. Confusing the issue of paternity—making it a subject of speculation—is the point. The book's frequent approach to the womb, first imaged horribly as Morgan le Fay's prison, finally moves above ground—the uterine retreat is now universally desired. Yet Launcelot's occupation of the site, of all such sites, prefigures Morgan's return to Merlin's cave (where Merlin's magical power is magically restored to him on condition he be disguised as a woman), all electrified but eventually as dark and odoriferous and deathly as Morgan le Fay's dungeon.

The pervasive desire of the book is not so much to have intercourse with the mother; that is merely a means to the womb, sex drive in support of death drive; the compulsive desire of the book is not yet to be born, to be unborn. The mechanicalness of the holocaust plot is merely equal to the mechanization of the world that Morgan creates as his fetid environment, and the object is suicide, prenatal suicide, death (thirteen centuries) before birth, sui-abortion. If the mechanism of the plot is ad hoc in the extreme, nevertheless it can be summarized this way: the joke aborts. Morgan originally gets into trouble making a joke about Sir Dinadan that Sir Sagramor misinterprets (Sir Dinadan had himself been making a joke whose direction Morgan had wished to reverse); the knights have the last laugh. Always a joke or cleverness on Morgan's part reacts against him, as when in flight he sends word to the pursuing officer to meet him at the end of the alley, assuming that the officer would suspect a trick and follow Morgan into a newly closed cul-de-sac. The officer innocently does go to the alley, and arrests Morgan.

This repeats the structure of an earlier maneuver, when Morgan climbs a tree with the King, then clambers to a neighboring tree to elude the pursuers; one of the crowd, by simple mistake, climbs the wrong tree, that is, the right tree, and discovers them. Here is how Morgan analyzes his miscalculation: "The best swordsman in the world doesn't need to fear the second best swordsman in the world; no, the person for him to be afraid of is some ignorant antagonist who has never had a sword in his hand before" (CY, 247). Morgan's error is to presume, despite his training at the Colt Factory, the golden spike of the American conjunction of war and industry, that war is a duel of wits, a rational contest in two senses, and that he is the superior duelist. Yet Morgan's whole project is to put an end to chivalry, to tournaments, to duels, and to replace them with baseball contests whose contestability is demonstrated by the death not of one side or the other but, before Clarence takes over, of many fine umpires. (Morgan's project of ending chivalry is premised on the duel, just as Ransom's campaign to restore it implies brutality to women.) What is the self-defeating logic at work here?

Twain has been wondering why his life has had precisely that logic:

every scheme backfires, every joke introjects. The dismay of Huck Finn after his practical joke on Jim is nothing compared to the penitence felt by Twain after the *Atlantic Monthly* dinner of 1877 when he told his apparently insulting anecdote about Emerson, Longfellow, and Holmes in their presence. The anecdote was in fact designed to turn prophylactically against himself, but the prophylaxis failed to protect (like Hank's evasive, too clever schemes) and Twain was humiliated. In the wake of that dinner, Twain begins to believe that his basic impulse must be suicide, that all his insults must be insulting to himself, that all his jokes must be jokes on himself, that all his bitterness must be self-hatred circuitously arriving at its destination. Writing to Howells about the speech, Twain says that his "sense of disgrace does not abate. It grows. I see that it is going to add to my list of permanencies—a list of humiliations that extends back to when I was seven years old, & which keep persecuting me regardless of my repentancies." The echo of "permanencies" and "repentancies" is a clue that Twain's provocations and his guilty abasements were a single, self-punishing psychic phenomenon. In *A Connecticut Yankee*, Twain universalizes the syndrome; in these terms the paradigmatic war must be a civil war. The logic necessarily appears accidental, irrational, perverse in the terms of Edgar Allan Poe; the self that is killed cannot face the self that kills. Twain feels "persecuted" by his own act.[44]

In terms of war theory, Twain's hypothesis amounts to this. War is the result of self-division; it is a self-consuming appetite. The history of warfare is not, therefore, a prolonged decline from the duel. Twain's essential war is on the Hebraic, not the Greek, model: America is the new chosen nation if that means that war, as in the Old Testament, must always be potentially introjected, civil, self-dividing. (Twain is on both sides of the American Civil War; the Arthurian Civil War is suicidal.) The duel is the invention of men to externalize warfare, to keep the opponent of one's violence, one's primary masochism, alienated. Only an opponent diametrically opposed keeps the arc of violence from being exactly 360°. I say "invention of men" advisedly—when, at the end of the book, Morgan writes that his defiant army consists of "fifty-four what? Men? No *minds*" (it consists of himself plus fifty-three boys, "as pretty as girls, too" [*CY*, 308, 311]), he brings to a period the book's oxymoronic pretense that you can manufacture men, that what Hank Morgan embodies and proselytizes for is masculinity.

As in *Private History*, the precise location of manhood with respect to war is obfuscated: Morgan wants to be a man and a duelist (superior in the ratio of antique warfare), but his own mechanization of warfare and masculinity prevents it. It has always been boyhood that he is after (baseball is boyish rather than manly), or rather unisexual childhood (the girlish Clarence = the vanished Clemens), or rather prenatal pre-sexuality. Manhood consists finally in chivalry, defined as the desire for a rational fight. This is to say that manhood is a convention; if man is a machine whose machine instinct is toward unbirth, then chivalry has to be ephemeral, a delaying anti-mechanism. The attempt to put an end to chivalry is therefore to crush the fleeting institutionalization of a rational, beautiful masculinity, a (fictive) masculinity compatible with the fiction that produced it, and to return men unwittingly from the Greek to the Hebraic world (*God the all-terrible!/ Thou who ordainest,/ Thunder thy clarion/ and lightning thy sound!*)[45] beyond ratio, even if explosives and electricity have replaced the thunder and lightning of a militant and infinite God.

In advance of World War I, Twain believed that the desire to be unborn would produce accidental death on a titanic scale; after World War I, Freud reproduced the theory. In Twain's brilliant depiction of massive repetition compulsion (a machine is a hominoid that is compelled to repeat, e.g., the machine gun), Morgan vacillates from birth to death to rebirth to redeath, always seeking and delaying death, and the Civil War is continually passed over: Merlin puts Morgan to sleep from the sixth century to the 1880s. Or better say that the Civil War is subsumed. Instead of the Civil War as the historical crisis of masculinity, we get a perpetual, universal, mechanized atrocity, a civil war of all mankind always, the pluperfect closure of an apocalypse before history. The repressed Civil War returns everywhere, which implies a realism of absolute, cynical pessimism, and entails a war more Hellish than Sherman's because peace is not peace. Peace is Maya after all. This is realism, but it is realism that cannot pose as the best hope for a progressive, post-war literature; its metonymic justification has refuted, exploded, itself.

If the lesson of realism is that a realist needs to remember to forget, along with Ransom, the whole question of sides and parties, and the names and details of actual battles, then naming a battle may be the first step of transcending realism. Chancellorsville, probably the historical model of Stephen Crane's battle in *The Red Badge of Courage*, was not a typical example of modern warfare; to a military historian, its distinguishing feature seems to have been the breakdown of Northern telegraphic communication, not to mention semaphore signaling and, due to heavy winds, balloon and telescopic observation. It was fought to a large extent blindly; for this reason, among others, an atavistic frontal assault resulted in a very costly Southern victory.[46] But though it was a premodern battle, it hastened the transition to modernism in *The Red Badge of Courage*, it moved literature beyond Twain's dead end of realism. The first paradox is that the premodernity of the battle made it more susceptible to Crane's modernist sensibility. The second is that it was by representing the Civil War *more* directly than James, Twain, or Howells had treated it (by a kind of frontal assault) that Crane transcended realism.

The epistemological crisis of the book was suggested by the epistemological crisis of the battle: if a battle cannot be comprehensively viewed from any position, is it in any sense a single battle at all? War, says Raymond Aron in a précis of Clausewitz, "is a totality which is defined by a dominant characteristic rather than by a motley collection of separate features."[47] Then, from Crane's point of view, there *is* no Civil War, there

are only private campaigns, as the realist hypothesis of a unifying of histories meets its extreme counter-hypothesis. Does this make all the book's
observations (from anywhere rather than from the opposition—from a
companion, a corpse, a campfire) *un*realistic? What is the epistemological
value of observations that are immeasurably dominated by imagination and
partiality? On a single page Henry hears stories, which may be true or
false, tries a mathematical proof of his own bravery, questions his beliefs,
sees possibilities, tries literally to see, tries to assemble information, tries to
sort fact from whatever is its opposite, and falls into skepticism.[48] It is not
merely that knowledge is hard to come by; it is that no one knows what
knowledge is, what its marks are, what the organ for receiving it is, how
one knows when one has it.

  Henry's problem is that his imagination is typically one step ahead of
reality; given that reality is what always straggles one step behind, imagination can never be falsified. All we need to realize, however, is that Henry's
problem is Crane's—that is, imagining a Civil War that needs to be made
congruent with the Civil War—to understand that it is an opportunity
for modernism, an opportunity to outgrow realism. When an imaginary
Chancellorsville *becomes* Chancellorsville, realism loses its rationale.

  We get the clue we need to how this might be accomplished in the
weird appropriateness of Crane's metaphors. Not that there are not many
brazenly unfit metaphors, as if the conflict in question were the war of
literature and reality—but the truly revelatory tropes are so appropriate as
to be tasteless. For example, the sleeping soldiers are "lying deathlike in
slumber" (*RB*, 66); Garfield's horrible mistake is reversed in a horrible
metaphor. Or: Henry's "disordered mind interpreted the hall of the forest
as a charnel place" (*RB*, 69). A soldier's protestation of truthfulness cooper-
ates in the project: "I hope to die," he says. "Sure as shooting" (*RB*, 85).
This is not a descendant of Howells's militarization of everyday life; it is a
militarization of military life. The attempt is to find metaphors that vouch
not only for the power of imagination but also for the powerlessness of
imagination to create anything that will not eventually be realized. Death is
generally the subject of Crane's bizarrely apt metaphors; death is the always
only imaginary and the only always realized experience.

  That a symbol will find its reality is one of the lessons of *The Scarlet
Letter*, on which *The Red Badge* is a meditation, borrowing not merely its
diurnal structure but also its romancer's prerogatives. Henry feels after his
cowardice that "letters of guilt [were] burned into his brow." Later, he
pictures "red letters of curious revenge" (*RB*, 47, 92)—*Red Badge* is an
aggressive masculine revision of Hawthorne's book, a masculinization of
romance (rather than a masculine repudiation of romance) as the prerequisite of Crane's modernism.[49] The book is inconceivable without two monuments of realism—*The Charterhouse of Parma* and *War and Peace*—and
their depiction of war as disarray. But neither of those books truly transcends Homer, at least in the sense that in both cases the disarray is framed.
Crane needed Hawthorne's romance to learn how disarray can be not so

much contained as symbolized; *The Scarlet Letter* teaches that a symbol has the equivalent literary position to clothing, that is, on the border between interior and exterior, exteriority that takes the shape of what it encloses, a frame's nightmare liquidification.

Henry's red badge is precisely the interpenetration of subject and object that Henry James sensed but did not wholly credit in his visit to the Civil War wounded. Wounds, says the tattered soldier of Crane's book, "might be inside mostly, an' them plays thunder" (*RB*, 53). That wounds are both inside and outside is a physical fact that turns epistemological when Henry finally receives his badge: "He saw the flaming wings of lightning flash before his vision" (*RB*, 60). This *is* a vision, or almost—the flaming wings of lightning suggest an inchoate mythologization of the battlefield, a partial descent of the beautifying goddess, who later is incarnated as the American flag: "It was a goddess, radiant, that bended its form with an imperious gesture to him" (*RB*, 90). That is not to say that Henry did not literally see his vision. The wound is a hybrid of visionary and visible fact—superfluously visible and visionary, since of all the visions that flash before eyes, the most redundantly appropriate one is a flash.

The wound is simultaneously part of the war and a representation of it. It is an independent empirical fact and, as a badge, a symbol of an empirical fact, a symbol of itself; just as Hester's "A" after she had embroidered it both symbolizes and is an example of her Artistry and Ability; just as the host that appears in the most famous of Crane's metaphors is both the crucified Christ and a symbol of the crucified Christ, a wounded body and the Word. Realism flounders before this modernist doctrine of the real presence: language represents reality by structuring reality as a system of representations. This means that both the metaphoric and the metonymic tacks of fiction are unnecessary. War is not the worst but the most inviting place for representation, because wounds are where flesh bleeds into symbol.[50] In death, accordingly, subjects go over completely into objects. Henry is "looked at by a dead man" (*RB*, 42), which means more, apparently, than that Henry imagines the corpse's vision; is the looking subjective or objective in such a quietly Gothic phrase as, "A house standing placidly in distant fields had to him an ominous look" (*RB*, 23)?

If realism is essentially a substitution for the most important event of the realists' era, then Crane's modernism is founded on the discovery that the best "substitute," as Crane said, for "nature and truth" is "nature and truth"; the romance strangely unalienated in Crane's declaration of his realistic lineage can be redeemed, through Hawthorne. *The Red Badge of Courage* manifests an assurance that James in *The Bostonians* could only approach: that in death if not in woundedness, one's inward war exactly equaled the outward war. The gap made necessary the view from elsewhere that was the basis as well as the bane of James's realism. For the noncombatant whose life began after the combat was over, the closing of the gap allowed the appropriation of the Civil War for the purpose of turning romance into, not realism, but modernism. As opposed to Howells's metonymic method, the inevitable and problematic model of war-conversion among realists, Crane's method does more than make of its own art a metaphor of war: tenor and vehicle trade places, exchange qualities. Symbols are wounded. Swords *include* words:

> The simple questions of the tattered man had been knife thrusts to him. . . . His late companion's chance persistency made him feel that he could not keep his crime concealed in his bosom. It was sure to be brought plain by one of those arrows which cloud the air and are constantly pricking, discovering, proclaiming those things which are willed to be forever hidden. (*RB*, 54)

> He had a conviction that he would soon feel in his sore heart the barbed missiles of ridicule. He had no strength to invent a tale; he would be a soft target. (*RB*, 64)

> The speech pierced the youth. Inwardly he was reduced to an abject pulp by these chance words. (*RB*, 77)

If Henry Fleming tries to depict, on Crane's behalf, the war, the war more successfully depicts him:

> As he hastened, there passed through his mind pictures of stupendous conflicts. His accumulated thought upon such subjects was used to form scenes. The noise was as the voice of an eloquent being, describing. (*RB*, 43)

To imagine war, imagine war imagining you. If war is the subject, we are its objects. Who is writing? Hell is writing.

3

Goddesses on the Battlefield: The Combatant Novels of Tourgée, Cable, and De Forest[1]

Must realism always follow romance? Not necessarily—not in Shakespeare. I allow myself a considerable definitional latitude here; but so does Howells, when in a paean to Shakespeare he finds in *Macbeth* and *Hamlet* adumbrations of his own realistic art (despite ghosts, since Shakespeare believed in them), but singles out *The Winter's Tale* (along with *Pericles*) as a play he would have been willing to sacrifice.[2] The American sequence is, if anything, slightly counter-intuitive, as if Thoreau's directive to build our castles in the air first, and the ground up to meet them second, were standard operating procedure, with the proviso that realists, having raised the ground to a sufficient elevation, would raze the castles.

So why does nineteenth-century American realism in fact follow nineteenth-century American romance? The implicit answer in all the American texts we group under the realism rubric is: because disillusion presumes illusion. In an essay on J. W. De Forest, Howells makes a witticism that I will drain of its humor for my own purposes: "these people of Mr. De Forrest's [sic] are so unlike characters in novels as to be like people in life."[3] The implication is that we need literary unreality in order to recognize reality by contrast. American realism, as a movement, could not have done without romance (as variously defined as the particular realist project for which it serves as foil); if Twain, James, and Howells have very little in common to abstract for the sake of a positive formal definition of realism, a negative one is suggested by the similar deployment of Sir Walter Scott, Transcendentalist ideality, and *Tears, Idle Tears*.

That realism is identified by its disillusion is at least part of the lesson learned from the example of Tolstoy; *War and Peace* was the paradigm that Civil War realism would have posited if it had existed. Evidence that Tolstoy was the model for this non-existent genre is that Howells was persistently concerned by the inability of any American to equal Tolstoy's scope.[4] There was a single work that suggested that something might be accomplished in America along Tolstoyan lines: De Forest had published *Miss Ravenel's Conversion from Secession to Loyalty* two decades before realism had become a cause. After the outbreak of literary hostilities, the highest claim that Howells could make for the book was that it might be mentioned in the same paragraph with *War and Peace*, the only American war book comparable to the Russian book in the breadth of its truth-telling.[5] But in a correspondence with Howells, De Forest modestly admitted that his own realism fell short of Tolstoy's: "Let me tell you that nobody but [Tolstoy] has written the whole truth about war and battle. I tried, and told all I dared, and perhaps all I could. . . . I actually did not dare state the extreme horror of battle, and the anguish with which the bravest soldiers struggle through it."[6] To understand why we had no great American realist of the Civil War, with one near miss, the place to start is not with why we had no Tolstoy, an absurd question, but rather with what conditions available to Tolstoy were unavailable to our own combatant novelists.

Though I cannot briefly enumerate every "reality effect" in *War and Peace*,[7] I can begin to outline why Howells and De Forest valued it. The most pertinent approach is by way of Auerbach's intuition that Russian realism was born out of an openness to new French and German ideas but a contempt for their basis. That is, the source of realism in Russia was continental modernism subordinated to its own native capacity for a spiritual egalitarianism that like French analysis could puncture fashionable unreality, but on behalf of a higher aspiration. *War and Peace* is Russian meta-realism: it is *about* what Auerbach posits as the origin of modern tragic realism (the Revolutionary and Napoleonic wars that reconfigured Europe) and the Russian attraction and hostility to it.[8] Howells also wanted realism to be founded on a finer ambition than the French, with ethical responsibility replacing spirituality as its motive.

Tolstoy provided the grandest conceivable model of realism as disillusion — as perpetual, as infinite disillusion, disillusion being necessary so long as flesh was not spirit. Tolstoy's agent of disillusion is Pierre, who replaces less plausible enthusiasms with more plausible ones in an open series of upward substitutions. War is critical in the ascent, since realism in Russia as in America was based on the premise that female society is a simulacrum. But war itself had to be de-romanticized, if God and not brutality was what femininity and fashion veiled. Pierre's faithless wife is Hélène: the turn on the Homeric allusion is that Pierre unlike Paris (like Andrei) goes to the war to *escape* his wife, not defend her, on the standard masculine model of flight. Nevertheless, Pierre *like* Paris stands for the subversion of the prestige of duels, though Tolstoy rejoices in the inconsequence of duels in his novel: duels by the nineteenth century were as dandified and artificial a form of brutality as social maneuvering, logistics, and conquest.

In peace, Pierre manages to turn the book's most critical duel into a fiasco. At the start of his confrontation with Dolohov, Pierre strays from the beaten path into deep snow, nevertheless manages to wound Dolohov with a random shot, then plunges into the woods muttering, "Folly . . . folly! Death. . . . Lies."[9] Without the intervention of a goddess, the inept party prevails. Pierre is also Tolstoy's agent for debunking the pretension of war itself to the rational beauty of the (successful) duel. In one of the few instances in the description of the Russian campaign that two individuals stand opposite each other, Pierre clutches a French officer by the throat, and the Frenchman clutches Pierre by the collar, while each wonders, "Am I taken prisoner or am I taking him prisoner?" (*WP*, 947). Such "duels" are less final, more contestable, than contests. Later, assuming to himself the responsibility for assassinating Napoleon, Pierre ends up saving the life of a stray French soldier. Two and a half millennia after Homer, Tolstoy provides the supererogatory proof that war is not rational.

To whom is he proving it? At least to Napoleon, posthumously: "It seemed to Napoleon that the principal significance of what was taking place lay in the personal contest between himself and Alexander" (*WP*, 1034). Tolstoy typically does not leave the point latent:

> Let us imagine two men have come out to fight a duel with swords in accordance with all the rules of the art of fencing. The parrying has continued for some time. Suddenly one of the combatants, aware that he has been wounded and realizing that the affair is no joke but that his life is at stake, throws down his sword and seizing the first cudgel that comes handy begins to brandish it. . . .
>
> The fencer who demanded a contest in accordance with the rules of fencing is the French army; his opponent who threw away his sword and snatched up a club did like the Russian people; those who try to give an account of the issue consistent with the rules of fencing are the historians who have described the event. (*WP*, 1221–1222)

The fact is, however, that Tolstoy has not found a way to register the war literarily except as a variation from the historians' duel—even the brilliant disarray of his battles could not hold our attention forever without the contrast—just as realism is a correction of romance. If Napoleon is vain to think of Alexander as his personal adversary, and Dolohov is proud to think that his measurable superiority will prevail against all irruptions of irrationality, and if Pierre is crazy to contemplate a personal confrontation with Napoleon, nevertheless Tolstoy conceives of his book as the staging of a duel between Napoleon and *himself*, or rather between Napoleon as representative of France and Tolstoy as representative of Russia, or rather between Napoleon as representative of French and Tolstoy as representative of Russian. France is vanquished a second time by Tolstoy's language, in contrast with the French language his novel subsumes: fancy Gallic virtuosity, martial or cultural, is defeated by the massive inertia of *War and*

Peace (luring us into its inviting vastness, overwhelming us by sheer natural potency).

When you get beneath the Russian—that is, the Frenchified—simulacrum, therefore, you get Russian; Howells hoped, after De Forest had once and for all de-romanticized the war, and he and his allies had de-romanticized literature, that what would similarly remain would be reality. Would it be American? Howells thought so: he quotes Daudet as envying Turgenev his "big untrodden barbaric language," as opposed to French, "language of an old civilization"; then he advises Americans to represent all the varieties of "true American" and to disdain the "priggish and artificial" attempt to write "English" ("English" is in quotes).[10] Howells's Tolstoyan hope is that American is to English as Russian is to French. Both sides of the Civil War spoke dialects of American, however, neither of which could claim to be standard, and both of which divided helplessly into sub-dialects. Howells knew this and celebrated it; nevertheless, "American" stays for him an oppositional term to "English." The corollary (which referring to "American" obscures) was that there was no language whose relation to American reality had even the plausibility of centuries of mutual adaptation. Auerbach notes that there are no "dialect regionalisms" in Russian literature;[11] but Civil War novelists precisely as Civil War novelists were adept at mimicking not just the duality but the plethora of racial and regional accents. A civil war is precisely the last place to look for the origins of a Tolstoyan realism.

What, then, is the solution to the riddle of why realism follows romance of those writers who, unlike the realists, felt the obligation to account for the Civil War? The answer evident in almost all combatant novels is: because the existence of sons presumes fathers. Sons may be disillusioned with their fathers; insofar as they are, realism may look attractive to them. Insofar as they worship their fathers, however, realism may look like a contemptible, because literary, compensation for being born later and weaker. Civil War combatant fiction was a "literature of sons": the concept comes from Klaus Theweleit, brilliant exegete of Freikorps literature,[12] and I hope that it will pay off in an analysis of why Civil War novelists would not make the commitment to the realism war that they had made to the real war.

To nominate George Washington Cable as the best combatant theorist of realism as filial degeneration, I have to take seriously two of his novels that are never taken seriously—but they are scorned by critics who are so assured that "realist" is an honorific that they value a boring novel like *Dr. Sevier* (with its tribute to Howells of an interminable apartment-hunting motif) above Cable's late, meretricious entertainments.[13] *The Cavalier*, Cable's first Civil War romance and his only best-seller, is often an inane book, but treating it almost respectfully will enable us to receive Cable's belief that it was better crafted than *The Grandissimes* as something other than critical senility, though the judgment is absurd.[14] The book includes, for one thing, an allegory of realism as merely the literary correlative of belatedness. Its hero is Dick Smith, who begins the novel by accepting a position as quartermaster's clerk in the hope that he can follow in the heroic footsteps of Ned Ferry, who graduated from that position to become the most feared cavalry scout in the Confederacy. But before he leaves on this quest, or *re*quest, Dick Smith dreams that "a young rat . . . [saw] a cockerel, whose tail was scarcely longer than his own, leap down into a barrel, gather some stray grains of corn and fly out again" and "was tempted to follow his example, but having got in, could only stay there" (*TC*, 3).

Ned Ferry is the alias of Edgar Ferry-Durand (he is a kind of Pierre Gustave Toutant Beauregard posing as Pete Gardiner); the difference between romance and realism approximates to the difference between his original name and "Dick Smith." (Romance is generally Creole French among combatant novelists; realism is commonplace Anglo-Saxon.) Dick Smith goes on to duplicate Ned Ferry's career very nearly. He loves the same woman, earns some of her more sororal affection, settles for a lesser woman but still an attractive one, and has a heroic run as a cavalry skirmisher. The whole progress is farfetched: why should the rank of quartermaster's clerk predict invariably, or even twice, a promotion to cavalry hero? Dick Smith's imitation of Ned Ferry's itinerary is presented first as a dream — a dream obviously of phallic competition — and it does not stop seeming like one when it switches from anxiety to wish-fulfillment. Insofar as Dick Smith can catch up with Edgar Ferry-Durand, realism can fulfill its dream of matching in masculine virtue a precedent romance. But Dick Smith never quite overtakes him: the novel's essence of womanhood, Charlotte Oliver, is always beyond his reach but not Ned's. Her ambiguous (though finally vindicated) morality, her preternatural charm, and even her final metamorphosis from war correspondent (and spy) to nurse are exactly what we would expect from a "literature of sons." (Theweleit diagnoses the typical Freikorps novel as a son's revenge against his mother's sexuality, which entails the imaginary transformation of mother into "white nurse" [*MF*, 99–100].) Dick Smith can never equal Ned Ferry, as being a clerk does not prefigure being a hero, as realism (a literary nation of clerks) can never provide an adequate masculine compensation for the lost heroism of modern war, just as sons can never precede their fathers to their mothers.

Even more precisely on the subject of secondariness is *John March, Southerner*, another of Cable's contemned novels. Fair loves Barbara. Barbara loves March. March loves Fannie. Fannie loves Ravenel. Ravenel loves himself. The three males are increasingly masculine; the two women are increasingly feminine. This is an outline of the catenulate romance plot that intersects the more or less realistic plot of the capitalist New South, and it would have been agreeable to align the two plots as follows: masculinity is in decline to the extent that capitalism infects the South. We can almost believe it. The least masculine male is Fair, an adventurer from Massachusetts who is in the South only on behalf of his father's and his own industrial opportunism.

That is the predictable point that we expect of post-war novelists: with speculative capitalism comes realism, defined as a subservience to the commonplace that entails a scorn for the pride of place given to the erotic appetite (as against money-hunger or power-hunger) in the romance. But Cable's point is subtler. Fannie does love Ravenel, mistaking his cynical, martial hauteur for sexual mystery, and is disenchanted, as if on behalf of realism. John March, however, is torn between two loves. He initially adores Fannie; he subsequently learns to love Barbara, another Southern belle, who in illogical desperation asks him to love her romantically as he might love a sister unromantically. March eventually agrees to marry Barbara, which means that not only the Northerner but also the book's paragon of a Southerner (identified in that capacity by the title) has a realistic side, reasonable, responsible, dispassionate, and the Southern woman appeals to it. Concerning Fannie's divinity March has been disabused—perhaps the lesson is that iconoclasm and practicality have spread from North to South—except that Barbara is never disillusioned with him. Further confusion: John March had become a businessman in the first place in service of his devotion not to Barbara but to Fannie; the only way to outduel Ravenel had seemed to be to outearn him. Meanwhile, the Northerner does ask Barbara to marry him as a compromise between a proposal and a proposition, but it is only a business proposition for *her* sake—he is irrationally in love and only wishes to finesse the fact that Barbara is not.

If we jettison the simple association of Northern capital with realism, and Southern landed chivalry with romance, what remains is an elaborate consideration of secondariness per se. John March is preoccupied with the subject on Cable's behalf. When Fannie suggests he try to love someone besides herself, he is astonished: "*I* love again!—*I?*—Ah! how little you women understand men! Oh, Fannie! to love twice is never to have loved. You are my first—my last!" (*JM*, 105). Which is to say that there is nothing secondary in the realm of romance passions—no realism follows. Later, however, John asks Barbara whether she believes that a "second love could ever have the depth and fervor of the first?" Barbara replies self-servingly that it can happen in the case of a man's love, but never in the case of a woman's—that in fact women do not take seriously a man's first love, which is generally inflated (*JM*, 328–330). Whether we are meant to take his second love as less fervid but more realistic, or just as fervid but more realistic, is ambiguous.

The book takes these institutions to be primary: war, property, and love considered as the conquest of desirable property by siege. The book's secondary institutions are business, money, and requited, contractual love. The primary terms are the elements of the Old Southern romance, the secondary are the constituents of the New Southern novel. Yet the book hardly ends with one side vindicated, or even demarcated. John March practices Heathcliffean capitalism on behalf of his first passion and to protect his property; his marriage with Barbara is fraternal for him but passionate for Barbara; the Northern capitalist's love is passionate for him but sororal for Barbara; business is presented as prolonged warfare, and people get killed in its prosecution. Infer that Cable did not merely collapse, out of aesthetic weariness, into romance when he was a resigned old literary trouper, as we are told.[15] (Nor did Tourgée lapse, in every novel of his career, into romance because of a deficiency of taste. These careers are considered as declinations partly on the realist assumption that in a healthy state of literature, realism comes second as disillusion — so that a late devotion to romance is perverse.)[16] Cable theorizes the relationship of romance and realism in his romances just as Howells does in his realism, but with less assurance that they are mutually exclusive, that only one has a purchase on post-war reality, that their historical moments are entirely distinct. I shall argue that a literature of sons will necessarily entail a generic eclecticism such as Cable theorize's, and that the Civil War might have been expected to produce precisely a literature of sons.

Conceiving of realism as disillusion has the advantage of implying a uniform reality beneath the simulacrum — since realism is most readily identifiable across distinct projects by this negative definition, we recognize realism indifferently whether the uniform reality is, for example, class-interest, corruption, or spirit. How in America does one manage such a faith? At the beginning of *Criticism and Fiction*, Howells endorses John Addington Symonds's hope that "unity of taste in the future" will be unsentimental, that "temporary partialities" will be transcended, that the "laws of evolution in art and society" will be recognized.[17] This vision is ostensibly future-oriented, yet the ideal is timeless. What is bad is "temporary." One might have thought that the "laws of evolution" teach nothing if not that *everything* is temporary, but Symonds's hope is in evolution as progressive revelation of an indivisible truth.

So Howells is almost right to remove whatever there is of attenuated temporality from Symonds's prophecy, paraphrasing it as follows: "That is to say, as I understand, that moods and tastes and fashions change; people fancy now this and that; but what is unpretentious and what is true is always beautiful and good, and nothing else is so."[18] This is Howells at his theoretical simplest — but not at his least pragmatic. What Howells wins by disregarding evolution even as revelation and collapsing all temporality into fashion is relief from the obligation to represent the Civil War. Similarly, Henry James, through the medievalist Ransom, ridicules the possibility of "new truths": because of the Civil War, realism must be the new literature for a new society in which nothing essential is new.

To return to Howells's "smiling aspects" misfortune one more time: it is tautological that if Dostoevsky's particular bleakness was founded on the trauma of being almost executed followed by imprisonment, then American writers had no right to it. But Howells generalizes that though "we have death too in America, and a great deal of disagreeable and painful diseases," nevertheless "this is tragedy that comes in the very nature of things, and is not peculiarly American, as the large, cheerful average of health and success and happy life is."[19] Howells wrote these words in 1886, twenty-one years after the Civil War, a single generation. (Dostoevsky published *Crime and Punishment* seventeen years after being condemned to death.) Tourgée was badly wounded in the Civil War (he was temporarily paralyzed) and spent four months in prison; De Forest contracted dysentery, apparently, leading to a lifetime of chronic diarrhea; these were of course more or less lucky outcomes.[20] In the "Editor's Study" version of the "smiling aspects" point, Howells tries to remember what dark, Dostoevskian past he is already forgetting: it is represented by the life of Harriet Tubman.[21]

If it is by a war-induced amnesia (a noncombatant shell shock, in F. Scott Fitzgerald's phrase) that we establish uniformity in time, how is uniformity in space achieved? De Forest complained that we could not have a comprehensive American novel—an American novel whose realism in one section was recognizable as verisimilar in another—because we are "a nation of provinces, and each province claims to be the court. . . . When Mr. Anthony Trollope commences a novel, he is perplexed by no . . . kaleidoscopic transformations and no such conflicting claims of sections."[22] Howells does not see that this is trouble for realism: if American fiction is not so capacious as Tolstoy's, Howells asks, summoning his own invariable touchstone, what is? Howells grants that our "social and political decentralization forbids" representing America as a whole. The genial inference Howells makes is the appropriateness of a realism of narrowness but depth.[23] There is, however, a perplexity for realism that combatant novelists had the wit to find disconcerting: realism depends on the legibility of signs. Uniformity in time or space is necessary to guarantee it. It is the plexus of European experience, as newly forced upon it by Napoleon, that produced continental realism according to Auerbach; Russian realism depended on both spatial and temporal continuity. Taking seriously the pseudo-unity of North and South, and the pseudo-duality of blacks and whites— taking seriously the Civil War and the absence of a correlative to, say, "the Russian people"—led inevitably to a belief in the dialectical contention of signs.

George Washington Cable's *The Grandissimes* is vivid on the dialectical, not to say the idiolectical, tonalities of truth. A parable of Reconstruction set in New Orleans in 1803 and 1804 (the parable is based on the Yankee acquisition of Louisiana and the antagonism of the new rulers to the customary treatment of blacks), the novel is about the convergence of three nationalities (French, Spanish, American), three races (white, black, Indian), three religions (Catholic, Protestant, voodoo). This neat triad of triads is of course neater than anything Cable dramatizes; for one thing, the elements do not correlate. Further: "American" means Yankee, but includes Scottish and English settlers; the French and Spanish nationalities combine in various percentages to form one aristocracy; white blood and black blood have mingled so thoroughly that blacks are occasionally whiter than whites (an anomaly also crucial to Tourgée and De Forest);

whites may even be proud of their Indian blood; blacks may partake of both Christianity and voodoo. Even more confusing, and more significant, is the array of languages: Creole French (which does not happen to equal "French spoken by Creoles"), Parisian French, American English, English spoken by speakers of pure French and English spoken by speakers of Creole French, and who knows what idiolectical variations beyond my linguistic competence. There is, to say the least, no Tolstoyan possibility of segregating the language of the soul from the language of the simulacrum.

It seems perfectly appropriate—and not an annoying device, as is charged—that the book is organized, or just as accurately, disorganized, by means of delayed information and a series of withheld stories. The most capricious seeming example is the suppression of the enlightening fact that there are two separate characters named Honoré Grandissime, both white in color but only one white in racial identity. But the reader's confusion is fitted to the obfuscations of racial taxonomy. The most significantly withheld story, dimly foreshadowed on several occasions before it is told to the protagonist three times in a single night, is that of the hunted, murdered, magnificent slave Bras-Coupé, which haunts every character in the book as it is manipulated to haunt us. Readers of this superb novel feel always a step behind the plot—and forcing us to endure that discomfort is what the novel partly exists to do. There is a truth, but we cannot quite get astride it; there can be no equating of the unpretentious and the true; truth is always caught up in suspense and partiality; such truths are truths *of* moods and fashions.

Albion Tourgée is the more persistent theorist of a reality so disunified that realism is impossible; but his truth is not comfortably relativized either, with the consequence that Tourgée's generic vacillation is more than a missed opportunity to be a realist. *A Royal Gentleman* is his best novel on the unsortability of versions of reality; in *A Fool's Errand* he infers from this the imbrication of genres; in *Figs and Thistles* he enacts a refutation of the realist faith in the legibility of signs in a uniform interpretive community.[24]

The preface to *A Royal Gentleman* includes several apologies for its status as a romance, though Tourgée also insists on its verisimilitude. One of his defenses is premised on the turmoil of "knowledge and ignorance, slavery and freedom, Northman and Southron, Caucasian and African": "Scarcely any age or nation presents so rich a field of romantic incident as the conflict of these forces" (*RG*, v). "Forces" is the right Tourgéan word: his idealism is always vulnerable to the encroachments of relativism, but different regions and races have interfering, rather than merely irreconcilable, mentalities. Later, Tourgée complicates the matter in the style of Cable: "Master and . . . Slave [are] united in a common destiny by that universal passion, love" (*RG*, vii)—which means that Tourgée coopts the love plot, staple of romances, on behalf of the politics, or more precisely the poetics, of desegregation. In the deconstructive novel that follows, the

Southern patriot will fall in love with the white-colored black slave, though the slave will spend part of the book freed.

In sum, Tourgée writes in his preface, "the story is the delineation of a romantic sentiment, having its root in slavery, but its flower and fruitage in freedom, and concerns itself with Slavery only in order to mark the growth of character under that influence. . . . It carefully traces only those unconscious influences which shape and mold mental and moral qualities, and through which *Slavery still lives and dominates*" (Tourgée's emphasis, *RG*, iv–v). The final defense of romance is that to contemplate the Civil War honestly is to understand that it was incomplete (the repeated point of all combatant novelists), which is not the same as implying, in the manner of realists, that it was negligible. Tourgée never centered a novel on the Civil War from the conviction that it was the outward and physical and chronological manifestation of what was more tragically inward and ideal and chronic. If this made him, in his own estimation, a romancer, I shall argue that the indiscreteness of black and white, slavery and freedom, north and south, antebellum and post-bellum made him something more interesting: knowledge and ignorance too, pace the realists, were as a consequence mutually permeable concepts, with odd implications for questions of genre.

A Royal Gentleman concerns the disastrous love of two white men for two black women, and of the disastrous adoration felt by these black women in return, not to mention an instance of a poor white woman adoring an aristocratic white man—the polyvalence of institutionalized sexism, classism, and racism prevents this tale of extravagant desire (bane of Howells's realism) from losing contact with reality. Instead of synthesis, as if these institutions could be transcended, this book is about "admixture," to use the repeated term. Tourgée is so concerned that we see that mixture itself is his strange theme that a verbal signal becomes a tic: old Manuel Hunter is "half gray" (*RG*, 9), has a "half-affected roughness of expression" (*RG*, 9) (and when he is in this half-state irritably calls his slave while "half-clad" [*RG*, 19]), drinks whiskey that is "more 'n half water" (*RG*, 11), and is "more 'n half of the notion" that slavery is detrimental to the South (*RG*, 159). His son Geoffrey Hunter "half wished [that his slaves] were all men" (*RG*, 25); he wishes this with "mouth shut quietly and firmly, the brow drooped, the eyes half closed" (*RG*, 25).

Why does this echolalia matter? The book is explicitly about "strange blending[s]" (*RG*, 7), about "ever-varying analogies and differences, agreements and conflicts" (*RG*, 10), about "hostile moieties" (a phrase to describe the United States, *RG*, 352). It is also about, at one excruciating moment, the nation's Capital "awaiting its future doom half-sullenly, half-hopefully" (*RG*, 358), and about the nation itself trapped between past and future, caught in "the connecting and dividing present" (*RG*, 358)—"connecting and dividing" being Tourgée's key conception, here expressing historically his determination to find an integer between unity and duality. Mainly the book is about the hostile moieties of black and white. Toinette, the slave heroine of the novel, tragic idolater of Geoffrey Hunter (proud

Southerner who merely loves her in return), is lighter skinned than her light-skinned mother, only perhaps a little darker than her master and capable of passing. Toinette cannot be treated "as an equal, nor did it suit [Geoffrey's] purpose to regard her altogether as a menial" (*RG*, 75). She begins as a doubly mixed category—as a result of her demi-freedom, she is "half child, half woman" (*RG*, 75)—and with education she moves halfway from sameness to difference: she develops "a demeanor neither of the servant nor of the equal, the outgrowth of her undefined position" (*RG*, 154).

And the mixed (indivisible, disintegrated) reality must necessarily be mirrored internally by the characters. When Toinette finds the injured Geoffrey and sees that he will not die, her celebration is awkwardly composed of "half sobbings, and half laughter" (*RG*, 335); when he does not recognize her, she excuses him on the grounds that, just awakening from unconsciousness, he is "only half himself" (*RG*, 336). The medical explanation of his failure to recognize her is that he is temporarily blind; but it is fair to say, given his love and contempt for Toinette, that half of himself is the most he ever is. When Geoffrey thinks back to the same period of coma and coming to, he recalls that he had heard Toinette "as he lay, half-dreaming" (*RG*, 367). That is his perpetual state, half-dreaming a love for Toinette, half himself insofar as he submits to its impossibility in the light of local standards. He can at best half-imagine what Toinette is worth, so that when he abandons her, he is only "half-aware of the terrible blow he had struck and of the fair field he had devastated" (*RG*, 380). What is threatened in this self-division, in this oscillation between static and ecstatic, is self-possession: "I would willingly give up all else for your love," he writes her, "but I cannot change my identity—I cannot lose myself" (*RG*, 445).

The hopelessly unsurveyable boundaries of race cause an internal division—or, rather, in Tourgée's world of ideal conflict, it is more accurate to say that internal divisions cause race. The figure of the black woman is a return of the Southern white man's repressed, just as the red (proletarian, Communist) woman arises from the id of the German Freikorpsman. Whites in Tourgée therefore feel haunted by blacks: the ghost-story/hidden-room mystery that keeps the plot plodding for half the book and that all critics half-justifiably despise is a romance element with a reason.[25]

The book is not completely a romance—passages about unnatural passions and, apparently, supernatural visitations give way more than occasionally to bland technical language concerning the legalisms of race and property. The book begins in Manuel Hunter's "private room, half [law] office and half library"—here transpires a "strange blending of business and leisure" (*RG*, 7) that might as well stand for the book's strange blend of law and lawless romance. Dialogue in this "romance" sometimes comes to this: "Will you loan me this volume?" "Certainly. The case is Robertson *et al. vs.* Carter and Others, page 592" (*RG*, 235). The book's voice is divided; so are the voices of its characters. Take Betty Certain, "a strange compound" (*RG*, 262) just as Belle, Toinette's mother, is a "strange compound" (*RG*, 281) (and the relationship of these strange compounds, sympathetic rivals, is compounded strangeness). Betty is strange insofar as she is propertyless and regal. She speaks words like "afeard" and "sorter," yet here is the elevation from which she remembers her love for the aristocratic Arthur Lovett: "I was to be allowed to bow at the shrine of my idolatry. . . . I murmured at my poverty and lowliness; yet I did not dream that it could be otherwise" (*RG*, 184–185). This latter diction is the result of her reading Shakespeare and Scott in Arthur's library. She maintains both accents in adult life; when she works herself into a passion, she "unconsciously" forgets the "vernacular of the 'poor white'" and her diction "show[s] something of the culture which her words [imply]" (*RG*, 174). Conversely, Manuel Hunter, when he is not speaking formally, slips into a vernacular that Northerners falsely associate only with "poor whites" (*RG*, vii).

In their extra-literary lives, Tourgée and Cable were both preoccupied with the necessity of reforming the educational system of the South. We can admire the radicalness of the program: without either blackness or black diction as a definitive mark of Negritude (Scott and the romance are partly redeemed if they elevate the diction of blacks and poor whites to an inhuman—therefore not class- or race-specific—level of artifice), with nothing necessarily to see or hear for the purpose of distinctions, what would remain of race? At any rate, a book in which single characters speak both in dialects that Howells might relish and in diction taken from Scott will not be a romance entirely. It is generically, as if genetically, mixed.

No book is more generically adulterated than Tourgée's most celebrated production, *A Fool's Errand by One of the Fools*. Advertised and usually received as "a brilliant romance" (*FE*, advertising section, 2), the book is still respected today for its realism. But it is more than just an admixture along the lines of *A Royal Gentleman*. The book has the tone of a romance mainly insofar as the KKK enters it—in case this seems to imply an impeachment of romance, suffice it here to say that the book counterpoises an equal and opposite romantic force when the heroic daughter Lily rides *against* the KKK. On the other hand, the book comes very close to the far horizon of realism—it approaches the documentary, with undigested letters and newspaper accounts from Tourgée's career as carpetbagger. The book also takes the form, occasionally, of an essay with charts. Howells says that realism needs to be a picture, not a map, but this book sometimes strays toward the cartographical.

In addition to all that is the weird allegorical element. The protagonist is regularly referred to as "the fool." But the concept "folly" (I do not need to prove) is unstable, and to be a fool in this book mean to be an idealist (*FE*, 118), a realist (*FE*, 129), a pessimist (*FE*, 151), an ignoramus (*FE*, 156, 216), a genius (*FE*, 3), an innocent (*FE*, 180), a Southern cavalier (*FE*, 262), a Southern thug (*FE*, 272), a genuinely wise man (*FE*, 338), and occasionally a genuine fool (*FE*, 68). Odder is the fact that "the fool" would not seem to have needed to be allegorized, since his already allegorical name is Comfort Servosse—though on inspection the Christian name is anti-allegorical, since the uncompromising Comfort brings relief to neither enemies nor friends, blacks nor whites, his family nor himself. The book is unwilling to rest even with an unstable allegory—it demonstrates the untrustworthiness of one of its own generic temptations. Part of the reason is that the South has provided its own allegorical epithet: even Tourgée refers to Servosse as "the carpet-bagger" (*FE*, 267), a negative Pilgrim.

The author refers to himself as a fool and is occasionally at one with his protagonist. Yet Tourgée describes the ride of the KKK with a poetaster's language that does not come from Servosse (it is regrettably his own), and his chart that compares Southern and Northern mutual prejudice seems to come from nowhere. Tourgée calls Northern soldiers neither "The Country's Hope" nor "Yankee vandals" (*FE*, 16); when the North turns against carpetbaggers, it cuts Tourgée off from the Northern definition of the term ("A man without means, character, or occupation, an adventurer, a camp-follower, a 'bummer'") as well as the Southern ("an incarnation of Northern hate, envy, spleen, greed, hypocrisy, and all uncleanness") (*FE*, 162). Harriet Beecher Stowe's response to the fickleness of language was to claim to have written a book that is not written, a hieroglyph. Tourgée could find his way to no similar illusion: denied Northern and Southern diction, he attempted to impersonate unlocatable intelligence itself, but more often seems merely déclassé. The book *arrives* nowhere. Lily does not marry the Southern Klan fellow traveler Melville Gurney, but she does not not marry him; the KKK is defeated (*FE*, 285) in one version of the conclusion and the refractory South triumphs (*FE*, 286, 292) in another. If James looks South for his realism and Twain migrates North, and Tolstoy resides on his own assured premises, this book floats between places, definitions, axioms, and, necessarily, genres.

The realist's geographical hope is that somewhere—for American realists, somewhere else—is a society that functions as a system of signs, though the simulacrum is in so clear an oppositional relation to the truth that both fashion and realism can read the identical signs similarly for different purposes, as Olive and Ransom read Verena. (This is a more corrupt explanation for why realism needs a precedent romance. Disillusion needs illusion not only as scapegoat but also as mentor.) Everything is legibly marked; clothing, manners, and diction are experimental data. This does not take seriously the mysteries that preoccupied Civil War combatant literature: the misleadingness of clothes and manners and diction (gentlemen could be barbarians, slaves could be refined), the liminal indistinctness of color, the metamorphic potential of education. The most brilliant problematization of the legibility of marks is Tourgée's disregarded, disrespected *Figs and Thistles: A Romance of the Western Reserve*. The "romance" is in two sections, with a crime mystery before the Civil War and a business scam after it (the Civil War, described in a tense, denotative prose unusual in Tourgée, makes its only substantial appearance in all his oeuvre as a kind of interlude). This looks like a historical separation of (mystery) romance as antebellum and (business) realism as post-bellum literature. Yet Tourgée lets us know that the *"fact* of war had sunk into insignificance in comparison with its cause and its consequences" (Tourgée's emphasis, *FT*, 187); and the same uncertainty of marks is worrisome on either side of the Civil War passages. Assume that the Civil War is insignificant as a way of quelling that preoccupation, and that the theme must have something to do with the war's cause and consequences.

There is once again the question of racial marking. For example, concerning the woman who raised the protagonist: "It was said that a trace of Indian blood—a suspicion of which her dark eyes, straight, jet hair and stealthy look might well justify—had given her the habit of sullen, intense moroseness" (*FT*, 31). A trace of black blood, on the contrary, had left Toinette racially unmarked in *A Royal Gentleman*; in the case of the allegedly Indian woman, Tourgée hedges the matter with Hawthornean coyness.[26]

The question of marking is not, however, strictly a racial issue in this book. The protagonist, Markham, runs away from home, believing he had murdered his grandfather and "thinking, ever since he began his flight, of Cain and the mark set in his forehead" (35). There are, in fact, welts on his back from his "grandfather's brutal blows," but they do not last and Markham, temporarily incognito, gets educated, Tourgée's preferred method for getting oneself remarked.

So the question particularizes from whether races are marked to whether individuals are marked—are all marks as potentially masked as racial ones? What is the existential equivalent of "passing"? The question then shifts to its avatar most fateful for realists (the skill of the book is in running all these variations together): is the truth marked? A robbery is committed at a bank, and private detectives are called in. But they get nowhere, because the breaking in was so unviolent that it "left no marks to guide those fellows" (*FT*, 121). Markham, an unfledged lawyer, bids to win some local fame by solving the crime, and his first clue is a footprint left by the criminal from a jump he had to take, a mark that indicates an identity. Later, Markham homes in by following that part of the theft that was "marked money" (*FT*, 169). Markham's faith is that truth is similarly marked; that is the entire content of his belief that truth "is mighty and will prevail" (*FT*, 445), that falsehood will not pass.

In the second half of the book, Boaz Woodley, Markam's surrogate father and victim of the first crime, himself commits a (white-collar) crime; the next problem for Markham and Tourgée is revealing it and clearing Markham of his apparent complicity in it. The chief clues are documents discovered on two separate occasions by Markham's wife Lizzie, identifiable as clues by the fact that she "recognized the handwriting" in both cases as belonging to Boaz Woodley. This is necessary because Boaz Woodley turns out to be Basil Woodson (never mind the details, which I have in any case forgotten), so that handwriting provides the inescapable truth of identity: the two ways in which marks are at issue in the book (are identities marked? is the truth?) converge.

Yet we do not leave the book feeling fortified in our trust in the durability of identity and the mightiness of truth. The handwriting issue is, as it turns out, illegible. The original bank crime, in which Woodley was the victim, turned on the possibility of forging Woodley's signature ("The signatures were so well executed that even Markham for a moment hardly thought of doubting their genuineness" [*FT*, 177]). Could it then reveal his identity? Woodley's handwriting is "as fine and delicate as if the hand that traced it were a lady's instead of a giant's—every letter as complete and perfect as if made by machinery; not a particle of shade, effort, or ornamentation about it" (*FT*, 139). This is incongruous. If the handwriting is as perfect as machinery, it can only conceal the effort taken to produce it; if it is as delicate as a lady's, ornamentation might have been one of its features; and a lady is not a machine; and Boaz Woodley is neither. Perhaps the individuality consists of its paradoxical attributes: this is the one signature in the world, maybe, that is feminine and mechanical, natural and masculine. At the very least we would still have to give up hope that handwriting is an entry to the soul. At the most, we would have to wonder how a mechanically perfect signature could be uniquely identifiable.

Meanwhile, we learn some interesting and dramatically irrelevant things about Lizzie's own handwriting: her letters are written in the "sloped style of penmanship known in that region as the 'Spencerian,' and regarded as the *ne plus ultra* of chirographic art"; it was being taught as if there were a "science and art of penmanship" (*FT*, 148, 149). Tourgée saunters for two pages along these lines, concluding: "Beauty or legibility it [the Spencerian style] had not except in his hands or that of a few masters; but it suited the American need, as being a rapid and easily-acquired system of thought-delineation" (*FT*, 150). If the male villain has a feminine hand, the female heroine has a masculine one (fast, unornamented, functional). But both are mechanical, both are reproducible, and neither reveals character. In addition, Lizzie's style of handwriting is usually illegible, though somehow at the same time useful for "thought-delineation." We might well wonder how perfectly ideas get physically embodied, turned into legible phenomena, in *Tourgée's* writing.

The detective's or psychologist's hope that a signature is indicative of character in actual extra-literary life is tantamount to the critical hope that a name, such as Markham, is revealing of character in a novel. Both are functions of the superstition that some signifiers are invested with meaning, though if naming is the author's one moment of true freedom, a signature is (analysts hope) fated. Boaz Woodley tries to escape his identity as Basil Woodson, but we should pay attention to his singular ineptness in the attempt. It is by the incredible carelessness of keeping his initials BW that he is uncovered; if the point is that he cannot rewrite his initial destiny, all we can see in it is that the author has kept himself free.

It is no surprise that the the book's danger is represented by Boaz Woodley's attempt to switch identities. From the beginning, character is conceived of as characterization, and every actor in the drama understudies all the roles. Burrill Andrus, Markham's grandfather, beats the young Markham with a stick; so Markham sets a snake on him; Burrill gets the snake off by submitting to a beating himself (the man who beats Burrill overdoes it to avenge Markham); and to extend the interchangeability of all roles to the animal and mineral kingdoms, the rod that is used to remove the snake "again and again . . . hissed through the air" (*FT*, 17), which means that the rod, as if by Aaron's divine metamorphosis, plays the role of the snake. Markham runs away thinking that he murdered Burrill; because of the boy's disappearance, all the village thinks that Burrill murdered Markham. Woodley is the victim of the first crime and the perpetrator of the second. Lizzie, who helps her betrothed in detective work, uses a spade to dig up the buried treasure; the absence of the spade becomes in turn a mystery that inspires theories (*FT*, 160). And her mysterious movements in pursuit of the stolen goods are always tracked in advisedly inappropriate language: "for two days, Lizzie Harper spent every moment she could steal, of night or day, in gazing upon the scene of the crime" (*FT*, 154); she "stole silently and quickly along the hall" (*FT*, 155).

Markham pursues the thief's itinerary to a clothing store where the thief had bought a suit (spending what *he* had stolen); Markham himself, weirdly, buys a suit. This makes clothing an illegible sign. The thief turns out to be Markham's college classmate, Horton, who is engaged to Lizzie's best friend while Markham is engaged to Lizzie. Horton redeems himself, under an alias, as a minister during the period that Markham is implicated, though falsely, in Woodley's scam. When Markham discovers Woodley's crime, he is blackmailed by Woodley to prevent his revealing it; when Lizzie discovers Woodley's old identity (he had stolen and forged like Horton, and had been falsely accused of murder like Andruss), she blackmails him (the indelicate word is not breathed) to protect her husband.

Almost nothing in this book is any more legible than Lizzie's handwriting, though that style of writing is supposed to be especially efficient; when some writing is legible, like Woodley's signature, it reveals nothing of what it names, and the name may be assumed. I am considering Tourgée's writing as in flux between these two paradigms. If clothing is shown by the incident of the suits to be unreadable, is what it veils more vulnerable to a realistic reading? Is a symptom an attempt of the body to be legible? When Woodley is ill, the physician "could hardly decide whether his symptoms pointed to recovery or speedy dissolution" (*FT*, 492). If writing is not necessarily legible, then symptoms are not necessarily symptomatic. Is Markham strangely descended from Woodley's first love? That can be answered: yes he is. But the fact, Markham is told, is meaningless: "whether you inherited the attributes and characteristics which attracted this strong nature from his first and probably only love, is a very interesting, even if quite insoluble, inquiry" (*FT*, 534).

We arrive by this late pseudo-revelation from Tourgée's preoccupation with the potential unmarkedness of race (as a question of the inheritance of attributes) at a more nearly absolute sense that an epistemology of the identifying mark is pernicious. (Perhaps the point of connection is in Markham himself: his name seems chosen to raise the issue of whether he carries with him the mark not of Cain but of Ham. What a nice joke on readers if the hero of this book, with his uncertain parentage, is part black.)[27] Is truth marked? We are not so sure; but "calumny, like death, loves a shining mark" (*FT*, 34). Is sex marked? This correlative question runs through the age of realism; the correlation more or less *defines* realism. The answer is complicated. Lizzie is the best detective in the book; she is the only character capable of facing down the daunting and resourceful Woodley; she blackmails him; she triumphs. She is more competent and intelligent and powerful than her husband, the Civil War hero. Why does Civil War fiction that is written by her husband's fellow veterans invariably take us from the unmarkedness of race—via the unmarkedness of truth, a refutation of the realist premise—to the unmarkedness of gender?

For the realists, the Civil War never began; for the combatants I have been considering, the Civil War never ended. In these conceptions they all contradict, in advance, William James, who considered the Civil War to be a prime example of war with perfect closure. *The Moral Equivalent of War* is as much about the necessity of discovering an *aesthetic* equivalent of war: James shares in the general "unwillingness of the imagination" to "envisage a future in which . . . the destinies of people shall nevermore be decided quickly, thrillingly, and tragically.[28] In fact, James is rather better at suggesting the moral equivalent than the aesthetic equivalent; at the border of Clausewitz's century and Scarry's, he anticipates Scarry in trying to imagine an ethically superior substitute for war, but follows Clausewitz in assuming the perfection of war's own finality. The response of Tourgée, De Forest, and Cable might run as follows. If the aesthetic equivalent of war requires thrilling and tragic historical decisions, then the Civil War itself was not the aesthetic equivalent of war. Each of them offered himself up in the futile hope of completing it: Tourgée and De Forest by moving South with Reconstruction, Cable by writing and speaking brilliantly on behalf of the new cause of civil rights.

　　The inability of Tourgée, De Forest, and Cable to leave the Civil War behind brings Klaus Theweleit to mind; the Freikorpsman whom Theweleit diagnoses may be defined as a German for whom World War I was not decisive (the Freikorps continued fighting against the Red Army in the Baltic and against German workers and others until their projects were absorbed into Nazism). Of course, in at least one sense the comparison is fantastically unjust: Tourgée, De Forest, and Cable were not Klansmen, who like Freikorpsmen turned their frustration against all participants in post-war social disorder and reordering. The Civil War combatant novelists I am discussing were the foes of the KKK—Tourgée's life was perhaps endangered by it.

And yet — Theweleit's book is not proposed as a study of proto-Nazis, rather of men. Not that all men are proto-Nazis, simply that the dividing line is never soothingly sharp. If that is an unwelcome point, at least let us note in respect for the Civil War combatant novelists that it is very nearly their own. A book such as *John March, Southerner*, written by Cable (who had been by the time of its writing a Northerner for a decade), refuses to make easy distinctions between Southerners and Northerners; De Forest's *Miss Ravenel's Conversion* features a Virginian cavalier who chooses the Union cause. To say that Southerners and Northerners are not clearly separable is not to say enough: not all Southerners in Reconstruction were Klansmen, and we want to hear from Tourgée, armed adversary of the Klan, before we make the Theweleitian point that the border between criminals and men of good will is just as permeable. Or perhaps we should call it the Lionel Tigerian point, since the Klan appears frequently in *Men in Groups* as a reasonably standard outcome of aggressive male bonding.[29] Tourgée is precisely the best source of the argument. Insofar as *A Fool's Errand* reads like a romance (and recall that Tourgée published several apologies for the genre), it does so to the extent that the Klan enters it:

> It was a chill, dreary night. A dry, harsh wind blew from the north. The moon was at the full, and shone clear and cold in the blue vault.
>   There was one shrill whistle, some noise of quietly-moving horses; and those who looked from their windows saw a black-gowned and grimly-masked horseman sitting upon a draped horse at every corner of the streets, and before each house, — grim, silent, threatening. (*FE*, 205)

> An Invisible Empire, with a trained and disciplined army of masked midnight marauders, making war upon the weakling 'powers' which the Wise Men had set up in the lately rebellious territory! (*FE*, 226)

> How lightly they told the tales of blood. . . . of warnings and whippings and slaughter! Ah, it is wonderful! (*FE*, 227)

The Klansman is an affront to realism because he is silent and invisible (almost an ideal force), because he is masked (almost illegible), because he is mysteriously gowned, makes blood flow, and rides in moonlight (almost feminine, yet hyper-masculine). The KKK calls out the romancer in Tourgée, whose exclamatory and alliterative powers especially are challenged, as if only such triplets as "masked midnight marauders" and "warnings, whippings, wonderful!" were equal to the real-life lyricism of the KKK.

How could the Klan not be attractive even to one of its most determined opponents, if in Tourgée's writing (and Cable's and De Forest's) there are everywhere signs that adult masculinity is a tantalizing ideal, that their literature therefore constitutes a literature of sons, and if the Klansmen are paradigmatic boy-men, conducting bloody initiation rites? If Freikorps literature is a literature of sons, then what else is, for example, *Figs and Thistles*? Markham is fatherless, so he attracts a series of father substitutes, especially the good father John Field and the sinister father Boaz Woodley. *The Cavalier* and *John March, Southerner* are both stories in which coevals, as I have suggested, are categorized as boys or men, and the protagonist in both is a boy. The protagonist of Cable's *Dr. Sevier*, invalid, noncombatant, chronically unable to stay employed, cannot survive without the help of the fatherly, eponymous Sevier. And De Forest's *Miss Ravenel's Conversion*, a book that needs to be considered as an approach to realism, is nevertheless another example of the type insofar as its protagonist Captain Colburne falls well short of the sexual maturity of his Colonel Carter.

Curiously, it is combatants who keep expressing, repeatedly, the failure of the Civil War to make them feel like men—as opposed to the realists, who having fled the war were able to generate a compensatory masculinity in a metonymic war (for realism in the 80s), as if a twenty-year sleep allowed Rip Van Winkle to pass his story-telling off as valor. The Theweleitian consequence is that the world cannot solidify for the veterans: if the difference between Freikorps literature and Civil War combatant literature can be framed in Theweleitian terms, it is that the tide the Freikorps opposes (femininity and egalitarianism, both imaged in one phrase as the "Red Flood"), the Civil War novelists ride. An "abolitionist," according to Southerners, was "one who was in favor of, and sought to promote, negro-equality, miscegenation, rape, murder, arson, and anarchy, with all the untold horrors which the people there believed would follow the uprising or liberation of a race of untaught savages, lustful as apes, bloodthirsty as cannibals, and artful as satyrs" (*FE*, 159): exactly the Freikorps vision, with abolitionists substituted for communists.

This is not Tourgée's view, of course, but on the other hand it is not a vision only alive in the recalcitrant South; the demarcations cannot be perfectly sustained, because it was the *fate* of demarcations in the Civil War to be unsustainable. Here is how Freikorps publicists put their inevitable metaphor. "The wave of Bolshevism surged onward," or "the Reds inundated the land," or "The Red wave surged onward" (*MF*, 229): the hope was that Communists and women could be dammed by a shared epithet. Theweleit explains that "the flood is abstract enough to allow processes of extreme diversity to be subsumed under its image. All they need have in common is some transgression of boundaries" (*MF*, 232). In this light, consider the evocation by Cable, civil rights spokesman, of what has been drowned in the Civil War:

> [John March] pondered again upon the present and the future of the unhappy race upon whom freedom had come as a wild freshet: Thousands must sink, thousands starve, for all were drunk with its [freedom's] cruel delusions. Yea, on this deluge the whole Southern social world, with its two distinct divisions—the shining upper—the dark nether—was reeling and careening. (*JM*, 40)

The black flood destroys first of all blacks—but also everybody else; liquidity within (drunkenness) and without (the deluge) overwhelms equally the shining upper and the dark nether, upsetting all solid categories; but if blacks are the first victims, what is triumphant in this inundation if not the dark nether? Therefore: the "old plantation slumbered on below the level of the world's great risen floods of emancipations and enfranchisements" (*JM*, 235). This is the red tide almost precisely anticipated. A contradiction (the Civil War's incompleteness could be experienced as a failed consummation or as an unmanning; the Civil War freed the slaves) begins to have the feel of a psychic coincidence. In combatant Civil War literature, the Southern awe before an unshackled black population becomes a general male awe before an unleashed femininity. Virgin land blackens in the black flood.

The central image of the combatant novel, insofar as it is romance, is the Woman on a Horse. This is not a prevalent image in Freikorps literature, though it appears. A report of "Spartacist women riding shaggy horses, hair flying, two pistols in each hand" (juxtaposed in the book with a painting by Henri Rousseau, "The War," featuring a spike-haired female with a sword on a spike-haired horse, mowing down men) earns this simple commentary from Theweleit: it is clearly "a product of fantasy, inasmuch as there were no such things as Spartacist women who rode around on shaggy horses" (*MF*, 72–73). There is, however, much on horses in Theweleit, as the only erotic objects that fascists can lovingly depict in their literature, and there is some equinophilia in Civil War romances as well.

The Woman on a Horse is so ubiquitous in Civil War combatant literature that her appearance in *A Fool's Errand* provokes this dismissive shrug: Tourgée's "incidents, when they left the realm of the conflict between struggling black and domineering white, were what Tourgée's feminine readers thought life should be, rather than what Tourgée knew it was: Lily Servosse made the traditional wild and heroic night ride to forestall a Klan raid in the nick of time, for example."[30] As if it goes without saying that a romance designed for women ought to have this particular feature. But why should reading women identify with riding women? Apparently they do: trying to capitalize on the success of *A Fool's Errand*, Tourgée used the figure again in his subsequent Reconstruction novel, *Bricks Without Straw*.[31] Edmund Wilson's comment that Tourgée was like the Southerners he opposed should be modified in view of the fact that in his books, only a girl is really equal to the Southerners he opposed.[32] In *Dr. Sevier*, Cable's heroine is a gentle flower of a woman, about whom the most that can be said is that she is stronger than her husband. So she has a heroic ride to New Orleans through Northern and Southern lines (she is shot at, the only military adventure of the book) to return to her beloved invalid, during which she is referred to humorously yet affectionately as "a good soldier" (*DS*, 397, 406). The book, however, was written under Howells's influence; therefore the ride is not at night, and the woman is unarmed.

The greatest of all the Women on Horses is Charlotte Oliver, who rides dangerously on various personal and martial errands. Here it should be mentioned that Theweleit, though he does not come across many women on horses, does feature *Flintenweiber* (rifle-women)—evil, promiscuous, castrating, subversive women with weapons—of whom Charlotte is ancestress. Actually, Charlotte is not evil, promiscuous, castrating, or subversive, but she seems to be all of these before becoming a "white nurse." (She gives up her previous profession of war correspondent. Female war correspondents are also threatening in *Miss Ravenel's Conversion*. What are women doing on the battlefield?)

Charlotte Oliver is not merely Charlotte Oliver, she is also Coralie Rothvelt—two names for an ambiguous identity. (Is she a Southern patriot or Northern spy? Promiscuous or pure?) The names are anagrams, suggesting that the contraries are indistinct, and I take Cable's trope as an invitation to note that "Charlotte Oliver" is a weak anagram of "The Cavalier." The ostensible cavalier is Ned Ferry—but the book insists repeatedly that Ned and Charlotte are romantic peers, equally ambiguous (they both have two names, one more foreign than the other), equally resourceful, passionate, sensual, and commanding. Add another ambiguity: is Charlotte masculine or feminine? *The Cavalier* was written after a post-Civil War book by Cable's warm friend Henry James, and Charlotte Oliver is a kind of anagrammatic mirror of Olive Chancellor. But Cable cannot dismiss Charlotte as unsexed—her masculine aura is part of her intense feminine appeal.

In a Civil War novel, we run across as many goddesses as heroes; Aphrodite—the fighting Aphrodite of *The Iliad*—is everywhere, stronger than Achilles or Mars. What Civil War novelists clarify about modern war, in not making an epic of it, is very similar to what Homer implies but disguises to *have* his epic. If war is still beautiful, it is because goddesses lend their grace to it. But that is an emasculated and illusory beauty, of the sort that art (on behalf of goddesses) supplies. (The goddess Charlotte Oliver appears on the battlefield as a writer.) What has been lost is warfare in which men face men in duels, so that beauty inheres in the rationality of combat. The same goddess who makes war beautiful enough to be narrated also makes it humiliating to the sons who look at her and are overawed. (Colburne, the metaphorical son of Carter and Lillie Ravenel in *Miss Ravenel's Conversion*, is actually referred to as Telemachus; the Civil War novel is a Telemachiad, with every Telemachus, in the presence of Penelope, hallucinating Aphrodite.)[33] Over four hundred women posed as men— as Homeric goddesses posed as men—to get into Civil War combat; women used feminine fashion (hoops, reticules, elaborate hairstyles) for espionage purposes. And Belle Boyd, who killed a Union soldier in her home, went on to pose as a "femme fatale" to get information out of Northern officers; she was famous for "midnight horseback rides through enemy lines . . . in the midst of enemy shelling."[34] She would seem to be the original of Charlotte Oliver; the only unrealistic aspect of the portrait is that Charlotte turns out to be innocent. What is dismissed as romance more honestly confronts the sexual carnival of the Civil War than realism.

Which leaves a final puzzle: how then does De Forest manage to become the only combatant to write a realistic novel in the Howellsian mode? The first clue is that there is a bad woman in *Miss Ravenel's Conversion*, willful, imaginative, and promiscuous. Naturally she is a Creole, Mrs. Larue. As a warrior, she has no power beyond her imagination: she "metaphorically" ties "Beast Butler [tyrant of New Orleans] to a flaming stake and [performed] a scalp dance around it, making a drinking cup of his skull and quaffing from it refreshing draughts of Yankee blood" (*MR*, 173). She is metaphorically the Woman on a Horse: "Some men can be driven by a cunning hand through flirtations which they do not enjoy, just as a spiritless horse can be held down and touched up, to a creditable trot. But Carter was not a nag to be managed in this way, being too experienced and selfish, too willful by nature and too much accustomed to domineer, to allow himself to be guided by a jockey whom he did not fancy" (*MR*, 137). Actually, he is ridden by Mrs. Larue eventually to his moral ruin. In war realism, the female rider is metaphoric; in war romance, she is real.

So we get our war realism. We know it is realism because (1) it exhibits the meta-realistic mark of realism, that is, it keeps protesting that it is not romance, in this case by not allowing Lillie Ravenel to go undisillusioned with the mercurial Carter, and arranging for him to be replaced by the solider Colburne; (2) it exhibits the formal mark of realism that things, when not veiled by regional romance, may be identified by their marks (the scientist Dr. Ravenel can see what is corrupt in Carter by observation on the model of his geologist's empiricism, though Carter is sometimes not "legible" to Colburne [*MR*, 195]); (3) it subscribes to the characteristic thematic protocol of realism, that it must traffic in the mixed, mediocre, and commonplace, with an attached meta-realistic claim. (Miss Ravenel and Captain Colburn "met in a merely friendly, commonplace manner. That is not the way that heroes and heroines meet on the boards or in some romances. . . . Melo-dramatically considered real life is frequently a failure" [*MR*, 128–129].)

In enumerating the realistic gestures of *Miss Ravenel's Conversion*, I do not mean to imply that realism can be considered as anything other than an "effect," as Barthes says; but the reality effect, insofar as certain American books are realistic, is not the result of the accumulation of unsorted stuff (signifiers that point at referents without the intervention of signifieds, the repressed signifieds returning as "realism"), but instead follows from the representation of romance within realism as the locus of unreality, leaving the remainder of the book associated by default with life. All realism is meta-realism; without the ingestion of romance—without, rather, the indigestion of romance—there is no realism. We accept this book as realism because it does what realistic books do—even the display of commonplace material comes in tandem with its metaliterary point—despite these undigested romance elements: the conflict of the soiled soldier with the solider soldier; the distinction of the evil woman and the innocent woman; the designation of the Creole woman as the embodiment of amoral sensuality.

My question becomes: how do you get a Civil War novel with inclinations toward romance to make the precise meta-realistic claims of a novel by Howells? Step one is to bracket the significance of the war that is at the center of the book. This has the effect of shifting our sympathy from the

Civil War hero (the romancer Carter, corrupt in peace but incorruptible in war) to the more staid but still manly Colburne, by analogy from romance to realism; it plants us more firmly in the commonplace earth. De Forest has no wish to claim that the Civil War itself was a commonplace occurrence. What is bracketed is a world of surreal inhumanity ("nearly supernatural in its horror," *MR*, 262) in which by alchemy even adulterers like Carter, a character whose amiable sordidness is a token of the alloyed reality of realism, can ride to their deaths (riding, not ridden) in unadulterated heroism. ("Balzac says that very corrupt people are generally very agreeable" [*MR*, 85], writes De Forest, a meta-realistic endorsement good enough for the creator of Bartley Hubbard, though unlike Hubbard, Carter dies heroically.) The war is *not* part of the mixed and mediocre reality that De Forest wishes to make the basis of his art (reality is mixed when company is mixed). The Gothic war with its epic heroes is largely a foil for his realism.

Critics do not like to acknowledge just how insignificant, how isolated, the Civil War is in this book. The claim is generally made that the Civil War does the important work of bringing Colburne to full, not irrevocably belated, manhood.[35] If that is true, this chapter is wrong, and Tourgée and Cable were merely eccentric or pathological in their sense of the relationship of incomplete masculinity, an unconsummated war, and generic impurity. A realism as masculine as romance *could* follow romance, at least — on this reading — according to one veteran.

I do not think, however, that Colburne is only masculinized by the war. He tells Lillie that "the war will give a manlier, nobler tone to the character of our nation," and clearly Lillie admires the manlier man before her (*MR*, 436). That is not all that she newly values, however. "She could not help admiring him, as he lay there, for looking so sick and weak, and yet so cheerful and courageous, so absolutely indifferent to his state of bodily depression" (*MR*, 435). What Lillie here admires in Colburne is what Colburne admires in Lillie: "I wonder that this [self-indifference] should seem hard doctrine to you," he tells her. "Women, if I understand them, are full of self-abnegation, and live through multitudes of self-sacrifices" (*MR*, 446). This adverts to the book's continuous if implicit comparison of going to war and giving birth (risking death to give new life, a "new birth of freedom," for instance), two modes of a Christian *imitatio* the association of which makes De Forest again reminiscent of Tolstoy.[36]

Lillie also reveres the mute obedience of a soldier: "You no more pretend to reason concerning your duties," Colburne tells her, "than a millstone troubles itself to understand the cause of its revolutions" (*MR*, 435). The unwitting echo here is of a remark by Dr. Ravenel about Lillie's infant. Lillie had wondered what the baby was thinking when he turned his head to the sky; "I presume he thought just about as much," laughs the father, "as the hollyhocks do when they turn their faces toward the sun" (*MR*, 415). The war masculinizes, the war feminizes, the war infantalizes. This is not implausible — Keegan, remarking on the infantalization of soldiers when they are near death, considers how often their cries are for "mother";[37] the effect of the Civil War in particular was, as a modern war, to devalue the independence of the soldier, while on the home front women were running households and businesses and entering new professions. The situation might have allowed us to predict a war literature by men for women, in which the appeal to women is in the similar nostalgia of sons and wives for the figure of the patriarch, a longing on the male side explicit enough to make Edmund Wilson worry that *The Cavalier*, despite Charlotte's love for Ferry, is a homosexual book because of Dick Smith's.[38] I am suggesting that the female market for war literature was not a cause of this generic eclecticism, rather an effect; the cause was war.

Another way that critics deny the war's insignificance in *Miss Ravenel's Conversion from Secession to Loyalty* is by disliking the title, since Lillie's conversion is only personal.[39] She first discovers that Northerners have more consideration for her private misfortune of having been raised in the South than Southerners have for the humiliation of her father's unionism. This begins to transform her. Her intense loyalty to her husband (who attracts her by virtue of his Virginian charm but fights for the North) forwards the transformation, and her final betrayal at the hands of Carter and Mrs. Larue and retreat to Colburne complete it. Surely, critics feel, this trivial process could not be the novel's central action.

If we ignore Lillie, what do we get when we concentrate on the Virginian, Carter? What causes *his* preference for loyalty to secession? All we know is that it has no important factor—perhaps it is merely out of the habit of West Point loyalty. At any rate, he leaves the lucrative peacefulness of his assignment in occupied New Orleans actually to do battle only from personal ambitions (*MR*, 167).

Granted that Lillie's father is a unionist for strong ideological reasons; evidence is that he throws himself enthusiastically into the cause of Negro labor and education in subdued New Orleans. The book would have made perfect sense if Dr. Ravenel's objection to Carter had been his Southernness; but Dr. Ravenel is confused by Carter's loyalty, as readers may be. So the father's chief concern in the book is apolitical. Lillie is poised between her father and Carter (between familial loyalty and secession) at approximately the same moment that she is balanced between political secession and loyalty—but there is no way of getting the personal and the political aligned. This last sentence makes the mistake of positing that there is any political dimension to her defection at all.

We get our commonplace realism by bracketing the Civil War. At the end of the book, however, two odd things happen, confusing our generic bearings. First, after Carter is killed in battle, Lillie is drawn to the somewhat less magnetic Colburne. This seems a triumph for realism—silly Lillie has learned the Howellsian lesson. But she chooses Colburne over a rich academic named Whitewood (as Barbara muddles genres by choosing the second most charismatic male over the third in *John March, Southerner*), and she chooses him simply for his greater magnetic pull. Whitewood has to grant Colburne's "superior conversational cleverness, and humbled himself in the dust before his honorable fame as a soldier" (*MR*, 453)—he grants about Colburne what Colburne had once granted about Carter. (Colonel Carter and Captain Colburne begin to look less chiasmic and more anagrammatic at this point.) In short, Lillie again follows her sexual instincts, and now the narrative voice approves: "How imperiously, for wise ends, we are governed by the passion of sex for sex, in spite of the superficial pleas of selfish reason and interest! What other quality, physical or moral, have we that could take the place of this beneficently despotic instinct?" (*MR*, 445). Yet that is the lesson of the romance novel (against selfishness, reason, and interest, against, that is, the new omni-capitalist order) that this protorealistic book had been trying to contemn, in condemning Carter on behalf of what came later and weaker. The instinct with respect to Carter was despotic but not benevolent, and was utterly superficial.

Meanwhile, as romance begins to prevail, the empirical and wise Dr. Ravenel becomes a romancer, a patriotic romancer as opposed to a traitorous, Southern romancer. He has read the European editorials expressing their enthusiasm for the Union victory, and he exults that "it is enough to make a spread peacock-tail sprout upon every loyal American" (*MR*, 443). Now Lillie tries to introduce a little realism. "The Europeans seem to have more enthusiastic views of us than we do of ourselves," she says. "I never thought of our being such a grand nation as Monsieur Laboulaye paints us. You never did, papa." He replies: "I never had occasion till now" (*MR*, 443). In his joy, he has lost the displaced scientific objectivity that had allowed him to taxonomize Mrs. Larue and Carter by their marks.

Dr. Ravenel goes on to find in the characters of Lincoln, Grant, Sherman, and Farragut grounds for "faith in the supernatural origin of humanity" (*MR*, 444). He "can now understand the Paradise Lost [sic], for I have beheld Heaven fighting with Hell" (*MR*, 444). *He* would not write a realistic war novel; he would write an epic. War is not Hell, war conquers Hell. In the face of his "lyricism," which seems more like epicism, Lillie drily considers the bottom-line implications of Miltonic war: "The National debt will be awful" (*MR*, 444).

What has occurred? By what mechanism does Lillie turn finally into the book's skeptical, practical, sardonic realist, and the scientist into the book's romancer, or lyricist, or epicist, at any rate, the book's *anti*-realist? The answer, insofar as I can make it out, is this: Dr. Ravenel, even after the war, is still engaged in the conceptual, the ideal, the spiritual conflict; Lillie, moving on, thought the war had been a private matter.

4

Temporal Form and Wartime: Modernism After World War I

As I Lay Dying, published in 1930 at the end of the two-year outpouring of World War I literature, begins far from the Western Front with Darl's observation, more or less, of his brother Jewel.[1] Jewel is fifteen feet behind him, walking up the path, so Darl must violate—or cause Faulkner to violate—a dictum of realistic writing (describe only when the visual opportunity presents itself) in order to tell us (or transmit, somehow, the thought to us) that Jewel wears a broken straw hat. Actually, he imagines someone in the cottonhouse observing Jewel's hat above his own head; he is visualizing what he cannot see behind him by imagining someone ahead of him visualizing it, himself an opacity that allows only Jewel's hat to be seen, yet curiously transparent in that it is Jewel who gets limned. This is not even one of Darl's best tricks; he is characteristically at all viewpoints at once, in his sister's mind, in Faulkner's mind, his own mind vulnerable to theirs. "It's like he had got into the inside of you, someway," says Tull. "Like somehow you was looking at yourself and your doings outen his eyes" (*ALD*, 119). His world has no interiors, no privacies, no depths; it consists of shards of vision, scattered on the surface of a mind.

It is not beyond Darl's resources, we infer, when, in the midst of the barn fire episode, he catches a fragment of the scene with remote precision: "The front, the conical facade with the square orifice of doorway broken only by the square squat shape of the coffin on the sawhorses like a cubistic bug, comes into relief" (*ALD*, 208–209). The frantic scene is transmuted into a geometric still life; the striking term, connecting geometry to art, is "cubistic." We might remember that e. e. cummings, in *The Enormous Room*, exhibits just such a nonchalant knowingness when he thinks of a wood-cut of "a tall, bearded, horrified man who, clad in an anonymous rig of goat-skins, with a fantastic umbrella clasped weakly in one huge paw, bends to examine an indication of humanity in the somewhat cubist wilderness whereof he had fancied himself the owner."[2] Cummings already proclaims himself an avant-garde painter and writer at the time of his incarceration in France during World War I (the subject of *The Enormous Room*), and he had already been to Paris to take the measure of modernism. We suspect, on the other hand, that if Darl is capable of a similar allusion, it must be because his mind is temporarily on loan to Faulkner's.

At nearly the last moment of the book, however, a few pages before the end, we learn that our contumely is wrong. We discover, almost too late, a fact so odd that we wonder what we had been making of the book in ignorance of it. Even when we come across it, it is a jagged fact to absorb. Darl, on his way to the asylum, is said to have "a little spy-glass he got in France at the war. In it it had a woman and a pig with two backs and no face" (*ALD*, 244). Darl has been to Europe; Darl, I presume, has been to Paris. Surely he was there on a spree, more like John Andrews in *Three Soldiers* than e. e. cummings; yet even Andrews returns to Paris with the serious intention of studying music. Is that why Darl went there? Perhaps we can imagine Darl, like many another American soldier, hitching a ride somewhere with Gertrude Stein; she likes his Americanness and invites him to the Rue de Fleurus. He tells her stories about American crazies. She introduces him to Picasso and Braque—hence, "cubistic."

One had thought of *As I Lay Dying* as a progress from the sticks to the city, from redneck ignorance to urban technology, from prehistory to modernity. The oddity is that Darl had already arrived, before Faulkner. The fact that Darl was in World War I makes the book seem superfluous— the largest experience of its main surviving character has been left out of the family history. One does not know as a result how to appraise what has been left in. Is the experience of the Bundren family parallel to Darl's in the war, so that Darl's insanity comes partly from the knowledge that there are no enclaves against modernity? Or a laughably retarded travesty of it? Or Faulkner's minimization of Darl's experience? If we are tempted to compare one confrontation with modernity and another, we are frustrated by the absence of any basis for doing so; a book stands against a remark. The question of this chapter might be put this way: what is the meaning of Darl's combat experience? Or: why does Darl have combat experience that has no meaning?

I reserve a full discussion of *As I Lay Dying* for the end of this chapter. I suggest here that for American writers as a species, what World War I made possible was the justification of a style. Begin with Bersani and Dutoit's axiom that "in the most general sense, we have narration whenever one thing is placed in front of something else which it partially blocks."[3] Then we might assume that what is narrated at the beginning of *As I Lay Dying* is the genesis not of style but of narrative itself. The problem is that the thing blocked is the thing seen. Jewel's hat is brought up to the surface of vision so that it sits just a head's length above Darl's head; Jewel is brought up with it, to confute perspective. Bersani and Dutoit posit their first premise of narration as against Assyrian sculpture that defuses narrative by mobilizing our vision multi-directionally on a surface; Faulkner's art also subverts, on a cubist authority, the hierarchies that are a necessary condition of narratives. I want to use that originary repudiation as an emblem of American modernist novels. What is deposed is the pre-eminence of the story; what is enthroned is an imperial style.

This is not the case with British war writing of the same period. Such memoirs as Blunden's *Undertones of War* (1928), Sassoon's *Memoirs of an Infantry Officer* (1930), and Graves's *Goodbye To All That* (1929), or such a novel as Aldington's *Death of a Hero* (1929), are stylish in the service of a narrative, as opposed to the American enlistment of narrative in the service of stylistic virtuosity.[4] Blunden's endangered pastoral equilibrium cannot be confused with Sassoon's dogged innocence or Graves's sardonic ebullience; but what I am urging is the essential weakness of these manners in contrast to the story they all tell.

All of these books, for one thing, are generically uncertain—much like the literature of Civil War combatants, especially Tourgée's. Blunden's *Undertones of War* begins with an apology for its manner ("I have been blamed for being too amiable over the old War" [*UW*, 6]); and throughout, any opportunity for relief from war horrors is taken as an opportunity for (even indoor) pastoral poetizing. ("I remember how Limberg-Buse and myself chirped and rarefied over some crayfish and a great cake, in a little side room of a miner's cottage, with vine leaves peeping in, and a flower-bed in front" [*UW*, 50].) In part I am retailing Fussell's well-known point about the ironic virtues of a remembered pastoral for putting war horrors into relief. I am also making an inverse point about how war experience is itself remembered after an interval of time: "Closely following the map, with my narrative, *then I hope much plainer than now*, Harrison decided that I had nearly been into Grandcourts" (*UW*, 122, my emphasis). The narrative has not only preserved but also accreted poetry over time; by the end of the memoir, irrepressible poetry finally takes over, in the form of a "supplement of poetical interpretations and variations."

Blunden's book seems to acknowledge that it is too well written. "Imagine," writes Blunden, the survivors' "message; they will never open their mouths, unless perhaps one hour, when the hooded shape comes to call them away, they lift from the lips of the extremest age a terrible complaint and courage, in phrases sounding to the bystanders like 'the drums and tramplings' of a mad dream" (*UW*, 51). Sonic effects overlap sonic effects the length of the sentence: the ugly fricative alignment of "message" and "mouths"; the edged consonance of "imagine," "message," "age," "courage"; the oxymoronic alliteration of "complaint and courage"; and the sonic chiasmus of the ultimate phrase. We might almost say about this what Bersani and Dutoit say about Assyrian sculpture: "One's interest moves between the geometric and the anecdotal at the very point at which the anecdotal center of the scene is being most strongly emphasized" (*FV*, 9).

Except that in Blunden's case, the geometric gets in the way of the anecdotal (the final chiasmus with its own allusion completes the muting of the terrible cry), as it does not in Faulkner (the scene, at the barn, *turns* geometric, shattered and cubistically reassembled).

As opposed to Blunden's practiced alliterations, Sassoon's are manic or hysterical. Sometimes Sassoon alliterates for a detectable purpose. (Onomatopoeia: "Almost at once the short preliminary bombardment began and the darkness became diabolic with the din and flash of the old old story" [*MIO*, 85]. Mock-nursery satire: "The big bugs back at Brigade and Divisional H.Q. were studying trench-maps with corrugated brows" [*MIO*, 67].) Usually he alliterates out of the anxiety, apparently, of having nothing literarily to do but tell his story. Nothing that I can think of justifies the random consonance of: "With an unsoldierly sigh I picked up my packages and plodded on in search of C Company, who were billeted in some buildings round a friendly farmhouse" (*MIO*, 55). Or of: "Wednesday morning was miserably wet. . . . [T]here was little else to be done, and solitude produced the sinking sensation appropriate to the circumstances. . . . At noon Barton came back from the Colonel's final conference of company-commanders. . . . We were told that all arrangements for the show were in temporary abeyance. . . . Was it the wet weather, we wondered" (*MIO*, 63–64).

Sassoon admits that he is auditioning styles; like Tourgée, he has a gothic manner, a documentary manner, a blunt essayistic manner. When he says that he wrote a letter to Aunt Evelyn in the "'happy warrior' style," he seems to be in control of the effect (*MIO*, 31); Graves, however, claims that Sassoon *authentically* "varied between happy warrior and bitter pacifist," even from paragraph to paragraph in a letter (*GTAT*, 244–245). Sassoon can write half a sentence that sounds like Hemingway before ascending into Keats: "The War's all right as long as one doesn't get killed or smashed up, I decided, blowing out the candle so that I could watch the moonlight which latticed the floor with shadows of leaded windows. Where the moonbeams lay thickest they touched the litter of drying lavender" (*MIO*, 137). Or he can observe a scene with the characteristic wit of F. Scott Fitzgerald: "'I've never met an Irishman with any more sense than that mouse!' he exclaimed. A mouse was standing on its head in the sugar-basin, which was made of metal and contained soft sugar. He eyes the mouse morosely, as though accusing it of Irish ancestry" (*MIO*, 42). Fitzgerald, however, would make of such a scene an emblem of his own preoccupation with the way excitements persist in finding inadequate correlatives. In Sassoon, it is a case of passing humor, and Sassoon seems to feel the unwitty necessity of dressing his story in pointless consonance (more sense, mouse, standing, sugar-basin, made of metal, soft sugar, mouse morosely).

Blunden's memoir keeps elevating into poetry; Sassoon's memoir, Fussell demonstrates, is a disguised fiction. Aldington's novel, conversely, is a kind of memoir à clef plus harangue. ("This book is not the work of a professional novelist. It is, apparently, not a novel at all" [*DH*, vii].) And it is impossible to sort out the generic impulses of Robert Graves's "memoir," *Goodbye To All That*. Graves started the book as a novel; possibly he gave that up because it seemed just as well to write nonfiction and lie. I believe and admire Graves's lies. He gives the impression of a man so honest that there is no point feigning it. Even after the war, Graves admits, he "still had the army habit of commandeering anything of uncertain ownership that I found lying about; also a difficulty in telling the truth" (*GTAT*, 254). So what does one make of the story that begins, "At Béthune, I saw the ghost of a man named Private Challoner, who had been at Lancaster with me," and which ends, "Challoner had been killed at Festubert in May"? In between, Graves admits of no doubts: "I could not mistake him or the cap-badge he wore" (*GTAT*, 106). Is this the truth, a lie, or a fiction?

The problem, in the case of all these books from the canon of British war prose, is how little highly literary men can add to the overwhelming fact. We might put the matter with slightly more subtlety by wondering whether the connection of violence and narrative is not too intimate, in Great War stories, for anything valuable in formal-historical demarcations. The connection of narrative and violence is the subject of the Bersani and Dutoit book I have been quoting. The Assyrian art that, they argue, re-presses narrative is always repressing, to be exact, narratives of hunting and war. But war, in the case of Blunden, Sassoon, Graves, and Aldington, nullifies or neutralizes style; it keeps making the style seem affected or gratuitous or weak. Graves is a liar, but why lie when reality itself keeps generating punchlines? "He picked up a No. 1 percussion-grenade and said: 'Now, lads, you've got to be careful here! Remember that if you touch anything while you're swinging the chap, it'll go off.' To illustrate the point, he rapped the grenade against the table edge. It killed him and the man next to him and wounded twelve others more or less severely" (*GTAT*, 169). Blunden and Sassoon verify the probability of such stories. It does not matter much who tells them, or in what avant-garde or rear-guard style.

I need a working definition of modernism, and the place to begin is perhaps Harry Levin's "cult of intransigent artistry."[5] The key for my argument is that each—nearly idiolectical—version of modernism is imperialistic, by which I mean that we credit a twentieth-century artist with participating in modernism if his or her style is so intransigent that it subsumes objects and audiences; replicating itself (making of itself a cult) seems to be its primary function. I am thinking of modernists as if they were actors of the type that enables the careers of countless mimics, as if we might say that Bogart and Cary Grant and Brando are modernists. It is not only that modernists can be parodied; it is that it takes no talent; we parody them because there is little else actively to do. The modernist style is a uniqueness that can only be duplicated; the first time we experience so strong an originality, it seems already a parody of some purer essence. The imperialistic gamble—like that of Kinbote fleeing Zembla in the meta-modernist *Pale Fire*—is that in self-division is self-multiplication.

To say that modernists are imperialists is to say that there is something bellicose about their use of style; yet a fact to contend with is the noncombatant status of most modernists and the loyalty of veteran litterateurs to anti- or non-modernism. (There is no pacifistic style of the 1920s; the only alternative is between inheriting the connection of violence and narrative or producing out of style's own resources an anti-narrative counter-force, for the purpose not of imitating war but of usurping its power.) For now, I only want to introduce what is not merely the noncombatant but also the typically American artistic response to World War I, by way of the imperialist styles of John Dos Passos and especially e. e. cummings. Of course, Americans did not have the seemingly endless trench experience that defined the English, French, and German memory of World War I. But when Americans did get a measure of the experience, they still saw in World War I basically a conflict of imagination and authority. The enemy is never the Boches (it is at least sometimes the Boches for English writers). The enemy is always the army, the police, and friendly governments.

John Dos Passos's *Three Soldiers* is an honorable attempt to avoid making style a principle of conquest.[6] Nevertheless, the two soldiers for whom artistic style is not a primary issue—Fuselli, who worked in an optical goods store in San Francisco before the war, and Chrisfield, the Indiana farmer—almost fail to appear in the second half of the novel. The musician John Andrews increasingly dominates the book. What is at risk for Andrews is a vision that descends from Walt Whitman: "'It's great to have your body all there, isn't it?' he said in a dreamy voice. 'Your skin's so soft and supple, and nothing in the world has the feel a muscle has. . . . Gee, I don't know what I'd do without my body'" (*TS*, 155).

Unfortunately (for the book), Andrews's vision of freedom seems to be compulsory and even, when title characters begin to disappear, cannibalistic. Chrisfield, for example, "had a sudden picture of himself in his old comfortable overalls, with his shirt open so that the wind caressed his neck like a girl blowing down it playfully, lying on a shuck of hay under the hot Indiana sun. Funny he'd thought all that, he said to himself." What is funny about it? "Before he'd known Andy [Andrews] he'd never have thought of that" (*TS*, 152), and Andrews could not have thought of it without Whitman. In this way, the book fails to get outside its own hatred of the army and the MPs: at precisely the point that the protagonist is most at large, readers are victims of the most secure incarceration. "Andrews forgot everything in the great wave of music that rose impetuously through him, poured with the hot blood through his veins, with the streaked colors of the river and the sky through his eyes, with the rhythm of the flowing river through his ears" (*TS*, 348). This extravaganza appeals to three of the five senses by means of three of the four elements (unless "veins" hints at the fourth); the indifference of elements and sensations is expressed in the hemorrhage of blood and river; the harmony of nature and expression is caught up in the anaphora of the sentence. The confluence of personal, natural, and literary style here is liberating for Andrews—he *is* his environment—but it is totalitarian for readers.

There is another character in *Three Soldiers* (not one of the three) who is devoted to freedom: Henslowe. Henslowe's emancipatory style is different. The poles of Andrews's experience are joy and despair; the poles of Henslowe's are sobriety and fun. When Andrews tries to remember, though it is difficult, that "there's any joy at all in life," Henslowe responds: "Rot . . . It's a circus parade" (*TS*, 233). In this mood, Henslowe might as well be e. e. cummings, and I'd like to turn to cummings's *The Enormous Room* for a *dis*honorable, I would say irresponsible, attempt to substitute a doctrinaire carnivalism for the compulsoriness of laws and authority. You do not have to approve of the arbitrary power of wartime governments to imprison innocent civilians, on the one hand, to resent, on the other, the smugness of cummings's imperialistic style.

The "enormous room" is, first of all, the French prison that holds four or five dozen civilians, many of them aliens, indefinitely without trial during World War I. Cummings presents the room as a cross between a zoo and a madhouse; his account vacillates between hatred of the government that unjustly condemns him and delight in the company of eccentrics who have been similarly condemned. "It's a circus parade," cummings might have said; but I am not sure that that would be such a tribute to the animals and clowns that do the parading. The tribute is to the mind, cummings's mind, that finds in misery or monomania or barest self-maintenance a dignity absent from power and authority. Cummings tells us explicitly, in his introduction of the 1934 edition, that the "enormous" object he was contemplating, "something more unimaginably huge than the most prodigious of all universes," is "the individual"; and that in his subsequent book, *Eimi*, "Eimi" is "the individual again; a more complex individual, a more enormous room" (*ER*, viii).

Cummings wants us to believe that he believes in the prodigiousness of the individuality of each prisoner; what comes across is how sympathetic is the mind that can discover itself in all of these individualities. Cummings's allegory, ostensibly modeled on *Pilgrim's Progress*, seems to be about the growth of his own consciousness to the scope of the world; he is the saving and punishing God of his enormous room.

> Frequently I would discover so perfect a command over myself as to easily reduce *le promenade* to a recently invented mechanism; or to the demonstration of a collection of vivid and unlovely toys around and around which, guarding them with impossible heroism, funnily moved purely unreal *plantons*, always absurdly marching, the maimed and stupid dolls of my imagination. (*ER*, 308)

A modernist mind gets outside the war, the war prison, the government, the guards—and imprisons them in a self-commanding imagination that mechanizes and maims. Other modernist attempts to escape the war I find more attractive, but always the delicacy is how to replace war narratives with a potent style that, conquering history on behalf of a peculiar temporality, is not merely a mimetic violence.

"Everyone dies" is the definitive close of a war narrative; even the narrator's death can be arranged, as in *All Quiet on the Western Front*. Hemingway includes in *For Whom the Bell Tolls* the story of the partisan Kashkin, "dead since April." "'That is what happens to everybody,' Pablo said, gloomily. 'That is the way we will all finish.'"[7] The slide from an intransigent platitude about mortality to an informed prediction is one of Hemingway's favorite moves. "They won't get us," Frederic Henry says, "Because you're too brave. Nothing ever happens to the brave." "They die of course," Catherine replies. "But only once," Frederic says (*FA*, 139). War is, in a sense, the perfection of narrative: it is by now clear enough, after the work of Bersani and Dutoit and Peter Brooks, that narratives are attracted to death or violence.

The problem for literature is the sameness of war narratives. Graves, Sassoon, and Blunden are quite different personalities, but one gets expert at foreseeing how anecdotes of a certain trajectory are going to land. Hemingway is preoccupied with the attraction of narratives not merely to deaths but to deaths that are redundant. Even the distinction between brave and cowardly deaths that Frederic Henry alludes to cannot be sustained. If a coward (according to misremembered Shakespeare) dies a thousand deaths, then "the brave dies perhaps two thousand deaths if he's intelligent. He simply doesn't mention them" (*FA*, 140). Here is a Hemingway sketch in its entirety:

> We were in a garden at Mons. Young Buckley came in with his patrol from across the river. The first German I saw climbed up over the garden wall. We waited till he got one leg over and then potted him. He had so much equipment on and looked awfully surprised and fell down into the garden. Then three more came over further down the wall. We shot them. They all came just like that.[8]

From one point of view, this is the consummation of narrative. Narrative is all there is: no characterization, no atmosphere, no style. From another, narrative has entirely degenerated. One German (to whom three sentences are devoted) becomes three Germans (two sentences) become all Germans (one sentence). A rejected ending of *A Farewell to Arms*—"That is all there is to the story. Catherine died and you will die and I will die and that is all I can promise you"[9]—might as well read, "That is all there is to stories."

The discovery—with which Hemingway struggled all his career—that the tendency of narrative is the preclusion of narrative casts a gloom on Peter Brooks's proposal of a Freudian narratology. As adapted by Brooks, the Freudian masterplot may be summarized as a delayed death-seeking, the delay assuring that all life will seek "the right death, the correct end."[10]

If not for that corollary, living would be unaccountable. The assumption is that Freud needed a death instinct to meet the challenge of World War I, and in fact the shell-shock neuroses of traumatized soldiers create the first demand for a new theory in *Beyond the Pleasure Principle*. But in the shadow of Hemingway's work, the Freudian/Brooksian theory is inexplicably optimistic. A true response to World War I would be a theory of the short-circuit, a theory of why humans might seek a death utterly wrong, not in accord with their lives, not at the end of a satisfying life story.

Writing a World War I narrative, on this line, is difficult because nothing could be easier: let the plot simply do what it wants to do without hindrance—everyone dies—and you have a perfect non-existent novel. In Brooks's terms, this would amount to a rhetorically impossible plot of a single extended metaphor, if the narratological equivalent of the Freudian paradigm is the delay of metaphor by metonymy. Everyone, according to Hemingway's degenerate war narrative, is alike; the world is a momentary metaphoric complex. Hemingway's style is the sign of his revulsion from this deadly notion. Insofar as the ideal of modernism is opposition to the hegemony of narrative by means of a charismatic idiolect, then the essence of Hemingway's modernism is an endless metonymic spiral. This seems wrong, since on any account, metonymy is the principle of narration itself: according to Jakobson, the metonymic tendency creates a "purely narrative context."[11] But left to its own devices, metonymy would get a narrative nowhere: "Following the path of contiguous relationships, the realist author metonymically digresses from the plot to the atmosphere and from the characters to the setting in space and time" (*SW*, 255). In Peter Brooksian terms, only metaphoric closure can keep metonymy plotted. The essence of the Hemingway style is the entrusting to metonymy of so much freedom as to threaten continually the narrative pursuit of death.

Hemingway's purest metonymic production is at the beginning of his career, so I wish to analyze backwards across the sequence *For Whom the Bell Tolls*, *A Farewell to Arms*, and *The Sun Also Rises*. The procedure would be question-begging (why assume any work by Hemingway to be purer Hemingway than another?) if it were not a commonplace that *The Sun Also Rises* is Hemingway's best established contribution to the canon of perfectionist modernism; if *The Sun Also Rises* is not the purest Hemingway, it is the purest modernism *in* Hemingway, which is its sole interest to my argument.[12] At a glance the sequence shows a pattern. A book centered on (the Spanish) war follows a book about a temporarily successful escape from (the Great) war, which follows a book that has no combat in it at all, though its effects are multifarious. If backwards toward *The Sun Also Rises* the books are decreasingly centered on combat, they are also decreasingly fascinated by heroics. In *For Whom the Bell Tolls*, both Jordan and Maria are exemplary in their fashion; in *A Farewell to Arms*, the heroine, though initially neurotic, is a martyred saint at the end, but the hero, if kind and knowledgeable, is homicidally ineffectual; all the main characters of *The Sun Also Rises* are warped and wounded. Reading backwards, the books are also decreasingly aimed toward death: Robert Jordan is fated to die; Catherine Barkley's death seems contingent; no major character dies (a circumstance explicitly defended in a draft of the novel) in *The Sun Also Rises*. The analysis, then, will try to explain a modernism that withstands the narrative attraction to brave doomed men and women, its attraction, that is, to short-circuiting metaphoricity.

The digressiveness of metonymy, on the other hand, moves always in the direction of immortal nature: you are all a lost generation (metaphor), but the sun also rises (metonymy). Another version of Freudian narratology—Bersani and Dutoit's formalism of the fetish—permits a first approximation of how Hemingway might avoid the metaphoric closure that Brooks, following Freud, sees as furnishing an *appropriate* close to a life but which Hemingway, after World War I, feels to be the literary equivalent of all catastrophic short-circuits. What Bersani and Dutoit argue is that since desire is always an inadequate substitute for a need, desires have no metaphoric connection to their source. It is therefore crucial to an analysis of desire that a fetish is not a phallic symbol. It is, so to speak, a phallic metonym. A life in pursuit of metoynymic fetishes does not approach a first term (such as the inorganic state), and the life of desire is never, as a result, one-directional (rounded off by a metaphoric connection of end to beginning). Bersani and Dutoit, like Hemingway, sense a premature foreclosing of desire in the satisfying narrative ending, not an appropriate object of it. Like Hemingway, they therefore prefer an endless (beginningless) metonymy.

Though granting that Freud is not quite sure that a fetish is the opposite of a phallic symbol, Bersani and Dutoit are wrong then simply to disregard his reservations. Freud is tentative about how precisely a fetish is chosen, which may be a hesitation about the extent to which a fetish can forestall castration anxiety if it is not phallic at all. When Freud considers the likelihood that the cause of a particular choice of fetish may indeed be that it is phallic, he concludes that "this may happen often enough, but is certainly not a deciding factor." When he hypothesizes what *is* the deciding factor in such cases as shoe or foot fetishism, he can only assert that the chosen object "owes its preference as a fetish—or a part of it—to the circumstance that the inquisitive boy peers at the woman's genitals from below." What is the other part? Freud admits that he does not claim "that it is invariably possible to discover with certainty how the fetish was determined."[13] I go into the inevitably mimetic anxieties (what is the origin of the unoriginal?), because the first term of the metonymic series of human activities taken up by *The Sun Also Rises*—which includes bullfighting, boxing, hunting, fishing, football, tennis, swimming, cycling, bridge, adultery, sadistic joking, adolescent joking, and writing—is not quite absent from the book. It is war (as the moment of castration, along with the self-disavowing demonstration of an attractive masculinity that finds evidence in the castration). But I shall maintain that the sequence of activities in the novel is fetishistically metonymic, and that that is why *The Sun Also Rises* does not open on the "joke front." Proceeding from *The Sun Also Rises* to *For Whom the Bell Tolls*, with its perfect equivalence of beginning in (the position of) death and ending in death, is a fall at once into war literature and into metaphor.

The technical question of *For Whom the Bell Tolls* is how to keep the narrative from collapsing too soon. The opposite might appear more plausible: as the narrative takes increasingly daring excursions from Jordan's consciousness, the ostensible point is that to supply the full context of even a simple combat operation, you have to initiate an endlessly ramifying analysis. Still, it is hard to see how that fact distinguishes war from anything else. If Hemingway had strayed into Cohn's holiday with Brett or Frances's last days in Paris, *The Sun Also Rises* would have been richer and also would have fallen apart. *For Whom the Bell Tolls* does not fall apart because of the intense centeredness of its action, and Hemingway labors to keep the star from immediately imploding. In any event, Hemingway's project to inflate the roughly seventy hours of the book with all the interest of a life of three score and ten *years* is not completely successful. (That all the essence of a marriage has been compacted into several days with the extraordinary Spanish girl, Maria, is famously unpersuasive.) In effect, Hemingway is working to make Jordan's death feel appropriate in the Freudian/Brooksian sense, but the strain is undisguisable.

As against the impressive elaboration of the seventy hours, Hemingway does not conceal the powerful constriction of Jordan's life. The book begins with the clause, "He lay flat on the brown, pine-needled floor of the forest." As we feel the righthand bulk of pages diminishing, the book makes sure we feel a corresponding closure making its approach with an increasing literary speed, comparable to the acceleration of the deaths in the garden at Mons. Chapter thirty-seven begins, "Now Robert Jordan lay with the girl"; Chapter forty-three begins, "Robert Jordan lay behind the trunk of a pine tree"; the third-to-last sentence of the book begins, "Robert Jordan lay behind the tree"; and the last sentence is, "He could feel his heart breaking against the pine needle floor of the forest" (*FWBT*, 1, 378, 431, 471). The effect is more than a nice sense of completion. In the insistence is the implication that nothing for Robert could have been altered, as if all foreshadowing represented the shadow of death. Early in the book Pilar reads death in the lines of Jordan's palms. She is reading, prophetically, the last lines of the book.

What Hemingway in effect narrates over 400 pages is the collapse of narrative, as the literary analogue of the short-circuiting of all good lives. The artist surrogate of the book is not Jordan (only an apprentice writer) but Pilar: when Pilar tells the story of the execution of the fascists in Pablo's town, Jordan thinks, "If that woman could only write" (*FA*, 134), and takes her unblinking realism as his model. We take, as a consequence, her narrative as an emblem of the book. Pablo had devised, as Pilar narrates it, a memorable way of executing the fascists of his town. One by one they are to be led out of the *Ayuntamiento*, and forced between two lines of

Republicans (armed with flails) until they arrive at a cliff over which they are all to be hurled. Once again, fate may be read in lines; but the lines disintegrate. First comes the mayor, who walks through a good portion of the gauntlet before the men start to beat him, and they have to improvise a way of getting him over the cliff. Second comes the detested mill and feed store owner, who shamefully has to be set in motion down the line with a club and then runs until falling just before the precipice. Third is the brave landowner Don Ricardo, who insults his torturers and so is quickly clubbed to death.

To this point each death is customized. But Don Ricardo's courage stirs the mob to an undifferentiated anger, and when the the cowardly "annoyer of girls" (*FWBT*, 112), Don Faustino, tries to imitate Don Ricardo, the crowd decides to humiliate him (by not beating him) before pushing him over the cliff. Now the crowd loses its ability to distinguish humans altogether; when Don Guillermo, a fascist but otherwise respectable, emerges, they taunt him indiscriminately. "They had had such success joking at Don Faustino that they could not see, now, that Don Guillermo was a different thing" (*FWBT*, 117). A fat grain buyer, insurance agent, and money lender appears next; the blood-drunk crowd rushes him, jumps on him, and beats his head on the "stone flags of the paving of the arcade and there were no more lines but only a mob" (*FWBT*, 121). Finally the executioners storm the *Ayuntamiento*: "I saw the hall full of men flailing away with clubs and striking with flails, and poking and striking and pushing and heaving" (*FWBT*, 125). All who are murdered in the melee are put in a cart and dumped over the cliff en masse.

The breakdown in the lines equals the breakdown in the capacity of the people to manufacture appropriate deaths; the most vivid narrative in the book concerns the short-circuiting of narrative. The aesthetic challenge of the novel is to generate a story out of the demise of story. In less formal terms, the challenge is to test whether a tragically abrupt death can be made to feel appropriate. But death eventually makes nonsense of any distinctions that keep our interest in reading—or in living—alive. If the Russians are forced to abandon Madrid, the wounded Russians have to be killed; the presence of these corpses would not implicate the Soviets, because "nothing proved a naked dead man was a Russian. Your nationality and your politics did not show when you were dead" (*FWBT*, 238). *For Whom the Bell Tolls* stops just before Jordan's death. If it had continued a single page longer, the book would have reduced to the absurd. It would have made nonsense of itself: it would have narrated the death of no one in particular.

The fact that *A Farewell to Arms* does extend the extra page is token of the courage of its analysis of narrative's attraction to premature death. The book makes a program of its metonymic impulse. There are almost no metaphors in it at all. Yet the book begins and ends with metaphors, as if to literalize the metaphoric connection of beginnings and endings in properly rounded narratives. On the second page of the book is this grotesque yet oddly predictable simile: "the two leather cartridge-boxes on the front of the belts, gray leather boxes heavy with the packs of clips of thin, long 6.5 mm. cartridges, bulged forward under the capes so that the men, passing on the road, marched as though they were six months gone with child" (*FA*, 4). This does more than adumbrate the death of Catherine in childbirth; it levels birth and death, men and women, war and peace. Death storms the womb: Catherine Barkley's child is dead in the third paragraph of the novel, his story as short-circuited a narrative as can be imagined. He is twice dead at birth.

The second-to-last sentence of the novel contains another of Hemingway's rare metaphors. Henry insists on seeing his dead wife, but it "wasn't any good. It was like saying good-by to a statue" (*FA*, 332). This is a tasteless metaphor, but it is perfectly justified. In an early scene, Henry had visited Catherine at her hospital, formerly the villa of a rich German. Everywhere there are marble busts, in the office, along the hall. "They had the complete marble quality of all looking alike. Sculpture had always seemed a dull business—still, bronzes looked like something. But marble busts all looked like a cemetery" (*FA*, 28). Presumably Catherine is not merely statuesque at the end but also marmoreal. Hemingway has done something exceedingly complex exceedingly simply: he intimates that Catherine is already absolutely non-Catherine because (1) she is inhuman, marmoreal, in her death from the moment of dying; (2) she is like all other corpses in the way all busts are alike; (3) she resembles busts that are reminiscent of cemeteries; (4) she has become metaphorizable no matter the vehicle; (5) her final metaphor reminds us of early paradigms of likeness so that her death is aesthetically an ending.

The death becomes a meta-artistic matter: the corpse is a statue but statues are inferior art. They have no temporal dimension—even walking along a hall of marble busts lends no temporal interest to them, since the experience does not change. We sense that Hemingway does not merely use metaphor to suggest an appropriate close to a metonymic narrative. He imitates the short-circuiting of a young life by allowing metaphor an absolute refutation of metonymy. In one rejected ending of the story, Hemingway tries to tie up all loose strands. (What happens to Rinaldi and the priest and the rest?) He floats a Gertrude Steinian flourish: "I could tell what has happened since then but that is the end of the story. END." Then he tries a more apologetic tack: "You can stop a story anytime. The rest goes on and you go on with it. On the other hand you have to stop a story. You have to stop it at the end of whatever it was you were writing about" (*HFW*, 47). What if what you were writing about does not have an end? You can close—you can effect closure—if your subject is early death.

In contradiction of the Freudian/Brooksian model, Catherine's death does not take its time. "The world breaks everyone and afterward many are strong at the broken places. But those that will not break it kills. If you are none of these you can be sure it will kill you too but there will be no special hurry" (*FA*, 249). When Henry writes that they "knew the baby was very close now and it gave us both a feeling as though something were hurrying us and we could not lose any time together" (*FA*, 311), we recognize what is hurrying them. The otherwise disconcerting fact that Catherine, despite her heroic spirit, dies quickly (once unconscious, "it did not take her very long to die" [*FA*, 331]) turns out to indicate that the heart of twentieth-century as opposed to Victorian narrative is the inappropriateness of the form of death. I associate her speed at dying with a local aesthetic matter as well: Hemingway's novel reads extremely fast (it is no trouble to read the 300 pages in a day), a fact Hemingway was aware and proud of. Hurrying toward death is hurrying toward the back cover.

In contrast is the famous, the mockable, Hemingway style, on display at the beginning: "In the late summer of that year we lived in a house in a village that looked across the river and the plain to the mountains. In the bed of the river there were pebbles and boulders, dry and white in the sun, and the water was clear and swiftly moving and blue in the channels" (*FA*, 3). A story that begins this way threatens merely to circulate. Michael S. Reynolds demonstrates that it is possible to say exactly what year, and almost certainly which village (*HFW*, 87–91), but the reader's experience of the passage is not to realize yet even that there is a war on. Metonymy rambles, as Jakobson describes, in the direction of atmosphere and environment. The passage is almost more than metonymic; it is reminiscent of a variety of aphasia that Jakobson calls "similarity disorder" (from which the metonymic pole derives), in which purely grammatical words like conjunctions, prepositions, pronouns, and articles dominate. Another occasional symptom of aphasiacs of this type is that though they have the ability to name "primary hues—red, yellow, green, and blue," they cannot apply these terms to related hues. It is as if, in this passage and a more striking one in *The Sun Also Rises* with which I shall close this discussion of endlessness, Hemingway is trying to treat the visual field as a design of colored patches, impervious to any perspective imposed by a super-sensual mental activity. The essence of narrative, on the contrary, in putting one thing ahead of another.

The book's metonymy quite frequently takes the form of a willful digressiveness, as on the ways to eat spaghetti (*FA*, 7); Hemingway explicitly makes the digression an emblem of a peacetime aesthetics. When he goes on leave, Henry does not visit the priest's beloved Abruzzi, which hurts the priest's feelings. He tells the priest that "it was what I had wanted to do and I tried to explain how one thing had led to another" (*FA*, 13). (In war, by contrast, all roads—even roads apparently away from the fighting—lead to doom.) Similarly, when an ambulence breaks down, removing itself from the war, the diagnosis is that "It is not good. One thing after another" (*FA*, 16).

Thus the sections of the book in which Catherine and Frederic seem to escape the war are, at long last, simply metonymic:

Outside, in front of the chalet a road went up the mountain. The wheel ruts and ridges were iron hard with the frost, and the road climbed steadily through the forest and up and around the mountain to where there were meadows, and barns and cabins in the meadows at the edge of the woods looking across the valley. The valley was deep and there was a stream at the bottom that flowed down into the lake and when the wind blew across the valley you could hear the stream in the rocks. (*FA*, 289–290)

This dizzying passage might be contrasted with a slightly later idyll imagined by Hemingway's precise coeval, Vladimir Nabokov. In "Cloud, Castle, Lake," Nabokov's "representative" tries to flee Nazi Germany to a country cabin looking out upon a perfectly trinitarian (or, as Nabokov says, dactyllic) scene: in the air is a cloud, on the ground is a lake, mediating them from ground to air is a castle, and the cloud is reflected in the center of the water. The scene stays identical as the hero circles the lake, which either means that the wind has blown the cloud in perfect correspondence to the walk or that time has halted. But in Hemingway's scene nothing is reflected in anything else, and the wind and stream move constantly and the road spirals. This is not about arrested time but eternally circulating time.

The opposition of hyper-metonymic style and super-metaphoric war means that there can hardly be a truce between them; there turns out to be no separate narratological peace. The relation of war activities to peace activities must, therefore, itself be a warfare of metaphor and metonymy. Once in Switzerland, Catherine and Henry walk and ski, and Henry boxes, as if strenuous activity and even violent male competition are conceptually proximate to war but not essentially like it. Much is risked in the proximity; when Catherine asks, early on, "*Do* we have to go on and talk this way?" (*FA*, 18), she registers the will-to-power of Hemingway's style. What I have called the metonymic method might be redubbed the fetishistic method; sport or style substitutes for a missing term their resemblance to which is uncertain rather than certain and negligible. But the alternative to Catherine and Henry's Scarrian peace is the original war of perfect inhuman metaphoricity.

Is peace a metaphor of war? World War I is spatially invasive: Catherine dies in Switzerland simultaneously with a German breakthrough. It is temporally *per*vasive: "There is no finish to a war" (*FA*, 50). Every activity becomes war activity. Fergy tells Catherine and Frederic that they will never marry: "You'll fight before you'll marry." "We never fight," they protest. "You'll die then," she says. "Fight or die. That's what people do. They don't marry." Then she relents for a moment. "Maybe you'll be all right you two. But watch out you don't get her in trouble. You get her in trouble and I'll kill you" (*FA*, 108). The three alternatives are dying, fighting, and getting pregnant (followed by murder). All turn out to be one thing after all. This is metaphor run riot: every action leads to death, and style cannot, finally, escape it.

In *The Sun Also Rises*, Hemingway seems not yet to have arrived at this impasse; what postpones it (though this is a false solution) is the emblematizing of the Hemingway aesthetic ideal by way of bullfighting: Romero's "purity of line" as opposed to the "false aesthetics of the bull-fighters of the decadent period" (*SAR*, 168, 215). Whenever there is a duel, there is the temptation of a metaphorical connection of war with style itself: violence is performative for Romero as for Achilles, and personality lives in their gestures. Nevertheless, one end of the equation is missing: if there is a connection from the bullfight to the prose, is there one from war to the bullfight? There is at least a metaphoric connection from the war-castrated Jake to the steers. If Romero's aesthetic ideal is expanded as follows— "holding the purity of line through the maximum of exposure"—and if sincerely working in the "terrain of the bull" gives the "sensation of coming tragedy" (*SAR*, 168, 213–214), then what war, bullfighting, and writing have in common is an ideal of grace at risk.

I cannot do more than allude here to Hemingway's lifelong lucubration on whether war and bullfighting are alike; and whether, if they are, bull-fighting and boxing are alike; and if they are, whether boxing and all other sports are alike; and whether war and hunting or fishing are alike; and if *they* are whether war essentially resembles tranquility. War and bullfighting require grace under castration-anxiety, but the killing of an animal is spirit-ually superior to the killing of a man. Anselmo, representing one of Hem-ingway's moods, thinks in *For Whom the Bell Tolls*: "How could the *Inglés* say that the shooting of a man is like the shooting of an animal. In all hunting I have had an elation and no feeling of wrong" (*FWBT*, 442). This would quarantine war from bullfighting, hunting, and fishing. Further, Romero's ideal of oneness with the bull is just what modern warfare, since the advent of machine guns, tanks, and mustard gas, prohibits. Or should the line be drawn between bullfighting and boxing? The black boxer in Vienna is a noble savage, but Cohn is contemptible. (The book seems to admire *big* boxers and despise small ones who fight smaller—Cohn is a middleweight trained as a featherweight—a distinction muddled in excised portions of the manuscript that celebrate Ledoux.) A passage in Baker's bi-ography makes the series a Great Chain: Hemingway wanted to "teach his readers how to fish or shoot or watch a bullfight or a revolution."[14] In the manuscript of *The Sun Also Rises*, Hemingway devotes as much expert attention to boxing as to bullfighting, but perhaps he omits the boxing exposition on the judgment, also recorded in Baker, that "boxing looked pale beside this great sport" of bullfighting (*H*, 129).

We need to know, finally, whether the series arrives at writing. In an early poem, Hemingway turns his typewriter into a machine gun:

The mills of the gods grind slowly,
But this mill
Chatters in mechanical staccato,
Ugly short infantry of the mind . . . .
(*H*, 90)

However, this passage about war writing ends in categorical inconsequence:

> In the war in Italy when I was a boy I had much to fear. In Spain I had no fear after a couple of weeks and was very happy. Yet for me not to understand fear in others or deny its existence would be bad writing. It is just that now I understand the whole thing better. The only thing about a war, once it has started, is to win it — and that is what we did not do [in Spain]. The hell with war for a while, I want to write. (*B*, 337)

A disquisition on war writing turns into — apparently — an absolute demarcation (wars are for winning, not writing). This recalls the introduction to *Men at War*: "Learning to suspend your imagination and live completely in the very second of the present minute with no before and no after is the greatest gift a soldier can acquire. It, naturally, is the opposite of all those gifts a writer should have."[15]

I have wandered this far from *The Sun Also Rises* for a reason: we cannot tell the relation of war to all the manifold activities of *The Sun Also Rises*, variously murderous or bloody or violent or competitive, because war is missing from the book. The logical starting point of the action is Jake's injury. Instead, the book begins with Cohn's boxing, followed on the next page by his football, followed on the next page by his tennis, followed on the next page by his bridge, followed closely by his novel-writing, as off we go on a chain of some kind, whether metaphoric or metonymic who can tell?

Not only is the war itself missing from *The Sun Also Rises*, but allusions to it are also excised from the notebook version of the novel wherever possible. Two passing references to Jake's recovery with Brett are cut out.[16] Their very triviality makes it significant that Hemingway sees fit to remove them: he is determined to connect the present peace and the past war only when necessary. One result is mystification. "The Boulevard Raspail always made dull riding. It was like a certain stretch on the P.L.M. between Fontainebleau and Montereau that always made me feel bored and dead and dull until it was over. I suppose it is some association of ideas that makes those dead places in a journey" (*SAR*, 41). It is not that the notebook passages explain the emotion precisely, but the additional language is revealing. "It may be something outside of the actual country some sort of connection that we do not know about that makes these ~~connections~~ blank spaces. . . . That ~~patch of hatred I have for no not hatred, rather a sort~~ scar of blank unenjoyment, is probably what Gerald [i.e., Robert] Cohn had for all of Paris" (*SARF*, 147). The replacement of "connections" by "blank spaces," of "patch" by "scar," of "hatred" by "blank unenjoyment" all suggest that the fact of castration has intruded at specifiable locales.

Also excised are several pages of notebook writing devoted to an impressionistic history of the relationship of Brett and Jake, a history of war and castration continued by a compulsion to repeat. ("She had wanted to kill off something that was in her and the killing had gotten out of control.

Well she had killed it off in me" [*SARF*, 398].) In censoring all of this, Hemingway attempts to excise history from the book. Something like a castration of castration is effected, such as Bersani and Dutoit describe in the case of the fetishist who cuts off his vision just before the scene of imagined cutting. In Hemingway's story, "Now I Lay Me," war avoidance is almost precisely fetishistic, with metonymic remembering substituted for metonymic seeing. "On those nights I tried to remember everything that had ever happened to me, starting with just before I went to the war and remembering back from one thing to another. I found I could only remember back to that attic in my grandfather's house. Then I would start there and remember this way again, until I reached the war."[17] The result of this negativing of negativity is not that the war is forgotten but rather that whether the war stands in metaphoric or metonymic relation to the events of the book is rendered moot. This fetishism makes possible a book that closes (like a bullfight) and does not close (like an unconsummatable romance).

Oddly, Jake Barnes alleges, in an omitted remark, that he is glad that he has been emasculated: "Somehow Duff [Brett] could hurt me now but it could not hurt me much. I realized that it was lucky that I was not whole and well. That seemed a rotten way to look at it compared with the heroics I used to work up in nineteen sixteen and seventeen but it did me a lot of good" (*SARF*, 400, see also 593). I might even venture that the various analogies between Jake and Cohn manifest the fancy of being emasculated from the start—or at any rate symbolically castrated, circumcised. I think Hemingway (or Hemingstein, as he nicknamed himself) was toying with the idea that either Jake was born a Jew or is part Jewish or fantasizes that he is a Jew. At Jake's uncle Jake's funeral, the younger Jake is preoccupied with his uncle's "high, gallant, hooked purple nose" (*SARF*, 49). The uncle with the unciform nose is first called Rafael or Ernest or Rafael Ernest (crossed out—but at this moment Hemingway realizes he is talking about the hero's namesake) and is next called Jacob, at which moment the hero's name itself becomes Old Testament.

What benefit would it have been to locate Jake's symbolic castration before the war, before, very nearly, his life? Castration becomes an imaginary matter, and it becomes impossible to specify the first moment of acknowledging it, so as to loose the metonymic desires that both incorporate and disavow the loss, from boxing to bridge to writing. Still, beginning the novel with a real Jew's avocations prepares the fetishistic metonymy more simply and cunningly; the contrast in either case is to beginning and ending the book with bullfighting, a metaphoric device, since bullfighting is presumed to resemble war, and since closure works by equivalence. In fact, Hemingway's manuscript does begin and end with the bullfight (Paris and Burguete are flashbacks). It is a clumsy structure, ensuring that we do not care about all the self-destructive drunks we immediately encounter. Nevertheless, what Hemingway writes in defense of the awkwardness is not just special pleading. We hear more than we are in a position to understand, so Jake says: "Probably any amount of this does not seem to have anything to do with the story and perhaps it has not. I am sick of these ones with their restrained writing and I am going to try to get in the whole business and to do that there has to be things that seem as though they had nothing to do with it just as in life" (*SARF*, 51). Hemingway's bullfight is a metaphoric beginning that inevitably leads (since we are given information at the beginning only comprehensible from the end) to an apology for metonymy.

At the other end of the novel, Hemingway wants his bullfight but not one that leads the story to the perfectly metaphoric conclusion of *For Whom the Bell Tolls* and *A Farewell to Arms*. He is tempted not to describe the bullfight at all: "This is not a story about bull fighting. There is not any big final bull fight scene. Guerrita [Romero] does not get killed" (*SARF*, 530). Rather than circle, like the two war novels, from scenes that are pregnant with death to scenes that deliver it, this book cuts the bullfight at the beginning and eschews the bullfight death at the end.

The novel starts with Cohn, which has the benefit of taking the focus off Jake and the emasculating moment. These lines are crossed out in the notebook: "It looked as though I were trying to be the hero of this story. But that was all wrong. Gerald [Robert] Cohn is the hero. When I bring myself in it is only to clear up something" (*SARF*, 143). Then Hemingway or Jake adds: "Or maybe Duff [Brett] is the hero or maybe Niño de la Palma [Romero]. He never really had a chance to be the hero. Or maybe there is not any hero at all. Maybe a story is better without any hero" (*SARF*, 447). Hemingway is struggling to realize that he has done something astounding in beginning the book with a character who is dismissed before the end, in making the dramatic climax of the book the triumph of a bullfighter who is a ficelle, and in ending the book with just the sort of squared incompleteness appropriate to the *n*th encounter of a castrated man and a nymphomaniac.

Just as the vivid bullfight beginning immediately leads to a defense of waywardness—that is to say, a metaphorical structure leads to an apology for metonymy—so war, in its capacity for either actual (Jake) or symbolic (Mike) emasculating, enables the escape from Brett that Hemingway makes explicit in the draft and exemplifies in the final version of the novel by means of the fishing interlude. Fishing has the effect of making war seem, to the Englishman Harris, lovely and jolly in retrospect; the related male predatory bonding of the episode is an acknowledgment of how thoroughly it takes castration—as in the original "Rip"—to escape subservience to women. To fish is to fetishize; it is an acknowledgment and denial of castration at once, the purest peaceful metonym of war in the category of male death sports. The bus ride to Burguete is an excursion into an almost monastically pure Hemingway metonymy, narrative entirely enlisted to the revelation of a visual field of colored patches. But the village named at the end of this passage is where Roland dies (betrayed by stepfather, accidentally injured by friend) in the *Chanson de Roland*; what needs to be known and repressed, since the flight must avow and disavow its fear, is that the Frankish invasion of Spain came under attack, not from Moslems, as the poem says, but from Christian Basques: otherness is not the enemy, sameness is.

> We went through the forest and the road came out and turned along a rise of land, and out ahead of us was a rolling green plain, with dark mountains beyond it. These were not like the brown, heat-baked mountains we had left behind. These were wooded and there were clouds coming down from them. The green plain stretched off. It was cut by fences and the white of the road showed through the trunks of a double line of trees that crossed the plain toward the north. As we came to the edge of the rise we saw the red roofs and white houses of Burguete ahead strung out on the plain, and away off on the shoulder of the first dark mountain was the gray metal-sheathed roof of the monastery of Roncesvalles.

The Great Gatsby is the best title of all the novels of American high modernism.[18] Even after repeated readings of the book, the title still haunts. Substance and accidents are in a relation of intense mutual exacerbation: Great Gatsby is both a name to gossip about and an essence to approach. I grant—it increases my admiration—the perfectly insinuated meretriciousness of the title. "Gatsby" is intriguing for reasons known to Gatsby himself when he saw in the appellation a romantic improvement on "Gatz." "Great" is the most debased word in the English language; the final slogan of the last political campaign—"The Great Newness"—will capture the American Gatsbian confusion of upward mobility and eschatology. Furthermore, when "The" is placed before "Great" and combined with x, where x is a name that ends with a hard "i," the personage thus self-created is generally a magician. If one literary scholar ought to be alive to how generously the word "great" panders to the desires of advertisers and demagogues, it is Paul Fussell, diagnostician of the emptying of political language, author of, as it happens, *The Great War and Modern Memory*.

I am not taunting Fussell. If the yearning for something unutterable has had a historical object in this century, it is World War I; the word "great" in "The Great War" is a pointedly inarticulate gesture. Rather, I am italicizing Fitzgerald's audacity. How, seven years after the close of the Great War, could anyone believe that a single man might be larger than his milieu; that he might represent an ideal cause worth sacrificing for; that his dream of repeating the past might conceivably survive the unsurpassable historical marker of modernity; that his death along with that of his assassin might be aptly termed a "holocaust"?

The answer to these questions will allow, I believe, a better model of the American relation of modernism and World War I than the rival extant paradigms. Neither Paul Fussell nor Modris Eksteins is primarily concerned with *American* modernism, and the American experience of World War I was of course less devastating than the European experience. Still, I can get at the American modernist's relation to the Great War by means of a cri-

tique of the symmetrical blindspots of Fussell's and Eksteins's analyses.[19]
Neither of them is quite satisfactory in answering why modernists were so
infrequently combatants and combatants so infrequently modernists. Neither Fussell nor Eksteins, in short, is in a tactical position to discover how
Fitzgerald's ingenuous dream of being the greatest novelist who ever lived
could come closest to realization in a novel about greatness so soon after
World War I should have made the terms of that ambition unspeakable
forever.

Fussell's book is not as embarrassed as Eksteins's by the fact that the
set of modernists and the set of combatant authors overlap so narrowly: his
book is *about* that curiosity. What Fussell elaborates is just how dependent
combatants were on antiquated forms (myths, antitheses, pastoral conventions) for coming to terms with the really new and evidently subliterary.
More troubling for Fussell is that modernism was well under way in advance of the Great War. Fussell's first chapter on Hardy is memorable and
exciting, but I am not sure what it precisely means. Though the first subtitle
of the chapter is "Thomas Hardy, Clairvoyant," Fussell will not vouch for
his own epithet. The third paragraph begins: "As if by uncanny foresight,
Hardy's volume [*Satires of Circumstance*] offers a medium for perceiving
the events of the war just beginning" (*GW*, 3). What is the weight of "as if"?
Later, Fussell begins a quotation with the phrase, "as Hardy prophesies";
nevertheless he stipulates, a little farther down the page, that he is "not
really arguing that Hardy, the master of situational irony, 'wrote' the Great
War" (*GW*, 7). I am unable to restate what Fussell *is* really arguing, and
the section on Hardy ends, with an overly optimistic adverb, "Clearly, there
are some intersections of literature and life that we have taken too little
notice of" (*GW*, 7).

Deep into the book, Fussell seems to make the subtle claim for Hardy
that the first chapter darkly indicates. Discussing Housman, Fussell writes
that "it is remarkable the way *A Shropshire Lad*, like Hardy's *Satires of
Circumstance*, anticipates, and in my view even helps determine, the imaginative means by which the war was conceived" (*GW*, 282). This implies
that Hardy can be an antebellum modernist because post-war modernists
learned to see the war through his vision. Perhaps Fussell means even more
subtly to imply that prophecy inverts approximately to this: in the Borgesian manner, modernists retrodict their prophets. (Is that not the best gloss
on Robert Lowell's comment that "one feels Housman foresaw the Somme"
[*GW*, 282]?) This sort of special pleading works—that is, keeps modernism
in place as an appalled response to the war—if there are only a few excep-
tions to the rule that World War I came first, so that Fussell can assert
that from our perspective, "the literary scene [before the war] is hard to
imagine."

> There was no *Waste Land*, with its rats' alleys, dull canals, and dead men
> who have lost their bones: it would take four years of trench warfare to bring
> these to consciousness. There was no *Ulysses*, no *Mauberley*, no *Cantos*,
> no Kafka, no Proust, no Waugh, no Auden, no Huxley, no Cummings, no

Women in Love or *Lady Chatterley's Lover*. There was no "Valley of Ashes" in *The Great Gatsby*. (*GW*, 23)

On the other hand, there *was Ubu Roi* without four years of trench warfare, there was Gertrude Stein, there was Apollinaire. And why, if the subject is so capacious as "modern memory," should we be concerned only with writers? There were Isadora Duncan, Nijinsky, Picasso, Stravinsky, Schoenberg. What sort of book would you write if you were struck by how much of modernism did not wait for the authority of the Great War? Possibly you would write something like Modris Eksteins's *Rites of Spring*. And you might argue, like Eksteins, that modernism was neither an artistic adaptation to the horror ushered in by the Great War nor a prophecy, but rather a manifestation of the same mentality. Art (in some of its avatars) and World War I (or some attitudes toward it) were similarly ecstatic, irrational, amoral, mythic, suicidal, technicist, revolutionary, anti-bourgeois, anti-social, and totalizing.

If this sounds unconvincing, I am glad. In order to make the argument work, Eksteins needs to mix and stir an element of surrealism, a bit of cubism, a snippet of Dada, a phase of international modernism, whatever is most irrational or suicidal or violent wherever he finds it. The use of evidence is consistently strained; to get Stravinsky and Nazi kitsch related (Eksteins involves modernism with German belligerence through both wars) requires an unflagging tendentiousness cum tin ear. There are asseverations that might have gone either way: when the audience of *Rite of Spring* rebels, it is *Rite of Spring* and not the audience that anticipates hysterical German crowds. To package all his strewn analogies of war and art, Eksteins is necessarily hazy. "Avant-garde has for us a positive ring, storm troops a frightening connotation. This book suggests that there may be a sibling relationship between these two terms that extends beyond their military origins. . . . Nazi kitsch may bear a blood relationship to the highbrow religion of art proclaimed by many moderns" (*RS*, xvi).

From Eksteins's point of view, Fussell's combatant English non-modernists are to be congratulated for their Englishness as well as their non-modernism: not only is modernism a blood relative of the Great War, it is in (some familial) relation to the specifically German bellicosity. There are two Great Wars in Eksteins: the good Victorian bourgeois war fought by England and the revolutionary, modernist war fought by Germany. This division, which inspires Eksteins to be the first historian to see something wise and profound in the British sense of war as a continuation of soccer in foreign fields, depends in its unnuanced form on scholarly litigiousness. The Christmas truce of 1914, begun by Germans on Christmas Eve, must in principle be a British phenomenon; Eksteins only manages to assert, desperately, that the key point is that the truce was not *Prussian* in origin (*RS*, 109, 133).

You might think that if what Eksteins means by World War I is exclusively the Boche World War I, then his connection to modernism would be in jeopardy, since he admits that only Dada of all forms of modernism had an important German component. When you examine what makes Germany the modernist nation par excellence—its idealist heritage combined with its accelerated industrialization and urbanization—you can only conclude that its "blood" and "sibling" relationship to modernism cannot be founded on a common ancestry. On what else?

If history is monolithic, if literary history is simply a part of it, then Fussell and Eksteins have the two purest solutions to the puzzle: what does World War I have to do with modernism? Either it followed it, aghast but adaptive, validating the prophecies of those who came before, or it prefigured it, a fraternal enthusiasm. What if, on the contrary, we imagine a competition for history? What if the Darwinian premise of literary history is that disciplines and genres need to establish their specific grounds of survival? Then you can imagine a writer asking, implicitly, this question, raised in different ways by Eric J. Leed and John Keegan: why, precisely, do you need World War I to determine or validate or even express the form of your response to modernity, if the industrialization and secularization of modern life were proceeding noisily and dangerously apace without it?[20] (Hardy did not need to be a prophet.) Fitzgerald as usual brings out the smug obtuseness in Hemingway: "The reason you are so sore you missed the war," Hemingway writes Fitzgerald, "is because war is the best subject of all. It groups the maximum of material and speeds up the action and brings out all sorts of stuff that normally you have to wait a lifetime to get."[21] Even Hemingway, however, developed a charismatic style in fact to slow down the action; modernist style is recalcitrant to the velocity of history.

The Great Gatsby corresponds to *The Sun Also Rises*: its technical perfection seems to entail that if its narrator as well as its protagonist served in World War I, their combat experience needs to be largely tacit. World War I is deleted from drafts in much the same way in the two novels. *Tender Is the Night* is Fitzgerald's version of *A Farewell to Arms*: in both, much messier, books, not the protagonist but a surrogate dies, as Great War violence frustrates the pursuit of a separate peace—corollary of a stylistic Utopia—in, first of all, Switzerland. In Fitzgerald's case as well as Hemingway's, the relation of the modernist aspiration to war is an irreducible tension; in both cases, the triumph of style is measured by how suavely the Great War narrative can be subsumed. If you had not read Fitzgerald's biography but had made deductions from *This Side of Paradise* and *The Great Gatsby*, you might have inferred that their author had served in World War I but could mime an Olympian dismissal of it, though if you had read *Tender Is the Night* only, you might have surmised that its author avoided World War I but was nearly overwhelmed by it.

When Fitzgerald began writing *The Great Gatsby*, he seems to have been under the impression that the Great War was its context. This would have been a departure from *This Side of Paradise*, in which World War I is an interlude, and *The Beautiful and Damned*, in which World War I is a moment in the proliferation of disarray. According to *The Beautiful and*

Damned, chosen individuals, as emblems of civilizations, reach a summit of beauty and then decline without the necessary intervention of catastrophes; Anthony Patch's theory is that beauty attained its apotheosis in Swinburne, which makes World War I merely a token of post-Victorian dissolution (*BD*, 421). But in *The Great Gatsby*, Fitzgerald begins by believing that he is, after all, above all, the novelist capable of registering the impact of the Great War on modern memory.

The detritus of this conception is scattered in the published version of the novel. Gatsby and Nick meet for the first time (unwittingly) when Gatsby apparently remembers Nick from Europe; Nick initially explains his counter-pioneering expedition East in terms of a Great War unsettling of his Midwestern provinciality; the fact that Tom Buchanan is not a veteran may explain why his masculinity is not entirely spent. But the original manuscript makes the war much more generally and peculiarly the criminal agent in these kidnapped American lives. The war is used to explain not merely Nick's but also Tom and Daisy's deracination: "Why they came East I don't know—perhaps for the same reason I did, searching among unfamiliar surroundings for that vague lost stimulus of the war."[22] How exactly had they been stimulated by the war? Daisy at most had been stimulated by soldiers in uniform; Tom's life is represented as a gradual fading of his college football stardom.

Even odder is Fitzgerald's original evaluation of Gatsby's war experience. In the novel as published, World War I is exclusively, to Gatsby, an opportunity for a forlorn heroism while he is waiting to regain his paradisal Daisy. In manuscript, his heroism is another thing. Nick asks Gatsby what he wants ultimately to accomplish.

> I want to turn the world upside down and give people something to think about. I don't care how much people talk about me or hate me. Just so I could make them admire me, make everybody admire me—like my company did in the war. They knew I was a good man. They gave me a watch! (*GGF*, 176)

Fitzgerald comes back to the surprising adequacy of military life to Gatsby's ambitions—it is not a mere, immediately regretted, improvisation on his part.

> In the cold dawn when his company formed under the last stars he found again the wild exhilaration of his youth and his frosty breath would come fast with excitement as he barked the roll-call. At first like so many young men in those days he thought he would stay in the army permanently. He was happier than he had ever been—the effort and the goal were so austere, so lucid, so complete. (*GGF*, 220)

This passage—without the bathos of the watch, it rises to the Fitzgeraldian sublime—concerns Gatsby while he is still in training and just before he meets Daisy; but the war, even after Daisy, is not precisely anti-climactic according to the manuscript: "He had an instinct for the business and in a long war he might have gone far" (*GGF*, 223). The sentence is quietly amazing: the relevance of a long war for Gatsby ought solely to be the distance (across an ocean rather than a bay) it keeps him from his vision. But Fitzgerald at the outset believes that war might have been, if it had lasted, a magical backdrop of Gatsby's Platonic self-conjuring. This view had to be excised, or the book would have been nonsense. Gatsby has to build his glorious, pathetic dreams on all the lost beauty of the world, not any of its available misery.

Army dreams can come in aesthetic form: war discipline is "so austere, so lucid, so complete." This is war as duel, as bullfight; but Fitzgerald has a higher aesthetic aspiration, so grand it transcends (rational) aesthetics. One of the most telling descriptive moments of *The Great Gatsby* is this physiognomical report on Gatsby's menace, when Tom makes insidious allusions to Gatsby's corruption: "an indefinable expression, at once definitely unfamiliar and vaguely recognizable, as if I had only heard it described in words, passed over Gatsby's face" (*GG*, 121). The oscillation is obvious: the "expression" is indefinable yet definite yet definitely unfamiliar yet recognizable. The outcome of this rolling oxymoron is that Nick moves to the level of his own readers, who are (as if) doubly distanced by the translucence of words. If the inference is that language permits only second-hand recognitions, perhaps we can understand the compatibility of Fitzgerald's scorn for the clichés of plebs ("I lay down and cried to beat the band all afternoon" [*GG*, 35]) with his own indulgence of higher clichés ("I was . . . simultaneously enchanted and repelled by the inexhaustible variety of life" [*GG*, 36]).

In *The Beautiful and Damned*, similarly, Fitzgerald has linguistic contempt for Mrs. Gilbert, who believes that "Bilphism isn't a religion. It's the science of all religions" (*BD*, 76). Fitzgerald notes that this was

> the *bon mot* of her belief. There was something in the arrangement of words which grasped her mind so definitely that the statement became superior to any obligation to define itself. It is not unlikely that she would have accepted any idea encased in this radiant formula—which was perhaps not a formula; it was the *reductio ad absurdum* of all formulas.

The joke—the echo of "the science of all religions" by "the *reductio ad absurdum* of all formulas"—is uncomfortable. Who more than Fitzgerald is attracted to the radiant formula that holds the mind definitely yet is "superior to any obligation to define itself"? If *The Great Gatsby* proves anything about language it is that words capture us not by denotation but by charm. All style in Fitzgerald is meta-style; and the point about style is that it takes over when representation grants its own disability. Style does all the work when no correlative ever succeeds in objectifying an idea, when nothing ever successfully represents anything, when aesthetics has to assume all the attributes of negative theology. The reason that Eucharistic language surrounds Gatsby ("A wafer of a moon was shining over Gatsby's house . . . . A sudden emptiness seemed to flow now from the windows and the great doors, endowing with complete isolation the figure of the host" [*GG*, 56]) is that the book takes its model of representation from the scholastic duality of substance and accidents. There can be no resemblance whatever between the accidental bread and the substantial Christ. In the abyss between God and body echo all the aspirations of style.

Fitzgerald establishes the opposition of the substantial (incarnate but not fully carnal) Gatsby and the accidental (corruptible) Gatsby by means of *accidents*. Gatsby must be ritually consumed, like the last delicacy of his parties, at the end of a series of accidents: the car "shorn of one wheel," its wheel (in another phrasing) "amputated" at the end of a riotous night; Tom's accident, driving with a previous mistress, which "ripped a front wheel off his car"; Myrtle's accidental death, which has the effect of making her "left breast [swing] loose like a flap," and which has the mirror effect on the car of doing damage to its "front right fender" (*GG*, 54, 78, 138, 161). The outcome is that "the laden mattress moved irregularly down the pool. A small gust of wind that scarcely corrugated the surface was enough to disturb its accidental course with its accidental burden" (*GG*, 162).

All these accidents are curiously fateful, culminating with the killing of a mistress by her lover's wife, the sequel of which is the sacrifice of what was always fatedly sacrificial (so that the "accident" is redubbed a "holocaust"). Fitzgerald has noticed that the advent of the automobile is a revolutionary phenomenon in social history: for the first time, homicide becomes, predominantly, accidental. Yet what Fitzgerald as author adds to the novelty is the subtracted intention; the death drive manifests a death drive, an aesthetic demand for completeness. What the essential effect of the Fitzgerald style amounts to—its aspects are the transubstantiation of fashion into truth, voyeurism into romance, time into form, cynicism into vision, gossip into literature—is the replacement of what is accidental with what is determined: in time but not of it.

What is squeezed out is history. Literary desire that is made to move between the disturbing glamour of Fitzgerald's prose and all that that prose cannot capture—as between Truth or Beauty and gossip about what is whispered on the other end of Tom Buchanan's phone or what transpires in Nicole Diver's bathroom—cannot find any fascination in war. Time is either entropic—so that lives as a statistical matter tend toward dissolution and the anticlimax of *The Great Gatsby* is Nick's remembering that he is thirty—or it is typological, and the climax of *The Great Gatsby* is Gatsby's passion. Fitzgerald is either concerned (in every novel) with the passing of youth or he is concerned (as he says in *The Beautiful and Damned*) with what is "older than history" (*BD*, 414). If this is the scope of Fitzgerald's design, how might World War I be aptly remembered?

> I graduated from New Haven in 1915, just a quarter of a century after my father, and a little later I participated in that delayed Teutonic migration known as the Great War. I enjoyed the counter-raid so thoroughly that I came back restless. (*GG*, 3)

Convert the war into a migration west and a return east, and it is no more thermodynamically significant than the perturbations of several related characters whose story Nick flattens this way: "Tom and Gatsby, Daisy and Jordan and I, were all Westerners, and perhaps we possessed some deficiency in common which made us subtly unadaptable to Eastern life" (*GG*, 177), hence Nick's re-return west. But if Gatsby's sacrifice is a holocaust, then a book called *The Great Gatsby* can distract us from a history of pointless driving back and forth, accidental victims beneath its wheels, the last excursion of which was "known as the Great War."

World War I is conjecturally great in *Tender Is the Night*; nevertheless it is again missing, which both emphasizes its importance (it is the context even of lives lived in the asylum, as it were, of a separate peace) and makes it possible for Fitzgerald to seek alternative contexts and etiologies. The book has, of course, two versions. The original published version begins with the blinding of Rosemary Hoyt by Dick's post-war brilliance; the Malcolm Cowley edition begins earlier and prosier with Dick Diver's studies during World War I. I prefer the Cowley edition; it demonstrates more conclusively that the subject of *Tender Is the Night* is whether social violence is what is necessarily sublimated in a creative career, Diver's or Fitzgerald's.[23]

The Cowley edition begins with Dick Diver's eccentric personal history during the Great War. Though he ends up in uniform (serving briefly with a neurological unit), he contributes nothing to the cause; the existence of the uniform itself is nonetheless crucial, since Nicole sees him in it and addresses him briefly thereafter as "Mon Capitaine." More strange is that "in 1916 he managed to get to Vienna" (*TN*, 20), of all places, in order to study with Freud who, no doubt, shares with Dick his suspicions about the compulsion to repeat and the death instinct, which Dick apparently both internalizes and forgets. Wartime and its immediate aftermath are referred to as Dick's "heroic period" (*TN*, 20), but the term has its treacheries; he seems to have agreed cordially with the judgment that he was "too much of a capital investment to be shot off in a gun," but "years later it seemed to him that even in his sanctuary he did not escape lightly" (*TN*, 19). Diver was wounded by his failure to be wounded, to earn his remasculating red badge, to be a hero during his heroic period.

On the other hand, one of Fitzgerald's most daring, if incompletely realized, ideas is that Nicole did suffer sufficiently in World War I, despite her summary opinion that "the war is over and I scarcely knew there was a war" (*TN*, 30). She had been raped by her father as a girl, which leads to fantasies "almost always about men going to attack her, men she knew or men on the street, anybody" (*TN*, 33). The guilty father, to find his wounded daughter institutional help, "run[s] the submarine blockade and bring[s] his daughter to Switzerland," as if she were Catherine Barkley fleeing war, "on a United States cruiser" (*TN*, 33). Of course the father, even more inevitably than Frederic Henry, carries the war wherever he goes; Nicole writes letters to Dick "of a marked pathological turn" "up to about the time of armistice," and writes "entirely normal" ones thereafter (*TN*, 25), as if men in general had to call off their attacks for her to feel the relief that they were not attacking *her*.

So when Dick pretends that he understands warfare—touring the Somme battleground near Thiepval, he finds himself "full of excitement . . . to make them understand about this" (*TN*, 124)—the fact that "actually Abe North had seen battle service and he had not" is far from the only irony. Back in Paris, we catch a glimpse of Nicole "reading over the guidebooks to the battlefield that Dick had brought along," and Fitzgerald adds acidly that Dick "had made a quick study of the whole affair, simplifying it always until it bore a faint resemblance to one of his own parties" (*TN*, 128). The question is what this resemblance could mean to Nicole, somehow as invisibly disabled as Abe. Why did Dick Diver throw the most consequential of all his parties? He confesses to Rosemary: "Maybe we'll have more fun this summer, but this particular fun is over. I want it to die violently instead of fading out sentimentally" (*TN*, 105). The Somme resembles Dick's parties not because the Somme was glamorously orchestrated. We know, thus, that Dick's masterful sociality is a kind of generalship manqué, that the point is to establish his tactical brilliance. It is at this party that Nicole suffers her first post-war collapse, leading to the duel of McKisco and Tommy Barban.

Once again, Dick Diver does not actively participate in the violence that fascinates him; he may be a general, but McKisco and Barban do all the fighting, and only Nicole gets hurt. (Diver's study, "A Psychology for Psychiatrists," diagnoses the typical analyst who is "a little crippled and broken," who chooses his profession as compensation, and by virtue of his choice has "won his battle without a struggle" [*TN*, 43].) Dick is left to make of his entire life an attenuated, marital Great War: "he scented battle from afar, and subconsciously he had been hardening and arming himself, hour by hour" (*TN*, 167). In his professional life, meanwhile, Dick is treating a woman—diagnosed as experiencing "nervous eczema," "a living, agonizing sore"—who claims to be "sharing the fate of the women of my time who challenge men to battle." She concludes: "You pick a set-up, or else win a Pyrrhic victory, or you're wrecked and ruined—you're a ghostly echo from a broken wall." "You are neither wrecked nor ruined," Dick answers clinically. "Are you quite sure you've been in a real battle?" (*TN*, 203–204). But Diver is hardly entitled to make this condescending distinction between real and sexual warfare. Wedlock is a war of attrition, of which the trenches are everywhere.

I seem to be arguing that what is lacking in Dick Diver is no trait but rather World War I itself. But that is not precise, because the violence that seeks Dick Diver is energetically sought by Abe North, who is a veteran. Even combatants are unsatiated by the violence of World War I, for reasons that need explaining. The assault of violence itself homes in this way (as in *Gatsby*, but finding the wrong target): McKisco and Barban's duel; a friend's shooting of an unknown Englishman at the train station; the murder of the black man in some sort of affair of Abe North's; the murder of Abe North. It is odd that Abe should be compelled to seek violence rather than Diver, an oddity subtly explicated in the final passage on Abe. Dick slept deep and awoke to a slow mournful march passing his window. It was a long column of men in uniform, wearing the familiar helmet of 1914, thick men in frock coats and silk hats, burghers, aristocrats, plain men. It was a society of veterans going to lay wreaths on the tombs of the dead. The column marched slowly with a sort of swagger for a lost magnificence, a past effort, a forgotten sorrow. The faces were only formally sad, but Dick's lungs burst for a moment with regret for Abe's death, and his own youth of ten years ago. (*TN*, 220)

Here is a double displacement—a double trivialization—of significance. World War I is nearly a "forgotten sorrow" inspiring "only formally sad" faces; Abe North's pathetic death restores the pathos of World War I; and Dick Diver's self-pity gives meaning to Abe North's death. North's murder represents Diver's aging, just as Gatsby's assassination is the emblem of Nick Carraway's thirtieth birthday.

The inference is that no more than Abe North could Dick Diver have expressed his undirected violence adequately in World War I. That North had served is most tellingly emphasized during the visit to Thiepval where, prophetically, North says (in contradiction of Dick's kitschily dramatized vision of the Somme as his own personal tragedy): "There are lots of people dead since and we'll all be dead soon" (*TN*, 124). This actually endorses Diver's view that dying gradually is as tragic as dying young, though it draws the opposite inference that neither is particularly tragic. At any rate, there is no end of dying, and no death is late enough. World War I seems, in these peculiar terms, a normative event, a sign of dissolution (as on Anthony Patch's theory) rather than, say, a purgation.

This is Abe North's view and Diver's, and it seems to be Fitzgerald's. But Fitzgerald is clear enough that adequately expressed violence is good for the soul. It is just that World War I was the wrong occasion. The correct moment for Diver is, as it turns out, immediately after the party at which Mrs. McKisco observes Nicole's collapse. She is eager to scandalize; Tommy Barban silences her; Mr. McKisco springs to his wife's defense; a duel is drunkenly arranged. It is Abe's opinion that "this fight is between two men—what Tommy needs is a good war" (*TN*, 112). What every man needs, apparently, is a good war, a war that is enacted "between two men," which is to say not a mass war of attrition like the Great War, but an aesthetically satisfying war, a duel. The duel, with pistols, is fought, and though it is a rather Tolstoyan affair with no injuries, the results are entirely beneficial. Tommy, for one, eventually wins Nicole. After he has finally achieved intercourse with her, they hear a cannon shot from a battleship sounding a recall. This is followed by an echoing knock at their door; some women want to use the balcony to wave farewell to their naval lovers. One of the women

pulled and ripped at her pink step-ins, and tore them to a sizable flag; then, screaming "Ben! Ben!" she waved it wildly. As Tommy and Nicole left the room it still fluttered against the blue sky. Oh, say can you see the tender colour of remembered flesh? — while at the stern of the battleship rose in rivalry the Star Spangled Banner. (*TN*, 316–317)

At this moment Francis Scott Key Fitzgerald confronts Francis Scott Key, his celebrated ancestor (cousin of his great-grandmother),[24] nationally revered for writing a battle poem while he sat out the battle. Fitzgerald also sat out the battle; but in an image he fantasizes, with considerable disgust, what license it might have gained him to fight it.

Meanwhile, McKisco turns into a successful, if unoriginal, novelist.

> "I've done nothing yet," he would say. "I don't think I've got any real genius. But if I kept [sic] trying I may write a good book." Fine dives have been made from flimsier spring-boards. The innumerable snubs of the past were forgotten. Indeed, his success was founded psychologically upon his duel with Tommy Barban, upon the basis of which, as it withered in his memory, he had created, afresh, a new self-respect. (*TN*, 226)

It does not require a jeweler's eye to pick out the word "dives" in this passage. Dick Diver should have fought the duel; when he warns Rosemary that he is inalterably in love with Nicole, and adds that he means "active love," it can only seem a non sequitur that he concludes: "it [their love] was responsible for that crazy duel" (*TN*, 144). How precisely was Dick's active love for Nicole responsible for his own passivity as Barban defended Nicole's honor and McKisco his wife's? Can Diver be imagining that his rival fought on his behalf? At any rate, Dick's success is inherited by the two disreputable duelists: brutal Barban gets love and money, the mediocre McKisco gets money and fame.

Meanwhile, Diver circles from oblivion to oblivion: in Chapter one, he, "like Grant, lolling in his general store in Galena, is ready to be called to an intricate destiny"; in the last chapter, Nicole hopes that his career is "biding its time, again like Grant's in Galena" (*TN*, 22, 334). The optimism of the latter prediction is not comforting. The Grant metaphor if it does allegorical work makes us consider the meaning of a career that moves from nowhere through a heroic period and then through corruption to disgrace; perhaps we can assimilate this sort of revolution to the death drive. I think it is preferable to consider the Grant metaphor as insufficiently justified and weightless, along with all the other Civil War metaphors. Why is Abe North (at one stage of the composition "Abe Grant") "Abe North"? He gets mixed up with blacks and is murdered; is that enough? Why is a Diver child named Topsy? ("You tell me my baby is black" [*TN*, 67]?) Perhaps it is plausible that a Southerner named Clay appears. But why should there be a (motion-) picture maker named Brady?

Fitzgerald was preoccupied with the Civil War; the sort of question I have been raising about *Tender Is the Night* could be asked about *The Great Gatsby*: why is Gatsby's party attended by Ulysses Swett and Stonewall Jackson Abrams? (The names reenact the historical bathos.) Among Fitzgerald's juvenilia are two stories about the Civil War, "A Debt of Honor" and "The Room With the Green Blinds."[25] The latter is about the death (many years after the purported execution in the barn) of John Wilkes Booth, with whom Fitzgerald's father had a remote connection (the mother-in-law of one of his father's cousins, Mary Surratt, was implicated in the assassination). And one of the more direct Civil War allusions of *Tender Is the Night* is to Mosby's Raiders, who also had a connection to Fitzgerald's father. At a restaurant in Paris, Dick observes a party of gold-star mothers, and admires "the maturity of an older America. . . . Momentarily, he sat again on his father's knee, riding with Mosby while the old loyalties and devotions fought on around him" (*TN*, 168). Fitzgerald's father (born 1853) had helped, in his youth, a Mosby sniper to escape capture.[26]

All of which means that there once existed a dignified war, a sacred and tragic conflict, which might have served as an object of Fitzgerald's filial, tardy ambitions. The Civil War, in Fitzgerald's imagination, was war as duel, as the next-to-last war always is. Historically too late for the opportunities of a beautiful history, Fitzgerald's style seems always to seek greatness not in any object, however historically momentous, but in the capacity of rhetoric itself to invoke what cannot be precisely measured or dated.

> She smiled, a moving childish smile that was like all the lost youth in the world. (*TN*, 40)

> She thanked him for everything, rather as if he had taken her to some party, and as Dick became less and less certain of his relation to her, her confidence increased—there was that excitement about her that seemed to reflect all the excitement of the world. (*TN*, 41)

> Now there was this scarcely saved waif of disaster bringing him the essence of a continent. (*TN*, 42)

This Gatsbian, eucharistic language is the inevitable result when the subject is excess but the principle of the mode is economy. Fitzgerald stakes his literary style on the beleaguered hegemony of Dick's magnificent, punctilious social style, and the point in both cases is that between the local glamour and its absconded referent, nothing so grotesque and limited as a Great War can intervene.

> But Dick's necessity of behaving as he did was a projection of some submerged reality: he was compelled to walk there, or stand there, his shirt-sleeve fitting his wrist and his coat sleeve encasing his shirt-sleeve like a sleeve valve, his collar moulded plastically to his neck, his red hair cut exactly, his hand holding his briefcase like a dandy—just as another man once found it necessary to stand in front of a church in Ferrara, in sackcloth and ashes. Dick was paying some tribute to things unforgotten, unshriven, unexpurgated. (*TN*, 160)

It is remarkable how immediately this passage moves from dandy to saint, preening to mortification, factory to monastery, fashion to eternity, what can be perfected to what cannot be forgiven, personal expression to the unsayable, modernity to the Middle Ages. The key to Dick's style as well as Fitzgerald's is incommensurability. Dick's

> excitement about things reached an intensity out of proportion to their importance, generating a really extraordinary virtuosity with people. Save among a few of the tough-minded and perennially suspicious, he had the power of arousing a fascinating and uncritical love. The reaction came when he realized the waste and extravagance involved. He sometimes looked back with awe at the carnivals of affection he had given, as a general might gaze upon a massacre he had ordered to satisfy an impersonal blood lust. (*TN*, 94)

So war—mass, impersonal war, not war as duel—is a fit emblem of the aesthetic ambition after all? Only if the general moves out of motives larger than tactics, larger than strategy, unmoored from policy, out of personal ambitions so compelling as to be impersonal and ahistorical. This is total and absolute war as a function of aesthetic desire. Would Ulysses S. Grant qualify? North states at Thiepval that "General Grant invented this kind of battle at Petersburg in sixty-five."

> "No he didn't," [Dick insists]. "He just invented mass butchery. This kind of battle was invented by Lewis Carroll and Jules Verne and whoever wrote *Undine*. . . . Why, this was a love battle—there was a century of middle-class love spent here. This was the last love battle." (*TN*, 125)

The apothegm is of course only a typical Diver opinion; but we may observe that the characteristic extravagance of Fitzgerald's prose only lasts as long as Diver's professional and social success (all my examples come from the first part of the book), as if we can be dazzled by Fitzgerald only as long as we are dazzled by Diver.

> "You want to hand over this battle to D. H. Lawrence," said Abe.

Which reveals that it was with some historical self-irony, some acknowlegment of what is falsified in taking war as a matter of lust and love and literature, some awareness of the risky arrogance of his longstanding allegiance to the Utopia of style, that Fitzgerald reaches torward the Great War with his own hand.

Assume it is true that Faulkner's first three novels were apprentice work, succeeded by the two masterpieces that make the case for Faulkner's stature as a high-formalist modernist (followed by other novels that may be better or worse than *The Sound and the Fury* and *As I Lay Dying* but which lack those books' virtuoso perfectionism). It follows that what had to be sacrificed in the fulfillment of Faulkner's most purely modernist aspiration is World War I. Faulkner's first novel, *Soldiers' Pay*, centers on a grotesquely scarred, progressively blind ex-aviator who barely resists fading into death for almost the length of the book; Faulkner's third novel, *Flags in the Dust* (published as *Sartoris*, cut one-fourth by Faulkner's agent), is about another aviator who seeks his unwillingly postponed death after World War I, only with more self-destructive élan. Faulkner sets out on the belief that his obsession with decay, constriction, and self-violence needs the historical basis of World War I. It is too facile to argue that the modernist claim is premised solely on the discovery that the war, on the contrary, was not an integral part of the project. The force of World War I had to be rechanneled; by mentioning, too late in *As I Lay Dying* to affect our conception of the book, that Darl was in the war, Faulkner marks the point at which history becomes form, or, more accurately, where time itself gets stylized.

The centerpiece of Faulkner's formal achievement in *As I Lay Dying* is Addie's coffin. Its shape is actually drawn in the novel; it is an ideal of rectilinear craftsmanship that the book brings to account. We hear the racket of its construction by Cash as the background noise of the first phase of the book. Most of the evidence indicates that Addie is comforted by the sound of her own coffin getting assembled, though Jewel, her most passionately devoted son, is tormented by the noise into a furious onomatopoeia. "It's because he stays out there, right under the window, hammering and sawing on that goddamn box. Where she's got to see him. Where every breath she draws is full of his knocking and sawing where she can see him saying See. See what a good one I am making for you" (*ALD*, 14). Addie would have to be ambivalent about the coffin, not merely for obvious reasons, but also because what it must signify for her is both the rigid obtuseness of men (whose linear language it memorializes) and the interpermeability of life and afterlife that only women can intuit. The woman's supervision of her own burial is, in any case, so vivid as to make us celebrate again Faulkner's peculiar gift.

Yet the soldier's self-detached, self-observant preference for death is standard in Great War memoirs—for example, at the beginning of Sassoon's: *"as for me, I had more or less made up my mind to die"* (*MIA*, 9). (Anse on Addie: "She's a going . . . . Her mind is set on it" [*ALD*, 29].) Even the premature, pre-posthumous experience of one's own coffin is a not infrequent occurrence in World War I literature. Without Faulkner, we might have concluded that the device was purest Remarque: "On the way [to the front] we pass a shelled school-house. Stacked up against its longer side is a high double wall of yellow, unpolished, brand-new coffins. They still smell of resin, and pine, and the forest. There are at least a hundred. . . . The coffins are really for us. The organization surpasses itself in that kind of thing."[27] As in Faulkner, nature is mobilized as gothic machinery. Such effects are in fact neither uniquely Faulkner nor uniquely Remarque. "Winterbourne [writes Aldington] peered through and saw that the whole of the inside had been cleared of débris, and was stacked with quantities of wooden objects. He shaded his eyes more carefully, and saw that they were ranks and ranks of wooden crosses. Those he could see had painted on them R.I.P.; then underneath was a blank space for the name. . . . Excellent forethought, he reflected as he filled his bucket and water-bottle; how well this War is organized!" (*DH*, 325).

I am not arguing that Faulkner was a crypto-war novelist or a plagiarist (all these passages were published between 1928 and 1930) or even unoriginal. I believe instead that some of the same passions that made him seek the self-destructive glamour of the RAF would drive his fiction; and that his failure to get even so far as his first training flight necessarily affected the form of his novels (one of Faulkner's most powerful fictions was the unpublished one that he had flown in the Great War and had crashed);[28] and that what is most useful to observe is how history is transformed, how temporality is formulated, as a modernist ambition transvaluates modernity.

In his first novel, *Soldiers' Pay*, Faulkner discovered the technique of making his narrative spiral around an almost mute character whose death seems a perfection of the immobility of his last days.[29] That Donald Mahon muddles the demarcation between death and life is a point made repeatedly, as if Faulkner does not yet trust his reader: "The man that was wounded is dead and this is another person, a grown child"; "Yes, that was Donald. He is dead" (*SP*, 118, 182). Mainly, Donald sits dying, but by the end he lies dying; just before his ultimate death he is yielded a single section in which to recall the circumstances of his wounding (recalling it permits him finally to die as a medical matter). That lives after combat can feel anti-climactic and attenuated is an empirical fact (Faulkner treats it again in "All the Dead Pilots," all of whom, except for John Sartoris, are physically alive). The question I raise is what it can do for Faulkner's modernist style, once the condition of nearly but not absolutely mute moribundity is wrested from all the dead pilots, once, that is, it is established that an old woman can take the seat apparently reserved for veterans.

The benefit of the convention in *Soldiers' Pay* is that it generates an anti-sexual erotic force that can serve as a gravitational center for the book's narrative. The novel is an asexual voyeuristic farce, composed of prying entanglements without copulation. Little Robert (kid brother of Cecily, betrothed of Donald) is obsessed with seeing Donald's scar; but when Gilligan and Mrs. Powers (the moral foci of the novel) accidentally espy Robert naked, he immediately sets to spying on *them* for his fickle sister. So it goes. "But what if they do see me?" worries a character named George on his way to a tryst with Cecily, and then runs into a rival also on the way to Cecily: "Whoever it was [it turns out to be Januarius Jones] did not want to be seen" (*SP*, 237). Every voyeur is the enemy of all voyeurs.

The character who sees the least is of course the returned aviator, Donald, fully blind halfway through the book. The discovery that he is blind is observational comedy. His father (the rector) has tried to ignore his son's condition; the doctor says sharply, "How you didn't know it I can't see" (*SP*, 167). The doctor cannot see why the rector could not see that the aviator has not been able to see. Donald's friends comfort his father with the hope that Donald's vision might be restored. "Yes, yes," the father says, "Let's get him well and then we can see" (*SP*, 168). He is hoping for a restoration of their own sight. On the other hand, the character who never fails to see, who catches everyone in every act, is the loathsome Januarius Jones, a sort of hyper-conscious Snopes. He is programmatically devoted to unwatched watching: "He considered moving beyond her so that she must face the light and leave his own face in shadow" (*SP*, 222). Occasionally he is himself caught: "Then, stooping, he peered through the keyhole"; but the act is performed under "Gilligan's detached, contemplative stare" (*SP*, 138).

There are five young men in the novel. One of two who did not fight in World War I is Januarius Jones, so we can be confident about the association of blindness specifically with combatants and seeing with civilians. Since Jones is also the most sexually determined of the men, it is tempting to read in blindness a symbol of war's castration. But that is not exactly right: no woman is attracted to the odious Jones, and three women, for three different reasons, wish to marry Donald, though none, it is true, is much interested in him physically, except Mrs. Powers who is attracted to his scar. One version of sexuality has been replaced by another. Post-war, noncombatant sexuality is sexuality as pornography, a sexuality of degraded, manipulative looking. All sensation is reduced to sight. The other of the two noncombatants—George—is described as experiencing "all his life [going] into his eyes leaving his body." Again: "He had lost his body. He could not feel it at all. It was as though vision were a bodiless Eye suspended in dark-blue space" (*SP*, 148, 236). To have been in air combat is apparently to have seen enough; to have missed air combat is to be reduced to a Transcendentally aerated scopophilia.

What is combatant, aviator sexuality? Not to fly is doubtless to remain a child, a virgin. The cadet Lowe, like Faulkner, is trained as a pilot but the war ends on him, and he returns to his mother. To fly is to have elevated sex, of course, but of a particular species: "Do you know how falcons make love? They embrace at an enormous height and fall locked, beak to beak, plunging: an unbearable ecstasy. While we [this is Jones speaking] have got to assume all sorts of ludicrous postures, knowing our own sweat" (*SP*, 227). The sine qua non of unfallen aerial love-making is not, however, its homosexuality or its violence. When George runs into Jones as they both stalk Cecily, they begin fighting—"clawing and panting"—but since both trysts are illicit (Cecily being engaged to Donald), they are forced into an intimacy when Cecily's father happens by: "Crushing themselves against the brick wall, they lay in a mutual passion for concealment" (*SP*, 239). This is the noncombatant, earthbound form (they are compared not to falcons but to ostriches) of male violent homoeroticism. The glory of aviator (falcon) sex is apparently its arrogant visibility, which amounts to a fearlessness of anti-climax: "The falcon breaks his clasp and swoops away swift and proud and lonely, while a man must rise and take his hat and walk out." Falcon intercourse (if Faulkner is derived from falconer, which sort does he experience?) is without the shame of detumescence.

That is the pathos of the fact that after the war is over, an aviator's life is only anti-climax, as in "All the Dead Pilots." To receive one's wound in an air battle is to have confirmed one's masculinity and to have lost it in a single rite: one loses one's virginity and one's sex in the heights of divine intercourse. (The red badge is again the signature of the emasculating and remasculating goddess.) There is an inverse fetishism at work here: blindness is the sign that one does not need to look for metonymic alternatives to lack because one has never been fully satisfied except by one's castration; one's own castration is one's pride, because to lose something means once to have had it, and one knows that one has had it only in the risking of it, and the risking and losing of it are Olympian. The young Robert's fascination with Donald's scar is castration envy; the perpetual cadet and virgin Lowe is sure (rightly) that Mrs. Powers (the emasculating, remasculating goddess herself) will always love Donald rather than himself because of the wound. "If I had wings," thinks Lowe, "and a scar"; then the two desiderata become one: "His scar: his wings" (*SP*, 47). The desirable Mrs. Powers is herself metaphorically scarred ("She raised her face, her pallid face beneath her black hair, scarred with her mouth" [*SP*, 42]). For these inverse fetishists, it is too late for castration anxiety; re-attachment anxiety is more their syndrome.

We are diagnosing the poverty of Faulkner's imagination for trench warfare and his continual fascination with the air war. We may add the historical dimension to this psychologizing: the air war is also the sign of loss as what one takes one's pride in (the lost thing but equally the losing of it). Faulkner depicts air combat as knighthood, as the last possible moment of Southern romantic medieval chivalry. The obese Jones, in an early foreshadowing of his falcon remarks, improvises a rhapsody on weightlessness: "If a man, if a single man, could be freed for a moment from the forces of gravity, concentrating his weight upon that point of his body which touches the earth, what would he not do? He would be a god . . . he would thunder at the very gates of infinity like a mailed knight" (*SP*, 62–63). He is not alluding to aviators—but the odd simile (why imagine weightlessness in metal armor?) conjures them. When Gilligan refers to "the old bunk about knights in the air and the romance of battle" (*SP*, 41), he is not belittling the chivalry of air combat. He is ruing the fact that no modern woman is attracted to it.

Faulkner is not superimposing a Southerner's romance on modern warfare without justice. The end of air dueling can be dated with some precision.

The year 1917 was marked . . . by an increasing development of the method of fighting and flying in formation, which tended to replace the Homeric combats of individual champions . . . . Henceforth, knight-errantry yielded to tactics and air-fighting gradually assumed the more developed forms of warfare, although carried out on a different plane. By the end of the war an attack was often delivered by formations of fifty or sixty machines which manoeuvred—the actual squadrons compact—with the aim of breaking up the enemy's formation.[30]

In 1917 the Homeric style of war, in decline since 1000 B.C., at long last took leave of the Western world. A modernist first novel, we might guess, could barely stay afloat on the ebb of its supremacy. How many books could generate narrative interest on the formal assumption that any climax — sexual, aesthetic, historical — has to be always already foregone?

In his third novel, then, Faulkner tries to make the belated dying at least active and violent. Bayard Sartoris, hero of *Flags in the Dust*, imagines that like his brother John, "he too was dead and this was hell"; civilian life is Hell because the Sartoris theology, from the Civil War to World War I, projects a Heaven of "martial cherubim."[31] Bayard's position is a prefiguration of Addie's; his character is a prefiguration of Jewel's: proud, self-torturing, anti-social, and mean. He rides a horse with the same combination of cruelty and masochism; but unlike Jewel, Bayard also drives a car. And unlike Jewel, he flew planes in World War I. His monomania has a historical component, and transforming it again leads to the high modernism of *As I Lay Dying*.

That its hero's pursuit of death (or the confirmation of death) is passionate helps to make *Flags in the Dust* a much better novel than *Soldiers' Pay*, but it also threatens its unity. If *Soldiers' Pay* is centripetal (Donald Mahon is a black sun), this book is centrifugal (it could not be published until it was cut). As Bayard Sartoris careers around town and countryside in his car, he almost literally keeps running into people, and the book works the same way.

What Faulkner uses to unite the book is a redundancy of image, the responsibility for which lies about halfway from Faulkner to young Bayard. Old Bayard, grandfather of the protagonist, fleeing Yankees as a youth, sees in his reflection in the spring "the cavernous sockets of his eyes . . . and from the still water there stared back at him for a sudden moment, a skull" (*FD*, 82). This connects to the "rusting skeleton of a Ford car," whose "two lamps gave it an expression of beetling patient astonishment, like a skull" (*FD*, 123). When young Bayard gallops past Narcissa Benbow, whom he will marry, on his way to a painful accident, he "remark[s] for a flashing second a woman's face and a mouth partly open and two eyes round with serene astonishment," later recalled as "two eyes round with a grave shocked astonishment" (*FD*, 120, 126). At the *next* memory of the woman Bayard recalls her "two eyes round with grave astonishment, winged serenely by two dark wings of hair" (*FD*, 134). Then we hear of the "fallen dark wings of her hair" moved upon by air "with grave coolness" (*FD*, 138). The skull is the car is the woman; the woman has wings and falls like an angel. Young Bayard's car accelerates "on a roar of sound like blurred thunderous wings" (*FD*, 105). Pedantic Dr. Alford's hair, something like Narcissa's, is parted into "two careful reddish-brown wings" (*FD*, 111) (the point is to reveal the skull); the horse on which young Bayard is injured "burst [out] like unfolding bronze wings" (*FD*, 119); the literary Horace Benbow is "borne aloft on his flaming verbal wings" (*FD*, 154).

There are wings everywhere, associated with skulls, speed, falling, and burning, because Bayard, flying with John, knew John was in trouble (we eventually learn) when he saw "the flame streaming out along his wing" (*FD*, 239), and Bayard is not satisfied until he dies flying an experimental plane, which crashes after its wings come off. The point is that the book's unity is staked on the uncanny repetition of an event. Every moment is the original (shall we say historic or prehistoric?) moment over and over. (The climax as in *Soldiers' Pay* is in advance of the book, but the action of the novel is mimetic of its tacit ante-climax.) Time passes, and each new month is noted, but the coherence of the novel is a function of Bayard's "Hell": the timelessness of traumatized memory. In this way masculine time never lasts more than the "sudden moment," the "flashing second."

Feminine time is something else; as the focus of *Flags in the Dust* shifts, so does Faulkner's historical sense. By the end of the novel, the subject is not Bayard's suffering but his great-aunt Miss Jenny's and his wife Narcissa's. There is a moment in every Great War memoir when the returning soldier is informed—much of course to his disgust—that the sacrifices on the home front have been heroic. There is a comparable moment in *Flags in the Dust*.

> "Men cant seem to stand anything," she [Miss Jenny] repeated. "Cant even stand helling around with no worry and no responsibility and no limit to all of the meanness they can think about wanting to do. Do you think a man could sit day after day and month after month in a house miles from anywhere and spend the time between casualty lists tearing up bedclothes and window curtains and table linen to make lint and watching sugar and flour and meat dwindling away and using pine knots for light because there aren't any candles and no candlesticks to put them in, if there were, and hiding in nigger cabins while drunken Yankee generals set fire to the house your great-great-grandfather built and you and all your folks were born in? Dont talk to me about men suffering in war." (*FD*, 45–46)

This passage, however, differs from the Great War cliché because there is no man around to resent it. Miss Jenny speaks these words to Narcissa, who produces a baby on the day her husband crashes and dies. The correspondence of birth and war is made almost explicitly: Narcissa surrounds her infant with "wave after wave of that strength which welled so abundantly within her as the days accumulated, manning the walls with invincible garrisons" (*FD*, 349). (The first wife of Bayard, a Sartoris in spirit and then in name, dies in childbirth—and as a spiritual Sartoris she fails to protect her baby who also dies—during World War I.) Woman's warfare is chivalric but defensive: Narcissa "thought how much finer that gallantry which never lowered lance to foes no sword could ever find, that uncomplaining steadfastness of those unsung (ay, unwept, too) women than the fustian and useless glamor of the men that theirs was hidden from" (*FD*, 350). The oddity is that Faulkner foreshadows the anti-masculinism of Lynn Hanley. Women are victims of war not only because of wartime privations but also by virtue of the lives they must thereafter endure with men warped or ruined forever.

I see in the refocusing of *Flags in the Dust* a transition to *As I Lay Dying*. I am not merely arguing that you have to replace young men with young and old women as the center of your concern for the sake of transcending war as the inevitable context of fiction. I am suggesting that one temporality is replaced by another in *Flags in the Dust* to make possible the stylistic supra-historicity of *As I Lay Dying*. Male time seeks climaxes and catastrophes (male time is a traditional narrative), so that after World War I, all that can be left for men who have outlived their story is a perpetual repetition of the catastrophic moment in a life otherwise of perfect bathos. Female time, however, is an "accumulation" of days and a slow-motion, "steadfast" translation of life into death. Male time is infinitesimal and infinitely thin; I shall argue that female time is, in *As I Lay Dying*, thick and clotted. It is wartime that must be transcended in order to make possible Faulkner's modernist subordination of narrative to style.

One aesthetic pole of *As I Lay Dying* is represented by Cash's coffin; Darl's cubist still life of the burning barn captures the same ideal. This is one aspect of the transcendence of narrative in *As I Lay Dying*. There is a counter-ideal; the book is a surfeit of mud and blood and guts, a satiety of everything that the coffin is supposed to hide or withstand. This is primarily (though not quite exclusively) the female element in the book: Addie whips the students so that her "blood and their blood [could] flow in one stream" (*ALD*, 164); Dewey Dell conceives of her relation to Peabody as, "He is a big tub of guts and I am a little tub of guts" (*ALD*, 56). When Jewel rides by the wagon on which Addie's body is carried and causes a "gout of mud, back-flung [to plop] onto the box" (*ALD*, 102), the stylistic duality of the novel gets its emblem.

I should mention in this connection the related vertical vs. horizontal coordination of *As I Lay Dying*. Anse, Addie's husband, is proud of his rooted verticality: "When [God] aims for something to be always a-moving, He makes it longways, like a road or a horse or a wagon, but when He aims for something to stay put, He makes it up-and-down ways, like a tree or a man" (*ALD*, 34–35). Cash, making Addie's coffin, reminds us that "in a house people are upright two thirds of the time. So the seams and joints are made up-and-down"; on the other hand, the seams and joints of a bed are sideways; the coffin, the vector of his own admirably wooden uprightness and Addie's prostration, is made with seams and joints on a slant (*ALD*, 77–78). But Addie spends the whole book supine, which is her destiny and not just her misfortune. Alive, Addie "would think how words go straight up in a thin line, quick and harmless, and how terribly doing goes along the earth, clinging to it" (*ALD*, 165).

Eric J. Leed, in *No Man's Land*, describes the mythical topography of the Great War as having two axes: first the aerial to underground axis (airplanes, trenches, mines); second the horizontal axis (rear areas, reserve trenches, front, No Man's Land, enemy front, enemy reserve, enemy rear). We may generalize that in most of Faulkner's explicit Great War writing what interests him is the vertical scheme. The myth of the flier is a myth of air as "the last home of chivalric endeavor" (*NML*, 134) — above fragmentation and constriction. Visions of burial are the underside of Faulkner's vertical imagination. In "Ad Astra," Monaghan remembers his father who made "a million dollars digging sewers in the ground. So he could look up at the tall glittering windows and say . . . every man is the slave of his own refuse."[32] In "Crevasse," a detached group of soldiers gets trapped in an infantry version of Poe's maelstrom, except that for the immaculate death of the whirlpool is substituted a death of "rotted flesh" and manure: "The scream ceases; he hears the voice of the wounded man coming thin and reiterant out of the plunging bowels of decay: 'A'm no dead! A'm no dead!'"[33]

So we may consider *As I Lay Dying* as the surfacing of Faulkner's excremental vision, and the vision is so reminiscent of World War I trench mythology that it is as if he turned away from the Great War to get closer to it. Leed's book exists to make the point that war is not the opposite of peace, a release of bestiality or a regression to the primitive. War in the trenches was hardly a release; the "civilization" from which soldiers are said to escape was already, by 1914, industrialized, oppressive, and dangerous. Rather, the terms of war are taken from peace, and war functions as a kind of ritual by which the structures of normal life in society are defamiliarized, though rituals eventuate in reintegration and war is a perpetual alienation. Call war an anti-rite, and you begin to get the essential connection to Faulkner.

What particularly marks *As I Lay Dying* as an anti-rite is its liminality, which is never (anti-ritualistically) transcended. The liminality of rituals, Leed says, "is closely analogous to the position of men in war. . . . A youth undergoing initiation is . . . spoken of as 'dead' to the things of the past, and may be treated as his society treats a corpse — buried, forced to lie immobile in a pit or a ditch. The initiand is identified with the earth, with pollution and corruption" (*NML*, 17). Leed's combat illustration of the liminal experience of pollution (i.e., the nauseous transgression of categories) is particularly suggestive: an officer is knocked by a shell into

> the distended abdomen of a German several days dead. The young officer knew, before he lost consciousness, "that the substance which filled his mouth and produced the most horrible sensations of taste and smell was derived from the decomposed entrails of an enemy." It would be difficult to find a more complete violation of the distinctions which separate the dead from the living, friend from enemy, rotten from edible . . . . (*NML*, 19)

Except, I hasten to add, in *As I Lay Dying*. (The key sensations of Great War novels and *As I Lay Dying* are olfactory, as opposed to civilian voyeurism.) "In war," Leed concludes, as if also discussing Addie's demise, "death lost the perfect, abstract clarity that it normally enjoyed as the brief moment between life and not-life" (*NML*, 23).

Addie is considered by Peabody to be dead in her "No Man's Land" ten days before her actual death, and seems to be alive for a comparable period between the moment of medical death and burial. The half-dead Addie and the half-quick foetus in Dewey Dell are the two leaks in the solidity of Cash's coffin. That foetuses are not quite alive and that corpses are not quite dead are unnerving notions; they suggest a world in which identities and elements are chronically impure, never identical and never elemental, a psychotic or excremental world. And the pathological Bundrens, whose minds are semi-permeable, move with comic horror through elements epitomized by the "runnel of yellow neither water nor earth" (*ALD*, 48). Perhaps nowhere in actual World War I literature is polluted trench life, a miasma of mud and guts and decomposing bodies, rendered better than in *As I Lay Dying*, which nevertheless minimizes almost to nullity Darl's experience in the war, so that his hysteria cannot be diagnosed as shell shock. *As I Lay Dying* ought to be the title of the unwritable Great War memoir recovered from No Man's Land.

That it is not means that we need finally to say how the facts of polluted horizontal life in World War I trenches are converted by Faulkner into the impure elements of his style. First, Addie turns suffering into a linguistic matter; when she is allowed words in a single section, she speaks mainly about words. Anse, courting and marrying and impregnating Addie, "had a word, too. Love, he called it. But I had been used to words for a long time. I knew that that word was like the others: just a shape to fill a lack; that when the right time came, you wouldn't need a word for that any more than for pride or fear" (*ALD*, 164). This itself is a Great War issue; Hemingway and Fussell make the same point about such words as "gallant" and "glory." But Addie does not want a simpler, more straightforward diction; she does not endorse Hemingway's vocabulary of place names, which seems to allow a direct contact of signifiers and referents, as Barthes describes the realist illusion. "I would think about [Anse's] name until after a while I could see the word as a shape, a vessel, and I would watch him liquefy and flow into it"; her own female shape "where I used to be a virgin is in the shape of a   " (*ALD*, 165). The blank space responds to the drawing of the coffin: words are interrupted twice, narrative is subverted twice, by the borders of the page, its prose justifications and margins.

This explains why the language of *As I Lay Dying* is occasionally so thick and coagulated (as against the "thin line" of words that are "quick and harmless"). All the key words of the novel are repeated, or transmuted, or juxtaposed with cognates and homonyms, as if to clot the linear thinness of the prose sentence. Dewey Dell is pregnant, so the trees are "swollen, increased as though quick with young" (*ALD*, 72). Then:

"Yes, sir. It will rain some more."
"It come up quick." (*ALD*, 82)

"It's been there a long time, that ere bridge," Quick says. (*ALD*, 83)

"A fellow can sho slip quick on wet planks," Quick says. (*ALD*, 85)

After this remark, the rain (that comes up quick) is imagined as the cause of a natural abortion (the cotton and corn will be "washed clean outen the ground"); while the men discuss this, the women's singing begins "to swell" (*ALD*, 85).

The word "quick"—associated first with thinness and inconsequence—thickens to suggest birth, injury, and abortion. The turns on the word "bore" suggest nurturing, endurance, and violent penetration. As in this flurry, all within one page:

> And the next morning they found [Vardaman] in his shirt tail, laying asleep on the floor like a felled steer, and the top of the box bored clean full of holes.

> And when folks talk [Anse] low, I think to myself he aint that less of a man or he couldn't a bore himself this long.

> Cora said, "I have bore you what the Lord God sent me." (*ALD*, 69–70)

Later the contrary suggestions of the word are compressed into two sentences by the preacher Whitfield. "It was His hand that bore me safely above the flood, that fended from me the dangers of the waters. My horse was frightened, and my own heart failed me as the logs and the uprooted trees bore down upon my littleness" (*ALD*, 170).

The word "lie" is the most freighted of the story; Addie's variations on the word are the most virtuosic.

> I would lie by [Anse] in the dark . . . . (*ALD*, 166)

> Then I would lay with Anse again—I did not lie to him. (*ALD*, 167)

> With Jewel—I lay by the lamp, holding up my own head, watching him cap and suture it before he breathed—the wild blood boiled away and the sound of it ceased. Then there was only the milk, warm and calm, and I lying calm in the slow silence, getting ready to clean my house. (*ALD*, 168)

The point of confusing recumbency, mendacity, and coitus (non-intercourse, false intercourse, intercourse) is not merely to clot the prose; not merely to muddle life and anti-life; not merely to suggest the coexistence of intimacy and isolation; tenses (as with the "bear," "bore" constellation) have been thoroughly confused in the process. Is the "lay" of the title grammatical? (The quotation is from Agamemnon in *The Odyssey*; Agamemnon is dead with unshut eyes [*FB*, 248–249].) Or is it the present tense slang (combined with the redundant Renaissance pun)? Or is it the ungrammatical present? "Lay" is used ungrammatically for "lie" throughout the novel, though not by the former schoolteacher Addie, unless "then I would lay with Anse" is an instance.

Time itself is thickened: present and past lie by each other on the surface of the novel. Coagulated by the prose, time does not flow. The antithesis is the ethereal linear thinness of geometric space with which Darl begins the book: "the path runs straight as a plumb-line . . . to the cotton-house in the center of the field, where it turns and circles the cottonhouse at four soft right angles" (*ALD*, 3). But wherever women (and Darl late in the book) confront empty space, they convert it immediately into the density of time: "Now it begins to say it. New Hope three miles. New Hope three miles. [And then Dewey Dell adds the apparent non sequitur:] *That's what they mean by the womb of time: the agony and the despair of spreading bones, the hard girdle in which lie the outraged entrails of events*" (*ALD*, 114). (Converting space to time converts hope to despair, in this case Dewey Dell's hope of undoing what she had done, of being able to reverse, since time is irreversible, her pregnancy.) Darl becomes the spokesman of the conversion. "We go on, with a motion so soporific, so dreamlike as to be uninferant of progress, as though time and not space were decreasing between us and it" (*ALD*, 101). Crossing the river becomes a journey through a peculiarly imagined time: "It is as though time, no longer running straight before us in a diminishing line, now runs parallel between us like a looping string, the distance between the doubling accretion of the thread and not the interval between" (*ALD*, 139).

To convert space to time is to make it irrevocable: no true closure is possible, no returns, and no geometries. And then time is looped—that is to say it is not imaged as a time *line*, reconverted to space—so it does not run thinly from *a* to *b* like a Hemingway sentence. Faulkner's modernist experiment is not an attempt to spatialize time; it is an attempt to temporalize space. The form of the novel might be called temporal form. Faulkner wants time itself (but not the linear time of narrative) to unshape, to disclose, the novel.

By the moment it is revealed that Darl had fought in World War I, any climactic, catastrophic notion of history has been rendered irrelevant. For the climactic time of World War I, which makes male lives in Faulkner's novels anti-climactic, Faulkner substitues the "womb of time" in *As I Lay Dying* (*ALD*, 114): Bundren sons are as unsexed as sons in *Soldiers' Pay*, but the reason is not their pre-castration but their incomplete births. If male temporality (as represented in the two post-war novels) is punctual, the traumatic repetition of catastrophic moments, so that World War I defines a man once and for all, then female temporality is a continuum that blurs even the decisiveness of the moment of death. By associating his novel with female temporality, Faulkner can free his modernism from the catastrophe of his time.

A coda: Faulkner was not, as it happens, done with World War I at the publication of *As I Lay Dying* or shortly thereafter. There is *A Fable* to consider, which might be rated as Faulkner's last major work or his most ludicrous mistake, or both. The book concerns a French mutiny—instigated by Christ and his disciples—in May 1918. Why so late? The dangerous French mutiny actually occurred in May 1917, which might have seemed a better time for it to Faulkner, since it would have halted the war sooner. Granted that ending a war half a year early would be a mercy if 5,000 soldiers were dying a day; nevertheless, it is hard to see the *millenarian* value of a strike to end the war so close to when it would have ended without divine intercession. Here is, I think, the critical passage. The paradox of the mutiny is that

> by mutinying, the regiment had stopped the war; it had saved France (France? England too; the whole West, since nothing else apparently had been able to stop the Germans since the March breakthrough in front of Amiens) and this [mass execution] was to be its reward; the three thousand men who had saved France and the world would lose their lives . . . .[34]

The mutiny, had it been successful, would have saved France—no, France and England—no, the West—no, the world. Granted that this might have been the local view, somewhat hyperbolized, in early 1918 (the March breakthrough had already been stopped east of Amiens at the time of the novel). But how can this be taken seriously from the perspective of 1944 when Faulkner began the book or 1953 when he completed it? With or without the mutiny, the Germans would be stopped and the armistice concluded in a few months.

The answer is that from the point of view of 1944, the war was still in progress—Germany was not yet stopped, and not merely France and England but also America was threatened. From the point of view of 1953, the world itself was in jeopardy, since the war with Germany had fostered the Bomb. (The Bomb was Faulkner's Nobel era preoccupation.) Catastrophic (male, Christian) historiography was verisimilar after all. World War I could not be transcended. It could not be subsumed into a competing version of time. The climactic death that was not quite universally experienced in the Great War had to be sought until it was produced. The world is a Sartoris; it seeks as if typologically an apocalypse in mimetic pursuit of an earlier passion. Faulkner's modernism was premised on an error. The Bomb represents the triumph of narrative violence over style.

5

The Postmodernization
of World War II

Fifty million people were killed in World War II.[1] If that is the first sentence, what could be the second? There is nowhere to go, except to add that writing the sequel is the obligation of postmodernism.

I have hardly done justice to war in this book about, purportedly, war; I notice, for a small example, that I have failed to specify where Hemingway got his war wound, or its nature. It hardly makes sense to evoke, one last time, the wars that have not been so much evoked as evaded to allow the formal development of post-war literary movements. But World War II (as a practical, moral, and aesthetic matter) was inescapable: literati even in America, the landscape of which was not cratered, the towns and cities of which were not gutted, the civilian population of which was never massacred, were unable to conceive of a place free of the war, the literary equivalent of which would be beauty, form, style. Why go on writing?

World War II was inescapable because it was deeply terroristic. The destruction of 40 percent of the Jews of the world is the paradigm, though the massacre (revived by Germany as a principle of warfare for the first time since the seventeenth century) had no strategic point (SWW, 288–289). Forty thousand British subjects were killed in the Blitz, which was followed by the V-1 flying-bomb and the V-2 rocket attacks, killing several thousand more (SWW, 100, 582). In the Warsaw uprising, 200,000 citizens, combatants and noncombatants, were killed (SWW, 482). A million Leningraders died of starvation during the siege of their city (SWW, 198); of the over five million Russian prisoners (who retain rights of civilians once captured),[2] 3.3 million died (SWW, 187).

In the strikes and retaliations conducted by British Bomber Command, civilian casualties became "the measure of strategic bombing success" (the rationale seems to have been to inspire a proletarian revolt) (*SWW*, 419, 421): Lübeck (important in *Gravity's Rainbow*) was entirely burned in 1942 (*SWW*, 422); everything in central Cologne was burned down but the cathedral (*SWW*, 423). All of this by fire-raising methods; in the Hamburg conflagration of 1943 (the core temperature of which reached 1500° Fahrenheit), 80 percent of its buildings were destroyed, as were 30,000 citizens, 20 percent of them children (*SWW*, 426). In the firestorming of Dresden in February 1945, the central event of *Slaughterhouse-Five*, at least 30,000 civilians (perhaps many more) were killed, without strategic justification (*SWW*, 515). Six thousand Berliners were killed by Bomber Command in the Battle of Berlin; one and a half million were left homeless (*SWW*, 428); 125,000 died in the final siege (*SWW*, 532).

In 1945, Curtis Lemay had 158,000 tons of bombs, mostly incendiary, dropped on the 58 largest Japanese cities, all wooden (*SWW*, 432). Eighty-nine thousand were killed in the March attack on Tokyo; 267,000 buildings were consumed, and the water in the city's canals boiled (*SWW*, 576). At Okinawa, between 70,000 and 160,000 (of the original population of 450,000) died in the fighting (*SWW*, 573). During the course of the war, Manila became a "ghost city as devastated as Warsaw" (*SWW*, 561). In August 1945, 78,000 citizens of Hiroshima and 25,000 citizens of Nagasaki were killed by atomic blast (*SWW*, 584).

Now for the bathos of the sequel: I hope it goes without saying that *The Naked and the Dead* (1948) and *From Here to Eternity* (1951) are the great war novels of the immediate post-war period; and that *Catch-22* (1961), *Slaughterhouse-Five* (1968), and *Gravity's Rainbow* (1973) constitute a revised tradition of the World War II novel. I chose the latter sequence as a sample without much thought, which I hope recommends the experiment, saves it from circularity. More than anything else I had in mind the fact that Vonnegut's, Heller's, and Pynchon's war novels are still read, and not by antiquaries—rather, I think, and this may be important, by high school and college students among others. Perhaps this merely testifies that anything after 1960 is contemporary; but my first hypothesis is that the Vonnegut, Heller, and Pynchon war books are postmodernist and that in their light we can classify Jones's and Mailer's novels as late modernist war literature. There was a modernist and a postmodernist World War II: the Second World War may have set the terms of post-war writing, but post-war writing conceived and reconceived the Second World War. The difference is in the rendering of inescapability—since inescapability is the shibboleth of all postmodern doctrine.

James Jones, like Norman Mailer, went to World War II to write the great World War II novel; no wonder *From Here to Eternity* begins in the modernist atmosphere Jones grew up breathing, though in *The Thin Red Line* he attempts something new.[3] (1) The expansive rhythms of *From Here to Eternity* are from Wolfe. I am unwilling to quote the best examples.[4] (2) The sexual jousting is partly out of Fitzgerald: "At [Fort] Myer all the boys hung out in Washington on their passes and he [Prewitt] hung out there too. That was where he met the society girl. He picked her up at a bar, or she picked him up. It was his first introduction into the haut monde . . . . She was a nice kid but very bitter and they had a satisfying affair . . ." (*HE*, 23–24).

(3) The aesthetic foil, against which Jones writes his long and soft-boiled sentences, is Hemingway. Three different characters make allusions to Hemingway. When Major Holmes quizzes his wife on her promiscuity, she responds that it is none of his business. "'I'm your husband,' Holmes said. 'It is my business.'" Karen Holmes rejoins: "You sound like a page right out of Hemingway" (*HE*, 792). The Harold Bloomian remark here can only be that at this dim-witted moment, Holmes sounds like a page out of a soap opera script. The problem is that Hemingway's influence is pervasive; the solution is to make Hemingway so pervasive as to be subliterary. The uneducated Angelo says: "Its like everything else in this world, you got to pay for what you get. You can pay for it by learning, or you can pay for it with experience once you learnt it, or you can pay for it with friendship. But you got to pay. Thats my philosophy. I read it in some book once." The reason Hemingway is declassed at this moment is that just earlier Angelo says he is "trying to induce the pizon [paisan] for some preparation [liquor] on the house." Prewitt replies: "To hell with that pizon. I got thirteen-fifty we can use for preparation. Induce him with that." When Angelo asks Prewitt to quit talking, Prewitt says, "Not without inducing some preparation" (*HE*, 354, 356). "Inducing" replaces "utilizing" when Jones attempts a hardboiled/inebriated poetics; Hemingway has to be declassed as strategic ingratitude.

Nevertheless, Jones manages, by the inflation of his terms, to do more than just commit the usual patricide: modernism and modernity as a whole are trivial if eternity measures the book's temporal scope. The basic opposition of the modernist American novel — the solitary endangered style against the overwhelming power — is so extremely portrayed in *From Here to Eternity* as to transcend modernism; what Jones is in fact depicting is a disparity of power that is, at the very least, monarchical. Granted that (4) the thematic borrowing is principally from *Three Soldiers*: the fragging episode; the opposition of music (Prewitt's bugling, Andy's guitar-playing) and the law (MPs, court martials, stockade). Yet the musical counterpoise has diminished almost to inaudibility. Prewitt has been forced to relinquish his role of bugler because of his adherence to principle, and picks up the bugle only once during the action, to play taps, whose "infinite sadness" is out of proportion to the function of signaling lights out, but proportionate to the demise of its own beauty (*HE*, 214). And the law is larger than in *Three Soldiers*; it is barely commensurable with the humanity it regulates and punishes. "What you got to do now is to remember that it aint nobody's fault. Its the system. Nobody's to blame" (*HE*, 351).

The proportion of power to beauty is so great that we jettison, finally, any modernist dream of an artistic asylum. The modern army is too large for modernism; it is too large for the century, for the episteme. Prewitt—the natural artist, thus offensive to the military—initially does nothing wrong, beyond refusing to fight for the boxing team. The ratio of the retribution, given the absence of a crime, is exorbitant. First Prewitt is broken, induced to rebel, and sent to the stockade. His official greeting there consists of his being lectured to as he receives, every time he makes a small error of protocol, "the butt of a grub hoe handle . . . into the small of his back above the kidney on the left side." The second time he is so punished, his testicles begin to ache; by the third time he is nauseated; by the fourth his back "hurt sickly all the way down to his knees and his mind was in a delirium of rage" (*HE*, 512–514). After the session, a guard congratulates him on earning only four hoe handle rebukes, one over the record. From there, of course, punishment gets worse—Prewitt's entombment in the Hole, for example. When a soldier named Berry refuses to admit cooperating with another prisoner's plan of escape by self-injuring, the Hole is too good for him. He is punched repeatedly; then he gets the hoe handle across the nose, causing blood to flow; then he gets the handle in the mouth, knocking out two teeth; then several more hours of this in private, so that when he reappears blood is flowing from different parts of his face (including his broken nose and his mouth when he coughs), his eyes are closed, and his ears are torn loose; when he still does not admit complicity, he earns more blows to the testicles and the small of the back; then much more of the same until he dies (*HE*, 626–629).

None of this is meant to reform Berry, or even serve as an example to others (it is an extravagant response to a novel crime—so that no legal or penal lesson can be inferred). It is a spectacle of the disparity of power between army and soldier. I have, of course, *Discipline and Punish* in mind; if the effect of monarchical punishment is the mark (the direct impression of power on the body) and the effect of reformist punishment is either the sign (the transparency of punishment as signifier to crime as signified) or the trace (the alteration of the criminal's behavior), then the army is king, and the guiding principle is the doctrine of the king's—or rather the officer's—two bodies.[5] To disobey an officer's command or wishes is an affront both to a person and to the body of the army—the corps. Revenge for an insult to the corps is administered directly to the individual flesh, and one can register power in the number and trenchancy of marks.

Where the army is sovereign, it is nonsense to insist on the survival of art as an exceptional state. "'In this world,' Stark said, 'today, nobody is left alone'" (*HE*, 204). Perhaps that is why Jones's prose is so bad. (He writes well at times: the sober, slightly off-center denotation of Prewitt's execution is a tour de force of restraint. And occasionally he tries to write well, as in Wolfean moments, and fails. Mainly he uglifies.) Perhaps also this accounts for Jones's utter repudiation of the metonymic method: the irrelevance of boxing to soldiering is the motive of the entire action. There is no escape outside masculinity, no Catherine Barkley, even on temporary loan; relations between men and women are wars that end in defeat for soldiers. The book is about a peacetime army that is in a state of thorough-going belligerency before Pearl Harbor.

One pre-war casualty is the suicide of Isaac Bloom, the book's Robert Cohn—except that he has no charming aspect, so that to dislike him is not necessarily anti-Semitic. In taking up suicide, Jones contemplates a pervasive World War II theme. It is partly a corollary of terrorism: the boundary between combatant and noncombatant was sufficiently blurred that no one, at the end of the war, could be certain of a return to civilian rights. There was a mass ritual suicide of Japanese officers and some civilians at the end of the war (*SWW*, 573); a large number of the civilian deaths in the siege of Berlin were suicidal (*SWW*, 532). In addition, curiously, there was a sense in which World War II suicides were tokens of pride (not disgrace) and the will to prevail (not submission to conquest). I am thinking of the kamika-zes, of course. But there is also the example of Frau Goebbels, who argued hysterically against Hitler's suicide; unsuccessful in this charity, she admin-istered poison to her six children as if it were a proud legacy (*SWW*, 528–529). Pynchon gives the paradox one more surreal twist: it is the explicitly suicidal black Hereros in *Gravity's Rainbow* (in some ways the Jews of the novel) who out-survive the Germans. So the aggressive suicidal philosophiz-ing of *From Here to Eternity* is a generic peculiarity.

When Catholic Angelo denounces Bloom's sin, Malloy comes to its defense:

> "Would you say a man in a Nazi concentration camp had the right to commit suicide?"
> "Hell yes."
> "Then why not a man in an American corporation?"
> "But thats differnt. He aint bein tortured."
> "You think not? And why not a man in the American Army?" (*HE*, 561)

This is odd because it is prompted by the death of a Jew, whose Jewishness is first terrifyingly magnified but then casually depreciated, as concentration camp fades into corporation and army. The conclusion of this line of argu-ment—"In our world, citizens . . . theres only one way a man can have freedom, and that is to die for it"—is that individual liberation depends on a complete indifference to individuality or liberty, to who or where you are, a Jew or not, in a concentration camp or not, at war or peace. Give me liberty and give me death. Malloy is preaching with Jones's endorsement a kind of Zen Marxism, which may be the only response to the indivisible, undialectical power that Jones describes. There can be no withdrawal to a Switzerland of style.

So "why write?"—the postmodern question—is transformed into the more fundamental, "how write?" Jones's answer is necessarily grandiose: by the force of an artistic project so immense and militant that it rivals the army as an absolutist hegemony. Jones conceived of his writing as a kind of Hole, a solitary self-confinement without sex or love or ulterior life. A veteran in a Jones story (1945) rejects a woman in a bar. "It isn't worth the trouble," he says. "I'm a writer. I'm writing a book about this war, and I'm really going to blow the lid off."[6] This not only means that writing has become the veteran's whole life; the method of his writing begins to mimic the subject of his writing, violent, insane, monomaniacal. Whose lid is blowing off? The veteran is Jones, as this dictum superfluously proves: "Every bit of energy consumed thru sex is energy that cannot be placed elsewhere" (*IE*, 89). Or again: "I have no family to raise . . . . Ive put all my eggs in one basket, sort of. And if I dont succeed in aiding the creativity of the world, at least a tiny bit, then my whole life is useless. I went down to 138 lbs because of it. I was constantly reminded of Wheelock's poem — 'There is a panther within my breast'" (*IE*, 88).

Creativity is more or less a direct transference of resources from the individual to the world; the world gains whatever is lost to the anorexic body. It is not that art seeks metonymically an alternative space (a space *beside* that of war): the bugling and guitar-playing of *From Here to Eternity* are pathetically homeless. Nor is art essentially *like* war; the violence of war is unpredictable and omni-directional, but the violence of art is introjected for the sake of creation at large. Art must take the army as its model; it necessitates a perfect discipline, a perfect order, a complete submission of the body, an imperial system to which every affront is aestheticide, tantamount to regicide. This is nearly postmodern; in opposition to the Foucauldian object of Jones's hatred (there is nothing outside the army's power) is Jones's Derridean project (there shall be nothing outside my text). The residual modernism resides in Jones's messianism: the world is not always already the Word but it will be.

Jones's psychiatric report — "He has disturbed dreams and is bothered by memories of combat, blood, stench of dead and hardships. Feels it was valuable to him tho as background for his writing" (*IE*, 69) — suggests how deliberately Jones conceived of his own body and mind as expendable troops in the war of war and art. Norman Mailer, as well, could harbor an artistic ambition so large as to threaten the mind and body of the artist, as if art were the army redeployed toward antithetical ends. Mailer also went to war on behalf of his literary ambitions — he had already written a play called "The Naked and the Dead," about a psychiatric hospital.[7] Nakedness and deadness were objective correlatives in search of a subject. Mailer's book like Jones's was conceived by a mind nursed on modernism, and again Dos Passos is a precursor, along with *Moby-Dick* and *Billy Budd*, modernist rediscoveries.

The Naked and the Dead is not so advanced as *From Here to Eternity* in this respect: Mailer envisions a "peace" to contextualize his "war." The "Time Machine" sections of his book, derived from Dos Passos, sketch regional and personal backgrounds for his soldiers, but this is at odds with Mailer's ventriloquized prophecy of perpetual conflict. "There would be this campaign and then another and another, and there would never be an end to it."[8] This is more than an estimate of the slowness of victory — of the sort calculated by World War I soldiers in unmoving trenches. A geologist could discern in Mailer's accretive novel these strata: World War I (absorbed through modernism, a formal source), World War II (witnessed, interrogated, origin of the book's vision of totalitarianism), Cold War (object of the book's ideology), World War III (predicted, source of the novel's inchoate eschatology). An apt title would have been *War and War*—but Mailer wants to confront Tolstoy on Tolstoy's own premises. When Gallagher's wife dies in childbirth, she expires in homage to *War and Peace*—her name is, pointedly, Mary. But then "peace" would have to be a meaningful category.

Mailer is torn throughout as to whether there is a world beyond war: in the American modernist tradition, the question is whether there is a sanctuary for style in the modern, military or paramilitary, world. Mailer begins *The Naked and the Dead* twice, on competitive assumptions. First:

> Nobody could sleep. When morning came, assault craft would be lowered and a first wave of troops would ride through the surf and charge ashore on the beach at Anopopei. All over the ship, all through the convoy, there was a knowledge that in a few hours some of them were going to be dead.

This is not unstylish, but it imitates stylelessness. "Nobody could sleep" is an abbreviation of the original—more Hemingwayesque—first sentence, "Nobody could sleep on the night before the invasion of Anopopei"[9]: the point of the concision is to galvanize readers, so that their nerves will feel something of what keeps the soldiers on edge. Then the factual second sentence, an imitation of reportage, and the third sentence whose last word drops like a weight.

There interposes a white space, and suddenly, as if on reconsideration, the book is mannered:

> A soldier lies flat on his bunk, closes his eyes, and remains wide-awake. All about him, like the soughing of surf, he hears the murmurs of men dozing fitfully. "I won't do it, I won't do it," someone cries out of a dream, and the soldier opens his eyes and gazes slowly about the hold, his vision becoming lost in the intricate tangle of hammocks and naked bodies and dangling equipment. (*ND*, 3)

This is essentially a rewriting of the opening paragraph. In place of "Nobody could sleep," Mailer writes by a vague specification that "a soldier . . . remains wide awake." It turns out that the soldier is not just anybody; but he is the Unknown Soldier momentarily, because Mailer is after a more hallucinatory, Stephen Crane-ish effect than his first paragraph had allowed. The second paragraph replaces "a first wave of troops would ride through the surf" with "like the soughing of surf, he hears the murmurs of men dozing fitfully." That the men pick up the rhythms of the ocean is implicit in the mock-clichés of the first paragraph (the wave rides through the surf), but in the eerier revision of the second paragraph, it is unclear whether the ocean is attuned to the soldiers or the soldiers are disturbed by a deep maternal, endlessly rocking discontent. (This effect is enhanced by the misplacement of "like the soughing of surf"). The first paragraph looks unblinkingly toward the dawn; the second paragraph is lost in the eternity of insomnia. Only the second paragraph could admit the explicit metaphor, the consonance, or the slightly precious, "soughing." This sentence is *written*, and its educated author has in mind the alliterative rhythms of the Anglo-Saxon epic. Both third sentences generalize; the third sentence of the belated paragraph envisions (though the vision is "lost" amid an intricate tangle of sonic effects) a general "nakedness," as the third sentence of the originary paragraph had foreseen (monosyllabically) the likelihood of mass death. We may call the dream style, then, the "Naked" style of the book, and the prosier prose the "Dead" style, or anti-style.

Mailer, once he had achieved celebrity with the publication of *The Naked and the Dead*, seems to have regretted its stylelessness: "I knew I was no stylist. I think one of the reasons I became a stylist was precisely because I had so poor a sense of style to begin with."[10] Certainly the high-charged metaphorist of later writing is not often recognizable. But if Mailer condescends to the stylelessness of this book, he has forgotten that the irrelevance of style is one of the book's themes.

> "The only thing to do is to get by on style." He [Hearn] had said that once, lived by it in the absence of anything else, and it had been a working guide, almost satisfactory until now. The only thing that had been important was to let no one in any ultimate issue ever violate your integrity, and this had been an ultimate issue. Hearn felt as if an immense cyst of suppuration and purulence had burst inside him, and was infecting his blood stream now, washing through all the conduits of his body in a sudden violent flux of change. (*ND*, 326)

Style—never *entirely* satisfactory—had in the modernist manner been equal to integrity; now Hearn disintegrates by infection and interior violence. There is no room for style in the army, and there is nothing outside the army. This is partly a political point, in the Frankfurt School mode: "'As kinetic energy a country is organization, co-ordinated effort, your epithet, fascism.' He [General Cummings] moved his chair slightly. 'Historically the purpose of this war is to translate America's potential into kinetic energy'" (*ND*, 321). Cummings makes speeches like this with some frequency, but they are all cartoons; Cummings is not much more than an adolescent dream of the wizard-fascist to whom the whining liberal can only submit. Hearn is as weak a figure fictionally as he is politically, and he does not come alive in confrontation with Cummings; he only lives by means of his antagonism to Croft, who better than Cummings demonstrates the hypothesis that the army is fascist and the army is everywhere.

Croft is a mere sergeant; but he is preoccupied with getting his reconnaissance mission over Mt. Anaka, and the obsession has grandeur. (It vivifies Hearn; it exacerbates all frictions; it energizes the writing.) Mailer has said that Anaka is the Moby Dick of his novel. You might have thought that Cummings should have been its Ahab, but making the analogy to

Croft brings all the inescapability of war—all its unrelaxing grip on the contemporary imagination—into the mind of middle America.

> As they [Croft's party] had got used to living in the jungle and being wet all the time, as they had forgotten what it was like to live in dry clothing, so they had forgotten now how it felt to draw an effortless breath. They did not think about it; certainly they did not think of when their journey would end. It had become all existence. (*ND*, 667)

For this reason, though army punishment is experienced as a corporeal marking, as in Jones, it is in Mailer a normal aspect of combat; you do not need to posit an artist with special integrity in order to demonstrate the torturing of a soldier's body. Mailer's book is superior to Jones's, a measurable advance on the *Three Soldiers* paradigm, and as distant as possible from *For Whom the Bell Tolls* in its decenteredness. There is no sensitive artist figure, no emblem of the book's artistry, no Switzerland of the fancy.

Insofar as there is an artist, it is Croft. This is astonishing: Croft is the best soldier in the book; Croft is a violent, almost nerveless, madman; Croft *is* the army. If Jones's project is to plunder all the inexorable, limitless, minute power of the army for the treasury of art, Mailer's is to discover a comparable power for art only in the very soul of the army. It cannot be a question of replacing one omnipotency with another. Jones believes his imagination can absorb the army's, but Mailer's is absorbed. That at the center of the army's imagination is something like Mt. Anaka—something whose fascination is beyond strategy and tactics, and which cannot be conquered by army logistics—is the only faith that Mailer can proceed on. If there is no imagination free of the military, then the hope must be that toward the center of its imagination is the only way out.

The final, late modernist, pre-postmodernist step in the closing down of the artistic alternative to war is taken by Jones in *The Thin Red Line*. Mailer thought that by its relative constriction Jones had surrendered his ambition to be the preeminent post-war novelist: Jones had "apparently decided to settle for being a very good writer among other very good writers. . . . He is no longer the worst writer of prose ever to give intimations of greatness" (*IE*, 208). What Mailer sees as lack of ambition is an ambition in harness. The book exhibits neither Jones's long-breathed, Wolfean sublime nor any of the random uglification of *From Here to Eternity*. It has no artist figure, so no artist figure to destroy. *The Thin Red Line* is a masterpiece of asceticism: it works on the tautological commandment that if there is no art outside the army, then there shall be no art outside the army. This is the war book that comes closest to having no context: there are almost no allusions to a time before or after war. The one character with continuous memories of a home life—John Bell—literally receives a Dear John letter near the end of the book and thereafter has no home life either.

There is, at the close of *The Thin Red Line*, the weakest and most cursory framing device imaginable. Here is the last paragraph in its entirety:

> Ahead of them the LCIs waited to take them aboard, and slowly they began
> to file into them to be taken out to climb the cargo nets into the big ships.
> One day one of their number would write a book about all this, but none of
> them would believe it, because none of them would remember it that way.
> (*RL*, 495)

"All this" is Guadalcanal; though the paragraph alludes to the fictionality
of memory—so that even so publicly famous an event as Guadalcanal is
hostage to it—the status of fiction is not elevated. Every character is a
fabulator. ("Doll had learned something during the past six months of his
life. Chiefly what he had learned was that everybody lived by a selected
fiction. . . . It was as if everybody made up a fiction story about himself,
and then he just pretended to everybody that that was what he was" [*RL*,
13].) This is so thoroughly true that the reader does not know which soldier
of C-Company is the future author. (I had thought, incorrectly, that it was
Bell, but Bell has nothing in common with Jones.) In this way the book can
make a fictional claim without clearing and occupying a separate space for
fiction outside or above the war. The novel fades away like an old soldier:
"One . . . one . . . none . . . none."

Nor does anything else transcend war. The preoccupation with ethnic-
ity of *From Here to Eternity* is largely dropped. (That Captain Stein is
Jewish matters for a while, then stops mattering.) The sexual sensationalism of both *From Here to Eternity* before this novel and *Whistle* after is
almost entirely sublimated into war experience: killing is intercourse, being
wounded is castration, staring at corpses is voyeurism with traces of onanism and masochism, bravado is exhibitionism. Different characters have
different terms for assimilating war to totalitarian peace: for Fife war is
business (*RL*, 40), for Walsh it is territoriality (*RL*, 49), for Bell (and
others) it is "Mathematics! Algebra! Geometry" (*RL*, 189)—that is, total
indifference. If there is no beyond of war, the impulse to fit that fact to any
rigid philosophical system would entail an immediate self-contradiction.
"There aint any choice," says Welsh. "There's no choice left for anybody.
And it aint only here, with us. It's everywhere. And it aint going to get any
better. This war's just the start" (*RL*, 79). When Blane is shot—"unluck-
ily"—he "bounced another five yards forward, and with three bullets
through his chest cavity did not die right away. He lay on his back and,
dreamily and quite numb, stared at the high, beautiful, pure white cumuli
which sailed like stately ships across the sunny, cool blue tropic sky." Then
War and Peace degenerates into *War and Nothingness*: "He was dimly
aware that he might possibly die as he became unconscious" (*RL*, 185).

This passage is typical: it allows Blane the most infinitesimal consciousness ("*dimly* aware" "that he *might*" "possibly" "die") and takes it away. At
the beginning of *Whistle*, the final book of the trilogy, Jones gets his revenge
against critics by calling attention to the continuity of characters through
the three books, noticed by no reviewers: Warden to Welsh (and now to)
Winch, Stark to Storm to Strange, Prewitt to Witt to Prell. After two books,
I had missed this myself, and my excuse is that what is most interesting

about *The Thin Red Line* is how little its characters have any interior lives
at all, let alone a depth that stays unstirred through changes of name and
circumstance.

Consider Warden/Welsh/Winch. As Warden and Winch, this sergeant
cares for his men; he is belligerent in *Eternity* to keep himself instrumentally
pure, and he is aloof and insensitive in *Whistle* even (sentimentally) to
provoke his hospitalized troops back to life. But in *The Thin Red Line*, he
(as Welsh) is a psychotic, bellowing, vile, intimidating monster who is
disgusted to find himself performing decently and heroically when the crisis
demands. Or take Prewitt/Witt/Prell. As Prewitt, this character is the poète
both manqué and maudit. But as Witt, easily Jones's funniest inspiration,
he is a half-cracked backwoodsman, who loves C-Company irrationally
but abandons it whenever its officers commit an outrage, joining another
company in which—to his amusement—he has at one point a different
rank, but which he in turn leaves whenever he misses C-Company too
unbearably, usually rejoining it in the middle of a battle or on a seemingly
untrackable jungle march. He is a monomaniacal, bigoted, comically demented character who would be one of Flannery O'Connor's best creations
if she had thought of him. Neither of these *Thin Red Line* incarnations has
any consciousness of what drives him, which is what makes the book a
kind of breakthrough.

Part of Jones's point is the irrelevance of his characters' psychic lives to
the army; and Jones can only contribute to their personal diminution, so
long as he adheres to his thesis that army life is all life, that war is peace.
The stylelessness of the book is perfectly intentional. When Jones tropes—
for example, to attack Hill 210 is "like walking down a bowling alley
toward the bowlers"—he takes care to stipulate that the metaphor is from
within the army: "and before the battle was over that is what it came to be
called: The Bowling Alley" (*RL*, 161). The emblem of the book is Bead's
killing, while out defecating, of his first Japanese soldier: because (this is
his own appraisal) of his "stupid incompetence, his foolish idiocy, . . .
whatever he did, done so badly and in such ugly style, gave no satisfaction:
action without honor, travail without grace" (*RL*, 163).

If this is the book's emblem, then incompetent and graceless writing is
an original achievement: Keck and Beck have a dialogue at one point (*RL*,
223); Doll and Dale feel mutual antagonism at another (*RL*, 228); Culp
and Culn have a little talk (*RL*, 472). And: Stein "motioned furiously to
Fife to hand him the phone, to take back up the call to Colonel Tall which
Tella's first screams had interrupted" (*RL*, 241). You cannot, without trying, write this badly: the pointless alliteration of furiously, Fife, phone; the
jingle of call and Tall; the juxtaposition of call and Colonel; the interference
of Tall and Tella; the attraction at a distance of Tella and phone. If this
seems conceivably accidental, I have statistical evidence that the bad writing
is at least at one moment intentional, or entropy is wrong.

Witt had sustained the powerful emotion of his leavetaking from Colonel
Tall. All across the long traverse from the old position on the third fold to

the jungle's edge, he kept thinking with fierce sentiment about what great, wonderful guys they all were. The Colonel, Captain Gaff who was not too high-toned to treat EM like an equal, Bell, Doll, Dale, Big Un, Keck (now dead), Skinny Culn. (*RL*, 309)

"Big Un" is Cash's nickname. What is improbable about the series: Witt, Tall, Gaff, Bell, Doll, Dale, Cash, Keck, Culn? In my phone book, the fraction of four-letter names is much below one in ten; let us be conservative and estimate the odds against Jones's series as $10^9 : 1$. Pick a number between one and a billion. In a book that treats death as an actuarial matter, can this be uncalculated?

Beck and Keck: Jones is, in *The Thin Red Line*, writing as if he were Samuel Beckett's illiterate younger brother. When Tella is wounded, there is much of Beckett in Jones's description: "Lying on his back, his head uphill, both hands pressed to his belly to hold his intestines in, he was inching his way back up the slope with his legs. . . . Inching was hardly the word, since Stein estimated he was making less than half an inch per try" (*RL*, 234). In calibrating the minimum point of humanity—how limited can motion be? how rote can gestures be? how long can the endgame last?— Jones meets Beckett at the gateway of postmodernism. The boundary is World War II: "Modern war. You couldn't even *pretend* it was human" (*RL*, 429). In consequent postmodernist theorizing, the category of "human" would cease to function, even as critique.

It was startling, once I had made my selection of delayed World War II novels, how lucidly they illustrated a phenomenon that might be dubbed the postmodernization of combat writing. But I should begin with the quality that I knew in advance was shared by *Catch-22*, *Slaughterhouse-Five*, and *Gravity's Rainbow*.[11] There is something adolescent about these books—brilliantly adolescent, I should add, to buffer the insult, though I hope to make the term analytically useful rather than dismissive. Take Pynchon's delight in the gross joke: when Mexico returns Jessica to Jeremy as if returning his lover to his father, his revenge is a verbal assault on the parental feast. "'Yeah, I could've done with some of that *pus pudding*, myself [contributes Bodine]. Think there'll be any of that?' 'No, but there might be a scum souffle!' cries Roger, 'with a side of—*menstrual marmalade!*'" (*GR*, 715). Or Vonnegut's literalization of the dream of flight from suburban adulthood by means of Pilgrim's Sci-Fi adventure in Tralfamadore. Or Heller's anti-parental, disestablishmentarian humor, emblematized by Yossarian's naked demonstration in the trees at Snowden's funeral.[12] All of these books are of course sophisticated as well—what I am calling "adolescent" is a kind of applied delinquency. But I think that the extent to which the term is appropriate equals the extent to which we intuit their postmodernity, just as without hesitation we recognize MTV, or cyberpunk, or the gynopunk of Kathy Acker, or monumentally prankish architecture as postmodernist.

Two facets of the adolescentness of these books are crucial. First: there is a sweet helplessness to almost all of Heller's, Vonnegut's, and Pynchon's characters. Vonnegut reports being told by his father, "You know—you never wrote a story with a villain in it" (*SF*, 8). Proof is how Vonnegut describes the aspect of the German who captures Billy Pilgrim: "It was the face of a blond angel, of a fifteen-year-old boy. . . . The boy was as beautiful as Eve. . . . Billy was helped to his feet by the lovely boy, by the heavenly androgyne" (*SF*, 53). The sweetness is not quite so overt and insistent in Pynchon and Heller, but you can locate it in such characters as Slothrop and Mexico and even Bodine in *Gravity's Rainbow*, and Yossarian, Dunbar, Doc Daneeka, and the chaplain in *Catch-22* (with whom Yossarian falls in love in the first line of the book). These characters are all ostensibly heterosexual, but they seem not to experience that condition as a code, a stance, an anxiety, and an ordeal. In *The Naked and the Dead* and *The Thin Red Line*, wounds confirm one's masculinity at the same time as they envaginate;[13] the combination of viciousness and victimage that is army life in general enrages most of Mailer's and Jones's soldiers. In Jones is the last modernist descent of the goddess who demands that her men prove their masculinity by castration. But Pilgrim, Slothrop, and Yossarian are adolescents who avoid the horrors of the interregnum by having no future, no idea of a succession.

Second (therefore): adolescent pathology is, in Erik Erikson's analysis, characterized by what he calls the "diffusion of time perspective," "a loss of consideration of time as a dimension of living."[14] Adolescents are required to sum up everything they have become and make it continuous with everything they are supposed to be—much of it radically different—in the future. One of the most surprising facts about the books of my sample is that they all involve time-inversion. Yossarian, trapped between an impossible innocence and an impossible adulthood, has frequent experiences of déjà vu, the (anti-) narrative principle of the novel, so that experience seems to precede itself, precede innocence; Slothrop can reverse stimulus and response, as if death might anticipate life; Billy Pilgrim time-travels from World War II to the 60s and flashes back, so that incipient adulthood, middle age, and death coexist in spatialized temporality (spatial time for Vonnegut is the view of time from space). A first take on this characteristic feature of the postmodern: humanity cannot stand too much history.[15]

If *Catch-22*, *Slaughterhouse-Five*, and *Gravity's Rainbow* are notably adolescent, it is equally obvious that they are all paranoid. "Delinquency" is the connecting term. In a passage that leaps from the battle pathologies of World War II veterans to the peacetime neuroses of the 60s (I shall get back to this connection), Erikson traces the history of the concepts "identity crisis" and "loss of ego identity." "Since [World War II]," Erikson tells us, "we have recognized the same central disturbance in severely conflicted young people whose sense of confusion is due, rather, to a war within themselves, and in confused rebels and destructive delinquents who war on their society" (*I*, 16–17).

This is the liberal view; the only permutation left out is the possibility that society wars on delinquents; but in a paranoid vision that rivals Pynchon's in scope and erudition, Foucault reevaluates the concept of delinquency. Surely, Foucault argues, the fact that for two hundred years prisons have produced, invigorated, and organized delinquency must mean that they are designed to do so. "The prison makes possible, even encourages, the organization of a milieu of delinquents, loyal to one another, hierarchized, ready to aid and abet any future crime" (*DP*, 267). Why? The objective is to eliminate the political dimension of crime; to allow crime to be infiltrated by political mechanisms that are adjusted to delinquency (prisons, psychiatric institutions, schools); to produce individuality as the object of this specification of control (*DP*, 276–277). Individuals are what institutions regulate; thus, "the child is more individualized than the adult, the patient more than the healthy man, the madman and the delinquent more than the normal and the non-delinquent" (*DP*, 193). The lower on the pyramid is the slave, the more individuality the slave can claim.

Armies, as James Jones observes, encourage (juvenile, adolescent) delinquency: officers prefer men who steal, who are sexually furious, who war on each other between battles. It may not be that they are trying to produce barbarians; they may be testing for specialization in the machine. All types of lawlessness are constantly under the surveillance of MPs and officers, and precisely a regulated delinquency rather than mutiny is the result. There is a hatred of the medicalization of criminality running from Jones through Heller to Pynchon: doctors are often sadists in Jones, but they are more subtly coopted and coopting in Heller and Pynchon. In Heller, individuality is Foucauldian—a preponderance of craziness, criminality, sickness, and adolescence—all channeled through the medical system so that the only alternatives are sullen cooperation (marked by adolescent rebelliousness but nothing serious) or, ambiguously, escape. (Yossarian refuses to commit himself to a fragging conspiracy, and his escape to Sweden is beyond the ken of the book.) Slothrop is the most complete example of how a perversion introduces the pervert to the medical/psychological disciplines (which also, in fact, began by producing it), how an extended adolescence may be channeled by the sex and behavior regulators, how little crazy individualism does for you besides putting you more at the mercy of your doctors.

Foucault's phrase for the disciplinary society is Pynchonesque: the "carceral city." At moments, he might as well be writing Pynchon criticism:

> The carceral network does not cast the unassimilable into a confused hell; there is no outside. It takes back with one hand what it seems to exclude with the other. It saves everything, including what it punishes. It is unwilling to waste even what it has decided to disqualify. (*DP*, 301)

"There is no outside": this is the characteristic statement of postmodernist paranoia. There is no outside of the carceral city, or the market culture, or the text.

In reducing Foucault to paranoia, I do not seem to be paying him much of a compliment. If it matters, I feel myself frequently entangled in Foucault's paranoia, though I take it that the Panopticon is the one British machine that is sufficiently Cartesian to have theoretical appeal in the French garden; the American system is based less on rationalization and surveillance of delinquency than on the toleration and commercialization of delinquent energies that are judged not to be cumulative, disciplined or undisciplined. And I do not seem to be much of a friend of postmodernism if I refer to it as a form of adolescent paranoia. Why I nevertheless gravitate toward both Foucault's critique of the carceral system and Erikson's analysis of adolescence is the shared reference to war as metaphor (perhaps war is what turns their objects into metaphor). The penultimate, climactic sentence of *Discipline and Punish* is a surprise revelation: "In this central and centralized humanity, the effect and instrument of complex power relations, bodies and forces subjected by multiple mechanisms of 'incarceration,' objects for discourses that are in themselves elements for this strategy, we must hear the distant roar of battle" (*DP*, 308). Which battle? Surely *Discipline and Punish* is a post-World War II text—a book whose vision is made possible by the next-to-last, second-best hope of total war. The war Foucault speaks of—out of cannon shot but within earshot—must be characterized by the military draft, by terrorism, by broadcast propaganda, by medical surveillance, by, in short, its multiple mechanisms of incarceration, its inescapability. French theorists are connoisseurs of occupation. Mailer and Jones had described a monarchical army, but the postmodernist revision of the same military of the same war is entirely carceral.

Similarly, Erikson's book attempted a "history of the present" (Foucault's phrase) insofar as it measured the degree to which the particular misery of the World War II soldier could be generalized in the 60s with respect to Vietnam-era adolescence.

> The term "identity crisis" was first used, if I remember correctly, for a specific clinical purpose in the Mt. Zion Veterans' Rehabilitation Clinic during the Second World War . . . . Most of our patients, so we concluded at that time, had neither been "shellshocked" nor become malingerers, but had through the exigencies of war lost a sense of personal sameness and historical continuity. . . . Therefore, I spoke of a loss of "ego identity." Since then [Erikson concludes, as I quoted him above], we have recognized the same central disturbance in severely conflicted young people whose sense of confusion is due, rather, to a war within themselves, and in confused rebels and destructive delinquents who war on their society. (*I*, 16–17)

The 60s delinquent fights World War II without weapons; the modern carceral society that creates delinquency does the same. Delinquency may be taken to be a psychological fact (as a pathological anti-social internalization of combat conditions) or as a political fact (as precisely the internalization of combat conditions that the state induces). Delinquent postmodernism is in either case the registering of contemporary history as an interior Second World War. The confrontation with history has been so profound that history has been psychologized—there is no longer the possibility of a merely personal pathology—and thus, apparently, de-historicized.

As unexpected as the discovery that all the books of my sample involve time-inversion was the recognition that they all involve the European war, as opposed to the Pacific war of Mailer and Jones. Was the war with Japan the modernist war, and the war with Germany and Italy a culturally subsequent event? The division is not merely coincidental because of the basis of postmodernism in terrorism. Japanese cities were terrorized; but neither Jones nor Mailer is concerned with that fact, less because of racism, I think, than because they did not live and fight among terrorized civilian populations. Slothrop, on the other hand, works and loves beneath the V-2 rocket (a delayed retaliation, Pynchon keeps suggesting, for the inaugural firestorming of Lübeck), and makes his way to Germany to see the destruction of its own cities. The humor drops out of *Catch-22* when Yossarian is asked to bomb an unwarned village innocent of military targets. Billy Pilgrim manages to make his way to Dresden in time to witness its destruction by firestorm. Both Pynchon and Vonnegut allude to Hiroshima (unlike Mailer and Jones), and the evaporation of Japanese civilians is in a sense the model of Slothrop's disintegration. When Slothrop finds a scrap of newspaper with the letters MB DRO / ROSHI, the Japanese city, Slothrop, and the text are all in the same approximate condition (*GR*, 693).

Other similarities fortify the sense of a new combat genre. (1) The interest in what may be slightly misnamed overkill. The American army demands in the postmodern combat novel more than one death from each soldier: destruction is separately psychological, physical, spiritual. Yossarian, Pilgrim, and Slothrop are not brave enought to die only once. (2) The anticipation of apocalypse. When Leni (from Lübeck) wishes to get rid of Franz, she thinks, "Let him look for flight out at the Raketenflugplatz . . . . Let him fly to the dead moon if he wants to" (*GR*, 162–163). The survivors of Dresden, according to Vonnegut, "if they were going to continue to survive, were going to have to climb over curve after curve on the face of the moon"; but, "there were to be no moon men at all" (*SV*, 179–180). The lunar landscapes connect wars II and III, if the genius of apocalypse is Wernher von Braun. (3) Black, or Yiddish, humor. The three novels make the point that (to invert Jordan Baker) we're all Jews here. ("What if we're all Jews, you see? All scattered like seeds" [*GV*, 170].) Morbid and subversive humor is shared by Puritans, Germans, and Africans in *Gravity's Rainbow*; Vonnegut is a German-American; Heller's Yossarian is of Assyrian descent. Each individual may be scattered, like Slothrop; every man his own diaspora. Genocide is, according to Jonathan Schell, our nearest approximation of apocalypse,[16] but black humor results when apocalypse is taken to be a personal insult. (4) From this perspective, time-inversion has a new resonance. Both *Slaughterhouse-Five* and *Gravity's Rainbow* make use of the device of the backwards-running movie. (E.g.: "So the assembly of the 00001 is occurring also in a geographical way, a Diaspora running backwards, seeds of exile flying inward in a modest preview of gravitational collapse, of the messiah gathering in the fallen spark" [*GR*, 737].) They seem to eschatologize Stephen Hawking's fantasy (it turns out not to be true) that at the end of the universe, backwards is the only way for time to run.

This tabulation establishes the existence of a postmodern combat genre; it does nothing toward justifying it. If the modernist World War I novel hopes (or despairs) that art can negotiate a separate peace, even if violence bleeds into the style that war is assumed to lack, then the modernist World War II novel hopes to find the possibility of style somewhere in military life itself, even if the army eventually crushes it whenever it blossoms among the men (*From Here to Eternity*), even if its exists as a self-contradiction at the heart of army violence (*The Naked and the Dead*), even if it (finally) only survives as what is tacit in the ascension of the graceless (*The Thin Red Line*). No such attenuated hopes survive in Heller, Vonnegut, and Pynchon. The beauty (peace)-ugliness (violence) spectrum drops out of relevance entirely. What is left is a meditation on reading.

Why is postmodern combat fiction allegorical? The hero of Vonnegut's book is Billy Pilgrim. "Billy" keeps the hero young; "Pilgrim" makes time-travel a fractured progress. This calls to mind "Slothrop's Progress: London the secular city instructs him: turn any corner and he can find himself inside a parable" (*GR*, 25). The answer begins with the structure of paranoia. It is as if Freud's Dr. Schreber hallucinates the allegorical elements of post-modern combat fiction: "he believed that he was dead and decomposing . . . [that] he went through worse horrors than any one could have imagined, and all on behalf of a holy purpose . . . that he was living in another world."[17] It sounds like a combination of Slothrop's decomposition in the Zone and Pilgrim's debarkation at Tralfamadore. Schreber believes that his physician "committed, or attempted to commit, 'soul-murder' upon him" (*SE*, 38); one thinks of Pointsman especially. Schreber is disoriented in time; he believes that there "has been a gap of vast duration in the history of mankind," of which there is no external evidence (*SE*, 69). The paranoiac cannot account for the apparent inefficiency of the apocalypse his vision has produced. Déjà vu, time-travel, and Slothrop's Pavlovian idiosyncrasy all allow the apocalyptic vision to find its correlative in the second, not the third, world war. Postmodern combat fiction is the literary vindication of Schreber's fantasies.

Especially pertinent is Schreber's belief that he is responsible for the end of the world, of which he is the only survivor. "He himself was the 'only real man left alive,' and the few human shapes that he still saw—the doctor, the attendants, the other patients—he explained as being 'miracled up, cursorily improvised men'" (*SE*, 68). Why does Yossarian survive, while most of his friends are destroyed seriatim, some by his inadvertence?[18] Why is Slothrop not killed; for what purpose do the doctors keep him running? (In Chapter 39 of *Catch-22*, Yossarian wanders Rome at night, and keeps confronting Catch-22; in Chapter 5 of a novel published a few years later, Oedipa Maas wanders San Francisco at night, regularly confronting the muted posthorn; the feeling of being the only living person among the nocturnal urban undead, finding signs of an unacknowledged apocalypse, is not limited to night or city in *Gravity's Rainbow*.) Why is Billy Pilgrim the only member of his lost war party to survive, while his incompetence is partly to blame for the death of the others? And why is he, later, the only one of a party of optometrists to survive the crash of their chartered airplane? The paranoia of the unworthily saved is the psychic cost of a pilgrim's progress.

Schreber's case begins with the love of his distinguished physician father, who was, Freud can only surmise, both adored and feared (*SE*, 51–52). Here I would like to go off on a tangent on the psychology of the creator of *Gravity's Rainbow*. The first item that needs accounting for is the mainly inexplicable love of men for their punishing fathers. I am thinking primarily of Enzian's love of Blicero, and also Gottfried's. "If he and Blicero are separated, what will happen to the flow of days?. . . . Will Blicero die *no please don't let him die.* . . . (But he will.)" (*GR*, 721). The love of Blicero is transformed into the adoration of the rocket, which is equal to the surfacing of Schreber's dreaded fantasy, "that after all it really must be very nice to be a woman submitting to the act of copulation" (*SE*, 13). That Schreber finds a way (through the God allegory) to accommodate himself to feminization makes him the ancestor not of Mailer or Jones but of the postmodern war allegorists.

On the other hand, the mothers and maternal figures of *Gravity's Rainbow* are truly daunting. Roger says that his "mother is the war" (*GR*, 39): what does he mean? Masochist Ernest Pudding visits Katje Borgesius in the guise of "Domina Nocturna . . . shining mother and last love" (*GR*, 232). When von Göll tries to comfort Slothrop about the future of Bianca, he says, "Bianca's a clever child, and her mother is hardly a destroying goddess" (*GR*, 494). Bianca's mother is Margherita, who has murdered Jewish children under the pretense that she is "Israel": "I wander all the Diaspora looking for strayed children. . . . And I will take you back, you fragment of smashed vessel, even if I must pull you by your nasty little circumcised penis" (*GR*, 478). If paradise is regained when, though it is night, the "sky will be milk" (*GR*, 133), a sort of allegorization of Maurice Sendak's ecstatic, "I'm in the milk and the milk's in me,"[19] then death for white men is its inverse: death, according to the first statement of the fantasy with variations, is tantamount to having one's head in feces while being anally raped by Malcolm X (*GR*, 63–65). To pursue the rocket consists for white men in wondering whether it might be more hygienic to submit as a woman to the act of copulation.

Paranoia in Schreber's case is allegorization: it begins with desire that stays targeted on the father; a simple allegorical translation is made to the older brother; brother is translated to doctor. Here intervenes a disturbance: to love one's doctor is to be homosexual. Thus an inverse projection: Schreber does not love the doctor, the doctor detests Schreber. (Sons may love fathers excessively in *Gravity's Rainbow*; doctors punish sons.) Why, however, is the issue of the doctor's emotions so invested? (The source of this medical paranoia in paternal memory is of course invisible.) It can only be God that abominates Schreber. God, as a matter of fact, wants to rape him, but this return of the homosexual wish is necessitated by the "Order of Things," the eschatological plan. At the end of this line of reasoning (at long last, weakly) is a Christ-fantasy.

These moments of the pathology may be abstracted. (1) Projection: the transparency of human to divine meaning. (2) Inversion: the derivation of punishment from love. (3) Conversion-anxiety: the existential indifference of retribution and salvation. (4) Detemporalization: the palliation of anxiety and pain by recourse to predestiny. (5) Higher-order recapitulation: the repression of the desire to be a woman is allowed to surface so long as God plays the male role; but this has theological repercussions almost as dire as the psychical repercussions of the original wish. (6) Reversion and retrojection: divine meaning is re-familiarized (Schreber is God's beloved son). All the elements of a Puritan allegory may be thus itemized (messianism softened to imitation).

Schreber's paranoia, like Foucault's, is an internalization of war: "In proportion as the object of contention became the most important thing in the external world, trying on the one hand to draw the whole of the libido on to itself, on the other hand mobilizing all the resistances against itself, so the struggle raging around this single object became more and more comparable to a general engagement; till at length a victory for the forces of repression found expression in a conviction that the world had come to an end and that the self alone survived" (*SE*, 73). As if according to Clausewitz's theorem that wars—as wars, not as instruments of policy—tend toward maximum brutality, all paranoias tend toward apocalypse. Conversely, World War II, it may be again noted, de-psychologized psychological categories, as Yossarian implies when he asserts that everyone is trying to kill him; he is told he is crazy, that no one is trying to kill him; Yossarian wonders why, in that case, they are shooting at him; the rejoinder is that they are not shooting at *him*; the final riposte is to wonder how that alters it (*C*, 17). In Nabokov's "Signs and Symbols," the paranoid subject of the story has an Aunt Rosa: "a fussy, angular, wide-eyed old lady, who had lived in a tremulous world of bad news, bankruptcies, train accidents, cancerous growths"—that is, she exhibits the quotidian symptoms of her nephew's more recherché paranoia—"until the Germans put her to death, together with all the people she had worried about."[20]

I referred to the "paranoid subject" of "Signs and Symbols"; actually, the diagnosis of that story is "referential mania." When the silent protagonist attempts suicide, he is said to desire "to tear a hole in his world and escape," that is, he is trying to rip through pages in which everything signifies. As much as Nabokov likes to believe that his predestined characters enjoy their lives under a Nabokovian deity, he usually portrays life in someone else's story (like Humbert in Quilty's) as a torture and a provocation. And the oddest fact about postmodern World War II novels is how textual-

ized are the lives led by its characters—they exist, they seem to acknowledge, in books. The experience of being in World War II is best translated
into literature not merely as an allegory, but as an allegory in which the
characters understand that they are allegorical. This is the logological
equivalent, as Kenneth Burke would say, of paranoia in a world that vindi-
cates paranoia.

In Paul de Man, allegory is where one necessarily arrives if one begins
with epistemological and textual sophistication.[21] I do not think postmodernist combat allegory works exactly his way, but it is useful to observe the
parallel structure of his "allegory" and Freud's "Dementia Paranoides" in
order to learn how to get from World War II terrorism to the textual phase
of postmodernism (both epitomized by *Gravity's Rainbow*, which is at the
crossroads of high, esoteric, international postmodernism and adolescent,
terrorized, exoteric American punk postmodernism).[22]

For de Man as for Freud, you start with a loss of local self-authoriza-
tion; de Man's Rousseau cannot depend on the self at all as a guarantee of
truth or intention (*AR*, 202–203).[23] Rousseau begins, in de Man's account
of *Julie*, with this first-order deconstruction; the alternative to authority
and intention might seem to be the free play of signifiers, but Rousseau
does not pursue that ignis fatuus, partly because it is no solution (it substitutes one referential simplicity for another), second because it terrifies him
(*AR*, 207–208) (as Schreber is terrified by the femininity according to which
he might have been simplistically dephallocentered). The most promising
solution to Rousseau's impasse is praxis or ethics (as opposed to reading)
combined with revelation (as opposed to reading)—in sum, allegory. So
Rousseau's problems are projected and inverted to the scope of the universe.
But ethics is itself a mode of discourse, it cannot back its own validity (*AR*,
206, 209), and the truth that would endorse it—God's revelation—turns
out to be unavailable except to reading (*AR*, 192–193). Rousseau's original, self-decentered problem is—like Schreber's—doubled in divinity; allegory is the home of the second-degree deconstruction (*AR*, 205); Rousseau's universe is as empty of self and love as Schreber's is empty of love
and other selves.

American combat fiction, on the other hand, begins with allegory, with
praxis-cum-theology, already inverted to the loveless, meaningless universal
paranoia that Schreber and Rousseau had to achieve. Projection, the principle mechanism of paranoia and allegory, is superfluous. The thing to be
explained, then, is why Vonnegut, Heller, and Pynchon work their way
backward to a version of meta-textuality. Vonnegut's book is the most
simply self-reflexive: it begins with a faux naïf referentiality ("All this happened, more or less" [*SF*, 1]) and then without hesitation begins to discuss
in writerly terms the arrangement of the story. "Vonnegut" is delighted
with the irony that he has thought up for the book's climax: the execution
of Edgar Derby—all Dresden destroyed around him—for stealing a teapot
(*SF*, 4–5). This does turn out to be the last event of the Dresden experience
that Vonnegut describes, but the effect has shifted. The ironic disparity is

not between the scale of the firebombing and the capital crime, but between war and literary satisfaction.

Catch-22 is almost a compendium of postmodernist self-reflexive techniques. Heller anticipates the comic proliferations of fiction within life that are the signature of Tom Stoppard:

> "Are you sure you didn't imagine the whole thing [the attacks of "Nately's whore"]?" Hungry Joe inquired hesitantly after a while.
> "Imagine it? You were right there with me, weren't you? You just flew her back to Rome."
> "Maybe I imagined the whole thing, too." (*C*, 407)

He is the inventor of John Barthian echolalia, the persistence of language after reality has absconded.

> "Now where were we? Read me back the last line."
> "'Read me back the last line,'" read back the corporal, who could take shorthand.
> "Not *my* last line stupid!" the colonel shouted. "Somebody else's."
> "'Read me back the last line,'" read back the corporal.
> "That's *my* last line again!" shrieked the colonel, turning purple with anger.
> "Oh, no, sir," corrected the corporal. "That's *my* last line." (etc., *C*, 80–81)

Heller anticipates some of Pynchon's/Slothrop's demonstration that signifiers can serve various masters, so that even proper nouns can be expropriated. "John, Milton is a sadist" . . . "Have you seen Milton, John?" . . . "Is anybody in the John, Milton?" (*C*, 100). In Pynchon this becomes: "You never did. [signed] The Kenosha Kid" . . . "Bet you never did the 'Kenosha,' kid" . . . "You never did '*the*,' Kenosha Kid!" (*GR*, 60–61).

And all the looking-glass double-going of Nabokov, Borges, and descendants is implicit in the title itself: "There was an elliptical precision about its perfect pairs of parts that was graceful and shocking, like good modern art" (*C*, 47). Like them, Heller hears in repetition compulsion the troping of death itself:

> "Help the bombardier, help the bombardier."
> "I'm the bombardier," Yossarian cried back to him. "I'm the bombardier. I'm all right. I'm all right."
> "Then help him, help him," Dobbs begged. "Help him, help him." (*C*, 52)

And:

> "I'm cold," Snowden said softly. "I'm cold."
> "You're going to be all right, kid," Yossarian reassured him with a grin. "You're going to be all right."
> "I'm cold," Snowden said again in a frail, childlike voice. "I'm cold."
> "There, there," Yossarian said, because he did not know what else to say. "There, there."
> "I'm cold," Snowden whimpered. "I'm cold."
> "There, there," Yossarian said. (*C*, 46–47)

As important as what Heller prefigures is what he post-figures; at least this is equally important if the case is that Heller is a postmodernist. All the books of my postmodern sample confess their tardiness in the history of literature, as Jones and Mailer do not. Heller manages, for instance, to get the name T. S. Eliot bouncing down one page and up the next (C, 37–38): "Name, for example, one poet who makes money." "'T. S. Eliot,' ex-P.F.C. Wintergreen said." "Well, what did he say?" "'T. S. Eliot,' Colonel Cargill informed him." "What's that?" "'T. S. Eliot,' Colonel Cargil repeated." "Just 'T. S.—'" "Yes, sir. That's all he said. Just T. S. Eliot." And so on for quite a bit longer. Capturing "T. S. Eliot" within single quotes within double quotes might be one way of epitomizing the postmodern resentment.

There is also in *Catch-22* an extraordinary implication of Emily Dickinson. Orr assures Yossarian that there are flies in Appleby's eyes. When Yossarian wonders why Appleby does not know it, the answer is, "How can he see he's got flies in his eyes if he's got flies in his eyes." "You've got flies in your eyes," Yossarian informs Appleby. "That's probably why you can't see them" (C, 47–48). What is the point of this running-gag reference to "I heard a fly buzz"? ("and then it was/ There interposed a Fly . . . and then/ I could not see to see.") The Vonnegut/Heller/Pynchon generation is a late regendering of a lineage that includes Anne Bradstreet, Dickinson, Christina Rossetti, and culminates in Plath and Sexton: the tradition is female, its rhetorical device is hysteron proteron, and its theme is living death.

It may be worth noting that James Jones was oddly fascinated by Dickinson. And the only poets explicitly quoted (I think) in *Gravity's Rainbow* are Dickinson and Rilke. Here is the second quotation from Dickinson:

> Ruin is formal, devil's work,
> Consecutive and slow—
> Fail in an instant no man did,
> Slipping is crash's law. (GR, 28)

Am I wrong to hear in "Ruin," "slow," "slipping," and "law" the elements of Tyrone Slothrop? This may be worse than a case of tardiness: could Slothrop (or Pynchon) feel as if he is born of a dead woman's words? Is this the intersection of postmodern belatedness with the fantasy of the Domina Nocturna ("shining mother and last love")?

This may be an excessively gloomy hypothesis. But in Heller's case, fabulation, that is, the making up of stories not professedly out of reality but confessedly out of language, the sense that all the enemies of the self are purely linguistic and so is the self, is precisely the characteristic mode of army history. Knowing oneself to be composed of words is an experience of mortality; it is the prematurity of that experience that the military finds congenial. When McWatt unintentionally flies his plane into Kid Sampson and then intentionally into the side of a mountain, Dr. Daneeka is supposed to be on board, accumulating flight time, so that for the sake of book-keeping clarity he is considered to be as dead as McWatt. In Heller's army, book-keeping generally produces reality; it is a type of book-writing. The result is that when we descend, in *Catch-22*, from allegory to first-order deconstruction, to the free-play of signifiers, we experience it with Rousseau's terror: "So many things were testing his faith. There was the Bible, of course, but the Bible was a book, and so were *Bleak House, Treasure Island, Ethan Frome,* and *The Last of the Mohicans*" (C, 293). A universal, empty fictionality merely opens up space for the army, which occupies it not by means of illiterate force, but by a knowing and radical deployment of fictionality itself.[24]

Gravity's Rainbow makes reference not just to Rilke and Dickinson but also to Hemingway, Lewis Carroll, the Rossettis, and Ishmael Reed. No simple statement about the nature of these allusions would be true; I wish only to make two points about them. First, the postmodern precursor who most dominates the book is Borges. "We are obsessed with building labyrinths," says the Argentine Squalidozzi about his countrymen, "where before there was plain and sky. To draw even more complex patterns on the blank sheet. We cannot abide that *openness*: it is terror to us. Look at Borges" (GR, 264). You might hope to find in this remark a tribute to Borges; what is a more complex patterning on blank sheets than *Gravity's Rainbow*? Yet Katje Borgesius is his namesake, and Katje is a highly ambiguous character: sadist and masochist, victim and torturer, agent and counter-agent, corrupt innocent. Borges is transformed into the Domina Nocturna: the precursor is mother-death. If there is something more labyrinthine than *Gravity's Rainbow*, it is the machinations of the war powers whom Katje serves. Borgesian complexity is caught up in *their* complexity.

Second: Pynchon therefore writes into his text a nostalgia for pre-writing, for oral poetry. The Argentines who want something more anarchic than Borgesian labyrinths move to the rhythms of *Martin Fierro*, the Argentine epic—written, of course, but featuring a "singing duel between the white gaucho and the dark El Moreno" (GR, 387), and a memorial of the pre-literate Indians that Argentina had exterminated. This is reminiscent of the "singing duel" that precedes the song of the Aqyn in Soviet Central Asia, where Tchitcherine had been exiled to impose literacy. The "singing duel" brings the duel's symmetry and balance (a "coming together of opposites" [GR, 610–611]) into the art itself; it is one degree more satisfying than a song *about* a duel; we return, by means of this oral genre, perfect unity of aesthetic war and dualistic art, to the forever occulted moment of cultural history, the last moment we cannot remember, just prior to Homer. (Tchitcherine "understands abruptly, that soon someone will come out and begin to write some of these [songs] down in the New Turkic Alphabet he helped frame . . . and this is how they will be lost" [GR, 357].) No wonder that the extremest form of self-conscious literary art—the postmodernist novel—is taken to be the appropriate setting of the extremest degradation of duel war into impersonal terrorism.

One of the attractions of oral culture is the presence of audience—which "sort of goes hmm" when the singing duel gets vicious, which laughs when the duel turns gentler, which takes to carousing after the song of the Aqyn. The village is remarkably united in its response to the performance art before it; at simpler moments, all Pynchon seems to wish for the world is that sort of togetherness-in-art. Leni, for example, speaks for a world of "'Metaphor. Signs and symptoms. Mapping on to different coordinate systems, I don't know . . .' She didn't know, all she was trying to do was reach. . . . Not A before B, but all together" (*GR*, 159). If "signs and symptoms" calls up Nabokov's referential mania, Pynchon grants it: "About the paranoia [brought on by Oneirine], it is nothing less than the onset, the leading edge, of the discovery that *everything is connected*, everything in the Creation, a secondary illumination — not yet blindingly One, but at least connected" (*GR*, 703).

The problem is that this paranoia is imperfectly distinct from World War II paranoia — justified, really terrorized, Yossarian, Aunt-Rosarian paranoia. The word "connected" has several possible meanings. Christian says to Enzian: "you're not even *connected* any more," and then "swings his fist at Enzian's face." Enzian feels the blow: "It hurts. He lets it," and says, "You just connected" (*GR*, 525). No doubt he means "made emotional contact," but the phrasing is poised to keep the pugilistic meaning of "to connect" unrepressed. This is not a book to argue that "only connect" is an unambiguously pacifistic motto. Is it possible to doubt that the best human connecting to date is what Pynchon calls the "cartelized state," set up by Rathenau whose legacy was the "demolishing [of] the barriers of secrecy and property that separated firm from firm" (*GR*, 164–165)? Is it possible to deny that the closest humankind has come to immortality — to forging Pynchon's ultimate community, undivided by death — is plastic? Only if we accept this (desperate) distinction: "The real movement [of industrial chemistry] is not from death to any rebirth. It is from death to death-transfigured. . . . But polymerization is not resurrection" (*GR*, 166). Or the distinction between unity and mere chemical "synthesis" (*GR*, 167). The book has trouble indicating what is meant by real unity, no trouble at all imaging violent connections (or business connections, as in *The Great Gatsby*). And every time it tries for the real thing, it is hostage to violence. Why can't Mexico's and Jessica's love — the only real hope of unity the book sponsors — survive the war?

Thus this series: (1) When Leni leaves Franz, his song is "Victim in a Vacuum!" There is a spoken interlude that begins: "All together now, all you masochists out there, specially those of you don't have a partner tonight . . ." (*GR*, 415). "All together" quotes Leni herself; the implication that there exists a community of loneliness is a cruel joke on Franz. (2) As Slothrop observes his own self-division, his inability to determine his own direction, this song appears: "How-dy neighbor, how-dy pard!/ Ain't it lone-ly, say ain't it hard" (*GR*, 677). The end of the song of loneliness is "Now ev'rybody." (3) And finally, the last words of the book, following a last song as the bomb falls: "Now everybody" (*GR*, 760). When Pynchon tries to imagine a contemporary community, a singing epic community with audience participation, all he can picture—in place of the duel—is the unity of nuclear holocaust. The illumination that is "blindingly one" sought by Leni, and the Kirghis light (available to oral poetry but not to writing) whose "light . . . is blindness," type the final atomic blast—"bright angel of death"—that ends the book (*GR*, 47, 358, 760). The only community that a written work can legitimately project is a community of perfect isolates, a community of the separately but simultaneously deceased.

If this is so, then what other procedure could there be for escaping the textual representation of apocalypse than escaping the text? On another planet, Billy Pilgrim learns the insignificance of death—Tralfamadore is a kind of trapdoor beneath combat fiction. Who knows where Slothrop ends up—not anywhere in particular, but at least not in *Gravity's Rainbow*. Pynchon writes that "neutral Switzerland" is a "rather stuffy convention," because "The War has been reconfiguring time and space into its own image" (*GR*, 257). Zurich is caricatured as a place of oblivious skiing businessmen ("hearing nothing of campaigns or politics") and "loonies on leave" (*GR*, 258–259). The parody is of Hemingway's and Fitzgerald's visions, respectively, of a beautiful elevated asylum.

Does Yossarian escape? The question is where to go. Perhaps the typical Heller joke is on the omnipresence and eternality of absence, as for example:

> "When didn't you say we couldn't find you guilty?"
> "Late last night in the latrine, sir."
> "Is that the only time you didn't say it?"
> "No, sir. I always didn't say you couldn't find me guilty, sir." (*C*, 82)

This is another *Catch-22* skit to which Tom Stoppard is indebted. Transform infinite non-existence to the non-existence of the Infinite, and you have a Paul de Manian allegory.

> "I thought you didn't believe in God."
> "I don't," she sobbed, bursting violently into tears. "But the God I don't believe in is a good God, a just God, a merciful God. He's not the mean and stupid God you make Him out to be." (*C*, 185)

Heller recognizes that paranoia is too simple a mechanism. There is no easy opposition to army and divine madness. From a world mocked by the absence joke, it is difficult to know how to go about absenting oneself. Certainly there is no escape into the imagination. *From* the imagination is closer to it: when Yossarian sits naked in a tree at Snowden's funeral, critics traditionally see a 60s, Hippie-ish protest avant la lettre.[25] But Yossarian is not protesting, he is repudiating; he is not making a symbolic plea for non-uniformity, he is taking off a literal uniform that does not symbolically refer to Snowden but is literally stained by Snowden. In short, the gesture is not significant. The desire is nakedly to act. That readers can only take the gesture as significant, however, turns the ethical act into an allegory of reading. Sweden is the book's Switzerland, except that it cannot be imagined. (Is it intentionally an echo of Snowden, type of the always present absence?) Yossarian, in flight from the army's fictionality, can do no more than name an alternative as if the name were a rip in the text to escape through.

Gravity's Rainbow, like *Catch-22*, imagines absolute incarceration in so many forms that it can only gratify postmodernists of every persuasion. Like Heller, Pynchon imagines war to be a function of international—borderless, ubiquitous, absconded—capitalism, to which there could be no dialectical response. At other moments power seems to be a deeper structure than money, and modern power takes the form of an internalized surveillance. In Hell, Stephen Dodson-Truck is "given the old Radio-Control-Implanted-In-The-Head-At-Birth problem to mull over" (*GR*, 542), but the true definition of Hell is the place of shame, the thing there is nothing outside of. "No, there's no leaving shame after all—not down here—it has to be swallowed sharp-edged and ugly, and lived with in pain, every day" (*GR*, 546). Or is the world a divine cryptogram, and the Hereros the "Kabbalists out here . . . the scholar-magicians of the Zone, with somewhere in it a Text, to be picked to pieces, annotated, explicated . . ." (*GR*, 520)? The Text "had to be the Rocket . . . our Torah." The spectre of scholarly annotation transpires through the very metaphors of the novel: "He gets back to the Casino just as big globular raindrops, thick as honey, began to splat into giant asterisks on the pavement, inviting him to look down at the bottom of the text of the day, where footnotes will explain all" (*GR*, 204). But *Gravity's Rainbow* like its world is bottomless.

The book is a nondenominational allegory; this does not imply that it means everything, it implies that it serves all paranoias. It seems to exist to give readers the experience of the world—of the world imagined as a war that does not end with victory, that is infinitely not a duel—rather than an alternative to it. What is the point of doubling the world if there is no escaping it? In *Catch-22*, "to disappear" is reclassified as a transitive verb, as in "Did they disappear him? . . . What will you do if they decide to disappear you?" (*C*, 410). Yossarian disappears himself, pre-emptively. In *Gravity's Rainbow*, it is unclear whether Slothrop disappears or is disappeared. Slothrop's fate is perhaps the ultimate extent of his victimage; on the other hand, he most resembles his creator at the moment of his disappearance. The postmodern hope is not exile, it is absence. In postmodern theory, the self appears only in the interstices of a network—side-effect of a textual aporia, epiphenomenon of an economic or penal system. Take away the system and you eliminate its subject. Postmodern fiction sufficiently believes this that it does not try to find the self a trans-systemic, transalpine refuge. But it converts war into literature to shadow the system, as if the text's final obscurity were a Zion into which the delinquent self, from its terrorized diaspora, might disappear.

6

Diversions: A Theory of the Vietnam Sports Novel

"Why not a smooth, orderly arc from war to peace?"
Tim O'Brien, *Going After Cacciato*

Play, Part I

(1955) Among the things that Vladimir Nabokov disdained, according to his introduction to *Bend Sinister*, were atomic warfare and the entire Orient,[1] which makes it unsurprising that the Korean War, fought on the sub-nuclear level and on only one Asian peninsula, left him cold. *Lolita* (whose action takes place between 1947 and 1952) hardly mentions the war (1950–53).[2] The war years are more or less the blank years of the novel (1949–52), the interlude of "Dolorès Disparue" (*L*, 231). When the action resumes, Humbert tracks Lolita to Dick, who—Humbert notes un-sympathetically—is hard of hearing, the result of an injury in "a remote war" (*L*, 249), probably Korea, though his friend Bill lost his arm in World War II. And when Humbert returns to Ramsdale, on the scent of Quilty, he is pointedly unmoved by the news that Charlie Holmes, old summer camp debaucher, was killed in Korea—the place and the war named for the first and only time. It would be easy to assert that the casualty is admitted into the book to stand for everything to which Nabokov is "supremely indifferent"[3]—except that Nabokov (even if identical with the author of the introduction to *Bend Sinister*) is not identical with Humbert Humbert. If Korea is merely the contingent token of all that Nabokov does not conde-scend to aestheticize, at least it serves in that capacity in a book that dis-plays the consequences of a murderous aesthetic solipsism.

(1966) In *The Crying of Lot 49*, Thomas Pynchon alludes to Viet-nam, in passing, twice. This seems short shrift in a book (a) published in

1966, and (b) much interested in the Civil War, World War I, and World War II.[4] Nevertheless, the book might have been called *Why Are We in Vietnam?*, on Norman Mailer's principle that a book on that war might be better off barely naming it. The clue to discovering Vietnam in—or Vietnam out of—*Lot 49* is observing, first of all, that the war between Squamuglia and Faggio illustrates no cunning rationality in history: both sides are devastated. Centuries later, during World War II, a company of Americans is wiped out by Germans on the Italian coast. One side loses the war, the other side—"cut off without communication"—loses the battle with such extravagance that no member of the company lives to celebrate the ultimate victory to which he contributed so negligibly. The Americans disappear "without a trace or a word"[5]—which certainly elicits the question of how anybody knows about them. Only one thing connects these two bits of catastrophic absurdity. Bones of combatants in the first war are used by Tristero for charcoal in pens, and bones of the dead GIs are used by Pierce Inverarity for charcoal in cigarettes. The plot of *Lot 49* imitates the plot of history; death is only the raw material of marketing and marking. The book's impossible project is to inscribe Vietnam only insofar as it leaves no trace or word.

(1968)   John Barth's *Lost in the Funhouse* is the Ultima Thule of self-reflexive metafiction.[6] The mythic preoccupation is *The Odyssey*, the postmodernist Ulysses is communication itself, whose arrival at any destination is always in peril. Nevertheless, the absence of an *Iliad* is on Barth's mind. ("Anonymiad" is the culminating story of a poet who invents writing while on an eventless adventure away from Troy during the Trojan War.) In the title story, Ambrose, too young to go to war (born, presumably, in 1930), visits Ocean City and its funhouse around 1943; there are signs everywhere of the war on, but the narrator, Ambrose/Barth, wonders: "What relevance does the war have to the story?" (*LF*, 92). The answer seems to be: it mirrors it.

> On account of German U-boats, Ocean City was "browned out": streetlights were shaded on the seaward side; shop windows and boardwalk amusement places were kept dim, not to silhouette tankers and Liberty-ships for torpedoing. In a short story about Ocean City, Maryland, during World War II, the author could make use of the image of sailors on leave in the penny arcades and shooting galleries, sighting through the crosshairs of toy machine guns at swastika'd subs, while out in the black Atlantic a U-boat skipper squints through his periscope at real ships outlined by the glow of penny arcades. (*LF*, 82)

This is, however, too treacherous a passage to use as an emblem: the author does not in fact write this mirror story, except insofar as he floats its scenario. It would be a silly story to write, but that does not prevent it so much as its self-importance. The funhouse of the story that does get written is disturbing not in its ludic contagiousness (its fictionality projected dangerously—browned out arcades somehow aglow—into the historical mirror), rather in its grim infectedness. The Barthian/Ambrosian narrative voice laments: "How much better it would be to be that common sailor! A wiry little Seaman 3rd, the fellow squeezed a girl to each side and stumbled hilarious into the mirror room, closer to Magda in thirty seconds than Ambrose had got in thirteen years" (*LF*, 89). Banal reality — a military-sexual complex — informs the funhouse.

Nabokov first dreamt the proto-*Lolita* in France, just before it was invaded, redreamt and rewrote *Lolita* during Korea. Pynchon wrote *The Crying of Lot 49* in the first year of significant anti-Vietnam protests (Oedipa, walking through Berkeley, breathes the radicalized air). Barth's collection of stories is high-Vietnam art. Nabokov mentions Korea once and there is one sad reminder of World War II; Pynchon alludes to Vietnam twice; Barth does not mention Vietnam at all. Is the Nabokovian moment of the American novel averse to combat fiction (1) because high-international postmodernism is superbly ahistorical, or (2) because history is the prey of textuality, or (3) because history is so hauntingly an apparition in the text itself that every formal gesture is a historical gesture?

Sports

If Nabokov is the pre-eminent advocate of the ludic novel, of literary creation as the word's superiority to history, then he ought to be the furthest thing possible from war novelist. Pynchon and Barth provide only two examples of the impossibility of writing Vietnam in the Nabokovian tradition: Donald Barthelme, in the metafictional questionnaire of *Snow White*, asks of presumably bored readers, "Would you like a war?"[7] Not all American postmodernism, of course, is Nabokovian (or Borgesian, international, rarefied) postmodernism. Nevertheless, though there were already something like 130 Vietnam novels by 1987, none to that or this moment has made a convincing claim to being the final, extensive, satisfying treatment of the war. Even Vietnam novelists themselves, at a conference dedicated to establishing and publicizing the vitality of the subgenre, "agreed that *the* Vietnam novel is yet to be written,"[8] despite the fact that through the 1980s *the* Vietnam film was released at approximately the rate of one every two years. The Vietnam film is sensuous bombardment diagrammatically framed; the postmodern Vietnam novel can be neither so crude nor so orderly. Such diversely excellent Vietnam novels as *Going After Cacciato*, *Why Are We in Vietnam?*, and *In Country* are combat writing by indirection: to transport us to Vietnam, they transport Vietnam to Paris, Alaska, and Kentucky.

Still — America makes available, between play and war, a compromise formation. American sports are oxymoronic to begin with — what is sport but beautiful belligerence? — and the American sports novel has served the impossible necessity of making Vietnam available to the postmodern novel. Bernard Malamud's *The Natural* and John Updike's *The Centaur* are pre-Vietnam, but taken together they illustrate the formal possibilities sport offers to Vietnam-era literature that is obsessed with the war it despairs of representing.

The Natural (written during Korea) concerns two peacetime eras, without the war dividing them.[9] But for a book about baseball, it is unduly violent; most of the crippling is just prior to the moment Roy Hobbs, the "natural" whose potentially brilliant career had been cut short fifteen years before by a nearly successful assassination, reappears on the scene. Walking into the equipment room to get his new uniform, Roy is addressed by the chatty equipment manager: "Caught me at an interesting moment. . . . I was reading about this catcher that got beaned in Boston yesterday. Broke the side of his skull." Then the equipment manager acknowledges his own team's desiderata: "Yeah, we been one man short on the roster for two weeks. One of our guys went and got himself hit on the head with a fly ball and both of his legs are now paralyzed." And "just before that our regular third baseman stepped on a bat and rolled down the dugout steps. Snapped his spine in two places" (*TN*, 42). A string of bad luck? This is more brutal misfortune than major league baseball will suffer in decades.

Granted that on one level of the allegory, what we have here is nothing historically specifiable, rather the seasonal confrontation of Parsifal and Death. (Going to bat, Roy swears that he will "murder" the ball; as he approaches the plate, the manager says, "Keep us alive" [*TN*, 210].) One of the athlete's functions is to play out the spectacular confrontation of life and death prematurely, when heroic exemptions are still possible; baseball players start fending off death around the age of thirty, which is why the book is framed by Roy's humiliation of "The Whammer" (aged 33) and his own humiliation (aged 34), and why the book turns out to be a meditation on another summer confrontation of Parsifal and Death, *The Great Gatsby*, in which Gatsby's martyrdom allegorizes Nick's thirtieth birthday. The two books are based on the same vision of green West and Eastern Waste, on the same paradox of Western pioneers moving East again, apparently in the direction of the past and rebirth but in fact toward decay. The shared vision, which almost necessarily turns men into boys and their fate over to murderous women, will place two separate infantalized heroes in two cars driving between Long Island and New York City, and will manage to have two separate women take over the steering and two homicides as the result (possibly imaginary in *The Natural*).

Finally, the analogy of the books involves the same allusion to baseball history: the fixing of the 1919 World Series, just before the action of *The Great Gatsby* and its historical correlative, is the climactic event of *The Natural*, transported three decades. After Roy is corrupted by the gamblers and the pennant is lost, a newspaper boy pleads, "Say it ain't so, Roy," because an apocryphal newspaper boy had implored, "Say it ain't so, Joe" to Joe Jackson after the 1919 scandal. If you throw Jordan Baker's cheating at golf into a consideration of *The Great Gatsby*, you get two powerful novels that stake their ironic grandiosity not merely on the decline of the athletic body toward death but also on the corruption of sport itself. Why should the mortification of American athletics appear to Fitzgerald—and to Malamud in turn—as necessary to their Arthurian-Eliotic parables of the decline of cultures?

The answer gets us to the relation of sport and war; the so-called Black Sox scandal, model for Malamud's climax, occurred at a crucial allegorical moment. We entered the war in 1917, we won the war in 1918, we belatedly suffered the degradation of the war in 1919. The bitterness of inheriting a bankrupt patrimony came to Americans a year late: the world war was fun for Gatsby and Nick, but the World Series made it possible for *Gatsby* to rewrite *The Waste Land*. As in Huizinga, what is at risk in modern civilization is the agon, the play-principle of civilization; it survives the Great War, but professional sport (as in Huizinga) is a more insidious enemy. When Malamud came to write his own allegory of war and waste land, the Black Sox scandal was simply transformed into the belatedly culminating event of the *next* world war—hence the rash of casualties just prior to Hobbs's return.

War is never mentioned in *The Natural*, but World War II intervenes nevertheless. A simple calculation puts this into relief. Sam Simpson, the scout who discovers Roy Hobbs, was a ballplayer from 1919 to 1921, a full-time scout in 1925. By the time he discovers Hobbs, however, he is only a scout insofar as he wanders the country looking for ballplayers on his own. Assume that a decade more or less has passed since 1925. Then he discovers Hobbs, who shows his genius by winning a baseball duel with the legendary Whammer, clearly Babe Ruth, who retired in 1935; but Hobbs is shot, not to complete his odyssey back to the majors, Malamud specifies, for another fifteen years. World War II is what, conspicuously, intervenes and disappears, like the Revolutionary War in the missing twenty years of "Rip Van Winkle," like Korea in the missing three years of *Lolita*.

Its intervention, though invisible, is unmistakable, because the vision that the antebellum Hobbs represents is a pastoral, romantic, Aryan affair: Sam's dream as a scout, which only Hobbs ever promises to realize, is of "twelve blond-bearded players," farmers, athletes, and supermen, playing titanic baseball on an unscouted farm (*TN*, 10). The corruption of Roy Hobbs is a fortunate fall, insofar as we do not buy into Sam's Aryan, agrarian, prelapsarian vision, or, to return to *The Great Gatsby*, Tom Buchanan's. Whether or not the fall is fortunate, the baseball story will be about, is virtually required to be about, the war that brought us to our urban, ethnic, mercenary present. The war that did that is every war; the baseball novel is our perpetual combat novel for novelists who missed the war, but got the parable.

The suspense of *The Natural* is whether it will be seduced by baseball's aesthetics of return: from adulthood to innocence, city to country, representation (legends and statistics) to history; basketball glamorizes the body in perpetual transition (history never solidifies, urban frenzy never relaxes, adolescence is eternal). In Updike's *The Centaur*, the emblematic sport of which is basketball, antitheses of the sort that Malamud's novel depends on keeping antithetical always mingle and refuse to detach.[10] It is unclear whether the book's Hebraic element (the Presbyterian, Hawthornean speculation) and the Hellenic element (the mythic frame) can be untangled. It is uncertain whether Updike's men are little lower than gods or little higher than animals: the centaur is a not wholly integrated but not wholly disintegrated (*half*-natural) monster, part god, human, and beast. The book chronicles the relation of a child-man and man-child, mutually compromised and inseparable.

Accordingly, Updike can make no Malamudian distinction of innocence and degradation, separable in principle even in a fallen world, or of war and peace. Both confusions come out at the basketball game, whose climactic vividness I hope justifies my taking *The Centaur* as a basketball novel. The basketball game is a monolith of Updikean sexuality—because of the closeness of the spectators to the exposed bodies on the court, the hothouse excitement of the packed bodies in the stands, the suggestiveness of the ball and skirted basket. The description of the game is suffused with sex: a player "drives in past the West Alton defender, and in a rapt moment of flight drops the peeper" (*TC*, 172). We register the "rape" in "rapt," the penetration, as they say, of the drive, the play of driving and flying, terms not only of transportation but of sexual transport, and the erotic vibrations of "drops the peeper." During the game, the centaur's son Peter decides to initiate himself into the truths of his girlfriend's body. He is anxious because his body is marred by psoriasis: not every body is a god's body, and Updike as intimately as Mark Twain knows that one truth of the human body is that it itches.

Penny's love, however, surmounts this difficulty, which I take it is responsible for the startling purity and grotesqueness of the vision immediately following the peace-in-war of the game. Caldwell père and fils leave the gymnasium; it is snowing outside, and Peter believes that "the multitude of flakes seems to have been released by a profanation" (*TC*, 190). How does a profanation entail a vision as consoling as the paraclete (of "an entire broadening wing of infinitesimal feathers")? The answer is that we have heard previously about a falling multitude of white flakes, as Peter scratches his decomposing skin. The universe magnifies and glorifies Peter's disease. If this is as sanctified a rottenness as can be imagined, it is an emblem of Updike's book.

So the novel, unlike Malamud's, has no before and after, prelapsarian and fallen: it lapses. There is no place for the American designation of war as fall, despite the fact that the book, written at the beginning of the 1960s, locates itself as a post-war novel. It takes place, more precisely dated than *The Natural*, in 1947, when post-war prosperity has begun: "The Esso and Mobil gas chains had both built service stations a few blocks away from the pike, and now that the war was over, and everybody could buy new cars with their war-work money, the demand for repairs had plummeted" (*TC*, 12). This is misleading, however, since Caldwell's demand for repairs of his car (and life) does not plummet, but increases to infinity during the

course of *The Centaur*—the car that keeps needing repairs is a '36 Buick.
And the war spills into post-war. A student named Ache (Achilles) survives
the war but is killed in a plane crash after it: "Isn't that funny? To go all
through the war without a scratch and then get nailed in peacetime" (*TC*,
167).

The inference is that the war has negligible impact on the events of the
novel. Caldwell, asked how long he has been a teacher, answers, "Fourteen
years. . . . I was laid off late in '31 and was out of work the whole year the
kid was born. In the summer of '33, Al Hummel . . . came up to the house
and suggested [getting a teaching job]" (*TC*, 101). The war, which began
when Caldwell was forty-five, merely represents four of the fourteen years
of his pedagogical futility in a world of "living corpses." In Roy Hobbs's
experience, the fallen world has replaced his agonistic Eden. For all we
know of it, he may as well have slept through the rupture, World War II,
as Rip Van Winkle slept through the Revolution, to awaken to newly
perfected venalities. Caldwell's world, on the other hand, is a perpetual
falling: "From Sky to Earth, they said, an anvil would fall nine days and
nights . . . . Perhaps now it was more, perhaps—the thought deepened his
sickness—an anvil could fall forever from Sky and never strike Earth" (*TC*,
218). He has been falling from 1933 to 1947, while Roy Hobbs was en-
tombed, and the war did not deflect his course.

The Natural does not mention war, but war is the subject of its allegory. *The Centaur* purports to register the effects of war, but finds war and
peace, like hate and love, mixed or compounded in every human gesture,
hence inappropriate as a special concern or referent of referents. A theory
of the sports novel needs to establish under what conditions it is crypto- or
pseudo-war literature, and to observe distinctions, war equally invisible in
either case, in the patterns of invisibility. A theory of the *Vietnam* sports
novel needs to do more. It needs to show how Updike's and Malamud's
quite particular purposes—after all, World War II did produce its candidates for *the* combat novel, *The Naked and the Dead, From Here to Eternity, Catch-22, Gravity's Rainbow*—required techniques of indirection that
would be useful generally during Vietnam. And it must show how those
techniques were manipulated by novelists who could not be so confident as
Malamud that the war was sufficiently distanced from their prose as to be
available for allegory, or share Updike's confidence (in *The Centaur*, at
least) that the war sufficiently informs life on the home front as to be
absorbed. *The Natural* and *The Centaur* are in control of their paradoxes;
during Vietnam, sports novelists seem as much victimized as energized by
the problematics of representing war in terms of peace.

Tennis, Baseball

The sports novel inherits its specific force from the ambiguities of sport
itself—the gift of anthropology to sports novelists is that there is no anthropological consensus as to what sport is. The problem begins with the anom-

aly that sport seems conceptually halfway between play and work; sport makes a continuum of what is, in our purest, pre-industrial dreams, a polarity. There is a riskier, more indispensable mediation that sport performs: it figures the relationship of art and war, a trickier function, since art and war are not antonyms.

What sport shares with art is the assertion of a quasi-sacred value free from utility and productivity.[11] On the other hand is the anaesthetic belligerence of the competition:

> Manifestations of the predatory temperament are all to be classed under the head of the exploit. They are partly simple and unreflected expressions of an attitude of emulative ferocity, partly activities deliberately entered upon with a view to gaining repute for prowess. Sports of all kind are of the same general character, including prizefights, bullfights, athletics, shooting, angling, yachting, and games of skill, even where the element of destructive physical efficiency is not an obtrusive feature. Sports shade off from the basis of hostile combat, through skill to cunning and chicanery, without its being possible to draw a line at any point.[12]

Thorstein Veblen's family likening is in Hemingwayesque increments, except that Veblen is unconcerned to find, migrating through the spectrum, a separate peace for literature. The inference is that sport is perfectly positioned for the aestheticizing of war and the militarization of art.

Even amateur tennis? Suppose that a character in a work of literature is identified as a tennis devotee (like Humbert Humbert, say); is it likely that its author wants us to think of him as a paragon of martial virtues? When the Dauphin sends Henry V a present of tennis balls, presumably he believes that thus to metonymize Henry is to disqualify him as a warrior or King. The simplest way to understand what ensues is to find evidence in Agincourt that Henry is no longer Hal, the boy at play. But that would be to make a simple distinction of sport and war that is not only invalid per se; to believe it would invalidate the drama.

The reason that tennis is instrumental is that Shakepseare is defensive, in the wake of realist skepticism, about the susceptibility of war to theatre;[13] if war cannot be represented by play, can it be represented by plays? In the Prologue to Act IV, for example, Shakespeare is confessedly unequal to the task of putting combat on stage:

> And so our scene must to the battle fly,
> Where—oh, for pity!—we shall much disgrace
> With four or five most vile and ragged foils,
> Right ill-disposed in brawl ridiculous,
> The name of Agincourt. Yet sit and see,
> Minding the things by what their mockeries be. (*CW*, IV. Prologue. 48–53)

All that Shakespeare can rely on is the cooperation of his audience, which is doubly tested: even a realistic representation would be a weak representation. But Shakespeare does more than apologize and beseech. The challenge to his audience is built into his play, so as to make criticism unpatriotic.

The Englishmen at Agincourt look little worthier, according to the drama, than their dramatic mockeries. Henry's lament is like a boast:

> We are but warriors for the working day.
> Our gayness and our gilt are all besmirched
> With rainy marching in the painful field.
> There's not a piece of feather in our host—
> Good argument, I hope, we will not fly—
> And time hath worn us into slovenry. (*CW*, IV. iii. 109–114)

That the English army will not fly is of course desirable, but it would have seemed to the French more likely that their unfledgedness signified "flat unraisèd spirits" (*CW*, I. Prologue. 9), a phrase that does not, however, refer to them, but to the play's own strategic modesty. When the arrogant French "behold yon poor and starvèd band" (*CW*, IV. ii. 16) and see such pathetic details—as if from the prop department—as the horsemen sitting "like fixèd candlesticks,/ With torch staves in their hand" (*CW*, IV. ii. 45–46), they may as well be the spectators of Henry's cavalry or Shakespeare's cast, mockers of mockeries.

If the audience scorns the play, they are equal in superficiality to the Dauphin and his entourage. What the French lack, the audience is manipulated to value: an imagination that is both productive ("Piece out the imperfections with your thoughts") and susceptible ("let us . . . on your imaginary forces work" [*CW*, I. Prologue. 23,18]). Between Shakespeare and his audience is an imaginary co-dependency, a community with reciprocal obligations: Shakespeare makes his own art the field of patriotism. In these terms, the tennis ball insult is not so much pointed as imaginatively flat. The French perceive, apparently, no relation between play and war, despite their own dedication to martial splendor. Henry sees a metaphorical relation:

> When we have matched our rackets to these balls,
> We will in France, by God's grace, play a set
> Shall strike his father's crown into the hazard.
> Tell him he hath made a match with such a wrangler
> That all the courts of France will be disturbed
> With chaces. (*CW*, I. ii. 261–266)

The conceit is not merely improvised for the occasion; Henry *believes* it. At the siege of Harfleur, Henry proclaims that "the game's afoot" (*CW*, III. i. 32). Justifying the execution of Bardolph for stealing, he pronounces that "when lenity and cruelty play for a kingdom, the gentler gamester is the soonest winner" (*CW*, III. vi. 118–120). If Henry had turned out to be no warrior, then the insistent metaphor would conclusively prove that a talent for tennis is congruent with a talent for poetry. Since he is victorious, the equation is as follows: to suspect nothing serious in Harry is to find nothing daunting in the English army is to conceive nothing belligerent in play is to consider nothing in *a* play to be adequate to war. The progression is from tennis court to royal court to Agincourt, and back from battleground to playground to playhouse.

I have not prejudged whether in fact tennis is sufficiently violent—or Agincourt sufficiently agonistic—to justify Harry's metaphorical, metamorphic leap. The case is best put as a rolling conditional: if tennis prepares for combat, then boyhood is preparation for adulthood, then a play can represent Agincourt. A standard supposition about sport, of course, even such a brutal one as boxing, is that whatever relation it has to war works precisely to make war less necessary or attractive. Was Henry V wasting his manhood on boyish pursuits like tennis, or was he preparing himself for conquest? Shakespeare's answer—it depends on the power of metaphor—is my answer also, that is, sport, like war on the one hand and literature on the other, is an aspect of the symbolic expression of a culture. The relationship of the three cannot be worked out in advance of cultural interpretation: the French at Waterloo will again fail to realize that specifically English imperialism is practiced on playing fields. The duplicity of sport, its prefiguration of violence and regimentation as against its descent from ludic joy, makes it an eternal shifter in the grammar of a culture, as this review of the anthropological scholarship gravely, hilariously, implies:

> The literature on athletics and violence generally suggests one of two things; [sic] that sports either lower violence levels in society by providing a significant cathartic experience for both participants and spectators [list of five studies follows] or conversely that they increase the incidence of such unstructured aggression [list of eight studies follows].[14]

"Like any other form of sacrificial prophylaxis," René Girard says, "prohibitions can on occasion turn against their users": if sports are meant to replace unstructured violence with violence against a scapegoat, how could they ever fully succeed, given the nearly perfect indiscernibility of the players or teams, and the impossibility of any final sacrifice of the outsider who looks exactly like an insider? "In the end the kudos mean nothing," Girard writes of the unsatisfying condition. "It is the prize of a temporary victory, an advantage no sooner won than challenged."[15] Contests are contests and not duels. Sport participates in the quasi-catharsis of pornography and the remembered nightmare: its double force is that it produces or exacerbates what it quashes or contains. The novelist who comes to the sports theme may do so exclusively to claim for art a moral equivalence to war, or exclusively to subject war to the moral superiority of the book, but no sports novel can avoid doing some of both.

The peculiar difficulty of sorting out which relationship to war the sports novelist favors—which way he reads the relationship of art and combat in his culture—is most vivid in the baseball novel.[16] Though it has its own resemblance to combat writing, the most striking fact about baseball literature is how arty it is. Even as moralistic a book as *Bang the Drum Slowly* glides from morals to metafiction with athletic ease: the book is unassuming yet persistent in its self-reference. The narrator (and fictional author) is a character named Author; he refers occasionally to his previous book, as well as to the present one; the book we are reading has two time frames, the time it is describing and the time of its writing, and within the latter frame we hear about the submission of early chapters, which we have read, to a literature professor for a critique.

Philip Roth gets involved much more flamboyantly in the labyrinths of fictionality in *The Great American Novel*, the narrator/fictional author of which is the sportswriter Word Smith, a concise amalgam of Red Smith, William Shakespeare, William Wordsworth, and Henry Wadsworth Longfellow, author of "The Village Blacksmith." The narrator discusses the "Great American Novel" in *The Great American Novel* with Hemingway; a discussion of the competition between Word Smith's attempt at the "GAN" and other candidates for the title follows. Unexpectedly, the book is comparable to Robert Coover's *The Universal Baseball Association*, in which Coover creates a fictional demiurge named J. Henry Waugh who sub-creates a fictional baseball league (which he also chronicles) which itself has a fictionalizing league historian.

It is not surprising that baseball, the most self-absorbed and literary of all sports, should produce metafiction almost naturally. But why should writers with referential ambitions, like Harris and Roth, have turned to baseball for its metafictional suitability? And why should Roth have done so in 1973—or, for that matter, why Coover in 1968—when the continuing war in Southeast Asia might have shattered any incipient self-reflexive baseball fantasy? Why was *Bang the Drum Slowly* turned into a movie in 1973, almost two decades after publication?

I do not mean that, in their self-conscious intricacies, these baseball novels have no contact with reality, or with war, at all. In every baseball novel, as in *The Natural*, there is too much bloodshed for anyone to assume that baseball is the entire subject. There are two ballfield murders in *The Universal Baseball Association*, and a wide assortment of diamond murders and maimings in *The Great American Novel*. (Roth's book takes place in 1943 and 1944—the war accounts for much of the weirdness of Patriot League pennant races.) War is a minor theme of *Bang the Drum Slowly*: we hear of the hero Bruce Pearson's incompetence in World War II, and the book's central metaphor is the card game TEGWAR (The Exciting Game Without Any Rules), the Shermanesque pastime that stands for the lawless cruelty that claims the Georgian Bruce Pearson's life.

On the one hand, we have the bookishness of metafiction, on the other, the paradigmatic extra-referentiality of the war novel, in every baseball book. At least part of the key to the paradox is provided by the advertising on the first page of *Bang the Drum Slowly* when it was republished, following the movie, in 1973: "Remember the 50s, when ballplayers were gods and the major leagues seemed like heaven? *Bang the Drum Slowly* is about those golden years." One should not need to commit all one's intellectual force to controverting bookjacket copy. I merely note that the ballplayers of *Bang the Drum Slowly* are not gods, the major leagues do not seem like heaven, and what the "golden years" amount to is the attenuation, cut off finally by Pearson's death, of pre–World War II America when a hick was still a hick. Still—there *is* something nostalgic about *Bang the Drum Slowly* that would be attractive in 1973—the bookjacket is correct despite itself. Despite Harris: as if a Borges parable, the novel published in 1973 is nostalgic exactly where the 1956 book was cynical. The players are mainly white, and mainly country boys. They have colorful nicknames. They are childish. Money is discussed, but rather small sums.

The antebellum baseball ethos is similarly, almost unwillingly, preserved in *The Great American Novel* and *The Universal Baseball Association*. This means that the baseball novel—even in the hands of writers like Coover and Roth, who are sardonic and antic, respectively, about the pastoral, prelapsarian pretensions of baseball and who are capable of concerning themselves with the football-loving President whose administration lasted from just after Coover's baseball novel to just after Roth's—is inevitably an exercise in mixed, but not mock, nostalgia. Roth's book takes place during a war, and his baseball season mimics it; Coover's is apocalyptic; neither book flees war to a pure pastoral utopia. This would have been bad faith in 1968 or 1973. But they have the war wrong. If Roth's book is set in World War II and Coover's in a numerological Armageddon, then what they both avoid is the war planted uncomfortably in every imagination without ordinal specification between the second world war and the third and final one—the anti-literary war that was fought while they wrote.

Vietnam was not absolute enough for their purposes; it was anaesthetic in its irrationality, impersonality, shapelessness, beginninglessness, endlessness. But it is missing—it is the thing not being written about—in every withdrawal from referentiality to signification. Roth's meta-picaresque follows a single hapless team, the Ruppert Mundys, whose ballfield has been turned over to the government for war use. To make them feel more at home wherever they have to play their games—since the whole season is "away"—an official at each park has been given a statement to announce by the league president's office: "Welcome Ruppert Mundys, welcome to _____, your home away from home! (PAUSE)." The "pause" is to allow an interval for neighborly cheering, but each official inevitably reads the word; the Mundys get to like it, and when an official at one park actually pauses, they are offended. Finally, a judicious ballplayer tries to calm everyone down. "A word," he says, "don't mean a thing that I could ever see. A whole speech is just a bunch of words from beginning to end, you know, that didn't fool nobody yet what's got half a brain in his head" (*GAN*, 137). Earlier, the league president had worried about the pernicious implications of radio broadcasts of games: "Why, the game might just as well not be happening, for all [listeners] knew! The whole thing might even be a hoax, a joke . . . . Furthermore, you could not begin to communicate through *words*, either printed or spoken, what this game was all about" (text's emphasis, *GAN*, 88). What the league president dreads is *The Great American Novel*, itself a hoax and a joke.

That literature was by its nature a hoax and a joke seemed to be the discovery of the 60s. But suppose Roth and Coover to be stymied by a repellent war; then conceivably we are led by the crazy bloodiness of these baseball books to conjure the unrepresented and anti-literary ghost itself. We might defend these books and their nostalgia by arguing that Vietnam, as endlessness, as inscrutability, as the final lapse of the agonistic element in war, was unavailable to the formal intelligence, so that allusions to other wars were a strategem to make Vietnam appear (like an apparition) as what has been lost to beautiful play. In these terms I admire the courage of writers who admit—the admission is in the nostalgia for reference veiled by metafiction—that the central event of their time, for all their high literacy, belonged to others—because of their high literacy it belonged to others—and so admire metafiction as the publication and sly redemption of their failure.

The violence of these baseball books indicates Vietnam—or at least prevents their inability to represent Vietnam directly from turning into the positive invocation of a pastoral Utopia. The violence of baseball metafiction is a locally necessary paradox: football brutality infecting even baseball and even the most academic of literary forms in the 60s. What nags at this rationalization is that metafiction does not merely represent violence contingently or dutifully, but enacts it gleefully. In this respect, the violence of pacific baseball, almost as peaceful as pacific tennis, in the hands of metafictionists is token of the violence that metafiction does to reality. Non-representational, self-congratulatory fabulation emblematized by its own violence to resistant reality was the *appropriate* technique of the Nixon era.[17] The Vietnam baseball novel resembles Malamud's *The Natural* in importing violence into the text the source of which it cannot name; but in the Vietnam book, as opposed to Malamud's, the violence is in the textuality.

Basketball

All basketball novels—like *The Centaur*—take betweenness as their aesthetic principle—they are entirely transition.[18] First, the basketball novel is the adolescent novel between the protracted innocence of the baseball book and the corruption of the football book. (Updike's Rabbit is a perpetual adolescent; the basketball players of Lawrence Shainberg's *One on One*, Jeremy Larner's *Drive, He Said*, and Coover's *The Origin of the Brunists* have unjettisoned late adolescent fantasies, anxieties, and dreams.) Second, it is most often the 50s book, in spirit, between the spiritually antebellum baseball book and the football book at home in the 60s. (*Drive, He Said*, just further than *Rabbit, Run* into the 60s—the rebel *almost* has a cause— assists Updike's book in attaching the basketball component to the Beat pun of car drive and sexual drive.) Finally, the basketball novel, situated between meta-literary baseball art and anti-literary football art, portrays the passing of mimesis.

Shainberg's *One on One* (not even distantly related to the silly movie of that name) is the classic case: as basketball is turned first into writing (the star center, Elwood Baskin, dreams about the newspaper accounts of his upcoming game almost to the point of missing it) and second into art (the hero fantasizes about a cement casting of the entire basketball scene, himself to be cast and never released, at the moment of one of his own jump shots), the passage of time brings Elwood back from verbal and plastic fancies to the game that has almost been fully supplemented. Meanwhile, predictably, onanism threatens to supplement intercourse: when Baskin imagines the moment when "suddenly you and the ball and the hoop are *together*, all of one piece" (OO, 38), the displaced congress is descended from that of Romero and the bull in *The Sun Also Rises*. The object of basketball like bullfighting is sex that does not notice what is missing. The subjective overcoming of limits and absences might be called onanism, and it might be called transcendence; when Baskin's fantasy psychoanalyst has an epiphany — "Internal and external will merge into a continual rhythmic flow!" (OO, 211) — he approximates what Emerson called "spirit." The question is whether the book reduces Vietnam to a solipsist's fantasy or whether the hero's subjectivity is capable of expanding its circle to include the geography of Southeast Asia.

For thirteen of its fourteen chapters, *One on One* never mentions Vietnam, though the book was published in 1970 and is set just before. *Love*, as in Barth's *Lost in the Funhouse* in general, and "The Meneliad" in particular, is the missing referent of the substitutions that begin with onanism. In a series of displacements from love to sex to art, where can war appear — is Vietnam the unrealizable reality that requires us to take *One on One* as nothing but Baskin's Barthian microcosm? Not entirely. The fourteenth chapter reveals retrospectively that Vietnam is a repressed pressure on the book, which finally becomes intolerable. In the cab ride to the game, the radio is on, and the news keeps referring to Vietnam — five separate times. It interrupts the novel as slavery breaks into transcendentalist testimony: the historical fact that defines the necessity and impossibility of individual ideal transcendence.

When Vietnam finally enters the book as its repressed subject, it is only revealed by means of radio reports of succinct meaninglessness: "the Marines were battering an outpost west of Hue"; "in Vietnam today American Marines report the killing of four hundred thirteen Communists"; "the Johnson peace offensive is continuing" (OO, 202, 205, 207). Vietnam appears only as the moment in the book's dialectic when reality has been most displaced by words, when you might as well call a war offensive a peace offensive. If the sports novel exists to make a continuum from art to war, then what basketball as a subject can primarily do for the subgenre is allude to war as the defeat of that mimesis on which the basketball novel depends. The basketball book simply lacks the power of the baseball book to make the missing reality itself its meta-literary impetus. If the basketball novel is the transcendentalist novel of sports literature, if it tracks the progress of the subject from private to public, then Vietnam can only make its appearance as what cannot be assimilated, as what is beyond the possibility of intercourse, as bad publicity.

John Updike cannot afford to submit to this inevitability without a struggle—Updike believes in "the irrepressible combinations of the real!"[19] This sounds Stephen Dedalian but is more Thoreauvian: Updike's books attempt to reconstruct Thoreau's "realometer," in order to measure the true meanness of the world and publish it, or else graph the world's evolution from ants to God. The problem is that between *Rabbit, Run* and *Rabbit Redux*, the world does not merely get meaner—it gets lost. *Present* Vietnam reality in *Rabbit Redux* is as irrecoverable as Rabbit's *past* basketball stardom in *Rabbit, Run*.

The first two Rabbit novels are a parenthesis around the 60s: *Rabbit, Run*, published in 1960, precedes its sequel by eleven years. From the first words of the novel, it looks two ways. It begins with kids at play, kids who will grow up into the 60s but who remind Rabbit of his high school basketball stardom in the 50s. "Boys are playing basketball around a telephone pole with a backboard bolted to it. Legs, shouts. The scrape and snap of Keds on loose alley pebbles seems to catapult their voices high into the moist March air blue above the wires" (*Run*, 7). No wonder that the founding gesture of the book is a description of basketball, the sport of the body panting to be soul. Fundamental reality exactly observed (Keds sneakers) and heard (on loose pebbles) is already elevated by tropes (seems to catapult their voices) toward firmamental reality (into the moist air blue). Rabbit joins the game, and can still *play*: "Then the ball seems to ride up the right lapel of his coat and comes off his shoulder as his knees dip down, and it appears the ball is not going toward the backboard. It was not aimed there. It drops into the circle of the rim, whipping the net with a ladylike whisper. 'Hey!' he shouts in pride" (*Run*, 8).[20] This sets off Rabbit's quest to fill the gap between memory and presence, desire and satisfaction, earth and heaven, by a series of sexual conquests modeled on this first one—both sadistic (whipping the net) and genteel (with a ladylike whisper)—on behalf of Updike's desire for representational fullness.

Rabbit, Run culminates with Rabbit's flight from the cemetery into the woods, which he conceives of as an emptiness to be filled: "He arrives between the arms of the woods and aims for the center of the crescent." This begins a long passage of dense Updikean description, mimicking the enveloping natural density: "Rocks jut up through the blanket of needles, scabby with lichen; collapsed trunks hold intricate claws across his path." Everywhere there are gaps—"places where a hole has been opened up in the roof of evergreen"—but everywhere the gaps are being filled: "berrying bushes and yellow grass grow in a hasty sweet-smelling tumble" into every hole. Rabbit's final vision, it is true, is that he has confronted the abyss and the abyss is Rabbit. "He feels his inside as very real suddenly, a pure blank space in the middle of a dense net" (*Run*, 245–246, 254). The net toward which he has been shooting (the phrase registers ballistic violence) is himself. Perhaps Rabbit can eke a moment of transcendence out of resignation to vacancy—to what Jeremy Larner calls, in a similar display of the invariant basketball metaphor, the "void of freedom" (*DHS*, 186). But the book has depended on continually filling it in—the book lives to the extent that Rabbit can reclaim his basketball prowess.

In *Rabbit Redux*, first paragraph, Updike is still filling in: "the granite curbs starred with mica and the row houses differentiated by speckled bastard sidings and the hopeful small porches with their jigsaw brackets and gray milk-bottle boxes and the sooty gingko trees and the baking curbside cars wince beneath a brilliance like a frozen explosion" (*Redux*, 13). Rabbit will not walk down a street in *Rabbit Redux* without the street getting described, serially, gaplessly, reality turning by means of a crystalline violence, a frozen explosion, into literature. But there is a crisis. *Rabbit Redux* is published in 1971, takes place in 1969; uncrystallized Vietnam is the context.

The problem is considerable, so long as Vietnam comes into the novel the way it comes into *One on One*: Rabbit watches the news. Rabbit has his hawk opinions, Charlie Stavros, lover of Rabbit's wife, has his dove opinions—the war is elsewhere. So Updike determines to "Bring the War Home" (*Redux*, 240). Rabbit has an early vision of his young lover Jill burned "like a napalmed child" by his semen (*Redux*, p. 142); when, finally, Rabbit's illiberal neighbors burn his house (in which he has been harboring not only drop-out Jill but the messianic black man, Skeeter), and Jill is killed, it is no surprise that Skeeter senses that the "war is come home" half-literally (*Redux*, 290). The lesson, as in *The Centaur*, is that sex and war, or sex as war, inhabits every human gesture.

This is, however, facile. Updike knows that for all the Angstrom family proficiency at killing children (one baby drowned, one girl incinerated in two books), they are no Viet Cong or Green Berets. So he introduces a character—Skeeter—who has been in Vietnam; this maneuver brings the war in so baldly that it seems an admission of failure. "Tell us about Vietnam, Skeeter," Rabbit says, at the beginning of Skeeter's informal, familial lecture series. Even this strategy—the novel turning into pseudo-memoir and pseudo-essay, as if granting its generic ineptitude—does not get the job done. The war resists verbal representation: "there is no word" for the peacefulness of the dead; Skeeter realizes, "I'm not doing it justice, I'm selling it short" (*Redux*, 223, 228). Vietnam is an orifice that cannot be filled, rather spews out of itself: when Skeeter begins to describe the war, it is as if "colored fragments pour down toward him through the hole in the ceiling." If the frozen explosion is a lovely metaphor for Clausewitz's absolute war, then the point about Vietnam is that it was all chance and politics and friction. The pouring fragmentation, the unwillingness of the explosion to freeze, is an affront to Updike's mimesis. "It was very complicated, there isn't any net," Skeeter says, "to grab it all in" (*Redux*, 227). Which means it is not susceptible to a pure shooter's prowess, that is, Updike's.

Updike's attempt to get the war integrated into the novel seems increasingly desperate—"to bring the war home," he resorts to purely verbal methods. The name Charlie multiplies. It is the nickname of the Cong, the designation of Skeeter's company in Vietnam, Skeeter's term of abuse for all whites including Rabbit, and the name of Rabbit's wife's Greek lover: it applies to Asians, blacks, mainstream Protestant whites, and ethnic whites, from Vietnam to America. But the war, for Rabbit, is what he has irrevocably missed. For Updike, consequently, it is a sign of the Protestant God—everything that Updike cannot contain. His purely verbal methods for bringing the war into literature fail to the extent that they are purely verbal. Vietnam falsifies his theorem that war is not essentially different from peace.

Vietnam is what Updike wants sport to represent, but the metaphor is always in trouble. The competition of Rabbit and Charlie Stavros for Rabbit's wife is described alternately, as if indifferently, in basketball and war terms. Basketball terms: "Now [Rabbit] sees [Charlie] as a type he never liked, the competitor. The type that sits on the bench doing the loudmouth bit until the coach sends him in with a play or with orders to foul" (*Redux*, 160). War terms: Rabbit says, "You intervened, not me." Charlie replies, "I didn't intervene, I performed a rescue." Rabbit rejoins, "That's what all us hawks say" (*Redux*, 161). The idea is that the two metaphors interchangeably render the mortal competition of daily life; if this is true, then doves are closet hawks. On the other hand, sport is precisely what prevents daily life from always replicating war. "In a room obliquely off the main room, a pool table: colored boys all arms and legs spidering around the idyllic green felt. The presence of a game reassures Rabbit. Where any game is being played a hedge exists against fury" (*Redux*, 107). Scared Rabbit is a closet dove.

Updike's funhouse menagerie of hawks, doves, rabbits, and spiders—Updike's mobile taxonomy of the ambiguity of sport—permits him to pretend he has a way of bringing the war home and to acknowledge that he does not. As basketball fades from this novel along with Rabbit's skill (all that is left of his prowess is his ludicrously old-fashioned set shot), Updike's confidence that his technique is adequate to the world fades pari passu. Sport had been his way of making contact with middle-American reality; but indescribable Vietnam *is* America. "Man don't like Vietnam, he don't like America," Skeeter says, and Rabbit seconds it, in rare agreement (*Redux*, 232). The full extent of the tragedy is that for Updike mortality is the inability to describe. He feels reality slipping from him the way Rabbit feels the diminution of his basketball skills: as death. If the baseball novel portrays Vietnam as what is masked in the turn to self-referentiality, the basketball novel is suited for a passing reference. For writers like Updike, that was the sort of dying they could do during Vietnam.

Football, the Hunt

Lewis Mumford's comparison of mass sports to war by virtue of their regimentation, non-spontaneity, and nationalism seems peculiarly fitted to football;[21] mass sports, he believes, rank only above war among the "least effective reactions against the machine"—which is to say that the reaction may be so weak as to constitute replication.[22] A black football player in Peter Gent's *North Dallas Forty* who seems to have been reading Mumford posts this sign: "MODERN MAN NO LONGER FEELS, HE MERELY REACTS. CREATIVITY HAS BEEN REPLACED BY CONFORMITY. LIFE HAS LOST ITS SPONTANEITY: WE ARE BEING MANIPULATED BY OUR MACHINES. THE INDIVIDUAL IS DEAD" (*NDF*, 158). Football—with its long bombs, blitzes, trenches, etc.—is a verbal compendium of twentieth-century war, so that the football novel ought to be the noncombatant's Vietnam novel.

The neat symmetry of the sports metaphor in terms of literary effects is simple to complete. If the baseball novel is meta-literary, the basketball novel anxiously literary, then the football novel is anti-literary. Language is in retreat: Billy Clyde Puckett, in Dan Jenkins' *Semi-Tough*, speaks of his "palatial apartment" until the adjective means as little to us as it does to him. Gary Harkness, the narrator of Don DeLillo's *End Zone*, stares at the phrase "When the going gets tough the tough get going" until "all meaning faded. . . . It was a sinister thing to discover at such an age, that words can escape their meaning" (*EZ*, 17). The football novel ought not to be quite a novel. *Semi-Tough* is supposedly spoken into a tape recorder, and *Why Are We In Vietnam?*, the apotheosis of the football novel, partly pretends to be a tape recording of its narrator DJ's "brain in the deep of its mysterious unwindings" (*IV*, 24). Apparently the football anti-novel sacrifices its own literariness to capture the Vietnam era.

And yet—for all the despair of the finest football novelist, Don DeLillo, that words are losing their meaning, nevertheless he refuses the available series of equations above: football = war = the death of language. Rather, he presents as the problem of novelists the appalling purchase that football and war in fact have on language. They are simultaneously the arenas in which (1) obsolete language is revived, and (2) contemporary language is invented. In facing this scandal, DeLillo brings all the dilemmas of the 60s sports novel to an extreme paradoxical acuteness.

The first point recalls Fussell: war and football still cannot get along without the vocabulary World War I should have outmoded. When a football player gets killed in an automobile accident, "a local minister called him a fallen warrior"—the pre-World War I name for a military corpse. "Death is the best soil for cliché," Harkness explains (*EZ*, 69–70); he might have added that wartime clichés are superior for all irruptions of death. Nor can we conclude that the obsolete vocabulary of ancient wars is inappropriate to modern wars, so long as it is dead language that men are dying for: "It was easier to die than admit that words could lose their meaning" (*EZ*, 54).

More insidiously, war diction is not merely passé (though revived) but also à la mode. The field of atomic war generates its own vocabulary, which is not without aesthetic charm. "I became fascinated," Harkness confesses, "by words and phrases like thermal hurricane, overkill, circular error probability, post-attack environment, stark deterrence, dose-rate contours, kill-ratio, spasm war. Pleasure in these words" (*EZ*, 21). The pleasure is uniquely satisfying because the language refers, at once, to the grossest conceivable eventuality and to no referent at all—thus Derrida characterizes nuclear language as "fabulously textual." (The aesthetic pleasure might well be in the vertiginous confrontations of hard, often Anglo-Saxon and immaterial, often Latinate, terms: stark deterrence, kill-ratio.) Football coaches have the same Adamic power as generals: the coach is the "maker of plays, the name-giver. We were his chalk-scrawls" (*EZ*, 118, 135). Generals and football coaches, together, "reinvent the language" (*EZ*, 85). It is not an irony that the Texas football school of this novel is Logos College.

Observe the darker reason that football books have to be anti-novels: not so much in imitation of the death of language in football and war—in wargames—as in obeisance to the preemption of language, traditional and contemporary, by wargames. The question is how a novelist can maneuver with respect to an invasive diction. DeLillo's preliminary answer is a 250-page allusion to silence. When we first hear about the late President of Logos College, who "was a man of reason," "who cherished the very word," we assume it is a joke that "unfortunately he was mute" (*EZ*, 7). Not entirely. Harkness's project is a sort of non-verbal oneness with the Texas environment, which, toward the end of the novel, he glimpses: "Beyond the window was that other world, unsyllabled, snow lifted in the wind, swirling up, massing within the lightless white day, falling toward the sky" (*EZ*, 189). Thirty-eight syllables, as it happens, to suggest zero.

At least one of the things DeLillo leaves to the silence must be suspected. DeLillo never mentions Vietnam, never names it directly. One player's girlfriend spends a night with a soldier on leave (from "Nam"), and the black star of the team explains why his barren room must have a radio: "The place where words are recycled. The place where villages are burned. That's my Indochina" (*EZ*, 239). Vietnam only exists in the novel as recycled words, twice nicknamed in this book about naming.

Has it been haunting *End Zone*—burning villages veiled in prose—or has the book successfully evaded it? What is the quality of the silence about Vietnam? If readers of this chapter have been seduced to conclude that it is unnecessary to mention Vietnam because football allegorizes it, they have been misled in just the way that DeLillo's readers may be. DeLillo does the reader the courtesy of clarifying the matter twice, in the words of the book's two most convincing theorists. First, Harkness himself: "The exemplary spectator is the person who understands that sport is a benign illusion, the illusion that order is possible. . . . The exemplary spectator has his occasional lusts, but not for warfare, hardly at all for that. No, it's detail he needs—impressions, colors, statistics, patterns, mysteries, numbers, idioms, symbols. Football, more than other sports, fulfills this need. . . . Here is not just order but civilization." And the eccentric Professor Zapalac, pure left-wing, is nevertheless attracted to General Sherman's tautology: "I reject the notion of football as warfare. Warfare is warfare" (*EZ*, 111–112, 164). Football has been aligned with nuclear wargames—the naming of the patterns of apocalypse—not war.

Quite as much as the baseball novelist who writes during Vietnam about World War II, and exactly like the baseball novelist who writes during Vietnam about an interior Armageddon, DeLillo avoids the war he might have invoked—though as a football novelist rather than a baseball novelist, he does not reinvoke the war as what he has eschewed. His position as a football novelist turns out to be unique not because he can approach nearer to Vietnam through the nature of his sport, rather because he cannot gauge the passing of reference or replace description with self-reference: the assumption among baseball and basketball novelists but not permitted among football novelists is that reality had formerly belonged to novelists like themselves. The football novelist, DeLillo suggests, is not allowed this belief or the consequent nostalgia or panic.

DeLillo is so admirably determined not to claim that he feels all the death of Vietnam in the death of his own art (as metaphorized, elsewhere, by the demise of pre-war baseball and 50s white basketball) that he makes the surprise gesture of identifying football *with* art—with impressions, patterns, mysteries, idioms, symbols—though not with representation. At the belligerent end of the spectrum from art to war that sport makes available, DeLillo tries to win it all back—football, sport, and at least imaginary war—though not Vietnam. His anti-novel is poised to assimilate the imaginary order of football and wargames into the passion for silence that their racket had seemed to inspire: the book's final twist is that their verbal inventiveness seems like DeLillo's a tribute to an unspeakable ideal, Clausewitz's absolute war, war removed from time. In the process, however, Vietnam, which baseball and basketball novelists manage paradoxically to display, paradoxically disappears. DeLillo accepts literary complicity in football and World War III but not Vietnam.

Norman Mailer's *Why Are We in Vietnam?* begins in Texas—which is the setting of every football novel I have named—and features as the father of the narrator one Rusty Jethroe, third-string football All-American in 1936 and 1937, current member of the Gridiron Club, the Dallas Cowboy Turtle Creek Cheering and Chowder, the TCU Boosters, and the SMU Boosters, who challenges son DJ to his first Oedipal showdown by means of a head-to-head running-tackling competition, and who takes DJ on the Alaskan adventure that is the subject of the book and the scene of their second Oedipal duel, on the premise that "the great white athlete is being superseded by the great black athlete" (*IV*, 110). *Why Are We in Vietnam?* starts where football novels leave off, and heads for Indochina.

Does it get there? On the final page of the anti-novel, Vietnam is mentioned twice, and the title seems decisive. If the title indicates that the Alaskan bear hunt is an allegory of Vietnam, then we learn that the war is a product of patricidal filial devotion, homoerotic homophobia, Negrophile Negrophobia, pious diabolism—each oxymoron indicative of white masculinity defeated and enraged—and the love of technology serving bestiality and anal aggressiveness turning into phallic aggression. That summary will have to serve as all the diagnosis Vietnam can get in this essay. The point here is that by virtue of these contradictions, the book portrays Vietnam as the quintessence of football—patricidal and filial, homophobic and homoerotic, Negrophile and Negrophobe, mechanical and primeval—as portrayed in all football novels.

But the book is not unambiguously an allegory of Vietnam, nor is the hunt unambiguously an extension of sport. Vietnam satisfies urges not satisfied by the hunt, which satisfies hungers not assuaged by football. The relation of the three activities might still be simple enough: they might be charted as increasingly hysterical attempts of white men to discharge primal instincts when the most sacred rituals of masculinity are conducted by blacks. If this were true, we could have the mediation of the football novel and the Vietnam novel accomplished neatly enough. At the last moment of *Why Are We in Vietnam?*, however, something peculiar happens. DJ announces that Tex and he are "off to see the Wizard in Vietnam"—first mention of that country and war. DJ immediately adds: "Unless, that is, I'm a black-ass cripple Spade and sending from Harlem" (*IV*, 208). This remark adverts to one of the book's occasional counter-suggestions: that Mailer is not ventriloquizing a WASP adventure inspired by fantasies about blacks but a black analysis or fantasy concerning WASPS. Deduce that Vietnam was generated out of the fictions that whites and blacks produce about each other—what would that mean? The crippled black—not only not going off to Vietnam but apparently not a daunting sexual threat—is inventing a white paranoia about blacks that only Vietnam can pacify?

It is not clear—and Mailer in an introduction admits he is not sure about his intention. We do not know what we need to know: is the bear hunt a white adventure or black fantasy of a white adventure? Will the bear hunt and Vietnam differ in the magnitude or the quality of their violence? A deeper obscurity, perhaps, is why the novel seeks to explain Vietnam in terms of the hankering of two white kids to fight, when white kids mainly did not volunteer. The book does not culminate in Rusty's love of Vietnam on behalf of the corporation (only DJ and Tex crave it) or any black's going off to the war (since if DJ is a black, he is a crippled black). The book was originally intended, Mailer tells us, not as preliminary to DJ and Tex's volunteering for Vietnam but to their metamorphosis into Mansonesque terrorists in Provincetown. It cannot be assumed that the switch has been successfully made.

The best reading of Mailer is that the book was not written to represent

Vietnam, rather, in his introductory terms, as "a diversion in the fields of dread" (*IV*, 5). This might mean that it is not so much about Vietnam as against it—that the hunt, which culminates in the pursuit of the bear by DJ and Tex without rifles, is not at all what leads them to Vietnam, but should have prevented that outcome. One mystery of the book's construction is the two-year blank interval between the hunt and the narration of the story followed by the decision to go to the war—possibly the solution is that it is not so much the hunt as the impossibility of reabsorption into Dallas society after the hunt, the paucity of appropriate Texan rituals rather than the Alaskan ritual, that drives DJ and Tex to war. The hunt might very well precede Vietnam not as a preface to it but as an inadequate prophylactic against it, as ritual violence that fails to ward off unleashed and unsanctified violence. The book might be taken as an attempt to redeem that failure: DJ and Tex are sent to Vietnam by Mailer not as a realistic appraisal of who went to Vietnam and why, but as a symbolic sacrifice the homeopathic power of which is intended to prevent our technological, anti-metaphoric, profane commitment to the war.

Can it be said that the allegory of the book is precisely *not* of Vietnam?

> We will never know if primitive artists painted their caves to show a representation, or whether the moving hand was looking to placate the forces above and the forces below. Sometimes, I think the novelist fashions a totem just as much as an aesthetic, and his real aim, not even known necessarily to himself, is to create a diversion in the fields of dread, a sanctuary in some of the arenas of magic. . . . By such logic, the book before you is a totem, not empty of amulets for the author against curses, static, and the pervasive malignity of our electronic air. (*IV*, 4–5)

And against Vietnam, of which Mailer does not "show a representation." If Veblen is right that predatory activity shades off from war to the hunt to games seamlessly, then this essay exists to reverse the perspective and climb from (tennis to) baseball to basketball to football to the hunt back to war. But the misdirection of the 60s sports novel provides that the closer you get to Vietnam the more it is distanced and withheld: people die violently in baseball novels all the time, almost never in football novels. We grasp Vietnam in sports novels, if at all, as the thing that made novels seem less powerful, less representative, than ever before. On the other hand, we might value the Vietnam sports novel as verbal homeopathy. As postmodernist novels incline toward the (modernist) "sanctuary" (as Mailer says) of textuality, textuality itself expands, so that the world is threatened, as if by book-burning. Mailer's Vietnam book reads the sports novel tradition that arrives at DeLillo, in which verbal bliss shadows the ecstasy of the contemplation of nuclear Armageddon. The homeopathic method is the converse of the metonymic method: by adding death to baseball as the formula of the baseball novel, and literary life to football as the formula of the football novel, sports novelists of the 60s brought the play of signifiers as near as possible to wargames as a diversion in the fields of dread.

Play, Part II

(1938–1939)   "A happier age than ours once made bold to call our species by the name of *Homo Sapiens*."[23] So wrote Huizinga, in Leyden, in June 1938. The sentence, the first one of his distinguished study, *Homo Ludens*, makes sense in its own terms; the problem is that it comes close to making nonsense of the rest of the book. It might seem equally appropriate to open the book with the declaration, "Only a happier age than ours would make bold to call our species by the name of *Homo Ludens*," in which case the book would last one sentence before folding. What would justify, in 1938, a book on Homo Ludens any better than a book on Homo Sapiens? The answer seems to be that by 1938 no one could claim that we had ever been, essentially, sapient; in 1938, Huizinga proposes that we had always been ludic.

The hypothesis makes the urgency of the book comprehensible. That the book was personally pressing is unmysterious: Huizinga was writing it while Hitler was preparing his assault on Europe; Huizinga was translating it into English and adding material after Hitler had invaded Poland; he was in fact killed in the invasion of Holland. But the book feels historically and politically urgent: "To fill in all the gaps in my knowledge beforehand was out of the question for me. I had to write now, or not at all. And I wanted to write" (*HL*, foreword). The sense of crisis in the early prose is despite the conceivable reservation that nothing could be more irrelevant to Hitler's Europe than a scholarly, humane, civilized, generous study of the play principle in civilization. Huizinga believed, however, that Nazism was attractive precisely because its brutality was masked as play.

The two elaborations of play that Huizinga cares most about are poetry and war. Play is so thoroughly beautiful that aesthetics represents the single threat to the autonomy of the category (*HL*, 7). And poetry is still, of all human activities including all other arts, the one that "remains fixed in the play-sphere where it was born" (*HL*, 119). The detecting of play in war is more difficult and controversial. Nevertheless: "who can deny that in all these concepts—challenge, danger, contest, etc.—we are very close to the play-sphere" (*HL*, 40). Shakespeare's Agincourt—a sacred event (this is indicated but not defined by its dedication to St. Crispin and St. Crispian), ruled off in time and space, where an insult is rejoined and glory is an object—might have been Huizinga's best demonstration that "Play is battle and battle is play" (*HL*, 41). It was the centrality to chivalric culture of tournaments and jousting that inspired *Homo Ludens* in the first place (*HL*, 104).

War is injuring and war is contest; clearly what is playful about war is exclusively the latter aspect. War is "very close to the play-sphere" insofar as it is "challenge, danger, contest." It is life conceived agonistically that best brings war into contact with play and hence with art: "On numerous Greek vases we can see that a contest of armed men is characterized as an agon by the presence of the flute-players who accompany it. At the Olympic games there were duels fought to the death" (*HL*, 49). If Burckhardt believed that a civilization, like the Greek, had no need of games if it had war, then Huizinga endeavors, on a Greek inspiration, to make the Scarrian idea plausible that a civilization has no particular need of war if every aspect of peace is thoroughly agonized.

Huizinga, however, was writing at the worst moment for proving that theorem. History seemed, in fact, to be moving in the contrary direction: civilization as play reached its summit in the eighteenth century, Huizinga comes to judge, and has been in decline ever since. This is doubtless the reason his book can seem zealous and strained. Huizinga is forced to be militant in his defense of play in this degraded and sobering epoch. The book is intellectually, politely aggressive and expansive. Play takes over, in successive chapters, law and war and metaphysics and poetry and myth and philosophy and art, until Huizinga finally surveys all of "Western civilization *Sub Specie Ludi*." I of course do not mean to identify Huizinga with the brutal expansionism that killed him. Nevertheless, he seems obliged to write as if conquering all the territory, domain by domain, that Nazism was devastating from the opposite side.

Another way to say it is that the conceptual uniting of war, play, and art is homeopathically close to what the Nazis were doing. In skirting that possibility, Huizinga is admittedly confused. As against German political theory, which describes the progression from peace to war as "the serious development of an emergency" (*HL*, 208), Huizinga argues that "it is not war that is serious, but peace." He immediately adds, "War and everything to do with it remains fast in the daemonic and magical bonds of play" (*HL*, 209). But that cannot be precisely put, because to nominate something as play, in this book, had never been to dismiss it as unserious. Yet: "we cannot deny that modern warfare has lapsed into the old agonistic attitude of playing at war for the sake of prestige and glory" (*HL*, 210). From sentence to sentence, it is not clear where Huizinga is going to come out.

Huizinga resorts to a desperate strategem. The Nazis are not playful after all; they are puerile. In some ways this demarcation makes perfect sense. War is ludic insofar as it is rule-bound (countries should declare war before invading other countries [*HL*, 208]), agonistic insofar as the enemy is respected (*HL*, 209), aesthetic if the political motive is secondary (*HL*, 210). In all these respects the Nazis were not playing. Yet Hitler's preference for the gamble is reminiscent of the play spirit (*HL*, 210). Huizinga might also have mentioned other facets of his appeal, like the excessiveness of his demagoguery. The only solution is to assert that the Nazis were playing at play, playing the "play-concept of war false" (*HL*, 210). The play element must not "be a false seeming, a masking of political purposes behind the illusion of genuine play-forms" (*HL*, 211).

This seems to me *ad hoc*: Huizinga admits that the "puerilism" of contemporary life had once seemed to him a "play-function."

> I have now come to a different conclusion. . . . [I]f our modern puerilism were genuine play we ought to see civilization returning to the great archaic forms of recreation where ritual, style and dignity are in perfect unison. The spectacle of a society rapidly goose-stepping into helotry is, for some, the dawn of the millennium. We believe them to be in error. (*HL*, 206)

The criterion of playfulness seems to me unmeetable: to rule out Nazis, you would have to rule out everything. In another context, the goose-step would not have seemed a despicable emblem; it would have seemed a genuine play element itself.

Huizinga has been playing a dangerous game. The game is intellectual homeopathy, and taken in enormous doses, the cure makes acquaintance with the disease. Huizinga wanted to carry sacred art into the domain of war, partly to condemn modern war for its apostasy. The line proved impossible to draw cleanly. Possibly Huizinga should have stuck by an earlier formulation, rather atypical of him, but typical at least of the dilemma war causes him.

> The noble life is seen as an exhilarating game of courage and honour. Unfortunately, even in archaic surroundings war with its grimness and bitterness offers but scant occasion for this noble game to become a reality. Bloody violence cannot be caught to any great extent in truly noble form; hence the game can only be fully experienced and enjoyed as a social and aesthetic fiction. That is why the spirit of society ever again seeks escape in fair imaginings of the life heroic, which is played out in the ideal sphere of honour, virtue, and beauty. (*HL*, 101)

That war is contest does not mean that war is beautiful, because war is injuring. The play-spirit does not really connect art and war; art *imagines* that the play-spirit connects art and war. The last two sentences of Huizinga's passage add up to this: because war is not beautiful, society fancies that war is beautiful. The beauty of war is a fiction, Homer's Athena's illusion. But to admit that is to concede that the book is less powerful than it had seemed; insofar as it made war beautiful it played playing false; the play-spirit does not provide a measure against which to condemn Nazi warfare, because the play-spirit had never really informed war. Homeopathy can endorse Nazi hypocrisy if it imports the play spirit where it does not naturally belong. If, on the other hand, war had ever been playful, it might, to that extent, be play for Nazis also.

(1984) The most sensational and influential section of Jacques Derrida's "No Apocalypse, Not Now (full speed ahead, seven missiles, seven missives)"[24] is the third missive, in which Derrida describes nuclear warfare as "fabulously textual" (*D*, 23), by which he primarily indicates that it exists only, until it occurs, as literature. (No actual war has ever been so out of proportion to previous wars as to make anticipation thoroughly imaginary; no other anticipated war ever inspired so much imagining.) Derrida of course is not attempting to make the phenomenon (the imagining) harmless: "For the 'reality' of the nuclear age and the fable of nuclear war are perhaps distinct, but they are not two separate things" (D, 23). This means that the voluminous literature of nuclear warfare — in the absence of any previous war that helpfully foreshadows it — is the sole guide of the actual diplomatic, technological, and military gamesmanship that has real and immediate as well as hypothetical effects.

This is the fullest textualization of warfare in history — possibly the textualization prevents anything beyond it. Derrida goes on to show how it is not merely that military affairs have been textualized; textuality has always, prefiguratively, been approaching nuclear war (D, 26–28). Since the seventeenth century, since the opening of the Age of Reason, literature has apprehended its own contingency; because its relationship to any referent is always creative, literature is exactly what could not survive a nuclear war. The reasoning here is a little odd, since Derrida has been considering *total* nuclear war, the thing that *nothing* human could survive; and he is not sure that literature's relation to the referent is peculiar. The tactic of positing a nuclear remainder that discriminates literature from non-literature is a thought experiment that might be restated this way. Suppose that only two people, a man and a woman of childbearing age, survived the war. It would be possible to fancy, in the next pulse of human history, Archimedean, Newtonian, and Einsteinian physics, but not Dante, Shakespeare, or Tolstoy. This may or may not be true; but since the seventeenth century, literature has conceived it to be true, that is, considered that it was uniquely contingent, susceptible to absolute annihilation.[25]

Though you might assume that this eventuality would be literature's horror, Derrida suspects that literature, like Hawthorne's Coverdale, longs for apocalypse: "Who can swear that our unconscious is not expecting this? dreaming of it, desiring it?" (D, 23). This is not, however, as necessary to his argument as the theorem that we (humanists) have been *depending* on it, at least insofar as we cherish literature, distinct from science, for its freedom. Derrida brings war to literature and literature to war, thus his running series of meta-tropes: what "weapons of irony" are appropriate to a conference on "nuclear criticism"? What would be its characteristic "arguments and its armaments, its modes of persuasion or intimidation" (D, 21)? The title — "seven missiles, seven missives" — turns out to be a kind of Heideggerian analogy, with overtones from Revelation, of the way that writing and weaponry are projected into the world.

What is the point of this assimilation? It is not to domesticate the possibility of absolute holocaust; it is not to create a bad conscience among humanists; it is not to win a Hellish glamour for literary theory. The answer emerges from three passages of Derrida's text that adumbrate his surprise ending.

First:

> For the "reality" of the nuclear age and the fable of nuclear war are perhaps
> distinct, but they are not two separate things. It is the war (in other words
> the fable) that triggers this fabulous war effort, this senseless capitalization of
> sophisticated weaponry, this speed race in search of speed, this crazy precipi-
> tation which, through techno-science, through all the techno-scientific inven-
> tiveness that it motivates, structures not only the army, diplomacy, politics,
> but the whole of the human *socius* today, everything that is named by the old
> words culture, civilization, *Bildung, scholè, paideia.* "Reality," let's say the
> encompassing institution of the nuclear age, is constructed by the fable . . . .
> (D, 23)

This is a fabulator's absolutism (like DeLillo's) in the image of absolute war,
a step beyond Huizinga's imperial playfulness in the image of imperialistic
puerilism. Nevertheless, it is perhaps less absolute than it appears. Derrida
first declares that civilization is "structured" by the fable, then that "reality"
is "constructed" by the fable, which is not quite to say that there is only the
fable. Otherwise, the words "senseless" and "crazy" would be impossible.
It is not clear to me how the words are possible in a civilization even only
"structured" by the fable, unless it is licit to say that a thesis structures its
antithesis. I doubt that that is what Derrida means either.

Second:

> No, nuclear war is not *only* fabulous because one can *only* talk about it, but
> because the extraordinary *sophistication* of its technologies—which are also
> the technologies of delivery, sending, dispatching, of the missile in general, of
> mission, missive, emission, and transmission, like all *technè*—the extraor-
> dinary sophistication of these technologies coexists, cooperates in an essen-
> tial way with sophistry, psycho-rhetoric, and the most cursory, the most ar-
> chaic, the most crudely opinionated psychagogy, the most vulgar psychology.
> (D, 24)

What makes nuclear war fabulous here is its combination of sophistication
and vulgarity, but I am not certain why. Derrida goes on to explicate the
passage as if he had only said that technology has to be mixed with *doxa,*
with opinion and opinion about opinion. In the passage itself, "missiles" is
aligned with "missives" in the technology part of the equation—Derrida's
missive is *all* sophistication—and is distinguished from not merely *doxa* but
vulgar *doxa.* Once again, terms of opprobrium imply that there is a structural principle in the culture (distinguishing sophistication from vulgarity)
after nuclear warfare (which does not recognize the distinction) has totally
structured it.

Third:

> I am thus choosing, as you have already observed, the genre or rhetorical
> form of tiny atomic nuclei (in the process of fission or division in an uninter-
> ruptible chain) which I shall arrange or rather which I shall project toward
> you, like tiny inoffensive missiles: in a discontinuous, more or less haphazard
> fashion. (D, 21)

If the text is itself a fission bomb, why "inoffensive"? This is all the more surprising in that a later passage, again associating missives and missiles, is careful not to suggest that that association reduces bombs "to the dull inoffensiveness that some would naively attribute to books. It recalls (exposes, explodes) that which, in writing, always includes the power of a death machine" (*D*, 29). If Derrida's paper was inoffensive merely insofar as no one was killed by it, he has made the rhetorical mistake of exculpating literature just on the brink of implicating it. I am tempted to believe that Derrida means "the opposite of offensive," that is, "defensive." But he does not say "defensive," nor does his essay care about any offensive-defensive distinction in the discourse of nuclear strategy. Perhaps he is being modest.

Why does Derrida keep exposing the attraction of nuclear war and textuality and then keep, in effect, denying it? The answer comes, at long last, in the movement from the fourth to the fifth missive. In the fourth, Derrida isolates the "destruction" in "deconstruction" (*D*, 27); he reveals deconstruction to be the theory of the nuclear age, which is equal to the epoch of literature. "Literature belongs to the nuclear age by virtue of the performative character of its relation to the referent." Then comes the surprise of the apothegm of the fifth missive: "*But we do not believe, such is the other version or the other side of the same paradox, in any thing except the nuclear referent*" (*D*, 28).

The referent repressed by literary history, repressed in order that literature might have a history, is absolute disappearance. Insofar as we had thought of deconstruction as attention to the free play of signfiers forming links with signifieds that turn into signifiers, we had thought of writing as unbounded. Even death could be absorbed into this formulation, since death can be denigrated to a significant event by survivors. But insofar as literature is essentially contingent, it always points to annihilation, the singularity at the end of signification: "The only 'subject' of all posssible literature, of all posssible criticism, its only ultimate and a-symbolic referent, unsymbolizable, even unsignifiable; this is, if not the nuclear age, if not the nuclear catastrophe, at least that toward which nuclear discourse and the nuclear symbolic *are still beckoning*: the remainderless and a-symbolic destruction of literature." In making annihilation the referent of literature, Derrida does not bring it into or up against literature: it is literature's only referent because it is "that unassimilable wholly other"; the relation is one of "incommensurability" (*D*, 28).

From this vantage, we have to return to all Derrida's puns of Ars and Mars and reread them. Literature is said to depend on "a project of stockpiling, of building up an objective archive over and above any traditional oral base," as well as on the legalities of authorship (*D*, 26). These two conditions define contingency: literary history is a development that moves not by closer approximations of the world but by the accumulation of unrepeatable, individually authored, events. What one picks out of this particular formulation, of course, is the term "stockpiling." It is not immediately clear what to make of it—until the revelation that literature aims at what it can never, by accumulation, annihilate: annihilation. "Stockpiling" indicates something outside of literature, more powerful than literature, wholly incommensurable with it, unsignifiable by it, but undermining it so definitively that you might as well say it is underwriting it. Literature stockpiles texts because it is radically vulnerable to destruction by stockpiled weapons. Derrida's logic is the logic of homeopathy ("strategic maneuvers to assimilate the unassimilable" [*D*, 28]): every move of deconstruction, as the theory best adapted to the precariousness of literature, is an attempt to reveal the resemblance of health and illness, up to and including the end of death and life at once. Derrida calls nuclear catastrophe the "absolute *pharmakon*" (*D*, 24). The logic of homeopathy turns poison into cure.

Stockpiling is the condition, Derrida says, of literature—that is, of writing—"over and above any traditional oral base"; epic is always excluded from what Derrida means by "literature" as such, not participating in its radical historical contingency. This book began with the insufficiency of oral poetry to modern, post-Trojan, war; literature is not so much sufficient to it as a progressive admission of its own ineptitude. At the near end of this epoch, the most admired literature has so lost the world as to resemble a technology for sacrificing it, just as the nuclear technology for sacrificing it almost dissolves entirely into literature. That is only to assert that literature as play, as beautiful contingency in the fields of fate, seeks to resemble what threatens it infinitely.

7

Family Likenesses:
War in Women's Words

The Civil War and Reality

Little Realism

What is the Civil War doing in the first volume of *Little Women*?[1] (1) Conceivably it is there as an autobiographical *donnée*. But Louisa May Alcott worked as a nurse for six weeks, while her father Bronson Alcott did not serve; in the novel, Mr. March does his duty, while Jo domesticates. Alcott defended the novel's realism as more than verisimilitude, rather as truth, so that the largest exception is an embarrassment, almost a metaphysical puzzle: "Mr. March did not go to the war, but Jo did."[2] *Mr. March* did not? *Jo* did? The Civil War causes the farthest straying from autobiography in a book that claims to alter nothing essential but names. (2) Conceivably it is there as a historical given. But the historical Civil War, as opposed to the March family's personal Civil War, hardly exists in *Little Women*: Mr. March falls ill; John Brooke, Meg's betrothed, is wounded without consequence between volumes; the family almost does not know anyone who was killed. So much for the national tragedy.

(3) A more sophisticated mistake is that the Civil War exists in *Little Women* for the sake of a female fantasy of liberated matriarchy. There is truth to this, but not enough. You do not need the Civil War to rid the Marches of Mr. March, the family's one male. Mr. March is at home for all of the second volume, but his absence is more pronounced. You might say that Volume 2 is a superior fantasy, because it proves that war is not crucial to dethroning patriarchs.

My solution to the riddle is that the Civil War, or rather its looming absence, is necessary to the disciplining of Jo, and that the name of the discipline is "realism." The Civil War is necessary so that Alcott can quarantine Jo from it. This is how Alcott keeps her novel "realistic," and it is not far distant from how the "realists" kept their novels "realistic." It is true that Alcott, unlike the realists, wanted to serve in the Civil War and did serve; but she tames Jo's extravagant enthusiasm for combat, so that the Civil War can be sequestered from her narrative as from the realists'. The corollary seemed inevitable that realism would depend on an extravagant commitment to apolitical piety, submission, littleness, and peace. That literary history does not agree proves that the male form of war evasion is the accredited—the sufficiently aggressive—form.

If one way to understand American literary history is as a negotiation with the history of war, then a final chapter on women's writing doubtless constitutes a marginalization. However, the tradition is already marginal with respect to war; the canon, insofar as it is an artifact of historical belligerency, is an argument for the priority of literary history to combat history with respect to which it would have seemed entirely secondary. Harold Bloom has remarked that feminism poses the first radical challenge to traditional literary history, because it would establish a pedigree that does not descend from Homer.[3] If Homer, however, inaugurates literary history as a problematization of the relation of war and beauty, then his descendents include not only Hemingway and Herr but also Cather and Wharton and Bobbie Ann Mason and Maxine Hong Kingston. At the head of the American female branch of the genealogy is *Little Women*, an inverse *Iliad* and *Odyssey*: the militant family awaits the return home of its (pious and unwarlike) patriarch from war. An inverse "Rip Van Winkle": the family makes use of war to free itself of its lovable ne'er-do-well. An inverse "realism": instead of an ersatz militancy, the book exhibits a real belligerency that is repressed.

Of the four March daughters, only two count. Meg is a vacuous figure; Amy is more vivaciously commonplace, but is still too mediocre to matter. Jo and Beth, however, are so close to the pulse of the book that you could almost say that Jo is the author of *Little Women* and Beth *is Little Women.* Yet—here is the mystery to be elucidated—Jo and Beth are more antagonistic than complementary, as if author and authored were antitheses. Beth's demise is the triumph of domesticity, and going to war, the only method Jo can imagine of getting out of the house, someone's house, is life itself. "I'm dying to go and fight with papa, and I can only stay at home and knit like a poky old woman," Jo fumes (*LW*, 10), falsifying in the process what her father is doing. (He is not fighting; he is a chaplain.) What is being half-repressed is the sexual reversal. When Meg says that "it was so splendid in father to go as a chaplain when he was too old to be draughted, and not strong enough for a soldier," Jo exclaims impulsively, "Don't I wish I could go as a drummer." This again comes too close to the real-life reversal, so Jo has second thoughts: "or a nurse, so I could be near him and serve him" (*LW*, 15). Though even nursing would be a feminist gesture (it was widely considered too difficult and indelicate for women, so that male nurses outnumbered female five to one),[4] Jo does not really want to nurse, and she does not really want to drum. "I always wanted to do the killing," she

almost says. Actually, she says, "I always wanted to do the killing part" —
she is contemplating a March family production of *Macbeth* (*LW*, 14).

The opposite of killing is dying; Mr. March gets sick during the war,
but Beth gets sicker. It is because Mrs. March is away tending to her
husband that Beth increases her contact with the poor, among whom she
contracts the disease that fatally ruins her health. You might have thought
that that makes Beth the one Civil War casualty of the novel; she is a
casualty, certainly, but a casualty of peace. Her death is caused by not
going to war, where Mrs. March does not fall ill. Beth represents the
"home-peace" of the book (*LW*, 10), the "sweet home-peace" that Jo is
always disturbing, "march[ing] off to bed," for example, refusing "over-
tures of peace" from feuding sisters (*LW*, 97). "Peace . . . is a true Celestial
City," Mrs. March teaches her daughters (*LW*, 18), which begins the process by which Beth's dying is made tantamount to her pacification. When
Beth starts to die, her "face looked so pale and peaceful in its utter repose,
that Jo felt no desire to weep or lament" (*LW*, 233). When she finally dies,
her "face [is] so full of painless peace, that those who loved it best smiled
through their tears, and thanked God that Beth was well at last" (*LW*,
514). After Beth dies, she is a "peaceful presence" in the household (*LW*,
556).

To be ultimately domesticated (a presence in the house forever) = to
die = to be at peace. No wonder war is attractive. And all these equivalents
are summed as "littleness." "Shy little Beth" makes friends (*LW*, 226); Amy
prays for her "gentle little sister" (*LW*, 244). Beth is the Little Woman par
excellence, the only one of the women who *stays* little. "Go then, my little
Book," Alcott writes in the first words of the adapted preface; the plot of
Little Women is a divine process by which Jo receives the spirit of Beth
so as to allow Jo, or Alcott, to author her own belittling. This is the
self-mortification by which Alcott believes herself to be reforming herself as
a realist. When Jo tries a new genre after her romances (a "small thing," a
"simple little story"), she has a disproportionately large literary success. "If
there *is* anything good or true in what I write, it isn't mine; I owe it all to
you [she says to her father] and mother, and to Beth." "So," Alcott adds,
"taught by love and sorrow, Jo wrote her little stories" (*LW*, 535). Beth
informs them; Jo's literary paradigm shifts from violent *Macbeth* to pacific
Beth; realism is constriction.

What had the Civil War offered Alcott or Jo that was so dangerous as
to entail this extreme oscillation to the side of domesticity, peacefulness,
and moral suicide? These journal entries of Alcott's all signal gender frustration. "I like a camp, and long for a war, to see how it all seems. I can't
fight, but I can nurse" (*LMA*, 104). More explicitly: "I've often longed to
see a war, and now I have my wish. I long to be a man; but as I can't fight,
I will content myself with working for those who can" (*LMA*, 127). A third
entry exhibits the origin of the anxiety that turns Mr. March into the family
volunteer: "I like the stir in the air, and long for battle like a warhorse
when he smells powder. The blood of the Mays is up!" (*LMA*, 132). Her

maternal blood is up. Alcott's desire to be a fighting man was not unique; over 400 women dressed as men to see combat, and many more expressed Jo's frustration.[5] Perhaps even her desire to go to war as a May was not exceptional, at least among literary women: it foreshadows the association of belligerence and motherhood in Cather and Kingston.

If the maternal is the martial, then what gender role does Alcott impersonate as nurse? A soldier says to her, "You are real motherly, ma'am," but he does not mean bellicose (*LMA*, 141). "So I set forth in the December twilight, with May and Julian Hawthorne as escort, feeling as if I was the son of the house going to war" (*LMA*, 141). In the hospital, women getting as near as they can to war meet men occupied with caring for and feeding other men. "Charley Thayer, the attendant, [is] patient as a woman with their helplessness" (*LMA*, 144). "Dr. J. haunts the room, coming by day and night with wood, cologne, books, and messes, like a motherly little man as he is" (*LMA*, 145). The hospital is a gender circus; also a carnival of class and familial roles. Concerning a Virginian blacksmith: "Under his plain speech and unpolished manner I seem to see a noble character, a heart as warm and tender as a woman's, a nature fresh and frank as any child's" (*LMA*, 142).[6]

When Jo submits to marriage with Mr. Bhaer, she takes on the only familial position the Civil War had prohibited, the daughterly wife (it had allowed Alcott to be maternal, paternal, and filial). The Civil War exists in *Little Women* as what has to be distanced if Jo is to inherit the spirit of Beth. Or perhaps "distanced" is exactly the wrong term. The Civil War has to be internalized; Jo has to die of it; Jo participates in its vast visitation not as soldier or nurse but as voluntary invalid.

The Civil War is internalized by Jo alternatively in the form of play and work, as if what is missing is the compromise formation, sport. (Though we are told that Jo "persisted in feeling an interest in manly sports, despite her nineteen years," her interest is only spectatorial [*LW*, 302].) When Jo occasionally tries playing at war, the absence of mediation by sport makes the whole experience queasy. The central event of the book's war play is the retreat to Camp Laurence, in which "Brooke is commander-in-chief; I [Laurie announces] am commissary-general; the other fellows are staff-officers; and you, ladies, are company." The word "camp" seems to be accreting two new meanings before our eyes. "The tent is for your especial benefit," Laurie continues, "and that oak is your drawing-room; this is the mess-room, and the third is the camp kitchen. Now let's have a game before it gets hot, and then we'll see about dinner" (*LW*, 155). The passage moves too quickly from war to recreation to refreshments. "The commander-in-chief and his aids [sic] soon spread the table-cloth with an inviting array of eatables and drinkables, prettily decorated with green leaves" (*LW*, 158).

The source of the queasiness is that Laurie is playing these delightful war games during the Civil War. As commissary-general, furthermore, he is not taking a belligerent male role even in the war analogue. We had been wondering about Laurie, of course, whose name is in fact Theodore, a name he gave up when the boys all called him Dora. (Laurie does not improve matters much.) He is brotherly and fatherly and sisterly. The Civil War does not straighten him out; he persists in using preciously arch war diction as if the book were determined not to have a bad conscience on his behalf. When Mrs. March goes off to minister to Mr. March, Laurie writes her: "All serene on the Rappahannock, troops in fine condition, commissary department well conducted, the Home Guard under Colonel Teddy always on duty" (*LW*, 214). We can only hope that this letter is destroyed lest mutilated soldiers at the hospital get a look at it.

What the Civil War offered Alcott is almost adequately represented by Laurie's polymorphous Civil War play; the problem is that this approach by way of male metonymy is kinder, gentler warfare than Jo desires. There is no killing in it. The only real alternative is for Jo to fight a self-Civil War, that is, to work herself to death. Mr. March writes to his wife an indirect message to his daughters as a sorority: "I know [they] . . . will do their duty faithfully, fight their bosom enemies bravely, and conquer themselves so beautifully, that when I come back to them I may be fonder and prouder than ever of my little women" (*LW*, 16). Only Jo picks up the war imagery. "I'll try and be what he loves to call me, 'a little woman,' . . . said Jo, thinking that keeping her temper at home was a much harder task than facing a rebel or two down South" (*LW*, 17). Conquering her own rebelliousness is both harder and easier for Jo than for the other girls (leaving aside Beth, who has surrendered to herself without a shot); harder because she has the most rebelliousness to overcome, easier because the effort requires a militant spirit. "Poor Jo tried desperately to be good, but her bosom enemy was always ready to flame up and defeat her; and it took years of patient effort to subdue it" (*LW*, 94). Finally, Beth's death completes the process; dying is Beth's only means of defeating Jo's insurrectionary spirit; and moral death becomes Jo's only method of spiritual self-surrender.

Giving up the Civil War (killing and polymorphous sexuality) for interior war (dying and daughterly submission) is at long last the fatal generic choice. One day Mr. Bhaer comes for his usual tutorial with Jo wearing a "paper soldier-cap on his head," placed there by a prankish young friend (*LW*, 435). Jo makes a gesture indicating her anxiety that the material for the hat is the "Volcano," the newspaper that prints her romances. "Yes, you are right to put it from you," says Bhaer observing Jo's reaction. "I do not like to think that good young girls should see such things. They are made pleasant to some, but I would more rather give my boys gunpowder to play with than this bad trash" (*LW*, 437). It seems about as likely that Jo's story is worse than gunpowder as that the paper hat will be taken for a real soldier's cap; but Bhaer is serious on behalf of Alcott's identification — like that of veteran litterateurs — of war and romance. Jo is inflammatory one way or another, so she throws her stories into the fireplace. "'Yes, that's the best place for such inflammable nonsense; I'd better burn the house down, I suppose, than let other people blow themselves up with my gunpowder,' she thought, as she watched the 'Demon of the Jura' whisk away, a little black cinder with fiery eyes" (*LW*, 438–439). That she imagines the fire expanding from hearth to home means that the alternatives for her have narrowed to domestic arson and self-immolation.

Jo becomes a realist; by this act of literary suttee, Mr. March is finally redeemed as an authority. (Jo's vocation is to nurse men—Laurie, Bhaer, her father—back to masculinity, as if the most common injury of the Civil War era were castration.) Why is her new story so successful? Mr. March knows: "There is truth in it, Jo—that's the secret" (*LW*, 535). As Jo turns Bhaer and March into men, Bhaer and March turn Jo, finally, into a literary Beth, and call the wreckage "truth." If "realism" is respectable at all, so is this outrage: how does Howellsian realism work if not by setting up romance as a straw man, then substituting for it a dedication to the mediocre, as if sending a substitute to experience the surreal excesses of the Civil War? What keeps Alcott from canonization is partly that, as a daughter, she cannot assume the compensatory postures of wounded literary sons.

Littler Realism

Reading *Gone With the Wind* with, to my surprise, increasing respect, I thought at times that I was in the presence of the single, great example of Civil War realism.[7] The book does more than make all the correct realistic gestures, though it does make them. Mitchell's novel is anti-literary in the Howellsian manner: Ashley is the literary figure of the book, and there is no escaping Rhett's consistent and Scarlett's final judgment that that entails weakness and ineptitude. When Charles Hamilton is being voraciously seduced by Scarlett, he notices that "her thick sooty lashes . . . were fluttering just like the eyes of girls in romances he had read, fluttering with timidity and love" (*GWW*, 128). Charles's misfortune is not to infer that Scarlett is a fake. *Gone With the Wind* exposes, in the realist manner, the sex in love, the opportunism in war, the cruelty of manners and taste, the idiocy of believing in romances.

The novel also is a distinguished contribution to the Twain school of realism. "Scarlett," says Rhett, "our Southern way of living is as antiquated as the feudal system of the Middle Ages" (*GWW*, 238). It cannot be saved; secession could not have been a success. Even Ashley knows this. ("Most of the misery of the world has been caused by wars. And when the wars were over, no one ever knew what they were all about" [*GWW*, 111].) Scarlett and Rhett concur; we might have thought of their lack of patriotism as selfishness and cynicism, but with Ashley's endorsement it seems merely commonsensical, unsentimental, and unromantic, to use the book's "realistic" vocabulary. Mitchell provides ample evidence for Rhett's two theories—the fool and the knave hypotheses—of why wars are fought. "It isn't the darkies, Scarlett. That's just the excuse. There'll always be wars because men love wars" (*GWW*, 258). Or: "there is never but one reason for a war.

And that is money" (*GWW*, 229). That war is Hell—that war is war and not a duel or ordeal—is proved finally in *Gone With the Wind* by the advent of the military realist himself, William Sherman.

Mitchell's book goes a great deal further than these tame realistic axioms, anomalous as it may be to find them assumed in a pro-slavery romance. *Gone With the Wind* is about taboos and the universal desire to violate them, these four in particular: miscegenation, incest, prostitution, and what might be delicately and impiously called loving one's enemy.

The taboo with pride of place in any war/plantation romance is miscegenation. Scarlett is assaulted by an emancipated black man. Though she invites this (riding heedlessly through the worst part of Atlanta), Scarlett is terrified and horrified by the attack (*GWW*, 780). "He was a mad stranger and this was a black darkness she did not know, darker than death. He was like death, carrying her away in arms that hurt" (*GWW*, 929). The double blackness implies that the horror of being raped by a black man is physical and metaphysical. Except: this passage concerns the marital rape of Scarlett by Rhett, who is always described as swarthy. Is Rhett somewhere in the racial neighborhood of quad- or octoroon? (The light man-dark man fantasy of Ashley and Rhett tends toward the extreme?) "He's the black sheep of a lovely family—oh, how could any of the Butlers ever turn out anything like him?" (*GWW*, 195). Is this in Southern code? Everything about Rhett's family background is oddly unsubstantiated rumor. At any rate, if intercourse with Rhett is intimacy with the blackness of blackness, it is necessary to add that Scarlett does not despise it.

> She was darkness and he was darkness and there had never been anything before this time, only darkness and his lips upon her. . . . Suddenly she had a wild thrill such as she had never known; joy, fear, madness, excitement, surrender to arms that were too strong, lips too bruising, fate that moved too fast. . . . Somehow, her arms were around his neck and her lips trembling beneath his and they were going up, up into the darkness again, a darkness that was soft and swirling and all enveloping. (*GWW*, 929)

Compare this passage: "Everything went black; she was caught up in the blackness of a storm. She was whirling around in a cutting, fiery wind while the fire was burning her flesh like a tormenting fever and she kept sinking down in the fire and fighting the blackness until every light went out like a candle and she fainted." Is this a description of being assaulted by a black man or being overcome by Rhett? Actually, a female slave named Vyry is being whipped by a white man in Margaret Walker's *Jubilee*.[8] Walker's book is occasionally a revision of *Gone With the Wind*; here what is demystified is miscegenation and violence. The romantic fantasy of the Southern belle conquered by swarthy Rhett is barely a veiling of the repressed fantasy of the Southern belle being raped by a black man, and the reality of miscegenation beneath that is the brutalization of innumerable black women by their masters. That the language of whipping and raping and rapture are so nearly interchangeable makes a self-evident feminist point, but I emphasize how permeable it makes the boundary between realism, romance, and pornography.[9]

Second taboo in this romance: incest. Scarlett loves Rhett because he reminds her of her father, just as she loves Ashley because he reminds her of her mother. At his best, Rhett's voice and his smell "of brandy and tobacco and horses" are comforting "because they reminded her of Gerald" (the father is always referred to by his given name) (*GWW*, 373). The more suspicious converse of this sentimentality is that after Rhett has been exiled from his wife's bedroom, he finds refuge in his daughter Bonnie's room; she "permitted no one but Rhett to undress her and put her to sleep in the small bed beside his" (*GWW*, 976). More scandalous yet is that after Bonnie's death he continues to share her bedroom with her: "An' w'en Miss Scarlett say she b'long in de pahlor in de coffin," Mammy says, "Ah thought Mist' Rhett gwine hit her. An' he say, right cole lak: 'She b'long in mah room'" (*GWW*, 982). These are words that cannot be spoken in a civilized diction. The Southern historical romance turns incest into necrophilia as inevitably as Southern sensationalism turns miscegenation into rape.

Third taboo in this plantation romance: prostitution. There is a literal prostitute in the book, Belle Watling, whose Christian name does much to implicate all the belles. Prostitution cannot be localized; not only Scarlett sells her beauty or her charms for money after the Civil War destroys the aristocracy. When Frank objects to Scarlett's use of convict labor, believing that it is "a traffic in human bodies on a par with prostitution" (735), the correct riposte would be, what is not on a par with prostitution once land (or husbands) cannot protect the bodies of Southern women from a mercenary world? What else besides her body can a woman use as "collateral" in a business deal with a man like Rhett? "I—I have myself" (*GWW*, 573). In similar straits, the young Northern woman, Jo March, sells her hair, which happens to equal her femininity. I said that a woman can only bargain with her body in business entanglements with a man like Rhett. I might have said: in most entanglements with most men. "You should have seen so clearly," Scarlet tells Ashley, "that you loved her [Melanie] all the time and only wanted me—like Rhett wants that Watling woman!" (*GWW*, 1002).

Fourth taboo, in this war/plantation romance: loving the enemy. To love Rhett is to love a man who does business with Northerners and Southerners, Democrats and Republicans, Klansmen and scalawags indifferently; even to adore Ashley is not quite to adore a Southerner enough, since the whole provocative Wilkes family enjoys going to Boston and New York for operas and museums, and imports "French and German books by the crate from the Yankees!" (*GWW*, 37). (Ashley can conceive of moving north with Melanie after the war.) In this sacrilege Scarlett is not the worst sinner. The O'Haras employ an overseer named Jonas Wilkerson, whom they have to dismiss when he impregnates a low-caste Southern woman out of wedlock. "What else can you expect from a Yankee man and a white-trash girl?" (*GWW*, 74). Later, during Reconstruction, Wilkerson is rich enough to make the "white-trash girl," Emmie Slattery, his fortunate bride, and seems about to steal Tara for her. There is enough consorting with the enemy by this time, and enough prettified prostitution, that it is hard to be outraged. Yet the oddly named Jonas Wilkerson (why come so close to substituting him for Ashley Wilkes as John Wilkes's son?) so enrages the insufficiently rebellious or rabble-roused Ashley that he wants to assassinate Wilkerson, as if to earn his father's name by imitating his father's namesake.

To treat honestly some of these themes (rape, miscegenation, incest, necrophilia, prostitution, treachery) would be to write as a naturalist; to bury these themes just below the surface (where I have, not much to my credit, dug them up) is to be a popular, celebrated, that is, a tasteful pornographer. Mitchell's triumph is to blur the distinction sufficiently that any retreat to sentimentality is gratefully accepted. She delegates Rhett to lead the retrenchment: when, in an effort to win his daughter Bonnie's entree into Southern-girl society, he reveals that he had (more or less secretly) fought for the South, he quiets all scandals at once. He may be swarthy, but he is white; he is a true family man, no admirer of Belle Watling; to marry him is not to espouse the enemy cause. And though the excessiveness of his devotion to Bonnie is remarked, everyone, including readers such as myself, is pleased to conclude that "there had to be something good about a man who loved his child" (*GWW*, 899). In Rhett's Atlanta "campaign" on his daughter's behalf, to which all the tattered Southern haut monde "capitulated" (*GWW*, 895, 898), everything that Sherman had taught Scarlett about the nature of life is inverted.

The sentimental project has its own interest. That a book so ruthlessly analytical can turn sentimental at all is a feat. It takes a change of intentions as radical as Rhett's and a duplicity as trenchant as Scarlett's. But the sentimental design is not merely a refusal of realism. If realism is predicated on the existence of a uniform reality beneath transient and local fads and conventions, then Mitchell's sentimentalism dares to premise that at its highest levels, life is a uniform simulacrum; reality is what changes from moment to moment and region to region.

Even within the South, even within Southern whiteness, how do you find unity in a book so acute about the differences between Georgian and less refined Southern cultures, between coastal and inland Georgia, old and new Georgia, white trash, poor whites, and gentry? Getting blacks and whites assimilated is easier. There is not enough realism with respect to slaves to generate a difficulty. "Negroes were provoking sometimes and stupid and lazy, but there was loyalty in them that money couldn't buy, a feeling of oneness with their white folks which made them risk their lives to keep food on the table" (*GWW*, 465). The virtue of slavery is that by quarantining blacks from money you save them from class hatred and mercenary self-interest. You cannot buy their loyalty because once you have bought them, slaves have no further personal relation to cash.

All other identifications require a less casual effort. The case that Scarlett *is* Tara, genetically, is strenuously made. Insofar as the land is "vital and earthy and coarse," it equals her father, and Scarlett as a physical being (these attributes "appealed to her" because "she possessed in some degree these same qualities" [*GWW*, 33]). Insofar as *terra* has been tamed—"the serene half-light over Tara's well-kept acres brought out a measure of quiet to her disturbed mind" (*GWW*, 30)—it equals her mother ("she . . . loved it as she loved her mother's face under the lamp at prayer time"), and equals Scarlett as an ideal self-conception. But to identify only with the country would cause an immediate disjunction between rural and city Georgia, so Scarlett is Atlanta as well: "Atlanta was only nine years older than she was . . . . Atlanta was of her own generation, crude with the crudities of youth and as headstrong and impetuous as herself" (*GWW*, 140). Earth, plantation, city: Scarlett as coarse father, cultivated mother, crude daughter.

There are other strange identifications. Twelve Oaks is "beautiful as a woman is beautiful who is so sure of her charm that she can be generous and gracious to all" (*GWW*, 96). Women are more than domesticated in Southern society; say that they are literally domesticated, or housed. The women who escape the house do so on a horse, as in all Civil War romances. By the preternatural unifying logic of *Gone With the Wind*, they must become horses. Mrs. Tarleton, horse-woman, tells Gerald about the birth of a new stallion: "He's a real Tarleton horse. He's as red as Hetty's curls." Camilla adds that he "looks a lot like Hetty, too," which Mitchell seconds by observing that Hetty "did have a long face." Hetty commences to pinch Camilla in revenge, causing Mrs. Carleton to apologize. "My fillies are feeling their oats this morning" (*GWW*, 91). Later, she dismisses the Wilkes as "overbred and inbred"; her favorite subject is "breeding, whether it be horses or humans." For the sake of the breed, she refused to marry her second cousin: "I bucked like a colt" (*GWW*, 92–93). No wonder Gerald considers her not just a horse-lover but a "centaur" (*GWW*, 90). Everywhere Mitchell looks, she sees more than family likenesses; she sees family onenesses. Parents are children are their houses are their horses are their slaves.

The book may be the greatest literary attempt in history to unify everything (including whites and blacks) against the threat of attack. Nationhood is identity; difference is invasion. Mr. O'Hara tells Scarlett: "only when like marries like can there be any happiness." Oddly, he is warning her away from Ashley; the logic appears when he goes on to remind her of the Wilkes's cultural connections with the North (*GWW*, 37). Wilkes himself agrees: "Love isn't enough to make a successful marriage when two people are as different as we are." He wants Melanie because "she is like me, part of my blood" (*GWW*, 119). It might seem that the disastrous contest and courtship of Scarlett and Rhett prove that their often remarked congruence can only result in incongruity. However, Mitchell ascribes their personal catastrophe to Scarlett's inability to acknowledge Rhett's principle that "like begets liking" (*GWW*, 335). His valedictory remark to her is that she has been "such a fool [not realizing] that there can't ever be happiness except when like mates like" (*GWW*, 928).

Mitchell, even in the throes of her allergic reaction to difference, understands that Southern unity is only a convention tacitly agreed to in the face of all real antagonisms (especially social and economic). *Gone With the Wind* is, confessedly, simulacrum nostalgia. "I want the outer semblance of the things I used to know," says—Rhett (*GWW*, 1021). The war brought home by Sherman reveals the contradictions in Southern society (some blacks turn against whites; trash try to supplant aristocrats; sisters turn on sisters in the competition for husbands with money; money flow is revealed to be integral to the permanency of land). But this is to say that reality is transient and piecemeal, and the romance, condemned as a kaleidoscope of moods and styles and fads, represents eternity, even if eternity is false and artificial.

Curiously, the conjuring of a preternatural unity is a convention of war fiction even among women not as dedicated as Mitchell to the survival of an artifically unadulterated society; and in all cases unity begins with uniform families. In *Gone With the Wind*, the O'Haras consist of a comical father, a strong mother, and three daughters (three sons have died in infancy or childhood); they bear a family likeness to the Marches, who consist of a mother and four daughters (the father is absent or absent-minded). In *Beloved*, the third of my examples of Civil War writing by women, the nuclear family consists of a mother, a living daughter, an undead daughter, the spirit of the husband's mother, an absent father, and two sons who disappear during the Civil War—before the time of the novel—without impact or trace. Consider my World War I sample: Willa Cather's family in *One of Ours* comprises three sons and no daughters; all Edith Wharton's families in *A Son at the Front* are composed of exactly one son (at the front); H. D.'s three women in *Bid Me to Live* have exactly zero sons (one woman has an abortion, one woman a stillbirth, the third abandons her children). There can only be one sort of family per book and the children must all be of one sex: call this the principle of the invariant family.

In a way that needs elucidating, one thing that war suggests to American women writers is the possibility of a world without difference; difference seems to begin with families that permit two sexes. Realists like Howells were also reliant on conformity, since realism depends on the positing of uniform interpretive communities. But women war writers have found themselves in the predicament of investigating the essence of division (war) and self-division (the will to preserve by killing, the need to injure on behalf of "home-peace," the necessity, in short, of contradictory male and female gendering) for the traces of absolute integrity. The identifying desire may be pacifistic; but the result may be a unity so strong that war is negligible as a threat to it; war may even (according to hawkish writers like Cather and Wharton) strengthen it. In Mitchell, the will to unity is ambiguous: identity is what one fights to defend, but identity is what is sacrificed in fighting for it. The paradox entails Mitchell's realistic romance.

Magic Realism

Gone With the Wind is an elemental book, and the three elements are air, earth, and fire. Ashley, admitting his inferiority to Scarlett as a way of establishing his difference, says that she is "as elemental as fire and wind" (*GWW*, 120). It is a surprising formulation, since Scarlett, fleeing Atlanta in flames, dreads that Tara is also "gone with the wind" (*GWW*, 390). The key is perhaps that Mitchell imagines the fickle elements to have different natures in different compounds. The second paragraph after the "gone with the wind" passage observes that "there was death in the air," that "no wind waved the trees" (*GWW*, 391). Wind is the principle of death when it fans the holocaust, the principle of life when it stirs the leaves. When Ashley after the fall of Atlanta sticks to his elemental compliment ("I love . . . your courage and your stubbornness and your fire" [*GWW*, 524]), we grant that the burning of Atlanta both unmakes and makes Scarlett. She is elemental yet mixed; she is Atlanta but in perfect spiritual sympathy with the burning of Atlanta. Scarlett seeks redemption from fire by fire.

As opposed to the destructive flames is "the indestructible red earth" (*GWW*, 482); Scarlett is that element also, insofar as she is "vital and earthy and coarse" (*GWW*, 33). It may not be possible to make consistency out of all this, but something seems to be working itself out. First of all, Scarlett inherits her earthiness from her father — she is genetically, elementally male. And Ashley, by comparing Scarlett with fire and wind, both admits his own inferior masculinity and correctly associates Scarlett not merely with maleness but with Sherman's pragmatic inhumanity. By these two elemental tropes, Scarlett's maleness is established in terms of feistiness and belligerency: she is male because combativeness is male. Now combine air and earth; they are the prototypical male elements if Irigaray is correct to describe male science as a "complicity of long standing between rationality and a mechanics of solids alone."[10] Scarlett, who is superior to her first two husbands and to Ashley in her hard-heartedness and -headedness and further in her talent for mathematical calculation, might be an emblem of that complicity. Irigaray points out the scandal of the tardiness of a theory of fluids. It is, she believes, the element of femininity that science can least reify and etherealize. Scarlett is manly in both its characteristic expressions, war and science; the misfortune of course is that she is manly but not a man.

Beloved is as elemental as *Gone With the Wind*, but it is as liquid a book as has ever taken place on land, more liquid even than *As I Lay Dying*.[11] Within one page, almost all bodily fluids and several non-bodily fluids are circulated. Sethe arrives across the river with her new baby; her mother-in-law, Baby Suggs, instructs a young woman "not to clean the [infant's] eyes till she got the mother's urine"; the woman (or perhaps Baby Suggs — the syntax is fluid) "cried into her cooking"; the next dawn, the infant "took her mother's milk"; Sethe's wounds, meanwhile, cause "roses of blood [to blossom] in the blanket covering [her] shoulders"; also meanwhile, Sethe's next-to-last daughter, Beloved, "dribbled clear spit into her face" (*B*, 92–93). A little of this might have seemed possibly charming; but in case the picture is not equivocal enough, remember that in four weeks, as if by menstrual cycle, Sethe will murder Beloved—"from the pure clear stream of spit that the little girl dribbled into her face to her oily blood was twenty-eight days" (*B*, 95)—and Sethe's infant will be nursed on milk mixed with her sister's blood. First among the horrors that Sethe is fleeing is the scientific plantation schoolteacher who measures her body and charts her behavior (she is property, like land, converted into statistics). The extremity of Morrison's liquid response makes her own ambivalence inevitable.

At stake is the possibility of a selfhood that is not masculine, that is not on the model that Scarlett O'Hara (or Jo March) is genetically poised to adapt when the men around her drop away. Men also fail Sethe—Halle, the spouse, disappears (with good cause, but still unheroically) at the moment of escape, so cannot protect her when the slave hunters come—but Toni Morrison's experiment is to see what would result from founding selfhood on different, unmasculine, premises.

Selfhood is traditionally conceived of as real property, like land, like Tara, or as chattel property, like slaves; but there is necessarily a flaw in all such conceptions. When Stephen Greenblatt goes to define the self—the self that is not historically specifiable—at the beginning of *Renaissance Self-Fashioning*, he lists its characteristics this way. "After all, there are always selves—a sense of personal order, a characteristic mode of address to the world, a structure of bounded desires [real property]—and always some elements of deliberate shaping in the formulation and expression of identity [chattel property]."[12] This means that selves are stabilizing (register the terms "order," "characteristic," "structure," "bounded") even when they are fashioned. Are these elements meant to be comprehensive? "A sense of personal order" might indicate what is private and conscious in selfhood; "a characteristic mode of address" might include what is public and conscious; "a structure of bounded desires" might suggest the point of contact of the public with the private and unconscious.

It is hard to say how systematic the itemization is meant to be: Greenblatt is not so much formulating as referring us to formulas already intuited. So when he merely wishes to recapitulate, he is not careful to get the triad exactly duplicated. What the sixteenth century fashioned according to its particular cultural logic is "a distinctive personality, a characteristic address to the world, a consistent mode of perceiving and behaving."[13] This is a more public triad, though item two is almost verbatim. "A sense of personal order" becomes a "distinctive personality," and bounded desires have shifted to consistent perceiving and behaving, what bounded desires act and look like. The point is not that in the sixteenth century the private aspects of selfhood were depreciated; the point is that selfhood does not need a precise definition, nor can it have one if the selfhood that is fashioned can go by the same name as the selfhood that is beyond fashion.

Selfhood is invented, in Greenblatt's sense, along with science at the border of science and literature, the tabulated and the narrated. This is another way of suggesting that selfhood must be hard enough to be resistant to temporal change and soft enough to be consistent with all temporal change. Moreover, it can only be tabulated once it is narrated: you cannot *begin* with a program to be definite (hard, rigid, abstract) about selfhood, because selfhood is the principle of definition that you are seeking to establish. (Similarly, scientific method cannot be used to prove the scientific method.) Definition always has to be partly free, improvised, indefinite.

Somewhere in the solidifying and measuring of self (in its reception of the two aspects of property) there has to be a liquid—in paradigmatic cases, an oceanic—crossing. The modern self in Greenblatt's analysis is imperialistic: self sails to America to conquer softness. This is definition in search of the indefinite. Morrison wonders if slaves, who came to America as property, as the objects of definition (the schoolteacher beats Sixo "to show him that definitions belonged to the definers—not the defined" [*B*, 190]), can have selves on an inverse program. Beloved is resurrected out of a river; Sethe has been told by Nan, the woman who raises her, that Sethe's "mother and Nan were together from the sea" (*B*, 62), as if they inherit their self-definition from their fluid origins. Womb and slave ship have been conflated, so that dispossession might, at least hypothetically, seem to equal perfect (shared) wholeness and oneness.

The issue is preternatural unity, as in Mitchell; the difference is that Mitchell conceives of an integrity of self and possessions, and Morrison an integrity of self and self in a relation of mutual possession and self-dispossession. "She's mine, Beloved. She's mine," thinks Denver of Beloved (*B*, 209). "I am Beloved and she is mine," thinks Beloved of Sethe (*B*, 210). Liquidity here implies a self without borders. It is as if Denver's nursing at Sethe's breast while Beloved bleeds into the milk implies a sort of circulation of fluid self of which nothing is ever lost. (Selfhood as solid property makes identity a zero-sum tabulation.) Late in the book, the three participate in a shared interior lyric; there are no quotation marks and no hard stops.

> You are my sister [thinks Denver]
> You are my daughter [thinks Sethe]
> You are my face; you are me [thinks Beloved, concerning Sethe]
>
> . . .
>
> You went in the water
> I drank your blood
> I brought your milk
>
> . . .
>
> You are mine
> You are mine
> You are mine (*B*, 216–217)

Morrison is drawing out the implications of a female trinitarianism: mother, daughter, holy ghost. (Actually, "holy ghost" itself divides into two indiscrete parts. Baby Suggs, still a spiritual presence, is always referred to as "Baby Suggs, Holy," and the ghost is the ghost. The two are inseparable; Beloved is the lost baby as adult, Baby Suggs the lost adult as baby.) Beloved (like "Baby," the term of endearment is applied to more than one character) is a sort of personified shifter; when the white girl Amy Denver helps to deliver Denver, we notice that "Amy" is "Beloved" translated. (Denver inherits her surname.) What the three Civil War novels I have selected have in common is the positing of a female trinity in the face of male divisiveness. Mrs. March, Jo, and Beth are also a consubstantial mother, daughter, and holy ghost. Mrs. March becomes the sainted Ellen O'Hara; Jo's masculine pugnacity takes a different form in Scarlett; and Beth becomes the shy, gentle Carreen. The Mariolatry of the O'Hara household is less heterodox than that of the Marches, since the O'Haras are Catholic. If the irreligious family of Sethe, Denver, and Beloved equally approximates a female trinity, it can only be the case that issues of war, in the hands of a female author, lead chronically to the same fantasy, regardless of race, religion, region, or era, though all these factors will shape the form of the fantasy.

The question is how you get from Civil War divisions and antagonisms to consubstantiality: the first thing to notice (not the only one, given *Gone With the Wind*) is that the Civil War is evaded in *Beloved* as much as in *Little Women*. The war is mentioned in *Beloved* about ten or fifteen times, but only to emphasize its negligible results, for example: "Talking of a war full of dead people, she looked happy" (*B*, 28); "the War had been over four or five years then, but nobody white or black seemed to know it" (*B*, 52); "Had she waited just a little she would have seen the end of the War, its short, flashy results" (*B*, 171). Here is the most arresting example:

> "Your love is too thick," he [Paul D] said . . . .
> "Too thick?" she said . . . . "Love is or it ain't. Thin love ain't love at all."
> "Yeah. It didn't work, did it? Did it work?" he asked.
> "It worked," she said.
> "How? Your boys gone you don't know where. One girl dead, the other won't leave the yard. How did it work?"
> "They ain't at Sweet Home. Schoolteacher ain't got 'em." (*B*, 164–165)

Sethe is arguing the point in 1873. Even if she had not escaped, and had not killed her daughter, they would not be at Sweet Home, and the schoolteacher would not have them. This goes beyond minimizing the Civil War; it is not to notice it occurred.

Sethe is not ignorant or insane. Nor is she merely making—though she is at least making—the point of several black (non-) war novelists: "Not only War is Hell."[14] A book such as Chester B. Himes's *If He Hollers Let Him Go* is at first glance as odd as *Why Are We in Vietnam?* in relation to its own war, World War II. The book is a war novel in which the protagonist only sets off for war on the last page. The point is that he has been in combat all along: "Is you ready to face the enemy" asks his friend as they drive to work.[15] There is a direct connection to *Beloved*: concerning the only black child in Himes's novel, the protagonist Bob Jones thinks, "if they really wanted to give him a break they'd cut his throat and bury him in the back yard before he got old enough to know he was a nigger."[16] If, to a novelist like Edith Wharton among others, war may be summarized as the sacrifice of children, then novelists who wish to memorialize slavery would not feel its compelling novelty. Toni Morrison could make, if she wanted, the Howellsian case that there are wars beyond the Civil War to fight, and on which to base an aesthetic. I think, however, that Morrison is making a peculiarly maternal point: her trinitarian denigration of the war is the result of a particular historical sense.

What Paul D means by saying that Sethe's love is too thick is that it is not discrete; her love flows through the veins of her daughters. Identities are so thoroughly permeable that to think of a daughter is to possess her; to be haunted by a daughter is to have the daughter alive in you, where she has always been. This is the meaning of "rememory"—memory in which the remembered thing does not fade, but grows in vividness in one's mind (as at Borges's idealist Tlön, where lost things, hrönir, are larger upon recovery). But Morrison does not want to refute time merely as a subjective perception, by rememory. "Thick love" leads to thick time on the model of *As I Lay Dying*: time that is neither entropic nor catastrophic, but gathers, coagulates. (Death is thus relativized in the case of Addie or Beloved.) Sethe says:

> I was talking about time. It's so hard for me to believe in it. Some things go. Pass on. Some things just stay. I used to think it was my rememory. . . . Someday you will be walking down the road and you hear something or see something going on. So clear. And you think it's you thinking it up. A thought picture. But no. It's when you bump into a rememory that belongs to some-body else. (*B*, 35–36)

Only male time moves individuals perpetually toward or away from catas-trophe: in female time, the catastrophic moment is always recoverable in the memory of a community. When Denver talks to Beloved "about people Denver knew once or had seen," she gives "them more life than life had" (*B*, 120). To remember the dead vividly is to resurrect them to greater life.

On this model, the Civil War is not the event men imagine it to be: the death of slavery, a new birth of freedom. The unpunctuality of time is confusing to men when they experience it. When Edward Bodwin drives to Sethe's house (Bodwin's old home) to pick up Denver (seeing him reminds Sethe of the slave hunters, which determines the book's closure), "it was his destination that turned his thoughts to time—the way it dripped or ran." The way, that is, it behaves as a liquid of varying consistencies. "Measured by the wars he had lived through but not fought in (against the Miami, the Spaniards, the Secessionists), it was slow. But measured by the burial of his private things it was the blink of an eye. Where, exactly, was the box of tin soldiers?" (*B*, 259–260). War time preserves history; time measured by the "burial of . . . private things" (i.e., as in rememory) is ahistorical. If men stay boys, warriors reduce to unaging tin soldiers.

Morrison is frank about what is sacrificed in the process of liquidifying self. The drinking of blood conjures Dracula as much as it invokes blood-sisterhood ("if I had the teeth of the man who died on my face I would bite the circle around her neck" [*B*, 211]). Sethe's inability to distinguish herself from her daughter might be diagnosed as parental narcissism ("when I went in," says Beloved, as if telling the Narcissus story from the point of view of the liquid reflection, "I saw her face coming to me and it was my face too. . . . I tried to join, but she went up into the pieces of light at the top of the water" [*B*, 214]). Before Paul D concludes that Sethe's love is "too thick," he thinks: "This here Sethe talked about safety with a handsaw [with which she executed Beloved]. This here new Sethe didn't know where the world stopped and she began. . . . It scared him" (*B*, 164). Granted that he is a man, but at the end of the book, Denver is allowed to experience the pleasure of "having a self to look out for and preserve" (*B*, 252). And if Sethe continues to believe that "the best thing she was, was her children" (*B*, 251), Paul D is allowed the last word, "You your best thing, Sethe," to which Sethe responds, "Me? Me?" (*B*, 273). The ghost evacuates, and Denver goes to college, despite the association of science, scholarship, and slavery.

Morrison's book had tried to model itself on the anachronistic confluency of its women. The Civil War was eliminated in the process: the book skips eighteen years from the escape (1855) to the return of Beloved and Paul D (1873), apparently on the example of "Rip Van Winkle" (it is Beloved who sleeps through the war but is reborn from the minds of her mother and sister). The novel is in the tradition of canonized war literature by men, and its avoidance of the Civil War might have been the first step of its realism. But the book may be classified as "magic realism," instead (perhaps on the model of "The Jolly Corner"), insofar as the various tergiversations of Civil War novelists produced American realism. If "Sweet Home" is an illusion of genteel slavery, the North cannot expose it; if the cause of freedom is an idealist's romance, that does not turn slave-holders into realists.

Toni Morrison begins with the wounding by which Henry James tried to marry realism and romance as a last resort. Bleeding is the condition of this magic realism; blood sharing is its quintessence. The schoolteacher has one of his students suck Sethe's milk; capturing her, he thinks of Sethe as the one who made "fine ink, damn good soup" (*B*, 149). In 1874, speaking to Paul D, Sethe says, "I made the ink, Paul D. He couldn't have done it if I hadn't made the ink" (*B*, 271). Sethe literally made ink for Schoolteacher, but the peculiar intensity here leads me to surmise: that even the milk of a black woman can be conceived of as black if there is such a thing as "black blood" (with which it mingles, as it happens); that Morrison sees in the spilling of Sethe's milk and Beloved's blood an emblem of her own writing; that if it is nourishing it may be nourishing the wrong people, and it may be simply an act of self-violence; that to deny her characters traditional selfhood may repeat the result of slavery (all the Pauls have one name to make them interchangeable); that if the self is to be removed from space and time, it needs something by way of compensation to prevent dissolution (Sethe, in all moments and places at once, sees in a friendly white face in 1874 the visage of slave hunters of 1855, and loses Beloved again); that the traditional name of that compensation is "realism."

World War I and Modern Beauty

Beautiful War

Willa Cather's *One of Ours* (1922), Edith Wharton's *A Son at the Front* (1923), and H. D.'s *Bid Me to Live* (1960, in process starting 1921) form a continuum from Cather's undeviatingly linear narrative to Wharton's more cunningly plotted narrative to H. D.'s fractured lyric; from Cather's untroubled bellicosity through Wharton's troubled bellicosity to H. D.'s contempt for the Great War; from Cather's immediate treatment of combat through Wharton's mediated combat to H. D.'s exclusive preoccupation with home-front conditions. Do we find evidence here of Peter Brooks's Freudian narratology? The perfect death of Cather's hero is the only apt culmination of his narrative; the good death of Wharton's title character is a somewhat less appropriate conclusion to her somewhat off-center plot; but H. D.'s book exhibits the compulsion to repeat as a fully textualized neurosis, as if to argue that the death drive, inscribed, does not produce actions so much as verbal tics.

One of Ours is startlingly straightforward: it does not even begin *in medias res*.[17] It begins in Nebraska on circus day, gives deliberate attention to matters of education and family and mating until the war arrives in the course of things, then it moves steadily toward its hero's achievement of manhood just before his death. There would not be much to say on the book's behalf, if the author's sex did not leave traces. This may account for the Gothic interlude before the war episodes, which suggests something more peculiar or perverse than a standard tale of masculinity, maturity, and martial sacrifice.

The oddest thing about the book is that Claude Wheeler, its protagonist and hero, is hardly a male according to Nebraska gendering. Nor does he go to the Great War seeking maleness. Rather, his masculine triumph of self-sacrifice is unmistakably a full development of his femininity. There are only sons—three of them—in the Wheeler family, in obeisance to the principle of the invariant family. The uniform sexuality of the siblings is designed in this case to foster an ideal of unisexuality, an ideal of manhood that, unhoused, is a triumph of womanhood. These proclivities define masculinity in Nebraska: the love of property, money, and machines. Claude despises all these things. It is not defined by the love of war: Claude's more conventionally masculine brother (more successful, less sensitive, more beloved of father) is a pacifist. *One of Ours* has to arrange reality so that only women are warriors.

Begin with the fact that Claude Wheeler tends to fall in love with mothers. "'It's almost like being a bride, keeping house for just you, Claude,' [Mrs. Wheeler] sometimes said" (OO, 78). When widowed Mrs. Erlich, mother of a family of boys like the Wheelers, "drew Claude aside and told him in excited whispers that her cousin Wilhelmina, the singer, had at last been relieved of the invalid husband whom she had supported for so many years, and now was going to marry her accompanist, a man much younger than herself," it is obvious that we are being prepared for a parallel eventuality (OO, 83). Nevertheless, Claude never does marry Mrs. Erlich, though that result is not avoided for the sake of a more appropriate marriage. Claude's marriage to Enid is a disaster. What occurs is not that Claude stops trying to marry mothers in order to have a wife. Claude stops trying to marry mothers in order to become a mother.

Enid, the woman Claude unfortunately weds, is measurably more masculine than he is: she takes over the driving when road conditions are dangerous; she beats Claude at chess. She is not merely unfeminine, she is anti-maternal: she forces Claude to have many hens but only one rooster because for business reasons she does not want her eggs to be fertilized (OO, 203). No surprise when this foreshadows her own attitude toward fertility, which she thinks of in terms of the pain of childbirth and Eve's sin (OO, 210). Meanwhile, Claude develops his maternal nature. A neighbor, Leonard, hates Enid for her policy on eggs; then he adds about Claude, "It's my opinion that she's got that boy cowed already" (OO, 204). How figurative is "cowed" in a farm setting? Only a few pages later, Claude feels tender sympathy for "his little Jersey cow, which came home every night with full udders and gave down her milk willingly, keeping her tail out of his face, as only a well-disposed cow will do" (OO, 206). Then Claude looks up: "The moon swam up over the bare wheat fields, big and magical, like a great flower." Glancing from the full udder to the full moon leads Claude's thoughts to Europe: is he "one of those people who are always discontented?" "Whatever his disappointments were, he kept them locked in his own breast" (OO, 213). Only Europe will relieve him.

I am charting an ascending difficulty: how to make World War I seem not merely a consummation of femininity but also a fruition of motherliness. First, it takes a feminine imagination not so much to understand the necessity of the war as to conceive of Europe at all. While men's thoughts are centered on the farm and can expand as far as the borders of Nebraska or the market at the outside, a woman like Gladys—whom Claude should have married—has her modest, trans-Nebraskan dreams: "A warm imagination helped her to find life interesting. She did, as she confided to Enid, want to go to Colorado; she was ashamed of never having seen a mountain" (OO, 152). When the war breaks out, it is Mrs. Wheeler who climbs to the attic "to hunt for a map of Europe,—a thing for which Nebraska farmers had never had much need. But that night, on many prairie homesteads, the women, American and foreign-born, were hunting for a map" (OO, 161). Why only the women? You might have assumed that Claude would escape to the war on the typical model of male flight; but since he is the oppressed

spouse, and since Enid is in China at the time anyway (not out of wander-
lust so much as the inability to see the difference between doing one's
Christian duty in Nebraska or China), the flight is a woman's, not a man's,
from domestication.

It follows that the war—calling out to those with imagination—is a
woman's defense of imagination and beauty. Claude, in France, is enam-
ored of both France and French patriotism, as exemplified by a dismem-
bered veteran. "How much it must mean to a man to love his country like
this, Claude thought; to love its trees and flowers; to nurse it when it was
sick, and tend its hurt with one arm" (*OO*, 387). It is true that Claude has
had his moments of nature-love in Nebraska; but it is the cultivation of
beauty, the maternal or at least disarmed nursing of beauty, that is peculiar
to France. Claude has his first moment of aesthetic bliss in a Catholic
church. "When he reached the choir he turned, and saw from behind him,
the rose window, with its purple heart" (*OO*, 342). If it has a purple heart,
it has been wounded in the war, out of which blossoms its full beauty.
Then the hour is tolled: "the revelations of the glass and the bell had
come almost simultaneously, as if one produced the other; and both were
superlatives toward which his mind had always been groping,—or so it
seemed to him then." Toward this harmony of time and space, of the
audible and the visual, of the momentary and the eternal, of woundedness
and perfection, is back toward his mother. "The purple and crimson and
peacock-green of this window . . . went through him and farther still . . .
as if his mother were looking over his shoulder" (*OO*, 343, the final ellipsis
is Cather's).

The beauty of the war is Catholic beauty; the experience of the beauty
of the war is Mariolatry; the aesthetic posture toward the war is submissive.
Claude has been struggling throughout the book "to subdue his own nature" (*OO*, 103), as if he were Jo March trying to resemble her sainted
mother. During a snow storm, his anti-desire finds an emblem: "he could
not help thinking how much better it would be if people could go to sleep
like the fields; could be blanketed down with the snow, to wake with their
hurts healed and their defeats forgotten" (*OO*, 223). For an incipient soldier, this is an odd aspiration. Claude hopes to forget defeat rather than
celebrate victory. The docile ideal ("There was something beautiful about
the submissive way in which the country met winter" [*OO*, 85]) extends to
the limit of suicide; infer that Claude's final act of superb heroism—charged
with holding the line against all odds, he runs in front of his trench to rally
his men—is an act of perfect self-control and obedience to duty and fate.
He dies a quiescent, almost non-violent death: "He was not bleeding very
much. He smiled at them as if he were going to speak, but there was
a weak blankness in his eyes. Bert tore his shirt open; three clean bul-
let holes—one through his heart. By the time they looked at him again,
the smile had gone . . . the look that was Claude had faded" (*OO*, 453,
Cather's ellipsis).

Finally, if Claude's wife Enid is aggressively infertile, as a spiritual if not a medical matter, then Claude's act of submission is equal to an act of procreation. David Gerhardt, concert violinist who dies just before Claude, puts it this way: "You remember in the old mythology tales how, when the sons of gods were born, the mothers always died in agony? Maybe it's only Semêle I'm thinking of. At any rate, I've sometimes wondered whether the young men of our time had to die to bring a new idea into the world . . . something Olympian. . . . Since I've been over this time, I've come to believe in immortality" (OO, 409–410, the first ellipsis is Cather's). Immortality equals the perfect confusion of motherhood and sonhood. The book itself ends with immortality, but we may imagine at what psychic cost. If narrative is so deeply attracted to war that post-war modernism consists in the discovery of idiosyncratic modes of interrupting or retarding time by stylistic force, then by what repressions and mutilations does a twentieth-century woman find her way by means of a displaced maternality back to perfect male, Christian, linear time?

The Gothic interlude of *One of Ours* takes place on the ship that brings Claude to Europe. A marine is telling the troops about the landing at Vera Cruz. "One thing there I'll never forget. . . . We went down into dungeons underneath the water, where they used to keep State prisoners, kept them buried alive for years." Claude sees in the marine's expression the hope that as a result of the European war, "the dungeons and cages would be broken open for ever" (OO, 290–291). The name of the marine is Albert Usher.

Cather's Usher hopes that the European war, in effect, is the end of the Gothic; listeners, including Lieutenant Bird, share his vision. The next morning, however, Bird has a severe nose-bleed, and in the afternoon he dies, as the influenza epidemic—"of a peculiarly bloody and malignant type" (OO, 292)—hits the ship. Its beginning is marked by the book's only historical asterisk: "The actual outbreak of influenza on transports carrying United States troops is here anticipated by several months" (OO, 292). The Gothic disease is the only disturbance of the historical linearity of the book. In the process it reconfigures the gender and family divisions of the ship. All victims are infantalized (big Tannhauser, "the giant baby of a long family," dies crying, "Mein' arme Mutter!" [OO, 300–301]); all survivors become white nurses. The atmosphere suggests a less benign femininity: there is a "sinister sunset"; "small, ragged black" clouds "hurried . . . up out of the sea" in "wild, witchlike shapes . . . as if summoned for an evil conclave" (OO, 293). The poor ship itself "seemed to wallow and sprawl in the waves, as he [Claude] had seen animals do on the farm when they gave birth to young. . . . [H]ow much misery she carried!" (OO, 300). The conjunction of the maternal in its benign, malign, and wretched aspects projects us, suddenly, despite Usher's vision, into the world of "The Fall of the House of Usher"-cum-*Narrative of A. Gordon Pym*. The oceanic disease calls up Poe's "red death" in tandem with Theweleit's "red tide": the anxiety of influenza is a woman's fear of being a part of the bloody disorder rather than its military repression.

Granted that World War I has its Gothic side: there is the hand that will not stay buried, for example (*OO*, 447–448), and Claude is at one moment buried alive by an explosion, except for his head and left shoulder (*OO*, 398). On the whole, however, the Great War is not underground for Claude, not claustrophobic or stultifying or excremental. The death ship takes care of the liminal and the polluted aspects of passage; war is for Claude an unburial. "Things are pretty tame at home," Claude says. "Tame?" says the aviator Victor Morse, who by the way is having an extramarital affair with a woman "old enough to be [his] mother," "My God, it's death in life!" (*OO*, 307–308). Cather's World War I is no endless, impersonal nightmare. Claude goes off to fight "a war without rage, with uncompromising generosity and chivalry" (*OO*, 248), and in fact that is the anachronistic war he finds. We are in the presence of a female fight, a war in which the son leaves home on his mother's business. But female power has to be sterilized against infection, witchcraft has to be sanitized, so sacrifice becomes assertion, trenches signify freedom, and martyrdom implies resurrection: "the war was life . . . . To be alive . . . was to be in the war" (*OO*, 416).

Peace is death in life; war is life in death. After Claude has been killed, Mrs. Wheeler comforts herself by reading Claude's posthumous letters, which keep coming for a while, and by reading the newspapers: "it seemed as if the flood of meanness and greed had been held back just long enough for the boys to go over, and then swept down and engulfed everything that was left at home" (*OO*, 458). The crossing of the ocean (with its tale of underwater death-in-life and its version of Poe's red death) becomes the crossing of the Red Sea; Claude transcends the red tide; even dead, Claude has arrived in the Promised Land. *Especially* dead: he is spared the bitterness of the returned soldiers. "But one she knew, who could ill bear disillusion . . . safe, safe" (*OO*, 459, Cather's ellipsis). If this elevates Claude into Moses, by a quick typological move he is elevated yet further. The servant Mahailey says, "Never you mind, Mudder; you'll see your boy up yonder." The last paragraph continues: "Mrs. Wheeler always feels that God is near, — but Mahailey is not troubled by any knowledge of interstellar spaces, and for her He is nearer still, — directly overhead, not so very far above the kitchen stove" (*OO*, 459). In these closing words, by this homey theology, Claude is rhymed with God.

It is not surprising. After a theological discussion in which Claude and Mrs. Wheeler agree that the only interesting character in the Bible who is not a sinner is Jesus, and Mrs. Wheeler, overlooking her son's compulsion to blaspheme, concludes that God may dwell "even in proud, rebellious hearts," the mother and son have a uniquely intimate experience. "For a moment they clung together in the pale, clear square of the west window, as the two natures in one person sometimes meet and cling in a fatal hour" (*OO*, 87). This is the language of love as well as schizophrenia: it is as if Cather is split between man and woman, soldier and matriarch, propagandist and Gothicist, and overcomes that divide by a death — by the arrival of another fatal hour—that returns the son to the mother. Achieving mature masculinity is finally to achieve oneness with the maternal.

It is a step beyond what Sara Ruddick envisages as the basis of a maternal pacifism. Concerning the Madres of Argentina, Ruddick begins by specifying that "The children, the absent ones, are *not* their mothers, who have decidedly *not* disappeared but are bodily present. Yet as the pictures the Madres carry suggest, the children are not, even in disappearance, apart from their mothers but, in their absence, are still inseparable from them."[18] Children cannot be sacrificed without protest; yet take the logic of maternal bonding to its limit, as Cather does, and they can be sacrificed without sacrifice. (In these terms, Sethe will always have her Beloved only if Beloved is dead.) The language of schizophrenia and romance is also theological: one nature in two persons is metaphorized as two natures in one person. What justifies Cather's commitment to linear violence is the divine di-unity of mother and daughter-son, which requires an antiseptic sacrifice and a rageless apocalypse.

Is War Beautiful?

A Son at the Front adheres to the law of the invariant family:[19] the third paragraph very nearly guarantees that Campton, the painter-protagonist, will eventually sacrifice "his son, his only boy" to the war (*SF*, 3); Campton's concierge has a single son killed at the front (*SF*, 185); we eventually get the news from the front that the great physician Fortin's son, "his only son, was dead" (*SF*, 119). Why do so many families have a single child, always male, always the appropriate age to fight, always eager to die? Part of the answer, the non-manipulative part, surfaces when Madeline Mayhew's boy appears: "Look here," says Campton, to this unknown youth who is his cousin, an American but eager to enlist, "if you're Madeline Mayhew's boy you're an only son" (*SF*, 106). Madeline Mayhew is in fact a misnomer, because she has married someone named Upsher, which makes her, appallingly, Madeline Upsher. In a book that uses the phrase "living burial" to describe existence in "occupied provinces" (*SF*, 122), this is perhaps (at least following *One of Ours*) no surprise. Something—doubtless something female—will be buried alive in this war book. A more explicit consideration is that if a single son dies, so does his family line; the Fall of the House of Upsher is the model for all paternal names that are extinguished by a single death.

This means that the book is arranged to contemplate the possibility of absolute endings—and conceivably the possiblity of origins as well. If Wharton was a feminist at all, and I think she was at least a feminist in her desperate refusal of the paths that American femininity was conventionally allowed to walk, she should have seen World War I as an Armageddon that promised a revelation, an unveiling.[20] Twenty-five thousand American women, most of them educated and middle-to-upper class, eager to find a useful alternative to marriage, went overseas as part of the war effort.[21] None of them, perhaps, found better work to do than Wharton: she employed a hundred seamstresses who had been displaced; she founded the American Hostels for Refugees; she arranged to get discounted groceries to refugees, provided daycare for them, and taught them; at the request of Belgium, she took charge of over 600 refugee children; she arranged benefits; she inaugurated a "cure program" for tuberculosis victims (eventually taken over by the Red Cross); she contributed; she rallied; she propagandized.[22] The precise contribution of World War I to the modern history of feminism is disputed: if the war itself raised hopes of political, professional, and sexual freedom for women, the post-war era was a retrenchment. I gather that the current tendency among historians is to emphasize the reaction.[23] But the war had unleashed on Wharton's part her most untamable energies, and she was not alone.

There was a problem, however, with merely asserting, in effect, that though ten million sons had to be sacrificed, though ten million houses had to fall, nevertheless women could hold history together by their newly liberated competence and force. It is not that this notion is too bloodthirsty for Wharton (she was no pacifist and decidedly no hand wringer); it is that the notion is not lovely enough. World War I called into question the appropriateness of beauty to the twentieth century for male authors, so that when Joyce wanted to write most beautifully he impersonated a woman (*women's* beauty could survive twentieth-century war), Nabokov a murderer (*destructive* beauty could survive twentieth-century war); the issue for Wharton is, rather, that beauty is traditional or non-existent, that catastrophic time cannot be literary time. Revolutionary time in the realm of religion is apocalypse, in the realm of politics, catastrophe, in the realm of ideas, science. But the essence of literature, Derrida says, is always postponed annihilation, so that there can be no such thing as revolutionary time in the realm of writing, except as a definitive threat. The question raised by Wharton—is it possible to imagine, by arranging the killing of only sons, the severing of the artistic heritage—turns out to endanger the validity of her own art, including the book in which the issue is revolved. There can be no question, in Wharton's mind, of a *feminine* literary heritage (Wharton's general though not universal scorn for female antecedents complicates all pro-feminist readings of her oeuvre).[24]

If the war that encourages feminist hopes also promises to destroy the male literary tradition, which *is*, to Wharton, the literary tradition, then feminist hopes have to be sacrificed so that the war can be redeemed. In the character of the bellicose Adele Anthony we can follow what happens to Wharton's feminism: the woman warrior is more male than the men of the book in order to arouse them to their potential—subdued in a feminine era—for beautiful, rational combat. In order to acknowledge the war but not be destroyed by it, Wharton feels the need of absorbing the war into traditional modes of beauty, of reconciling the Great War to its Homeric ancestry. This requires that she aestheticize male behavior at its most uncivilized; dying and killing have to be made to serve aesthetic unities and the survival of the tradition. Still—that the war that puts beauty and literature at risk needs to be revised as the war in which masculine beauty survives the feminization of culture makes the book more troubled, more paradoxical, less propagandistic, and more interesting than even sympathetic critics have allowed.

The positing of an authentic male artist as the protagonist raises all issues of war, manhood, and beauty to the surface. Suppose John Campton to be a great artist—he is at least not without artistic integrity—and the first inference is that beauty has nothing whatever to do with war. "No doubt the future was dark"—it is the end of July 1914—"But what could a man do, whose convictions were so largely formed by the play of things on his retina . . . . Paris was too triumphant a fact not to argue down his fears. There she lay in the security of her beauty, and once more proclaimed herself eternal" (*SF*, 26). Campton is characteristically blinded by too much vision; but it is not as simple as it first appears to condemn his insensate sensitivity. "Usually any deep inward trouble made him more than ever alive to the outward aspect of things; but this new world in which people talked glibly of sons in the war had suddenly become invisible to him" (*SF*, 70). The "inward trouble" is that a war means that his son might be killed at the front; the "outward aspect of things" is that people talk glibly of sons at the front. Suddenly, superficial and private look very much alike: private pain and public crises are blurred in wartime. The invisibility of war to the painter is either a limitation of his art (perhaps he sounds like a quaint belated impressionist) or its strength (to claim prescience or comprehension with respect to war can only be glib).

A Son at the Front never resolves the enigma, but the book has a tendency. The suggestion that it is a strength of art not to be able to envision war is increasingly arguable; then it is ironized; then it is satirized. When Campton wonders "What retribution devised by man could be commensurate with the crime of destroying the beautiful world?" we feel sympathy (*SF*, 222). When silly, selfish Mrs. Talkett urges that "we *must* save Beauty for the world . . . . after all, ugliness is the only *real* death, isn't it?" she is contemptible (*SF*, 224), but we are unsure whether to have contempt for her or her idea. Finally, when Campton has dealings with a pretentious crowd of pseudo-aesthetes who have "decided, for a certain number of hours each day, to forget the war," and shouts his approval of their determination "that beauty shall not perish from the earth!" (*SF*, 233–234), he bellows this Lincolnesque phrase, more appropriate to commemorate a battle at the scene of the battle, to drown out his final knowledge that beauty can have no sanctuary. Does that mean that war must be beautiful if beauty is to continue as a relevant category?

Cather's immediate answer would be yes; H. D.'s would be no; in Wharton, it takes a book's whole length to work the answer out. Cather presumes actually to describe the war; Wharton approaches the war, but she does not arrive, which makes her solution to the most basic of all artistic questions about war asymptotic. (Wharton in real life was more familiar with the front than Cather or Campton, but she suppresses her familiarity.) When George Campton is wounded, his father and stepfather drive to the hospital, which is to say toward the front. As they get closer, the war gets more real: "Had he ever before heard that sinister roar? . . . He could not be sure. . . . He cowered back in his corner. Would it ever stop, he asked himself? . . . Was that merciless thud forever in the ears of the dying?" (*SF*, 271). Closer: "Every crash of the guns seemed to tear a piece of flesh from his body; and it was always the piece nearest the heart" (*SF*, 275). Nevertheless, though the war becomes first available to Campton's senses, then to his flesh by way of his imagination, he never does arrive at the front. Moreover, when he arrives at his wounded son, he can hear the guns but not, so to speak, the war: the "isolation" of father and son is enforced by "George's weakness, and by his father's inabilty to learn from others what the boy was not yet able to tell him" (*SF*, 292).

I take Campton's approach to the front as a parable of the approach of beauty to combat: there is no place else to go, but can it ever quite arrive *there*? Does Campton = beauty? It would be helpful to know exactly what Wharton thinks of his painting, but everything Wharton says about it is delicately tuned. There are certainly signs that he is admirably old-fashioned in his integrity, his aestheticism, his hatred of technology. But "old-fashioned" is itself an interrogated term: to be old-fashioned (Wharton argues) means once to have been in fashion, though Wharton would like to believe that true art has no relation to fashion, in or out. Is there any art more compatible than Campton's with the war?

At a meeting of "The Friends of French Art," the pretentious aesthetes quiet down as the "pianist attacked Stravinsky" (*SF*, 329). One's first reaction is: poor Stravinsky. It is the only name of a modern artist in the book, so one needs to know what Wharton thinks of him. We hear no more. Does the pianist attack Stravinsky in the sense that he makes a violent—blunt and brutally approximate—assault on his music? Or is attacking him precisely what one should do with Stravinsky? Does Wharton share the view of Modris Eksteins that Stravinsky's violence is akin to the war's? Would that make Stravinsky's music beautiful in a revolutionary way? There is no saying. Toward the end of the book, Campton "attacked [Mme. Lebel] in oils" (*SF*, 373). Mme. Lebel is Campton's poor concierge, recently bereft of her only son at the front: there can be no second-guessing the decency of this art project. Once again, however, we do not know what to make of the verb. Campton is painting Mme. Lebel as the first step of his new determination to "shut himself up, for long solitary hours, in the empty and echoing temple of his art." Is his art an asylum or a place from which to launch attacks? Wharton's problem is that it has to be both.

As in the case of Fitzgerald, Hemingway, and Faulkner, the question of how art is to survive becomes a question of how to read time: if time is linear, then World War I is its catastrophe, and to survive it is an anticlimax. The single sentence of the first paragraph ends with John Campton "contemplating a battered calendar" that, according to the single sentence of the second paragraph, "marked July 30, 1914" (*SF*, 3). What calendar time informs us, retrospectively read, is that Europe is on the verge of wartime. The question is whether art implies any temporality that may be salvaged. Art should be a place of "transcendent bliss," as Wharton puts it on Campton's behalf: when Campton begins to paint again, "his first stroke carried him out of space and time" (*SF*, 227). Yet the temporality of the art world, as Wharton describes it, is tied inextricably to fashion, that is, to femininity. Beausite was once the fashionable painter; he paints a portrait of Campton's ex-wife, which she puts away on the advice of her new husband, because her "dress had grown so dreadfully old-fashioned" (*SF*, 16). This connects the fashions of high culture to the fashions of haute couture. Knowing how it goes, Beausite has trained his "three sons in three different lines of art so that there might always be a Beausite in the fashion" (*SF*, 157). Beausite could not have an only son at the front; fashion is never at risk. Typically, Campton is in fashion as well as out of it. He admirably refuses to become merely a portrait painter when he could make a fortune at it, but that is partly to avoid "turning out work that would injure his reputation and reduce his sales after the war" (*SF*, 130).

If art is fashion, then it will certainly avoid the catastrophe of the Great War, or any other holocaust, so long as there survive rich people with pretensions. The problem is that Wharton almost fails to be able to imagine any other continuity for art; yet World War I appears to be pure discontinuity. The only solution turns out to be very nearly Cather's.

A Son at the Front ends with Campton in his studio, working for the first time on George's monument. He had previously refused, but something shakes him:

> After he [a friend of the dead son] had gone the painter moved back to his long table. He had always had . . . lumps of clay lying about within reach. He pulled out all the sketches of his son from the old portfolio, spread them before him on the table, and began. (*SF*, 425–426)

With this beginning the book ends, on a peculiar note. An entirely new art form is introduced, as if painting has to be alienated at the last moment. The new art form is literally monumental. Monuments have the attraction of founding their immortality on mortality: Campton's marble (translated from clay) will redeem his sketches (which the painter, until this last gesture, had not been able to look at).

The book pulls together, at this last opportunity, only if it makes sense to build monuments, to translate ephemeral things (sketches, clay) into their opposite (sculpture, marble). So we learn that despite his growing remoteness from George, or in his growing remoteness, there had been a "close inextricable sense in which Campton had had his son" (*SF*, 421). They share, at the end, related privacies; or perhaps George's injury, though it keeps him distant, allows John's lameness to participate in the vast visitation. A friend tells Campton that George, by his injury, even before dying of it, has been "transfigured, say; no trans—what's the word in the theology books? A new substance": transubstantiation becomes the model of the translation from clay and sketches to marble monument (*SF*, 390). Though Campton had thought to wait until the end of the war "to find some new ground of communion" with his son (*SF*, 403), it arrives before the Armistice. George seems, at the end of his life, "part and substance of his father" (*SF*, 394); if death is to be transformed into beauty, the logic of tradition goes, then sons in their deaths have to rejoin their fathers.

The difference from Cather is that they are not dying into their mothers. In particular, George does not die either into his uncomprehending mother or even into Adele Anthony, the childless mother-figure of the novel, George's confidante, embodiment of Wharton's ambivalence. Adele, who had traveled to Europe to support her brother's unsuccessful artistic endeavors, is the strongest advocate of the capacity of the war for building beautiful characters; death becomes the ground of her passion for immortal beauty. She is a strange figure haunting the book; a combination of Jo March and Mrs. Wheeler, Adele is at first dismissed by John Campton as an "elderly virgin on the warpath" (*SF*, 85). Her psychic function is to make it obvious that art cannot survive on the model of *female* procreation. (Her motherly instincts are what the book buries alive—she is the real Madeline Upsher.) Adele's first object is to support brother rather than child in art, her second, to support a son's right to find in war a version of his father's aesthetic bliss. She is childless not by accident but by the nature of her character and commitment. Adele is the author of Wharton's book, which does not quite imagine war but knows that it had better be beautiful, if art is going to survive as more than fashion, which is to say as more than feminine.

Is Beauty Warlike?

In *Bid Me to Live*, H. D. goes so far as to grant the genetic disconnection of past and future: if sons in Cather and Wharton die into their fathers and mothers, children in H. D. are sacrificed before the war.[25] Julia (H. D.) has had what sounds like a miscarriage with overtones of abortion (on biographical evidence, it is a stillbirth, caused in H. D.'s opinion by Aldington's brutal announcement of the sinking of the Lusitania);[26] Bella (Dorothy Yorke) has had an abortion; Elsa (D. H. Lawrence's Frieda) has abandoned her three children. Yet this is not to say that the war has invaded private lives, or not at least unambiguously to say it: the pervasive decision not to raise children seems to be entirely personal, and it is to the personal that H. D. wishes to flee the war. *Bid Me to Live* is exclusively a home-front novel, though Rafe (Richard Aldington) occasionally brings the war on leave with him. H. D.'s question, as much as Cather's or Wharton's, is whether the family (or the private network as substitute family) is strong enough to absorb the brunt of the war without being a casualty of the war.

"Beauty is truth, truth beauty": H. D. wants to grant the urn's mystery, though the urn knows nothing of time. "But could this truth be beautiful? Maybe it was. They had shouted of honour and sacrifice for two years, three years now. This was winter or early spring but seasons revolved around horrors until one was numb and the posters that screamed at one at street-corners had no more reality, not as much, as the remembered Flemish gallery of the Louvre and the abstract painted horror of a flayed saint" (*BML*, 37). This seems to repudiate the possibility of aesthetic war—yet the remark is so deeply obscure that you begin to wonder whether the book's general obscurity is not principally an attempt to obfuscate the question. "Maybe it was" seems to have no rhetorical energy at all, especially compared to the subsequent passage on the war's horrors. But it turns out not to be the horrors of war that scream at H. D. so much as the horrors of war *posters*. Is it war or crude representations of it that have less reality than art? We seem to be saving Keats's motto by denying not merely the beauty of war but also its truth (its "reality"); what is *more* real, however, is another representation. Beauty is truth if the "truth" in question is a painting. Not merely a painting: a painting of violent horror. Beautiful representations of horror have more beauty and truth than crude representations of horror. We were looking for an opposition of combat and art, and we get merely this.

The book is a frustrated search for an oppositional term to war: the natural, the mythic, the personal, (which add up to) the beautiful. At Cornwall, "heather country," Julia walks "out of a dream, the fog and fever, the constant threat from the air, the constant reminder of death and suffering (those soldiers in blue hospital uniform) into reality. This was real" (*BML*, 146). If the opposition is to death, then Cornwall, where Julia goes off with the painter Vane (Cecil Gray), leaving Rafe and Frederick (D. H. Lawrence), is not more real by virtue of being more mortal, more pedestrian, more quotidian, rather the reverse: "some parallel in myth suggested itself to her as she ran a bare hand over the rough grey woven texture of her coat" (*BML*, 147–148). Reality is the capacity of such a coat to metamorphose: "It was a sign of something . . . a miraculous story of a fleece . . . . Any fleece; anyhow, golden" (*BML*, 148). The object is the same as in Mitchell or Morrison, miraculous elemental unity. "How many years had this path existed? She was one with its druid asymmetry as she trudged toward the sea" (*BML*, 152). Unity differs from publicity insofar as something is reserved, and what is reserved is precisely the mythic or sacred quality that can be seen but not violated. "Surely this room," Julia thinks while she is still indoors and still with Rafe and Frederick, "was open on one side; everything that went on here, it seemed to Julia, was public property, no privacy, yet with a sort of inner sanctity that public works of art have" (*BML*, 90). Beauty is the innerness of the exposed, the real emotion experienced by actors on stage, the mythic beneath the skin.

Beauty at least has to *face* outward; and that means it must front the war. How to be about the war but not of it—or rather how to be away from the war but still contain it—becomes the question of the book. The answer, as in Cather and Wharton, is life-in-death: but death, if we are to avoid finding only the war beautiful, must be an available aspect of home-front endurance. Julia's culminating experience of beauty in the book occurs at a movie theatre with Vane. The movie scene begins with nature: "Oddly, it was not America, there was the usual slope, hairpin bend, but it was Italy." "Hairpin" implies a road, and momentarily a car appears, possibly out of control but avoiding precipitous destruction. As the car goes down the mountain, all the audience "swerved and turned," Julia as well. "She was part of this. She swerved and veered with a thousand men in khaki" (*BML*, 123). At first you think that Julia must be at the movies with soldiers on leave. A thousand, however, is too many (she is with Vane, so she is not at a London theatre). The point is that she is experiencing annihilation—it is the moment of identity with the troops.

This is to come too close to reading the war for beauty, and too close also to perfect publicity. Consequently, the aesthetic emotion Julia is feeling turns out, as usual, to have its reserve. "She edged forward further, her eyes were adjusting, focussing to this scene of danger without. It was danger without. Inside she was clear, the old Greek *katharsis* was at work here, as in the stone-ledged theatre benches of fifth-century Greece." By a stroke the war is faced, internalized, repelled; Julia is freed of it; she returns from 1918 to classical Greece. The scene is set for the appearance of "Beauty"— now mystically protected from the squalor of the front. The first car is followed by a second—the war, which Julia thought she was confronting, is turned into a duel—and their destination, at first a mystery, is finally revealed. A goddess, as in *The Iliad*, is what causes men to risk death: "This was the answer to everything, then, Beauty, for surprisingly, a goddess-woman stepped forward. She released from the screen the first (to Julia) intimation of screen-beauty." Then H. D. explicates the pun: "Screen? This was a veil" (*BML*, 124). What is public suddenly is privatized.

The cost, however, is flesh. "There she was exactly incorporated, no screen-image. Here was Beauty, a ghost but Beauty. Beauty was not dead. It emerged unexpectedly in the midst of this frantic maelstrom. The Spirit moved, gestured" (*BML*, 125–126). Why "no screen-image"? "Beauty" is "exactly incorporated," because she is incorporeal to begin with, a spirit. If beauty is a spirit, then what one sees on the screen is not the screen (veiled) image of beauty (which would imply that beauty has a physical presence elsewhere) but beauty itself; to incorporate beauty is precisely to leave it incorporate—free of a corpus, or corpse. Beauty is not dead because beauty was never exactly alive. World War I cannot kill it because it was already a ghost.

The ghostliness of beauty—its ontologically anomalous position as sensed spirit, incorporated incorporeity, publicly displayed privacy, mortalized myth—is the repeated point of the book, its whole strategy. If beauty is what continues (as in Cather and Wharton), and World War I is the chasm of history, then ghostly half-life, the state of being undead, is the non-trinitarian solution. The book begins by comparing the "lost generation" with those who were even more badly victimized a half a generation older. "They had roots (being in their mid-twenties and very early thirties) still with that past" (*BML*, 7). This is H. D.'s and D. H. Lawrence's generation as opposed to Hemingway's or Fitzgerald's; the older generation's modernism can only appear as an apparition. There has to be continuity for there to be art, but continuity is only possible if death is already internal to what continues. "The ghost, whatever it was, was not dead": Julia is referring to the perseverance of her shared love with Rafe as Rafe goes off to war. "Ghosts don't, of course, die. That was it. It had been, even in the beginning, a sort of emanation" (*BML*, 22). When Bella, Rafe's lover, wants to discuss the dance of love and passion, she "might have been saying anything, it's a cold evening, or do you believe in ghosts? Ghosts? They were visibly about her, Rafe on the Appian Way, a cypress in the graveyard where they had laid a wreath of pink and white alternate camellias on Shelley's grave" (*BML*, 98). Is this ghostly memory of a grave a solution or a repetition of the problem?

Wharton's *A Son at the Front* begins with a calendar; *Bid Me to Live* begins: "Oh, the times, oh the customs! Oh, indeed, the times! The customs! Their own, specifically, but part and parcel of the cosmic, comic, crucifying times of history" (*BML*, 7). The "times of history" turn out, as always, to be Christian in type: linear time implies narratives of premature death, whether or not resurrection is possible, and apocalypse. H. D. attempts to Hellenize, and to live as if in a myth, or as if always in the process of turning life, moment by moment, into art. (This book is closer to aestheticized memoir than to roman à clef.) For Rafe and Julia to experience Michaelangelo fully is to *be* Michaelangelo—even to experience art as a tactile presence (like Campton at the end of *A Son at the Front*) is to be Michaelangelo: "the very touch of the fingers of Michaelangelo had been transferred to theirs. Their feet, their hands were instilled with living beauty, with things that were not dead. Other cities had been buried. Other people had been shot to death and something had gone on" (*BML*, 72). It sounds like Campton being "carried . . . out of space and time." Wharton wants to find a way to absorb private concerns into public history; for H. D., art exists visually in a public setting but must retain a private, tactile dimension.[27] Her attempt is to reserve something of mythic time within the world catastrophe.

Thus the identification of clocks and war: Rafe, about to leave for the continent, calls attention to his watch. "Oh, the—time," says Julia. "Time in prison, that time," she thinks, and says, "I can actually hear it ticking" (*BML*, 19). Later: "There would be this pause, then there would be the tic-tic-tic again that people said . . . were 'our guns'" (*BML*, 105). Am I wrong to think that this trope is suspiciously facile? Could it be so easy to assign war and history to the continent and reduce them simultaneously to this irritating ticking? The complication is that everything that H. D. tries to reserve on the inside of apocalypse is so destructive itself. It is Rafe's watch that is ticking:

> "Hullo, what's happened to it?"
> "Oh, it just went on ticking. They do."
> She peered through the fencer's mask into the bird cage [i.e., into the watch], she took up the watch, she shook it. "Maybe it's stopped."
> "Stopped?"
> "I mean, maybe it stopped at tea-time." She held it to her ear. True, she had heard its insistent insect tick-tick. The room was so quiet. Standing, she had heard above a table the voice of time on a table, the little voice that said, "It's time, it's time." The little demon or devil or daemon was alive. She knew of course that it hadn't stopped at tea-time.
> "Well, it's tea-time, anyhow."
> "Any time is tea-time," she said. (*BML*, 19–20)

The point is to acknowledge the willfullness of the anachronistic pretense. Julia fantasizes that time has stopped; the man, about to go to war, corrects her; she admits that he is right. The passage ends with her stand against schedules. Yet this is a forlorn insistence, because if anything is to be salvaged from the war, it has to be salvaged as a shared reality between Rafe and Julia. To adapt Tom Stoppard: a single vision is a hallucination, popular vision is the war; but what is it if Rafe and Julia together preserve an antebellum ghost?

There is just possibly a hopeless pun in "Any time is tea-time." I do not know when H. D. wrote that line in the several decades during which she composed the novel. Possibly after D-Day? Was she aware that in army parlance the day of the attack is D-Day, the hour of the attack is H-Hour—so that, in the army, any time is T-Time? At any rate, H. D. has an increasingly difficult job distinguishing what she is trying to preserve from what she is preserving it from: the repetition of tea-time, tea-time, tea-time itself picks up the clock's tick-tock. The book works by a kind of interpersonal balancing of power: Julia begins with Rafe. Rafe takes up with Bella, leaving Julia unmatched. When Frederick shows up with Elsa, Elsa plots to give Frederick to Julia to leave herself unencumbered to pair with Vane. But nothing gets concluded between Julia and Frederick, so Elsa does not get Vane, which means that Julia does. "Standing at the head of the stairs, [Julia] was herself now playing her own part in this curious mixed partners, dance of death? dance of life?" (*BML*, 108). It is a domestic version of recently discredited Realpolitik that is enacted in these shifting alliances. There is much mating, but no life is, literally, produced. Julia's lost baby begins to seem like an emblem of her role in the vast visitation. "Herself projected out in death, was that dead child actually. . . . It happened actually about identically with the breaking out of the war" (*BML*, 141).

There can be no salvation from catastrophe in a reserved private sphere because freedom (as opposed to "time's prison, that time") is a constant roiling. Lovers are, when perfectly free, chronically malcontent because what is freed is restless desire, and desires are multiple so long as selves are not whole. When Rafe says to Julia, "I would give [Bella] a mind, I would give you a body" (*BML*, 8), he means of course that he is himself divided, which is very nearly explicit in his précis, "I love you, I desire *l'autre*" (*BML*, 56). Julia in turn needs Rafe for the stability that selves dwell in, Frederick for the instability that selves feed on, Vane because he takes her away from Rafe and Frederick to the possibility of self-loss in nature. The constant fort-da rhetoric of the book begins to look like the sort of self-division that internalizes war, or which, projected, *is* war. "It's all so neat with Rico. But it isn't. Yet it is" (*BML*, 120). This seems like a modernist mannerism: certainly the narrative does not receive much impetus. Yet these are moments in which tick-tock repetitions pick up the death drive of the war. The repeated example of repetition is this one: "It was shut in her as other things were shut in her because 'the war will be over.' (The war will never be over.)" (*BML*, 12). Always a public voice is corrected by an internal voice. It is the private voice that knows that there is no privacy reserved from combat.

The intensifying realization is that the book's style, its disintegration of narrative, is itself an effect of the war, of wartime. "They were all having relationships, or would have—Rafe and Bella. Elsa had said, 'Yes, you and Frederico, that will leave me free for Vanio.' But that hadn't worked out. There was no sense in it. Given normal civilised peace-time conditions of course, all this could never have happened, or it would have happened in sections, so that one could deal with one problem after another, in due sequence" (*BML*, 139). It is peace that is linear.

If these modernist war novels by women are distinct from the modernism of Hemingway, Fitzgerald, and Faulkner, it is that they are more frank about their belligerency, less hopeful about the possibility of a stylistic asylum. Taken as a set, the lesson is that form and style will have to evolve their energy from the catastrophic formlessness and stylelessness of World War I. Cather's book is most linear and bellicose, but only because it seeks an immortal formal unity, a reunited trinitarian aesthetic. H. D.'s book is least linear and belligerent, but observes the indebtedness of fractured narratives to the violence of war. There is no question of an unwitting or automatic participation in violence; the fascination is in the struggle to grant one's implication in order to retain an artist's consciousness in an anaesthetic time.

Media and Immediate Wars

A Media War

Frankie (Frances) Addams of Carson McCullers's *The Member of the Wedding*, and Sam (Samantha) Hughes of Bobbie Ann Mason's *In Country*, are nearly continuous, as if Sam is Frankie five years older and forty years later: the verbal, eccentric, precocious, small-town, universal Southern boy-girl, girl-woman.[28] War (World War II, Vietnam) functions in much the same way for both of them: it represents escape, connection, completion, maturity. Nevertheless, something changes from World War II to Vietnam that radically alters the aesthetic ideal — *The Member of the Wedding* is the last American hope of combat trinitarianism, the female replacement for the masculine, rational duel as the aesthetic basis of war writing. Frankie Addams (mother dead in childbirth, father elsewhere) and Sam Hughes (father dead at nearly the moment of her birth, mother elsewhere) both improvise families, but only Frankie craves familial consubstantiality.

In *The Member of the Wedding*, the Nicene paradigm is ironized: Frankie wants to be so close to her brother (the soldier) and sister-in-law that she claims that *"They are the we of me"* (*MW*, 291), but no reader misses the pathos of the desire. Still, the trinitarian dream is not foreclosed. What Frankie envisions in war is the possibility of transcendent unity; what she misses is the possibility of immanent unity. During the course of the novella, Frankie maintains an intimate, touching relationship with the black servant, Berenice, and the child, John Henry; they spar endlessly, but when they sing, "their three voices were joined, and the parts of the song were woven together"; when they cry, "though the reasons were three different reasons," "yet they started at the same instant as though they agreed together" (*MW*, 359–360). When they share their Utopian dreams, they are God in three persons: "Sometimes their voices crossed and the three worlds twisted. The Holy Lord God John Henry West. The Holy Lord God Berenice Sadie Brown. The Holy Lord God Frankie Addams" (*MW*, 338). At the end of the piece, John Henry dies without preparation, suddenly, apparently insignificantly, of meningitis. But connoisseurs of the female war novel see the meaning: "She remembered John Henry more as he used to be, and it was seldom now that she felt his presence — solemn, hovering, and ghost-gray. Only occasionally at twilight time or when the special hush would come into the room" (*MW*, 391). Crypto-mother and crypto-daughter require a crypto-Holy Ghost; the revised war novel point is that you do not need a war to arrange it (Sam's brother is spending the war safely in Alaska). There is no remaining trinitarian possibility in the postmodern war novel, *In Country*; but the question again for the landlocked Southern girl is how much intimacy with the prematurely dead can be obtained on the Southern home front.

The particular reformulation of the question in *In Country* is how much of Vietnam is available to Sam Hughes — whose father was killed there — *mediately*, by means of the media. The Nabokovian pedagogical fantasy of reading a novel until it mentions another work of literature, then reading *that* until *it* mentions another work, might be tried out on Bobbie Ann Mason, low culture substituted for high. At every mention of a TV show or rock song, watch it or listen to it. Masculinity appears by way of Bruce Springsteen, cross dressing by way of Boy George. Also by way of Klinger from M*A*S*H, which Sam and her Vietnam-vet uncle, Emmett, watch every night.

Sam is trying to connect with her father, and the connection is mediated by two vets, Emmett and his friend Tom. Sam's connection with them is itself distanced, which is why mediation relies on the media. The easiest assumption concerning Sam and Emmett's obsession with M*A*S*H is that Sam is watching to get closer to Vietnam, and Emmett to get farther away. Lonnie tells Sam, "All that stuff on TV you and Emmett watch—it's just fantasy. It's not real" (*IC*, 187). But Lonnie is Sam's first boyfriend, not a veteran. Emmett himself vouches for the realism of M*A*S*H. "Burns reminded him, he said, of his C.O. in Vietnam, a real idiot" (*IC*, 25). In some ways, the show is uncannily suggestive. Sam notices that when Emmett works, he would occasionally "pause and touch his temple for a moment, waiting for the sensation to pass. It was as though he were listening to some inner music" (*IC*, 44). This comes to remind Sam of "the way Radar O'Reilly on M*A*S*H could always hear the chopper coming in with wounded before anyone else could" (*IC*, 50). When Sam asks Tom what he thinks about when he remembers Vietnam, he answers, "Oh, lots of things," and laughs "the way Frank Burns laughed the time he drove a tank into the women's shower" (*IC*, 135).

It is unspecified, always, how much of this sort of analogy Mason vouches for. The narrative voice stays close enough to Sam's consciousness that we cannot tell which of her desperate attempts to imagine Vietnam are successes. This is no defect; Mason is not posing as the expert on Vietnam whose expertise is the result of immediate acquaintance. Everyone—protagonist, author, readers—gets caught up in the question of how much mediated Vietnam *is* Vietnam. Insofar as we are to believe that Sam is not prohibited from understanding Vietnam, the master trope of the narrative is chiasmus. Increasingly, Western Kentucky begins to look like Vietnam to Sam; this may or may not be hallucinatory. Meanwhile, veterans remember Vietnam as home. Tom's memories of Vietnam are escaping, but "sometimes I feel homesick for those memories" (*IC*, 78). The odd word allows us to realize that when Emmett says he has been "homesick" for M*A*S*H "since the series ended" (*IC*, 33), he is homesick for Indochina. Finally, by means of Sam's father's diary, we get a direct report from Vietnam. Yet: "What if Charlie [the Cong] dropped in sudden? It would be like Sundays when company came and Mama went around grabbing all of Pap's clothes and all the toys strowed all over the living room" (*IC*, 203). And: "we're one fine team. If Hot Shot didn't get so mad we wouldn't be half as good as we are. He really knows how to run us. Just like Coach Jones in basketball" (*IC*, 204). This is metonymy even on the part of a combatant: Vietnam is mediated for everybody.

If Sam imagines Kentucky as Vietnam, and veterans conceive of Vietnam as home, that of course does not mean that Vietnam and home are alike. What it does imply is that concepts and paradigms can cross; Kentuckians brought to Vietnam some of Kentucky, but Sam sheds some of Kentucky when she directs her thoughts obsessively toward Vietnam. The intersection of the chiasmus occurs when Sam spends the night at the swamp, trying to get the exact feeling of "humping the boonies." It is uncertain how far she succeeds. She is scared (she hears a stranger—it turns out to be Emmett—approaching): "a curious pleasure stole over her. This terror was what the soldiers had felt every minute" (*IC*, 217). But "she felt no rush of adrenaline, no trembling of knees. She knew it was because she didn't really believe this was real, after all. It couldn't be happening to her. In a few moments, everything would be clear and fine" (*IC*, 218). What is certain is that Sam and Emmett trade perspectives. Emmett, finding Sam, thinks that she had "flipped out again," and tells her that "you scared me. . . . You might have considered that some people would be worried about you" (*IC*, 219). She had spent the book, until this moment, worried about *Emmett's* flipping out: the perfect chiasmus indicates that some of the consciousness of Vietnam has been transferred.

When Sam's friend Dawn gets pregnant, Sam, translating everything, can only think of it as an assassination: "Since Dawn got pregnant, Sam had been feeling that if she didn't watch her step, her whole life could be ruined by some mischance, some stupid surprise, like sniper fire" (*IC*, 184). Now Dawn will "live and die in Hopewell" (*IC*, 142)—mainly die, we take it. By the inevitable rhetorical logic, this makes the way that Vets are inhabited by Vietnam into a kind of pregnancy. "Emmett had Agent Orange and a sinister pain in his head. Dawn was having a baby" (*IC*, 159). What Sam is after (living with her brother as if with a husband, dating Tom, apparently attracted like a goddess to the wounded) is to be similarly imbued with death. At the end of the book, Sam arrives at the Vietnam War Memorial. "Sam doesn't understand what she is feeling, but it is something so strong, it is like a tornado moving in her, something massive and overpowering. It feels like giving birth to this wall" (*IC*, 240).

The chiasmus is comforting; the crossing of birth-death and death-birth is imitated by the structure of the book, which ends where it begins, with the trip to the wall. The cleverness of the book's beauty, however, is that it provides the satisfactions of closure and symmetry without sacrificing any of its desperate skepticism. If, at the swamp, Sam feels some of the insanity of Vietnam and Emmett tries to bring her home to peace and security, nevertheless the crossing is always in jeopardy, and the attempt to relocate Vietnam in Kentucky oscillates wildly from the beginning (Sam runs to the swamp to escape Emmett and Vietnam but brings canned pork and beans to imitate G.I. food). Similarly, Sam urges Dawn to have an abortion rather than be destroyed as if by (male) sniper fire (abortion equals escape from Vietnam), but "soldiers murdered babies. . . . [W]omen did too. They ripped their own unborn babies out of themselves and flushed them away, squirming and bloody" (*IC*, 215). Is the assertion of women's power a step toward or away from Vietnam? Sam's mother, who has freed herself from Vietnam by forgetting Sam's father, remarrying, having a baby, and abandoning her brother, Emmett, "raved about Geraldine Ferraro [it is 1984]: 'Women can do anything now, Sam'" (*IC*, 232). She is urging Sam to go to college—to get free of father, Emmett, and Vietnam herself. Nevertheless, when Sam is angered that she cannot dig a foxhole, she thinks that "that woman Mondale nominated could probably dig one" (*IC*, 224).

In women's war fiction, questions of war are posed as questions of family; if Sam's relation to Vietnam is fluid at every moment, so will be her relation to relations. When Sam's mother Irene leaves Emmett, it is portrayed (at a distance not far from Sam's consciousness) exactly as if she had abandoned her husband—an identification reinforced by the fact that Irene flees Emmett to Lexington, where a vet's wife later, similarly, escapes. Sam lives with Emmett as if his wife; Emmett tries to be fatherly (*IC*, 225); Sam tries to be motherly (*IC*, 153). When Sam finds herself attracted to Tom despite his emasculation, she wants him as lover, as father (*IC*, 174), as child (*IC*, 129), and as fellow soldier (*IC*, 124). Since father Dwayne was dead at Sam's current age, he is turned into a hypothetical date; since Tom is now older than her father at the time of his death, this makes him potentially fatherly (*IC*, 191); since Dwayne was more childish than Sam at the same age (*IC*, 179), father-figures can metamorphose into son-figures. If the fantasy of the trinitarian war novel is that sons can die into their parents, *In Country* is the postmodernization of the genre: a daughter, not a mother, tries to identify with not a filial but a paternal ghost, though she tries to make herself pregnant with it nonetheless; but every relation of age, sex, and family role is tried out, and every one of them is a mediation.

I began by comparing the intricacy of cultural reference in *In Country* to Nabokov for this reason: if it is Nabokov's passion to create a parallel universe that alludes to war only as what has been excluded from it, Mason's universe of artifacts may be either a way of blocking Vietnam or a way of capturing it. In this respect, *In Country* resembles the Nabokovian generation of male Vietnam writing in which sports mediate verbal play and warfare; Mason substitutes the family for the team as the agonized arena. The female war tradition, by way of variant aesthetic models, arrives at much the same point as the male war tradition. The distinction is that if Vietnam sports novelists wondered how invisible Vietnam can be allowed to stay without frustrating their historical homeopathy, Mason wonders how visibly she can conjure Vietnam without undermining her dogged loyalty to the possibility of formal relations.[29]

Immediate War

Joan Didion's *Democracy* takes the war novel as far as it can go in a certain direction: set around the time of the fall of Saigon in 1975, the novel portrays war as if just after the last moment in history that it could be located in space and time.[30] With the end of the Vietnam war, Didion's world (centered on the mid-Pacific, underneath planes that distribute contraband between Asia and America) is so thoroughly permeated by war that you cannot tell where arms-trading ends and legitimate business begins, or where business connections end and family relations begin; meanness is so pervasive that war seems a nostalgic formalization of human injuring, and the only manifestation of actual enduring love is on the part of the book's most shadowy and unattached dealer in weaponry. This is the furthest conceivable fall from duel warfare.[31] The surprise is that the context of *Democracy* is the context of Maxine Hong Kingston's *The Woman Warrior*,[32] which revives the dream of duel warfare, in the words of a female novelist.

The family of the narrator (call her Kingston) leaves China in the midst of war with Japan; Kingston is born during the American participation in the same war; the Korean War is part of her childhood (*WW*, 174); Vietnam, where her brother is serving, is the book's present (*WW*, 114). The Asian Theater of perpetual combat is the setting of her book as well as Didion's. But Kingston betrays very little interest in any of these wars—she is concerned with warriors rather than soldiers, with duels rather than terrorism and its technology. That bare statement, however, is not enough to explain the title. The book is divided into five sections, in which only the second, "White Tigers," is centered on a woman warrior.

You get closer to understanding the title by noticing that the first tale, "No Name Woman," is about a passive adulteress in China (her adultery is probably an aspect of her conventional submission to any man's desires), whose house is invaded by the outraged villagers, and who commits suicide, taking her child. Then comes the woman warrior chapter, pregnant with the motive of revenge against rich and misogynistic men (*WW*, 30). And toward the end of the final chapter, "A Song for a Barbarian Reed Pipe," a family is worried about bandits who threaten to invade their homes; this is followed by the concluding legend of Ts'ai Yen, another woman warrior. The book is framed, at any rate, by tales of invasion and women's revenge.

Even that structural symmetry is not enough to explain the title. Kingston frequently writes as if the book per se, and as a whole, constitutes revenge against two overlapping groups: men, white America. It is difficult to see, however, how it amounts to that. Reading as a white American male, I felt quite safe, at least at first, at least superficially. The pain of the book seems to stay centered without very much eccentricity at all on the Chinese girl and woman whom I am led to call Kingston. She is at most points of the book ashamed or overwhelmed or defeated or silenced. It is tempting to see in the woman warrior tales a merely ironic fantasy. If this were true, the book would collapse into bathos—I do not think it does. The title is not a clarifying act of taxonomy; it is a mystery to be approached.

Approach it this way: *The Woman Warrior* is a written text, but it feigns orality and presence. Everywhere the arbitrariness of signifiers is denied: puns are significant (*WW*, 185); naming is meaningful (*WW*, 192); ideograms resemble their signifieds (passim); chanting preserves the vibrations of voice on the inside of language (passim); perhaps origami is invoked to turn the paper itself of literature into things in the world (*WW*, 120). The most ambitious attempt of the book to be more present than a book is the frequent recourse to "talk-stories." "Talk-stories" are distinct from "stories" by virtue of the resonances of voice; in addition, the term "talk-story" is itself a kind of Englished ideogram. Talk-stories are conceptually precedent to any division of analysis and creativity. ("They"—the American teachers—"take stories and teach us to turn them into essays" [*WW*, 201].) They precede any disconnection of truth and fiction. (The mother, main talker of stories, is "a practical woman, she could not invent stories and told only true ones." Yet, after Kingston is adapted to American life, she considers Chinese to be "the language of impossible stories" [*WW*, 66, 87].) They precede any removal of artist from audience. ("I've watched a Chinese audience [at a recital] laugh, visit, talk-story" [*WW*, 172].) They are Homeric as Homer was experienced by an audience that did not doubt his story's truth or his creativity, both verified by his inspired presence.

If orality and duel warfare are metaphorically intimate, so that the whole Homeric declension is a function of improvised, merely metonymic connections of fallen (abandoned) literature to fallen (expansive) warfare, then *The Woman Warrior*, insofar as it is determined to be oral, ought to celebrate the duel, ought to *be* a duel. So it does, so it is. The duel warfare that Kingston learns as a woman warrior in her mother's story is natural: "Every creature has a hiding skill and a fighting skill a warrior can use" (*WW*, 23–24). Duel warfare is aesthetic violence: "When I get hungry enough, the killing and falling are dancing too" (*WW*, 27). It is distinguished from army warfare in both these respects.

> The old man [the woman warrior's tutor] pointed out strengths and weaknesses whenever heroes met in classical battles, but warfare makes a scramble of the beautiful, slow old fights. I saw one young fighter salute his opponent—and five peasants hit him from behind with scythes and hammers. His opponent did not warn him.
> "Cheaters!" I yelled. "How am I going to win against cheaters?"
> "Don't worry," the old man said. "You'll never be trapped like that poor amateur. You can see behind you like a bat." (*WW*, 30)

"Fights are confusing as to who has won," Kingston observes about the reality of contests as against the dream of a duel (*WW*, 51). I might go so far as to argue that insofar as the book pretends to be oral, it necessarily has to invoke the natural, rational, duel warfare of the oral tradition. Or that if it wants to duel, it needs to speak.

At all points, the oral project and the warrior project reinforce each other. "My mother told [stories] that followed swords-women through woods and palaces for years. . . . At last I saw that I too had been in the presence of great power, my mother talking-story. . . . I had forgotten this chant that was once mine, given me by my mother, who may not have known its power to remind. She said I would grow up a wife and a slave, but she taught me the song of the warrior woman, Fa Mu Lan. I would have to grow up a warrior woman" (*WW*, 19–20). Throughout this passage, it is unclear whether power is the subject of the story or a quality of it. Not the least of the sources of the talk-story's power is that among the distinctions that the genre does not recognize as absolute are gendered ones. ("I put on my men's clothes and armor and tied my hair in a man's fashion. 'How beautiful you look,' the people said. 'How beautiful she looks'" [*WW*, 36].) The fall of war, in which external female beauty replaces inherent male beauty as a motive, has not yet occurred. The generalization of this point is that before difference, language is action. "The ideographs for *revenge* are 'report a crime' and 'report to five families.' The reporting is the vengeance—not the beheading, not the gutting, but the words" (*WW*, 53). De Man says that history is a text, even when it poses as war. Kingston posits a world in which texts *are* war.

Kingston is anything but naïve. She knows perfectly well the writtenness of her tribute to orality. Her adopted American sensibility and her mastery of English entail the loss of Chinese presence. After the woman-warrior tale of "White Tigers" is a blank space, followed by:

> My American life has been such a disappointment.
> "I got straight A's, Mama."
> "Let me tell you a true story about a girl who saved her village." (*WW*, 45)

With Kingston's fall into scholarship comes simultaneously this admission: "I have no magic beads, no water gourd sight, no rabbit that will jump in the fire when I'm hungry. I dislike armies" (*WW*, 49). The naturalized, that is, denaturalized American demands distinctions between truth and fiction: "And I don't want to listen to any more of your stories; they have no logic. They scramble me up. You lie with stories. You won't tell me a story and then say, 'This is a true story,' or 'This is just a story.' I can't tell the difference" (*WW*, 201). Between imagination and analysis: "I learned to think that mysteries are for explanation" (*WW*, 204). All boundaries become desirable: "I continue to sort out what's just my childhood, just my imagination, just my family, just the village, just movies, just living" (*WW*, 205). This is a sentence you could find nearly verbatim in *In Country*.

Still, the book ends with "A Song for a Barbarian Reed Pipe," about the warrior-poetess Ts'ai Yen, who is kidnapped from her father, a "scholar famous for his library," by the barbarians, the Southern Hsiung-nu (*WW*, 207). She learns to fight barbarian style, which includes the use of singing arrows: "During battle the arrows whistled, high whirling whistles that suddenly stopped when the arrows hit true." Ts'ai Yen thinks that this "was their only music," until she hears their flutes. "They reached again and again for a high note, yearning toward a high note, which they found at last and held—an icicle in the desert. The music disturbed Ts'ai Yen; its sharpness and its cold made her ache." With the end of artistic yearning, with its consummation, its hitting home, music imitates the trenchancy of the arrows (*WW*, 208).

When Ts'ai Yen returns to civilization, "she brought her songs back from the savage lands, and one of the three that has been passed down to us is 'Eighteen Stanzas for a Barbarian Reed Pipe,' a song that Chinese sing to their own instruments. It translated well" (*WW*, 209). "Translation" means "transcription": from reed pipe to the instruments of Chinese civilization. The translation is not from language to language but is, so to speak, over the head of language. The translation, without, apparently, loss, is from musical weapons to painful music, and then from barbarian instruments to those of civilization.

Oral culture can be perfectly translated into writing insofar as words retain their capacity to sing and wound: Kingston's conservative and her avenging impulses are identical. We may not accept it—we are required to believe that the orality that precedes splitting (including gender divisions) is the agent of wounding (and revenge against males). But Kingston is aware of her paradoxes and her affronts to post-structuralist theory. I do not want to leave the impression, furthermore, that her strategy is merely rhetorical, that she is merely, brilliantly willful. There is a quite delicate program for restoring to beauty the capacity for wounding proximate bodies.

First, if much of the violence of men may be considered as an effort to restrain the red tide, to impose distinctions and hierarchies, then Kingston writes a woman's war book from *within* the red tide. *The Woman Warrior* is, as a whole, ambivalent about Chinese communism, but the object of the woman warrior herself is egalitarian. The baron who is the object of her revenge is discovered "counting his money." "Who are you?" he demands. "'What do you want?' he said, encircling his profits with his arms" (*WW*, 43). The woman's uprisings against profits is uniquely colorful: "we sewed red flags and tied the red scraps around arms, legs, horses' tails" (*WW*, 37). In the general ruddiness, individualism is no value; the new peasant ruler looks out at his new constituency, "a great red crowd" (*WW*, 42). The chromatic scheme takes on its sexual specificity when, during her training, the woman warrior menstruates for the first time (*WW*, 30), which seems to mark her initiation into warrior's as well as woman's society. The bleeding is projected onto the political landscape: "I bled and thought about the people to be killed." But of course women warriors are procreative as well as decreative, and menstruation opens up another potential: "I bled and thought about the people to be born" (*WW*, 33). Here is the prophetic uniting of all connotations: "Forebodingly I caught a smell—metallic, the iron smell of blood, as when a woman gives birth, as at the sacrifice of a large animal, as when I menstruated and dreamed red dreams" (*WW*, 34).

That this book is written as if from within the red tide is startling enough. The physical necessity of book-binding, felt as an analogue of foot-binding, and the aesthetic desirability of closure weigh as much against this outrage as against the spreading of Cather's oceanic interlude, or against Morrison's general liquidity. The book attempts a yet more difficult affront: the book is written as if from within the blood itself of the red tide, from within Cather's bloody violence or Beloved's wound whose source is Sethe's menses and whose destination is Morrison's ink. "We are going to carve revenge on your back," announces the father. First he "brushed the words in ink . . . . Then he began cutting." As the cutting progresses, the mother catches the blood—there is a holy grail aspect of this fantasy. When the cutting is finished, the woman warrior's parents nurse her "just as if I had fallen in battle after many victories." Somehow this participatory mutilation has already succeeded in its avenging purpose. The woman warrior, with mirrors, sees "her back covered entirely with words in red and black files, like an army, like my army" (*WW*, 34–35). This is a metaphor within a fantasy within a novel or memoir (?), yet the effect is to integrate writing with the wounded body itself. The red and black files mediate blood and ink, reading and warring, or perhaps the book is as divinely spoken, within its writing, as the New Testament.

A brief genealogy of this trope. *The Woman Warrior* begins with an adulteress who, even though punished within sight of her partner, refuses to implicate him; this leads to the revenge fantasy of "White Tigers"; the model for simultaneous penance, penitence, redemption, and revenge is *The Scarlet Letter*. The male dream of actually inscribing a woman's body with masculine values is turned inside out: the script begins to take on the character of the inscribed. *The Scarlet Letter* was written at precisely the moment that, in Margaret Walker's *Jubilee*, a runaway female slave is branded with the letter "R." Possibly Walker brings out a contemporary correlative of Hester's punishment; at any rate, punishment by marking is shown to be an attempt to rewrite—or rather to write in the first place—the female body; by writing *Jubilee*, the black woman takes up the pen as an act of repossession of her own flesh. Crane's wound is both symbolic as in Hawthorne and corporeal as in Walker; the wounded body is both body and text. The wound is a red badge of courage insofar as we accept the illusion, explicated from Homer to Mailer and Jones, that assuming the female mark is confirmation of masculinity.

Always the wounding is done by the enemy or oppressor, so that if the wound becomes the stuff of Hester's self-definition, Henry Fleming's self-fashioning, Walker's fiction, it does so by an act of reading against the author. Two women and one man produce their courage out of being marked as casualties; deeper into their flesh is deeper into their resources. In these respects Kingston produces something new. The language she bleeds in the legend is carved by her father, as a ritual of passion, consubstantiation, and community; it makes reference both to her menstrual blood and the blood of enemies, that is, to her mutually energized femininity and masculinity. If we are used to thinking of language as a symptom of self-repression, of self-loss, of self-difference—as a sign of internal woundedness—then Kingston's words are paradoxical, but the paradox works for producing her audience. The readership of a written text may be an absent multitude, out of the range of corporeal revenge; nevertheless, woundedness is the one thing that reaches us—that can reach us—unscathed. With this difference by virtue of the change of perspective: Kingston accepts her woundedness as the precondition of a warrior's Eucharist. "Even if I got killed, the people could use my dead body for a weapon" (*WW*, 34). The male reader will feel it as emasculation.

Three millennia after Homer, the goddess returns to the battlefield, her potency the capacity for infecting men with her woundedness. For three millennia, she had been blamed for the fall from the masculine, rational beauty of the duel; now she not only glorifies the Nicene militancy of Stowe and Mitchell and Cather and Wharton, but she furthermore reclaims the duel as her own. America has, by this time, embraced the fall from duel: only by reimagining Chinese legends can Kingston evade the American lust for dehumanized weaponry, as in *Democracy*, which is shadowed by the American fascination with unauthored texts. Only by positing an embodied, proximate reader in opposition to her authority can Kingston find a way to redirect her stigmata as the words of war.

Afterword

Bobbie Ann Mason and Maxine Hong Kingston may have appeared to be antithetical—but I wish to make explicit the single meaning of my double conclusion. I should begin with the full circling of the discussion that arrives only at Kingston: from the fall into war and literature under the aegis of goddess warriors, at the beginning of the study, to the reascent into duel and orality under the aegis of the woman warrior, at the end. I evaluated, in the last chapter, the affinity of women writers for war partly to anticipate Kingston's attempt at a metaphorical connection of war and literature, necessarily converted, in the process, to duel and talk-story. Nicene theology provided a model for the transfiguration of duality into unity, of splitting into wholeness, that would account for Kingston's fantasy of injury as an emblem not of the infantalization or feminization of men, but of the reunion of maleness and femaleness, child and parent. Death, as in Cather and Wharton, would on this analysis allow the perfect congruence of front and home front; the return of ghost to parent guarantees the restoration of war to beauty.

This appearance of epic circumnavigation should not, however, obscure Kingston's lucid certainty that her work is inescapably written, the correlative of which is that Vietnam rather than the duel represents the characteristic violence of her era. Kingston and Mason, for all Mason's obsession with mediation and Kingston's with immediacy, are deeply similar in their sophistication about the home-front literariness of all writing on war, even by soldiers in their diaries, in Mason's case, or by warriors in their "songs," in Kingston's. I intended Mason to stand for that late moment in literary history when mediation is so expertly and knowingly detected that war and writing are almost tenor and vehicle after all, insofar as the experience of war is shaped by the same cultural and aesthetic expectations as the experience of literature. But Kingston is so aware of this terminal belatedness that her passion to write a book that performs its own immediate violence prohibits anything more than an allusion or two to Vietnam.

This is as far into paradox as I can trace the historical argument; I have been at pains to establish—against contemporary tendencies that I shall briefly enumerate—that such paradoxes have arisen of necessity, because the structural difference of war and writing is always, identically for men and women, irreducible. I assert this, for one thing, against implication models of literature, at the apex of which is the claim of Armstrong and Tennenhouse that physical violence in the world and representational violence "cannot in fact be distinguished, at least not in writing." I am not sure of the meaning or force of "at least not in writing";[1] at any rate, my own position is that the violence of literature does not resemble—even *mutatis mutandis*—the violence of war, which creates unending complications, culminating in the intricacies of Mason and Kingston, for war and post-war writing. I think that the implication model is itself a token of the peculiar relation of literature and war after World War II, a more or less self-conscious version of homeopathy.

In order to argue that literature's violence does not resemble war's, I have denied that war is beautiful, which is primarily to deny, against the Clausewitzian position endorsed by the pacific William James, that it is beautifully *resolved*. The point is crucial because those theories that focus on literature's attraction to death—Brooks's attention to the narrative death-seeking of the ending, Bersani and Dutoit's attention to narrative violence that pursues a satisfying climax—similarly engage the psychology of closure. My gratitude to Elaine Scarry is therefore profound for demonstrating that even if literature is violent according to these retrospects, war is not. War does not beautifully conclude like a duel. You may value narrative violence or you may detest it; in any case, it is the sort of violence that war has not achieved since Troy.

There are other ways of claiming that war is beautiful. It has beautiful or brilliant aspects, of course, which are not overlooked even by Tolstoy. But everything has beautiful aspects, and the tangential beauty of war is a distraction from its essential feature, mangled bodies. The strategies of war may be elegant; this means that war is beautiful if it makes sense to assume that a ruined building is beautiful, the rubble of which, by its arrangement, indicates an admirable blueprint. Soldiers in war may conduct themselves beautifully, but I would prefer to say "bravely" or "selflessly," granting the aesthetic component of these terms, to quarantine the aesthetics of war per se from the ethics of its victims. I know nothing about these matters. What I feel entitled to assert is that you cannot deduce the formal beauty of war from the formal beauty of war or post-war narratives, which may be all we know of it.

This proved difficult to formulate in an atmosphere of exhilarating self-accusation, indulged in by both confessional militarists (war is *our* beauty) and Foucauldian theorists (literature is *our* war). It also proved difficult to say in an era when literature is treated (the contradiction often appears as a corollary) as if it were a non-agency, awaiting inertly the obligation of professors to stitch it into a favored historical quilt. But literature argues its relation to history before it arrives at academics; it is by virtue of historical recalcitrance that it survives.[2] Modern history is a competition for history, and literature is the saboteur of all historical monoliths, which is the perverseness of the fascination of historical monoliths for literature departments. I seem to employ the term "literature" as if it were still a powerful invocation; I merely observe for whoever cares that to simplify its place in history is to kill it. The war of war and literature, for one thing, will have a clear victor (war is a vastly prestigious integrator of history); it will have become a duel.

Notes

Introduction

1. See William Broyles, Jr., "Why Men Love War," *Esquire* 102 (1984), 55–65. "War *is* beautiful," he declares (62).

2. See Nancy Armstrong and Leonard Tennenhouse, eds., *The Violence of Representation: Literature and the History of Violence* (New York: Routledge, 1989), especially their introduction, 1–26. In the introduction, the editors associate themselves with the view that "writing is not so much about violence as a form of violence in its own right" (2). The premises are that violence may be invisibly omnipresent in the Foucauldian way, and that its particular literary form is "suppression of difference" (8). The editors are so careful to confess the literary implication in violence that they cannot acknowledge that some forms are more objectionable than others, though if violence is as general as they suggest, the necessity of that sort of distinction becomes paramount.

Foucault seems preliminarily willing to reverse Clausewitz and make policy the continuation of war. "Isn't power simply a form of domination? . . . Peace would then be a form of war, and the state a means of waging it." But he then refuses the simplification. "A whole range of problems emerges here. Who wages war against whom? . . . Is it a war of all against all? . . . All these questions need to be explored. In any case it's astonishing to see how easily and self-evidently people talk of warlike relations of power or class struggle without ever making it clear whether some form of war is meant, and if so what form." See Paul Rabinow, ed., *The Foucault Reader* (New York: Pantheon, 1984), 64–65.

3. See Walter Benn Michaels, *The Gold Standard and the Logic of Naturalism: American Literature at the Turn of the Century* (Berkeley: Univ. of California Press, 1987), 27. What makes this already famous remark uninnocent is that Michaels does not really mean that literature is a part of culture—the "part of" is misleading—he means that literature *is* culture. There is no space of opposition within a culture—no enclaves for dissent or even partial withdrawal; to be in the culture is to be of it, all of it. By this token, carried as Michaels carries it to its last destination, Marx himself would always give away, at the deeper levels of interpretation, his capitalist premises, not having had the fortune to be born into a Marxist state; anything oppositional would always have to follow itself. In my view, if Marx was not oppositional at all, he was oppositional enough.

4. Paul de Man, *Blindness and Insight: Essays in the Rhetoric of Contemporary Criticism* (Minneapolis: Univ. of Minnesota Press, 1983), 165. De Man's "Lit-

erary History and Literary Modernity," like my own study, is about the self-contradictoriness of literary history—its struggle away from itself toward the modern, its fall back into its own history. The weirdness intrudes with de Man's repeated judgment that one part of literary history—the movement away from itself—is impossible: no claim on novelty is ever sustainable. You can put this impossibility one way (literature is always futilely trying to join the world of action, of war and revolution) or another way (there *is* no novelty, no world of immediate action, to inhabit), but you cannot put it both ways. Or rather, in fact, de Man does, but the tendency of the essay is from the first to the second. The existence of all the past is what each present moment is forced to bear the weight of: there is only the present moment, but (as against the hope of modernity) it is full of texts rather than emptied out of them. In order thus to say that history itself is fully textualized, de Man finds himself having to assert, against the exile and return paradigm of literary history (which can "only be metaphorical") that "history is not a fiction." I would reverse this: other histories exist for literature to be in tension with, so that all history is not textual but *is* fictional. Science, for example, has as much right to its fictional version of history, in which the past is repudiated, as any other discipline.

5. Norman Mailer, *The Armies of the Night* (New York: Signet, 1968), 53. Mailer's quotation of Jean Malaquais begins by looking tautological: if the inferior novelist could read the mind of the superior novelist, then he would have the capacity to be superior to himself. But if Mailer meant this, he would also believe that the one mind a scientist cannot read is that of a superior scientist. No—Mailer is not merely defining inferiority. He is asserting that specifically novelists must be judged by what they can absorb, and the supreme novelist would be able to absorb everything. Experiencing war from every angle—including that of the dead—would be no particular difficulty, so that calling a book *The Naked and the Dead* would not be out of the question.

6. John Limon, *The Place of Fiction in the Time of Science: A Disciplinary History of American Writing* (New York: Cambridge Univ. Press, 1990).

7. Michael Herr, *Dispatches* (New York: Avon, 1968), 3–5.

8. Siegfried Sassoon, *Memoirs of an Infantry Officer* (London: Faber & Faber, 1930), 241.

9. This is Broyles's take on the story; I believe that Lynn Hanley, in *Writing War: Fiction, Gender, and Memory* (Amherst: Univ. of Massachusetts Press, 1991), takes Broyles's simplifications too seriously. In any event, she joins Susan Jeffords who, in *The Remasculinization of America: Gender and the Vietnam War* (Bloomington: Indiana Univ. Press, 1989), criticizes all masculine mystifications of the war experience, including, prominently, Herr's.

10. I heard Thomas Ferraro, in a lecture, use the term "bombarded" to describe the reader's condition in *Dispatches*.

Chapter 1

1. Washington Irving, *The Sketch Book of Geoffrey Crayon, Gent.* (New York: Signet, 1961). All references to this edition, abbreviated *SB*, will be inserted parenthetically in the text.

2. Only boredom itself puts limits on speculation about Irving's lifelong bachelorhood. Possibly he was traumatized by Matilda's death; possibly he was not. Possibly he was morbidly frightened of marriage; possibly he was merely unsuccessful at accomplishing it. At least it is certain that he had no grudge against matrimony as the result of having an intimate experience with a woman like Dame Van Winkle.

His mother was gentle (his father was severe); he was used to the kindness of women from childhood on. Anyone is free to speculate about the psychopathology represented in the imagery of "Rip Van Winkle" and deflected in the portrait of Dame Van Winkle. This merely removes from our attention—by an extra stage—the story of Irving's character's war evasion. For an attempt to normalize Irving's connubial behavior, see George S. Hellman, *Washington Irving Esquire: Ambassador at Large from the New World to the Old* (New York: Knopf, 1925), 47–57. For an overview of the line of criticism that finds the story sexually morbid, see William L. Hedges, *Washington Irving: An American Study, 1802–1832* (Baltimore: Johns Hopkins, 1965), 137–41.

3. See Hellman, 12.

4. Joel Barlow, "The Columbiad," in Vernon Louis Parrington, ed., *The Connecticut Wits* (Hamden, Conn.: Archon, 1963), 309.

5. Margaret Mitchell, *Gone With the Wind* (New York: Avon, 1936), 342, 405; Edith Wharton, *A Son at the Front* (New York: Scribner's, 1923), 285.

6. William Irving, Washington's father, named a son born in England William Irving Jr., but the son died just after birth. In America, he named another son William Irving Jr., who died within a year. The third son, named William Irving Jr. once again, survived. Only the survival of a son prior to Washington prevented Washington from being William. But Washington could hardly escape being a "junior" in this patriarchy—he is the Son of his Country if Washington is the Father of his Country. See Hellman, 5–6.

7. As an example, it is perhaps too clear. In general I argue that wars are not so much shunned by literature as revised or falsified or commandeered. This happened with the Revolutionary War: in *The Spy*, Cooper takes the question of liberty and gives it several twists (is it equal to the capacity for changing sex? for changing race? for changing identities? is it compatible with the pursuit of money?) that will be of interest to the self-consciously non-military literati of the American Renaissance. *Israel Potter* is another pseudo-Revolutionary tale of the impoverished hero whose spying promises freedom but delivers loss of identity. And of course Stowe adapts the association of freedom with cross-dressing and cross-racing.

8. Carl von Clausewitz, *On War*, trans. Michael Howard and Peter Paret (Princeton: Princeton Univ. Press, 1976). All references to this edition, abbreviated *W*, will be inserted parenthetically in the text. Elaine Scarry, *The Body in Pain: The Making and Unmaking of the World* (New York: Oxford Univ. Press, 1985). All references to this edition, abbreviated *BP*, will be inserted parenthetically in the text.

9. Conrad H. Lanza, ed., *Napoleon and Modern War: His Military Maxims* (Harrisburg, Pa.: Military Service Publishing, 1943), 85.

10. John Ruskin, quoted in Michael Walzer, *Just and Unjust Wars: A Moral Argument with Historical Illustrations* (New York: Basic Books, 1977), 25.

11. Klaus Theweleit, *Male Fantasies*, trans. Stephen Conway (Minneapolis: Univ. of Minnesota Press, 1987).

12. Eric A. Havelock, "Some Elements of the Homeric Fantasy," in Harold Bloom, ed., *Homer's The Iliad: Modern Critical Interpretations* (New York: Chelsea House, 1987), 94–96.

13. See John Keegan and Richard Holmes, *Soldiers: A History of Men in Battle* (New York: Viking, 1986), 77, 79.

14. Plato, *The Republic*, Bk. 10, trans. Paul Shorey (Cambridge: Harvard Univ. Press, 1963), 449, 451.

15. Homer, *The Iliad*, trans. Robert Fitzgerald (Garden City, N.Y.: Anchor/ Doubleday, 1974), 69–70. All further references to this edition, abbreviated *I*, will

be inserted parenthetically in the text. I use Fitzgerald's spellings when I am working from his translation.

16. Thucydides, *The History of the Peloponnesian War*, I, trans. B. Jowett (Oxford: Clarendon, 1881), 6–7.

17. Thucydides, pp. 8–9.

18. Aristophanes, *The Complete Plays of Aristophanes*, "Lysistrata," trans. Jack Lindsay (New York: Bantam, 1962), 303.

19. I notice that I have identified Homer primarily with Helen and Athêna as a beautifier of war; I wonder if I wish to argue that Homer is a woman. In *No Man's Land: The Place of the Woman Writer in the Twentieth Century. Vol. 1: The War of the Words* (New Haven: Yale Univ. Press, 1988), Gilbert and Gubar quote Harold Bloom to the effect that feminism could cause the first fundamental change in literary tradition by deflecting literary history from its heretofore inevitable origin in Homer. Gilbert and Gubar add that Samuel Butler in 1897 had already argued that *The Odyssey* was composed by a woman (131). I can add that in Siegfried Sassoon's *Memoirs of an Infantry Officer* (London: Faber & Faber, 1930), "David Cromlech" (Robert Graves) is quoted as opining that Homer was a woman (it is not specified that Graves means the Homer of *The Odyssey*, though he is probably quoting Butler, a favorite of his) (109). In passing I might mention that Bloom himself now posits a woman at the beginning of the *Hebraic* tradition. Without seeing the necessity of becoming fanatical about this, I do want to argue that literary history is transformed by a less flamboyant gesture than claiming that Homer (like "J") was a woman, if Homer was rather the first to grant anxiously how little war had anything to do with the beauty he was dedicated to. Then the literary tradition could include with equal justification both men and women. See Chapter 7.

20. Keegan and Holmes, 23.

21. For an "art of war" estranged altogether from the aesthetics of the duel, see Sun Tzu, *The Art of War*, trans. Thomas Cleary (Boston: Shambala, 1988). *The Art of War* reads like a point-by-point refutation of Homeric aesthetics; in its subtle endorsement of combat indirection, it seems completely writerly.

22. Actually, they were not invented but probably revised—and probably records were kept for the first time. E. Norman Gardiner, in his seminal *Greek Athletic Sports and Festivals* (London: MacMillan, 1910), believes that records must have been kept starting in 776—how else would Hippias or Aristotle justify their record-keeping claims centuries later (50–51)? Waldo E. Sweet, in *Sport and Recreation in Ancient Greece* (New York: Oxford Univ. Press, 1987), refers to the "reorganization of the games in 776" (4). There are many theories about the origins of festivals of games, some of them pertinent (funeral games transfer the power of the dead to the living?). I am not proposing my own theory, in asserting that Homeric games seem to arise from the decline of duel warfare. I am saying that that account makes sense of *The Iliad*. Gardiner does mention that festival innovations—as a result of the change of warfare—occurred at a much later date. In 520 B.C., the race in heavy armour, and in 496 B.C., the riding race (plus dismount and running race) are innovations from a nostalgia for "the system of individual warfare" (70–72).

23. "A people knowing war has no need of tournaments"; I add to Burckhardt's formula a proviso in the spirit of Huizinga, that that is only true if the war contains more of the tournament's agonistic beauty than the tournament. Johan Huizinga, *Homo Ludens: A Study of the Play-Element in Culture* (Boston: Beacon, 1955), 72–75.

24. Virgil, *The Aeneid*, trans. Robert Fitzgerald (New York: Vintage/Random House, 1980), 136–37.

25. The issue of the orality of Homer is of course vexed; the history of the disputation is clearly summarized by Hugh Lloyd-Jones, "Becoming Homer," *The New York Review of Books*, 39 (5 March 1992), 52–56.

26. Keegan and Holmes, 14.

27. Geoffrey Perret, *A Country Made by War: From the Revolution to Vietnam—The Story of America's Rise to Power* (New York: Random House, 1989). All further references to this edition, abbreviated *CW*, will be inserted parenthetically in the text.

28. See Fredric Jameson, *Postmodernism, or, The Cultural Logic of Late Capitalism* (Durham, Duke Univ. Press, 1991), 35–36. The three stages of capitalism come from Ernest Mandel.

29. See Jameson, xx–xxi. The third stage of capitalism was possible by the end of World War II, and was "crystallized" around 1973 at the end of the "great wave of 'wars of national liberation.'" So much for war in his book.

30. We learn for example that *Blow-Up* is modernist and *Blow-out* is postmodernist. At a seminar at the Center for Literary and Cultural Studies at Harvard, Jameson gave a paper that detached his aesthetic stages so completely from their supposed historical moments that it seemed to me an exercise in formal spatialization. Marjorie Garber made the embarrassing point about Shakespeare.

Chapter 2

1. William Tecumseh Sherman, *Memoirs of General W. T. Sherman*, notes (including this reference) by Charles Royster (New York: Library of America, 1990), 1115. All further references to this edition, abbreviated *MG*, will be inserted parenthetically in the text.

2. In *Just and Unjust Wars: A Moral Argument with Historical Illustrations* (New York: Basic Books, 1977).

3. Walzer, 4.

4. B. H. Liddell Hart, *Sherman: Soldier, Realist, American* (New York: Dodd, Mead, 1930). For Sherman's consistent dedication to the hard logic of war, see 310; for the opposition of this logic to "romance," see 426; for the description of Sherman as a "realistic idealist" (not in favor of punishing the South), see 410.

5. Michael Herr, *Dispatches* (New York: Avon, 1978), 289. All further references to this edition, abbreviated *D*, will be inserted parenthetically in the text.

6. Siegfried Sassoon, *Memoirs of an Infantry Officer* (London: Faber & Faber, 1930), 199.

7. Leo Tolstoy, *War and Peace*, trans. Rosemary Edmonds (London: Penguin, 1957), 937–38.

8. Quoted in Lynn Hanley, *Writing War: Fiction, Gender, and Memory* (Amherst: Univ. of Massachusetts Press, 1991), 74–75.

9. See Philip Fisher, "Appearing and Disappearing in Public: Social Space in Late-Nineteenth-Century Literature and Culture," in Sacvan Bercovitch, ed., *Reconstructing American Literary History* (Cambridge: Harvard Univ. Press, 1986), 155–88; and Walter Michaels, *The Gold Standard and the Logic of Naturalism: American Literature at the Turn of the Century* (Berkeley: Univ. of California Press, 1987). Fisher treats the embeddedness issue empirically: realists sampled the varieties of conspicuous self-production. Michaels treats the issue empirically and analytically: where else but embedded in a culture could realists have been?

10. Michael Bell, *The Problem of American Realism: Studies in the Cultural History of a Literary Idea* (Chicago: Univ. of Chicago Press, 1993).

11. William Dean Howells, *Years of My Youth and Three Essays* (Bloomington: Indiana Univ. Press, 1975), 201–03. Only in one clause of one sentence is there any hint of an interruption in the seamless transition from Howells's feelings of intense solidarity with the new soldiers to his seeking the consulate in Europe. He wishes to write a novel based either on the sublimity of soldier solidarity or "on the subjective riddle of one who looked on and baffled himself with question of the event" (202). Howells did, of course, express guilt about his flight from time to time; it is striking how often he did not.

12. See, for example, William Dean Howells, *My Literary Passions* (New York: Harper & Brothers, 1895), 165–66.

13. William Dean Howells, *Heroines of Fiction* II (New York: Harper & Brothers, 1901), 162; *My Literary Passions*, 223.

14. Kenneth Lynn, *William Dean Howells: An American Life* (New York: Harcourt Brace Jovanovich, 1970), 125. Howells is himself capable of this kind of judgment: had he attended more political rallies, he would have been a better realist (*Years*, 138).

15. See Everett Carter, *Howells and the Age of Realism* (Philadelphia: Lippincott, 1950), 76–87; and Harold H. Kolb, *The Illusion of Life: American Realism as a Literary Form* (Charlottesville: Univ. Press of Virginia, 1969), 91.

16. Daniel Aaron, in *The Unwritten War: American Writers and the Civil War* (New York: Knopf, 1973), arrives at a similar view of Howells's realism as a compensation for the missed Civil War, 132. Only this final position makes sense of Aaron's oscillations, on behalf of Howells's. For example: Howells uses his realism to expose the connection between chattel slavery and wage slavery (130); nevertheless, the North's victory ensured the triumph of realism (131). Is realism a Northern cause or not? Is Howells's literary philosophy best corroborated by a soldier (Grant) or a civilian (Lincoln)? I need to work out why realism cannot be contentedly *either* combatant or civilian literature, or the property of *either* North or South. It is always defined in terms of what it missed, especially the war.

17. William Dean Howells, *A Hazard of New Fortunes* (Bloomington: Indiana Univ. Press, 1976). All further references to this edition, abbreviated *HF*, will be inserted parenthetically in the text.

18. Howells, *Years*, 175–78.

19. See Edmund Wilson, *Patriotic Gore: Studies in the Literature of the Civil War* (New York: Oxford Univ. Press, 1962), 585.

20. Howells, *Years*, 194–95. Warner Berthoff, in *The Ferment of Realism: American Literature, 1884–1919* (New York: The Free Press, 1965), picks up on Pound's hint that individual freedom was a realistic (specifically a Jamesian) preoccupation, but continues on to a Howellsian warning that the fight for personal freedom has always postponed "the struggle to find a decent and manageable footing for human life and work (including the work of art) within the mass secular society and ungoverned technological order of modern times," 47. Part of the point of what follows in my essay is the signficance for realism of confusing these two orders of freedom.

21. The original of Lindau was killed once and for all in the Civil War. We might have expected Lindau therefore to have been killed outright in the labor fighting. See Howells, *Years*, 117.

22. Wilson, 662–63.

23. For Howells's preoccupation with this question, see William Dean How-

ells, *"Criticism and Fiction" and Other Essays*, ed. Clara Marburg Kirk and Rudolf Kirk (New York: New York Univ. Press, 1959), 68; or *Editor's Study*, ed. James W. Simpson (Troy, N.Y.: Whiston, 1983), 95–97; or Edwin H. Cady, ed., *W. D. Howells as Critic* (Boston: Routledge & Kegan Paul, 1973), 447–48.

24. Edwin H. Cady, *The Realist at War* (Syracuse: Syracuse Univ. Press, 1958), 7, 217.

25. Lynn, 113.

26. William Dean Howells, "Editha," in *Anthology of American Literature* II, 2nd ed., gen. ed. George McMichael (New York: Macmillan, 1980), 580–81. All further references to this work, abbreviated *E*, will be inserted parenthetically in the text.

27. Henry James, *Notes of a Son and Brother* (New York: Scribner's, 1914), 300. All further references to this volume, abbreviated *N*, will be inserted parenthetically in the text.

28. Aaron, 113. See also Wilson, 662; and Leon Edel, *Henry James: The Untried Years* (Philadelphia: Lippincott, 1953), 179–81, 219–21, 236–38.

29. Henry James, *Literary Criticism* (New York: Library of America, 1984), 52.

30. Howells, *"Criticism and Fiction" and Other Essays*, 51.

31. Wilson, 662.

32. Wilson, 654.

33. Henry James, "The Jolly Corner," in *The Short Stories of Henry James* (New York: Modern Library, 1945), 623. All further references to this story, abbreviated *JC*, will be inserted parenthetically in the text.

34. Edel, 170.

35. Henry James, *The Bostonians* (Middlesex: Penguin, 1966), 12. All further references to this work, abbreviated *B*, will be inserted parenthetically in the text.

36. Eric Sundquist, "Mark Twain and Homer Plessy," *Representations*, 24 (1988), 105–06.

37. Mark Twain, "The Private History of a Campaign that Failed," in *The Portable Mark Twain*, ed. Bernard De Voto (New York: Viking, 1946), 139. All further references to this work, abbreviated *PH*, will be inserted parenthetically in the text.

38. See Edward Hagerman, *The American Civil War and the Origins of Modern Warfare* (Bloomington: Indiana Univ. Press, 1988), especially the Introduction, xi–xviii.

39. Mark Twain, *A Connecticut Yankee in King Arthur's Court* (New York: Signet, 1963). All references to this edition, abbreviated *CY*, will be inserted parenthetically in the text. See also Walter Benn Michaels, "An American Tragedy, or the Promise of American Life," *Representations*, 25 (1989), 71–98. In his section on *A Connecticut Yankee*, Michaels concludes that manhood in Twain equals mechanicalness.

40. Baseball flourished during the Civil War: see George B. Kirsch, *The Creation of American Team Sports: Baseball and Cricket, 1838–1872* (Urbana: Univ. of Illinois Press, 1989), 80–85; or Harvey Frommer, *Primitive Baseball: The First Quarter-Century of the National Pastime* (New York: Atheneum, 1988), 8. Baseball was impeded by the Civil War but boomed after it: see Harold Seymour, *Baseball: The Early Years* (New York: Oxford, 1960), 40–41.

41. Whether baseball was masculine or juvenile was a constant concern. See Warren Goldstein, *Playing for Keeps: A History of Early Baseball* (Ithaca: Cornell Univ. Press, 1989), 4, 43–63. This dispute is critical to *A Connecticut Yankee*: are

Hank Morgan's endeavors on behalf of masculinity (as he claims) or boyishness (as his final predicament suggests)?

42. That baseball was not sufficiently "chivalric" bothered many of its early supporters; see Goldstein, 67. For sport as a continuation of the "spirit of emulation," compare Thorstein Veblen, "Modern Survivals of Prowess": "Manifestations of the predatory temperament are all to be classed under the head of the exploit. They are partly simple and unreflected expressions of an attitude of emulative ferocity, partly activities deliberately entered upon with a view to gaining repute for prowess. . . . Sports shade off from the basis of hostile combat, through skill to cunning and chicanery, without its being possible to draw a line at any point." The essay may be found in John T. Talamini and Charles H. Page, eds., *Sport & Society* (Boston: Little, Brown, 1973), 47.

43. "Throughout the decade [of the 1860s], when a club was doing well in the course of a game, its 'paper' was said to be offered at a 'premium' or 'above par'; if it did poorly, its 'paper' was offered at a 'discount' or 'below par.' If a club established an early lead, its 'stock' went up." See Goldstein, 71.

44. See *Mark Twain–Howells Letters: The Correspondence of Samuel L. Clemens and William Dean Howells, 1872–1910* (Cambridge: Belknap/Harvard Univ. Press, 1960) 212, 213. For Howells's account of the "amazing mistake, the bewildering blunder, the cruel catastrophe," see *My Mark Twain: Reminiscences and Criticisms* (Brooklyn: Haskell, 1977), 58–63.

45. See Mark Twain, *The War Prayer* (New York: Crispin/Harper & Row, 1968), n.p. This is the entire war prayer, shorter version.

46. Hagerman, 82–87, 133–35.

47. Raymond Aron, *Clausewitz: Philosopher of War*, trans. Christine Booker and Norman Stone (Englewood Cliffs, N.J.: Prentice-Hall, 1985), 269.

48. Stephen Crane, *The Red Badge of Courage* (New York: Norton, 1962), 11. All further references to this edition, abbreviated *RB*, will be inserted parenthetically in the text.

49. In drawing his own connection of Crane and Hawthorne, Richard H. Brodhead, in *The School of Hawthorne* (New York: Oxford Univ. Press, 1986), also quotes the "letters of guilt" passage. But contrast his conclusion that Hawthorne's presence in *Red Badge* is "strictly momentary, not sustained or deeply informing" (206–7).

50. For the simultaneous representation of war and representation of representation in Crane's *Red Badge*, see Michael Fried, *Realism, Writing, Disfiguration: On Thomas Eakins and Stephen Crane* (Chicago: Univ. of Chicago Press, 1987).

Chapter 3

1. These are the three writers who are grouped as prototypical realists in Everett Carter, *Howells and the Age of Realism* (Philadelphia: J.B. Lippincott, 1950), 76–87; in every case their writing is taken to be a cultural correlative of the Northern cause in the Civil War.

2. William Dean Howells, *My Literary Passions* (New York: Harper and Brothers, 1895), 76, 77.

3. William Dean Howells, *"Criticism and Fiction" and Other Essays*, ed. Clara Marburg Kirk and Rudolf Kirk (New York: New York Univ. Press, 1959), 210.

4. See *Criticism and Fiction*, 68; or William Dean Howells, *Editor's Study*,

ed. James W. Simpson (Troy, N.Y.: Whiston, 1983), 95–97; or Edwin H. Cady, ed., *W. D. Howells as Critic* (Boston: Routledge & Kegan Paul, 1973), 447–48.

5. *Editor's Study*, 96.

6. *Editor's Study*, 81.

7. The term is from Roland Barthes, "The Reality Effect," in Tzvetan Todorov, *French Literary Theory Today* (New York: Cambridge Univ. Press, 1982), 11–17. I propose my own version of the American "reality effect" below.

8. Erich Auerbach, *Mimesis: The Representation of Reality in Western Literature*, trans. Willard R. Trask (Princeton: Princeton Univ. Press, 1953), 458–59 (the origins of continental realism), 520–24 (the Russian version).

9. Leo Tolstoy, *War and Peace*, trans. Rosemary Edmonds (London: Penguin, 1957), 369. All further references, abbreviated *WP*, will be inserted parenthetically in the text.

10. *Criticism and Fiction*, 64–67.

11. Auerbach, 522.

12. Klaus Theweleit, *Male Fantasies. Vol. 1: Women, Floods, Bodies, History*, trans. Stephen Conway (Minneapolis: Univ. of Minnesota Press, 1987), 107. All further references to this edition, abbreviated *MF*, will be inserted parenthetically in the text.

13. I consider the following novels by George W. Cable: *The Grandissimes: A Story of Creole Life* (New York: Scribner's, 1883); *Dr. Sevier* (New York: Garrett, 1970); *John March, Southerner* (New York: Scribner's, 1898); *The Cavalier* (New York: Scribner's, 1901). Further references to these editions will be inserted parenthetically in the text, abbreviated *TG, DS, JM, TC*.

14. Cable wrote to Scribner that passages of *The Grandissimes* sunk "to a standard of literary workmanship to which I do not believe one page of 'The Cavalier' descends. I never before knew nearly so well just what I want to write or how to write it." Quoted in Arlin Turner, *George W. Cable: A Biography* (Durham: Duke Univ. Press, 1956), 316.

15. For example, in Turner, *A Biography*, 318. Edmund Wilson, in *Patriotic Gore: Studies in Literature of the American Civil War* (New York: Oxford Univ. Press, 1962), echoes this view, 594–95.

16. See, for a summary of this position, Otto H. Olsen, *Carpetbagger's Crusade: The Life of Albion Winegar Tourgée* (Baltimore: Johns Hopkins, 1965), 237–38.

17. *Criticism and Fiction*, 9.

18. *Criticism and Fiction*, 10.

19. *Editor's Study*, 41.

20. For Tourgée's troubled military career, see Olsen, 12–25; for De Forest's, see James A. Hijiya, *J. W. De Forest and the Rise of American Gentility* (Hanover, N.H.: Univ. Press of New England, 1988), 53–63.

21. The judgment that we can "hardly imagine such things now for the purposes of fiction" (*Editor's Study*, 41) is happily omitted from the section when it is reprinted as part of *Criticism and Fiction* (61–62), which proves that no memory is better than some. Howells forgets what he forgot.

22. John De Forest, "The Great American Novel," *The Nation*, 6 (1868), 29.

23. *Criticism and Fiction*, 67–69.

24. *A Royal Gentleman* (New York: Fords, Howard, & Hulbert, 1881, but published in 1874, in a more optimistic form, as *Toinette*); *A Fool's Errand by One of the Fools* (New York: Fords, Howard, & Hulbert, 1880); *Figs and Thistles: A*

Romance of the Western Reserve (New York: Fords, Howard, & Hulbert, 1879). I insert further references to these editions parenthetically, abbreviated *RG, FE, FT*. The phrase "interpretive community" is from Stanley Fish, *Is There a Text in This Class? The Authority of Interpretive Communities* (Cambridge: Harvard Univ. Press, 1980), which argues that truth within one such critical community is nonsense within another. I extend the concept to such interpretive communities as "Southerners" and "Southern blacks" in "The Integration of *Go Down, Moses*," *Critical Inquiry*, 12 (1986), 422–38.

25. "His readers must suffer through ridiculous plots and the clumsiest fictive devices before encountering passages of vigorous exposition in which Tourgée, the lawyer, historian, and prophet, overshadows the concoctor of chases, murders, captures, conspiracies, haunted houses, and secret wills." Daniel Aaron, *The Unwritten War: American Writers and the Civil War* (New York: Knopf, 1973), 194.

26. That blacks are marked is a Southern axiom. The Selma *Times* claimed to have a letter from a Negro of South Carolina who accuses G. W. Cable of stirring up trouble. The newspaper says: "We don't believe that any one but a sharp Negro could have written or did write it. The handwriting, the loose grammar, the postmark on the envelope, all mark it as a genuine document from the man it purports to have come from. Not only is this true of such external marks as we have named, but so is it likewise of its internal, essential substance." This is all quoted in Cable's essay, "The Silent South," reprinted in Arlin Turner, *The Negro Question: A Selection of Writings on Civil Rights in the South by George W. Cable* (Garden City, N.Y.: Doubleday Anchor, 1958), 91–92n. Of course the last claim begs the question. Curiously apt for the following discussion of *Figs and Thistles* is the slide from the hidden hypothesis that is actually being defended (blacks are marked, that is, by their blackness) to the somewhat more easily defended hypothesis concerning not a race but a specific document (this letter has the marks of being from a black man) to the quite legitimate search for clues as to the origin of the document (by means of the postmark). The strategy is to make less defensible claims by means of more defensible ones that look similar; but the strategy backfires, because the final step is so legitimate as to be falsifiable. Cable did trace the letter to its origin, where no such black man lived. All of these levels of remarking (racial marks, individual marks, marks as clues) are involved in *Figs and Thistles*. Also apt is the assumption that handwriting is a unique mark.

27. Thanks to Michael Bell for pointing out the syllable I had somehow managed not to accent.

28. Bruce W. Wilshire, ed., *William James: The Essential Writings* (Albany: State Univ. of New York Press, 1984), 355.

29. Lionel Tiger, *Men in Groups* (New York: Random House, 1969), 131–32, 154, 198–99.

30. Carter, 81.

31. See Wilson, 545.

32. Wilson, 537.

33. J. W. De Forest, *Miss Ravenel's Conversion from Secession to Loyalty* (New York: Harper & Brothers, 1939), 317. All further references to this edition, abbreviated *MR*, will be inserted parenthetically in the text.

34. Marilyn Mayer Culpepper, *Trials and Triumphs: Women of the American Civil War* (East Lansing: Michigan State Univ. Press, 1991), 39–41.

35. For example, Hijiya, 86–87.

36. For war as the male equivalent of birth, see Nancy Huston, "The Matrix of War: Mothers and Heroes," in Susan Rubin Suleiman, ed., *The Female Body in Western Culture: Contemporary Perspectives* (Cambridge: Harvard Univ. Press, 1986). Huston treats Homer's comparison of Agamemnon's wounded agony to labor (127n); mentions the relationship of labor and combat in Tolstoy (130); and writes the following sentence, suggestive of the Gettysburg Address: "How many revolutions have been compared to 'labor pains,' violent convulsions preceding the 'birth' of a new society?" (133).

37. John Keegan, *The Face of Battle* (New York: Viking, 1976), 194–95.

38. Wilson, 597.

39. Howells was the first to dislike the title, *Criticism and Fiction*, 211–12. Daniel Aaron agrees, 173.

Chapter 4

1. William Faulkner, *As I Lay Dying* (New York: Vintage/Random, 1930), 3. All further references to this edition, abbreviated *ALD*, will be inserted parenthetically in the text.

2. e. e. cummings, *The Enormous Room* (New York: Modern Library, 1922), 23–24. All further references to this edition, abbreviated *ER*, will be inserted parenthetically in the text.

3. Leo Bersani and Ulysse Dutoit, *The Forms of Violence: Narrative in Assyrian Art and Modern Culture* (New York: Schocken, 1985), 46. Further references to this edition, abbreviated *FV*, will be inserted parenthetically in the text.

4. Edmund Blunden, *Undertones of War* (London: Collins, 1965); Siegfried Sassoon, *Memoirs of an Infantry Officer* (London: Faber & Faber, 1930); Robert Graves, *Goodbye To All That* (London: Cassell, 1957); Richard Aldington, *Death of a Hero* (Garden City, N.Y.: Garden City Publishing, 1929). References to these editions, abbreviated *UW*, *MIO*, *GTAT*, and *DH*, will be inserted parenthetically in the text.

5. Harry Levin, *Refractions: Essays in Comparative Literature* (New York: Oxford Univ. Press, 1966), 291.

6. John Dos Passos, *Three Soldiers* (New York: George H. Doran, 1921). All references to this edition, abbreviated *TS*, will be inserted parenthetically in the text.

7. Ernest Hemingway, *For Whom the Bell Tolls* (New York: Scribner's, 1940), 14. All further references to this edition, abbreviated *FWBT*, will be inserted parenthetically in the text. I also insert parenthetical references to *The Sun Also Rises* (New York: Scribner's, 1926), abbreviated *SAR*, and *A Farewell to Arms* (New York: Scribner's, 1929), abbreviated *FA*.

8. Ernest Hemingway, *The Short Stories of Ernest Hemingway* (New York: Scribner's, 1938), 105.

9. See Michael S. Reynolds, *Hemingway's First War: The Making of A Farewell to Arms* (Princeton: Princeton Univ. Press, 1976). All further references to this edition, abbreviated *HFW*, will be inserted parenthetically in the text.

10. Peter Brooks, *Reading For the Plot: Design and Intention in Narrative* (New York: Vintage/Random House, 1984), 103. For a summary and critique of Brooks's and Bersani's positions, see Jay Clayton, "Narrative and Theories of Desire," *Critical Inquiry*, 16 (1989), 33–53.

11. Roman Jakobson, *Selected Writings*, II (The Hague: Mouton, 1971), 254–

55. All further references to this text, abbreviated *SW*, will be inserted parenthetically in the text.

12. Using "perfectionist" as a tautological adjective preceding "modernism" is my way of making Fredric Jameson's point that modernism is nostalgic, in pursuit of the "satisfactions of handicraft transfigured." See Fredric Jameson, *Postmodernism, or, The Cultural Logic of Late Capitalism* (Durham: Duke Univ. Press, 1991), 307.

13. Sigmund Freud, *The Standard Edition of the Complete Psychological Works*, xxi, trans. James Strachey (London: Hogarth, 1961), 155.

14. Carlos Baker, *Ernest Hemingway: A Life Story* (New York: Scribner's, 1969), 244. All further references to this text, abbreviated *H*, will be inserted parenthetically in the text.

15. Ernest Hemingway, ed. and introd., *Men At War: The Best War Stories of All Time* (New York: Crown, 1942), xxvii.

16. Matthew J. Bruccoli, ed., *The Sun Also Rises: A Facsimile Edition*, 2 vols. (Detroit: Omnigraphics, 1990), 220, 461. All further references to this text, abbreviated *SARF*, will be inserted parenthetically in the text. For a discussion of the drafts of *The Sun Also Rises*, see Frederic Joseph Svoboda, *Hemingway and The Sun Also Rises* (Lawrence: Univ. Press of Kansas, 1983).

17. Hemingway, *Short Stories*, 365.

18. F. Scott Fitzgerald, *The Great Gatsby* (New York: Scribner's, 1925). All further references to this edition, abbreviated *GG*, will be inserted parenthetically in the text. I also insert parenthetically references to *The Beautiful and Damned* (New York: Scribner's, 1922), abbreviated *BD*; and *Tender Is the Night*, Malcolm Cowley, ed. (Harmondsworth, Middlesex, England: Penguin, 1955), abbreviated *TN*.

19. Paul Fussell, *The Great War and Modern Memory* (New York: Oxford Univ. Press, 1975); all further references to this edition, abbreviated *GW*, will be inserted parenthetically in the text. Modris Eksteins, *Rites of Spring: The Great War and the Birth of the Modern Age* (New York: Anchor/Doubleday, 1989); all further references to this edition, abbreviated *RS*, will be inserted parenthetically in the text.

20. For a satisfying treatment of the continuities of World War I and peacetime, see Eric J. Leed, *No Man's Land: Combat & Identity in World War I* (New York: Cambridge Univ. Press, 1979). All further references to this edition, abbreviated *NML*, will be inserted parenthetically in the text. See also John Keegan, *The Face of Battle* (New York: Viking, 1976). Keegan ends his book with praise for Fussell. Nevertheless, Keegan writes in opposition to the "decisive battle" school of historiography (everything we have achieved we owe to crucial victories) of which Fussell may be said to be an inverse example. Keegan raises the question of why the modern world is repudiating war when the modern world is so much *like* war. "Men and women employed in continuous-process industries are made indirectly familiar with many . . . modern battlefield phenomena: they are to a considerable degree inured to very high constant noise levels and to emissions of intense light, they work in proximity to dangerous machinery and chemicals, including poison gases, and they are involved in high-speed automatic processes . . . [that] imitate in many respects the actions of modern weapons systems, such as automated artillery pieces, self-loading tank guns, machine-guns, flame throwers, rocket dischargers and the like. . . . Modern industry, moreover, teaches its work people—though the same lessons are learnt by almost all citizens, first in school and later as the *admin-*

istrés of the state's bureaucracy—habits of order, obedience and uniform behaviour" (318–19).

21. André Le Vot, *F. Scott Fitzgerald: A Biography*, trans. William Byron (Garden City, N.Y.: Doubleday, 1983), 220.

22. Matthew J. Bruccoli, ed., *The Great Gatsby: A Facsimile of the Manuscript* (Washington: Microcard, 1973), 8. All further references to this edition, abbreviated *GGF*, will be inserted parenthetically in the text.

23. Nevertheless, in the index of Milton R. Stern, *Critical Essays on F. Scott Fitzgerald's Tender Is the Night* (Boston: G. K. Hall, 1986), there are only eleven references to World War I, six from one essay. The one essay is Bruce L. Greenberg's "Fitzgerald's 'Figured Curtain': Personality and History in *Tender Is the Night*" (211–37), which does assemble the parallels of personal and European history (especially 212–16), but argues weirdly that "Dick's nineteenth-century ideals and sensibilities survive well into the twentieth century simply because they are not exposed directly to the shock of World War I" (217). I do not see in Dick's personality much that is worth preserving, and argue that his missing World War I is the sign, though not the cause, of his undoing. Alan Trachtenberg's essay, "The Journey Back: Myth and History in *Tender is the Night*" (170–85), observes usefully that the difference between *Gatsby* and *Tender* is that the former is mainly spatial and the latter mainly temporal; it also summarizes the meaning of the Grant parallel.

24. Le Vot, 3.

25. John Kuehl, ed., *The Apprentice Fiction of F. Scott Fitzgerald: 1909–1917* (New Brunswick, N.J.: Rutgers Univ. Press, 1965), 34–43.

26. For the biographical information concerning Edward Fitzgerald and the Civil War, see Le Vot, 5.

27. Erich Maria Remarque, *All Quiet on the Western Front*, trans. A. W. Wheen (New York: Fawcett, 1929), 99–100.

28. Joseph Blotner, *Faulkner: A Biography* (New York: Random House, 1984), 64–65. All further references to this work, abbreviated *FB*, will be inserted parenthetically in the text.

29. William Faulkner, *Soldiers' Pay* (New York: Liveright, 1926). All references to this edition, abbreviated *SP*, will be inserted parenthetically in the text.

30. B. H. Liddell Hart, *The Real War: 1914–1918* (Boston: Little, Brown, 1930), 316.

31. William Faulkner, *Flags in the Dust* (New York: Random House, 1973), 315, 37. All further references to this edition, abbreviated *FD*, will be inserted parenthetically·in the text.

32. William Faulkner, *Collected Short Stories* (New York: Random House, 1950), 415.

33. Faulkner, *Collected Short Stories*, 471.

34. William Faulkner, *A Fable* (New York: Random House, 1954), 125–26.

Chapter 5

1. John Keegan, *The Second World War* (Harmondsworth, Middlesex, England: Penguin, 1989), foreword. All further references to this edition, abbreviated *SWW*, will be inserted parenthetically in the text.

2. For the rights of captured soldiers, see Michael Walzer, *Just and Unjust Wars: A Moral Argument with Historical Illustrations* (New York: Basic Books, 1977).

3. James Jones, *From Here to Eternity* (New York: Avon, 1975); all further references to this edition, abbreviated *HE*, will be inserted parenthetically in the text. *The Thin Red Line* (New York: Scribner's, 1962); all further references to this edition, abbreviated *RL*, will be inserted parenthetically in the text. I also make a few references to *Whistle* (New York: Delacorte, 1978).

4. My favorite is a ramifying passage on a tree—"ancient thorny-fingered guardian" (*HE*, 97).

5. See Michel Foucault, *Discipline and Punish: The Birth of the Prison*, trans. Alan Sheridan (New York: Vintage-Random House, 1979), especially 130–31. All further references to this edition, abbreviated *DP*, will be inserted parenthetically in the text.

6. Quoted in Frank MacShane, *Into Eternity: The Life of James Jones, American Writer* (Boston: Houghton Mifflin, 1985), 80. All further references to this edition, abbreviated *IE*, will be inserted parenthetically in the text.

7. See Peter Manso, *Mailer: His Life and Times* (New York: Simon and Schuster, 1985), 70. Mailer also wrote (1942–43) a Pacific war novella, *A Calculus at Heaven*; see Hilary Mills, *Mailer: A Biography* (New York: Empire Books, 1982), 71.

8. Norman Mailer, *The Naked and the Dead* (New York: Rinehart, 1948), 12. All further references to this edition, abbreviated *ND*, will be inserted parenthetically in the text.

9. Manso, 105.

10. Manso, 119.

11. Joseph Heller, *Catch-22* (New York: Dell, 1961); all further references to this edition, abbreviated *C*, will be inserted parenthetically in the text. Kurt Vonnegut, Jr., *Slaughterhouse-Five, Or, The Children's Crusade: A Duty-Dance with Death* (New York: Dell, 1968); all further references to this edition, abbreviated *SF*, will be inserted parenthetically in the text. Thomas Pynchon, *Gravity's Rainbow* (New York: Viking, 1973); all further references to this edition, abbreviated *GR*, will be inserted parenthetically in the text.

12. See Sanford Pinsker, "Heller's *Catch-22*: The Protest of *Puer Eternis*," *Critique*, 7 (winter 1964–65), 150–62. Yossarian is to Pinsker a "perennial innocent"; this seems to me to exaggerate his inexperience.

13. This is explicit in *The Naked and the Dead*, 535; implicit, 356, 543, 573; the pain of the wound compared to childbirth, 536. See also *The Thin Red Line*, 348.

14. Erik H. Erikson, *Identity: Youth and Crisis* (New York: Norton, 1968), 169. All further references to this edition, abbreviated *I*, will be inserted parenthetically in the text.

15. Among the first to sever postmodernism from modernism, Harry Levin saw that World War II was "the Flood." And he sees adolescentness as one of its hallmarks, as in J. D. Salinger ("who writes so movingly of adolescent confusions, [but] has yet to free himself from them"), and John Updike (in whom "adolescence [is] so institutionalized that the old people's home of *The Poorhouse Fair* turns out to be merely another high school"). But he does not connect the historical fact to the psychological one. Harry Levin, "What Was Modernism," *Refractions: Essays in Comparative Literature* (New York: Oxford Univ. Press, 1966), 273, 278.

16. Jonathan Schell, *The Fate of the Earth* (New York: Knopf, 1982), 146.

17. Sigmund Freud, "Psycho-Analytic Notes on an Autobiographical Account of a Case of Paranoia (Dementia Paranoides)," *The Standard Edition of the Complete Psychological Works*, trans. James Strachey, XII (London: Hogarth, 1958),

13–14. All further references to this edition, abbreviated *SE*, will be inserted parenthetically in the text.

18. See Stephen L. Sniderman, "'It Was All Yossarian's Fault': Power and Responsibility in *Catch-22*," in James Nagel, ed., *Critical Essays on Joseph Heller* (Boston: G. K. Hall, 1989), 33–39. Sniderman attempts to make Yossarian *individually* responsible for many of the deaths and debacles of *Catch-22*. I would say rather that Yossarian's guilt is systematically produced.

19. Maurice Sendak, *In the Night Kitchen* (New York: Harper & Row, 1970), n.p.

20. Vladimir Nabokov, *Nabokov's Dozen* (Freeport, N.Y.: Books for Libraries, 1969), 71.

21. Paul de Man, "Allegory," in *Allegories of Reading: Figural Language in Rousseau, Nietzsche, Rilke, and Proust* (New Haven: Yale Univ. Press, 1979), 188–220. All further references to this edition, abbreviated *AR*, will be inserted parenthetically in the text.

22. Andreas Huyssen, in *After the Great Divide: Modernism, Mass Culture, Postmodernism* (Bloomington: Indiana Univ. Press, 1986), makes a firm distinction between modernism and avantgardism; post-structuralism turns out to be late modernism, and true postmodernism is descended from the avant-garde. This formulation insists on ideology at the expense of history. At any rate, Pynchon seems able to embody both the elitist textual and the anti-elitist punk turn of contemporary culture.

The punk turn of postmodernism has its post-structuralist dimension in William Gibson's *Neuromancer*, which is descended from *Gravity's Rainbow* in that (1) it goes further in imagining World War III as the necessary context of terrorized post-World War II writing; (2) it goes further into the punk fascination with pain and perversity; (3) it treats the "elitist" issue of how far fictionality extends into the world as a question of contemporary technology and politics.

Kathy Acker's gynopunk is similarly preoccupied with a moral World War III. ("Through holes of rats cockroaches nuclear waste garbage lids, the actual world is coming through. . . . At the end of time. . . .") She similarly is fascinated by pain and perversity; she similarly sees her fate as a (female) politicized version of *Lost in the Funhouse* or "There is nothing outside the text," witness some of her titles (*Don Quixote, Great Expectations*). She feels herself so trapped within male narratives that masochism is the necessary corollary of violence against men; if this seems a political *turn* in postmodernism, see again Nabokov's "Signs and Symbols." The quotation is from Kathy Acker, *Don Quixote* (New York: Grove, 1986), 194.

23. Here is de Man's version of *Foucauldian* paranoia: "Morality is a version of the same language aporia that gives rise to such concepts as 'man' or 'love' or 'self,' and not the cause or the consequence of such concepts" (*AR*, 206). It would be pretty to draw a chart putting the psychopathological on one side (paranoid self-evacuation), the socio-pathological opposite (terrorist war), and interpolating the most influential postmodernist philosophers, Derrida and Foucault, where the pathology has been sublated.

24. See Gary W. Davis, "*Catch-22* and the Language of Discontinuity," in Nagel, 62–73. Davis sees an ambivalence toward post-structuralist free-play fabulation: is it a mode of freedom (as in the case of Yossarian's generation of a Utopia named Sweden) or a mode of incarceration (a form of military violence against reality)?

25. See again Pinsker, for example, 152.

Chapter 6

1. Vladimir Nabokov, *Bend Sinister* (New York: McGraw-Hill, 1947), vi.

2. Vladimir Nabokov, *Lolita* (New York: Berkley, 1955). All further references to this edition, abbreviated *L*, will be inserted parenthetically in the text.

3. *Bend Sinister*, vi.

4. Thomas Pynchon, *The Crying of Lot 49* (New York: Bantam, 1966). I have been told several times that 1966 is too early to expect much on Vietnam. But it was in February 1965 that Johnson began bombing North Vietnam; the April demonstration in Washington attracted 20,000 people. Between December 1964 and October 1965, SDS membership increased from 2,500 to 10,000. In the spring of 1966, sit-ins began at universities across the country. And one of the key events in shaking American consciences, the self-immolation of Buddhists, is recorded in *Lot 49*. See Allen J. Matusow, *The Unraveling of America: A History of Liberalism in the 1960s* (New York: Harper & Row, 1984), 319–21.

5. Pynchon, 42.

6. John Barth, *Lost in the Funhouse* (New York: Bantam, 1968). All further references to this edition, abbreviated *LF*, will be inserted parenthetically in the text.

7. Donald Barthelme, *Snow White* (New York: Bantam, 1967), 82.

8. Timothy J. Lomperis, *"Reading the Wind": The Literature of the Vietnam War* (Durham: Duke Univ. Press, 1987), 42; the count of Vietnam novels comes from Lomperis.

9. Bernard Malamud, *The Natural* (New York: Pocket Books, 1952); all further references to this edition, abbreviated *TN*, will be inserted parenthetically in the text.

10. John Updike, *The Centaur* (Greenwich, Conn.: Fawcett, 1963); all further references to this edition, abbreviated *TC*, will be inserted parenthetically in the text.

11. See Richard Carlton, "Sport as Art—Some Reflections on Definitional Problems in the Sociology of Sport," in David F. Lancy and B. Allan Tindall, eds., *The Anthropological Study of Play: Problems and Prospects* (Cornwall, N.Y.: Leisure Press, 1976), 25–26.

12. Thorstein Veblen, "Modern Survivals of Prowess," in John T. Talamini and Charles H. Page, eds., *Sport & Society* (Boston: Little, Brown, 1973), 47.

13. G. B. Harrison, ed., *Shakespeare: The Complete Works* (New York: Harcourt, Brace & World), 1968), 734. All further references to this edition, abbreviated *CW*, will be inserted parenthetically in the text.

14. Kendall Blanchard, "Team Sports and Violence: An Anthropological Perspective," in Lancy and Tindall, 95.

15. René Girard, *Violence and the Sacred*, trans. Patrick Gregory (Baltimore: The Johns Hopkins Univ. Press, 1977), 154, 219.

16. I consider the following books under this heading. Mark Harris, *Bang the Drum Slowly* (New York: Dell, 1956). Robert Coover, *The Universal Baseball Association, Inc.: J. Henry Waugh, Prop.* (New York: New American Library, 1968). Philip Roth, *The Great American Novel* (New York: Holt, Rinehart and Winston, 1973); all further references to this edition, abbreviated *GAN*, will be inserted parenthetically in the text.

17. For an analysis of Nixon (in association with Mailer and Herr) as a kind of New Journalist, see Susan Jeffords, *The Remasculinization of America: Gender and the Vietnam War* (Bloomington: Indiana Univ. Press, 1989), 22–35.

18. I consider Robert Coover, *The Origin of the Brunists* (London: Arthur Baker, 1966); Lawrence Shainberg, *One on One* (New York: Holt, Rinehart and Winston, 1970), references to which, abbreviated *OO*, will be inserted parenthetically in the text; Jeremy Larner, *Drive, He Said* (New York: Delacorte, 1964), references to which, abbreviated *DHS*, will be inserted parenthetically in the text; John Updike, *Rabbit, Run* (Greenwich, Conn.: Fawcett, 1960) and *Rabbit Redux* (Greenwich, Conn.: Fawcett, 1971), references to which, abbreviated *Run* and *Redux*, respectively, will be inserted parenthetically in the text.

19. John Updike, *Roger's Version* (New York: Knopf, 1986), 56.

20. See *The Origin of the Brunists* for an example of the invariance of metaphorics within sports: the aging star, wearing a coat, is "Tiger" not "Rabbit," but he intrudes on a kids' game in March, his muscles seem to remember what to do, and his shot touches only net, at which moment he shouts with sexual pride.

21. Under the heading "football novel," I consider Dan Jenkins, *Semi-Tough* (New York: New American Library, 1972); Peter Gent, *North Dallas Forty* (New York: William Morrow, 1973), references to which, abbreviated *NDF*, will be inserted parenthetically in the text; Norman Mailer, *Why Are We in Vietnam?* (New York: Holt, Rinehart and Winston, 1967, preface 1977), references to which, abbreviated *IV*, will be inserted parenthetically in the text; Don DeLillo, *End Zone* (New York: Pocket Books, 1973), references to which, abbreviated *EZ*, will be inserted parenthetically in the text.

22. Lewis Mumford, "Sport and the 'Bitch Goddess,'" in Talamini and Page, 65.

23. Johan Huizinga, *Homo Ludens: A Study of the Play Element in Culture* (Boston: Beacon, 1955), foreword. All further references to this edition, abbreviated *HL*, will be inserted parenthetically in the text.

24. Jacques Derrida, "No Apocalypse, Not Now (full speed ahead, seven missiles, seven missives)," *Diacritics*, 14 (1984). All further references to this volume, abbreviated *D*, will be inserted parenthetically in the text.

25. Clausewitz believes that actual battle is to all other belligerent operations what cash payment is to credit, or gold to money. This causes Raymond Aron, in his book on Clausewitz, to wonder whether cold war might cause "permanent inflation," i.e., escalating threats of complete destruction, or, on the other hand, "permanent warfare." That writing has no backing on the model of gold is a premise of post-structuralism (I am necessarily thinking here of the work of Walter Michaels); by this similar route nuclear war meets "the text." See Raymond Aron, *Clausewitz: Philosopher of War*, trans. Christine Booker and Norman Stone (Englewood Cliffs, N.J.: Prentice-Hall, 1985).

Chapter 7

1. Louisa May Alcott, *Little Women* (New York: Modern Library, 1983). All further references to this edition, abbreviated *LW*, will be inserted parenthetically in the text.

2. Ednah D. Cheney, *Louisa May Alcott*, introd. Ann Douglas (New York: Chelsea House, 1980), 193. All further references to this edition, abbreviated *LMA*, will be inserted parenthetically in the text.

3. Harold Bloom, *A Map of Misreading* (New York: Oxford Univ. Press, 1975), 33. I was sent to this passage by Gilbert and Gubar's *No Man's Land*.

4. See Marilyn Mayer Culpepper, *Trials and Triumphs: Women of the American Civil War* (East Lansing: Michigan State Univ. Press, 1991), 315–28.

5. See Culpepper, 37–39.

6. Race may also be carnivalized. In her fever, Alcott was convinced "that I had married a stout, handsome Spaniard, dressed in black velvet." She could not escape an "awful fear of the Spanish spouse." Because of the black velvet, and because "Spaniard" in *Uncle Tom's Cabin* means "a black man passing," I think this is a fantasy of miscegenation (*LMA*, 146).

7. Margaret Mitchell, *Gone With the Wind* (New York: Avon, 1973). All further references to this edition, abbreviated *GWW*, will be inserted parenthetically in the text.

8. Margaret Walker, *Jubilee* (Boston: Houghton, Mifflin, 1966), 173.

9. What is most remarkable about Alston Anderson's *All God's Children* (Indianapolis: Bobbs-Merrill, 1965) is that it avoids the problem by treating miscegenation (in this case, the intercourse of a black slave and the daughter of his white mistress) as merely another thing that happens. The book is oddest, and oddly appealing, in featuring a black man who simply assumes his rights as an American (even before the Civil War) to vote, to live where he wants, to literacy, to have intercourse with anyone. How miscegenation is handled largely determines the subgenre of Civil War fiction; *All God's Children* is unique in treating it—incest as well—as a simple fact. It therefore has no genre to which I can attach it. Hence this footnote.

10. Luce Irigaray, *The Sex Which Is Not One*, trans. Catherine Porter (Ithaca: Cornell Univ. Press, 1985), 10.

11. Toni Morrison, *Beloved* (New York: Knopf, 1987). All further references to this edition, abbreviated *B*, will be inserted parenthetically in the text.

12. Stephen Greenblatt, *Renaissance Self-Fashioning: From More to Shakespeare* (Chicago: Univ. of Chicago Press, 1980), 1.

13. Greenblatt, 2.

14. Victor Daly, *Not Only War: A Story of Two Great Conflicts* (Boston: Christopher, 1932), epigraph.

15. Chester B. Himes, *If He Hollers Let Him Go* (Garden City, N.Y.: Doubleday, Doran, 1945), 12.

16. Himes, 5.

17. Willa Cather, *One of Ours* (New York: Knopf, 1922). All further references to this edition, abbreviated *OO*, will be inserted parenthetically in the text.

18. Sara Ruddick, *Maternal Thinking: Toward a Politics of Peace* (New York: Ballantine, 1989), 228.

19. Edith Wharton, *A Son at the Front* (New York: Scribner's, 1923). All further references to this edition, abbreviated *SF*, will be inserted parenthetically in the text.

20. See, for the nuances of Wharton's feminism, Sandra M. Gilbert and Susan Gubar, *No Man's Land: The Place of Women Writers in the Twentieth Century*. Vol. 2: *Sexchanges* (New Haven: Yale Univ. Press, 1989), 123–68. See also, for the poverty of alternatives available to American femininity, Frances L. Restuccia, "The Name of the Lily: Edith Wharton's Feminism(s)," *Contemporary Literature*, 38 (1987), 223–38.

21. See Dorothy and Carl J. Schneider, *Into the Breach: American Women Overseas in World War I* (New York: Viking, 1991), 1, 4–6.

22. See Schneider, 40–42.

23. Despite the prominent role given to World War I by the second volume of Gilbert and Gubar's *No Man's Land* in the joint history of modernism and gender politics, the first volume tells a continuing story from the middle of the nineteenth

century that nearly leaves war out. Compare *Sexchanges* to *No Man's Land: The Place of Women Writers in the Twentieth Century*. Vol. 1: *The War of the Words* (New Haven: Yale Univ. Press, 1988). Lynn Hanley, on the evidence of the first volume, congratulated Gilbert and Gubar for narrating a history of sexual antagonism that did not need to be focused on war; after the second volume she may have had doubts. But even *Sexchanges* has reservations about the extent to which the gains of war were permanent: Gilbert and Gubar set out to track the various explanations of the "political and economic revolution by which the Great War at least temporarily dispossessed male citizens of the primacy that had always been their birthright, while permanently granting women access to both the vote and the professions that they had never before possessed" (263). The hedge of "at least" mirrors the reservations of most of the contributors to Margaret Randolph Higgonet, et al., ed., *Behind the Lines: Gender and the Two World Wars* (New Haven: Yale Univ. Press, 1987). Michelle Perrot is typical in describing the advances in civil rights for French women at the turn of the century, but in also noting that "the war halted the momentum" (Higgonet, 54). Steven C. Hause discusses the post-war revival of masculinism and pro-natalism in France, 99–113. Karin Hausen describes the way that war widows had to be ignored in post-war Germany to maintain the illusions of male heroism, 126–40.

24. See Gilbert and Gubar, *Sexchanges*, 127.

25. H. D., *Bid Me to Live* (Redding Ridge, Conn.: Black Swann, 1983). All further references to this edition, abbreviated *BML*, will be inserted parenthetically in the text.

26. See Janice S. Robinson, *H. D.: The Life and Work of an American Poet* (Boston: Houghton Mifflin, 1982), 95, 103, 153.

27. World War I raises the issue of privacy in war uniquely well: though a world war, nevertheless life went on (in Paris or London), and *Americans* in Paris (Wharton) or London (H. D.) could choose to be more or less involved for much of the conflict. But I would like to use this footnote, awkwardly, to make a point about the relation of *black* writing to war; if the black tradition says repeatedly that peace, also, is Hell, the related assertion is that peace, also, is a *public* catastrophe. See especially Ann Petry, *The Street* (Boston: Houghton Mifflin, 1946). Set in 1944, the book refers to World War II perhaps five times, glancingly. The first and last times the word "war" is used, however, it refers to street violence (200, 416). The only example of *white* violence is a suicide, and it occurs in a mansion in the country, so that no one but the family witnesses it, and it is hushed up, revised as an accident. But all black violence, on the street or in apartments, takes place before an intimate, all-seeing, all-hearing, fascinated audience.

28. Carson McCullers, *The Member of the Wedding* in *Collected Stories of Carson McCullers* (Boston: Houghton Mifflin, 1987), 255–392; all further references to this work, abbreviated *MW*, will be inserted parenthetically in the text. Bobbie Ann Mason, *In Country* (New York: Harper & Row, 1985); all further references to this edition, abbreviated *IC*, will be inserted parenthetically in the text.

29. At every point that I see complexity in Mason, Susan Jeffords, in *The Remasculinization of America: Gender and the Vietnam War* (Bloomington: Indiana Univ. Press, 1989), sees simplicity (62–65). Jeffords believes that a preoccupation with the soldier's experience in Vietnam equals a mystification of masculine bonding; I wish to honor the importance of her point without endorsing the tendentious way she supports it, and without endorsing the view that certain objects of knowledge must be avoided per se. First, Jeffords attacks Mason for arranging that

Sam should reinforce—by the trip to the wall—the idea that American community equals masculine bonding. (Samantha becomes Sam to join the country.) But Jeffords cannot allow the reinforcement to be too strong, since a woman would be in on it. Thus (1): "Although women can 'understand' the war, it is only through men or books written about men's experiences, not from experience itself." This ignores the subtlety with which Mason contemplates the issue of precisely how internal Sam can make Vietnam, and how mediated the experience of it is even for soldiers. Jeffords simply does not believe Mason when she contemplates such issues; she seems to want to ignore the book to get at what Mason *really* means. Thus (2): "Sam's 'reunion' with her father is . . . only a superficial one that exists through the inanimate stone of the Vietnam Memorial." Jeffords does not quote any evidence that this is superficial; in fact, she writes that "now dead and reborn as 'Sam Alan Hughes,' Samantha Hughes is no longer excluded from Vietnam." Apparently the reunion simply must be superficial, given Mason's presumed implication in exclusive male thinking, and it must be profound, given Sam's conversion to masculinity. I gather that Jeffords leans toward the weakness hypothesis, though the opposite position has evidence to support it. Thus (3): "women who might have seemed strong at one point, like Sam Hughes, are finally forced into the position of being 'pitiable and contemptible' in order for the narrative to progress." The phrase "pitiable and contemptible" does not come from *In Country*; Sam may be, more or less, "pitiable" (the term would be inexact), but she is never contemptible, except in Jefford's rewriting of the novel.

30. Joan Didion, *Democracy* (New York: Simon and Schuster, 1984).

31. See Jeffords's discussion of the novel, 184–85.

32. Maxine Hong Kingston, *The Woman Warrior: Memoirs of a Girlhood Among Ghosts* (New York: Knopf, 1976). All further references to this edition, abbreviated *WW*, will be inserted parenthetically in the text.

Afterword

1. See Nancy Armstrong and Leonard Tennenhouse, eds., *The Violence of Representation: Literature and the History of Violence* (New York: Routledge, 1989), 9. About the qualification, three comments. (1) "At least" is an ambiguous hedge. (2) If it is only in writing that you cannot tell the difference between in-text and out-text violence, then in-text violence and out-text violence have been distinguished *ipso facto*. (3) "At least not in writing" seems to substitute (a) the indifference of *represented violence* and the violence of representation, for (b) the indifference of *violence in the world* and the violence of representation. But even in the former case, you can make distinctions; on Armstrong and Tennenhouse's own theory, represented violence may exist to make invisible the violence of representation, since the two violent agencies are likely to be politically opposed.

Conclusion: whether you look in texts or out, the violence of representation may be distinguished from all other sorts.

2. I tried to prove this in *The Place of Fiction in the Time of Science: A Disciplinary History of American Writing* (New York: Cambridge Univ. Press, 1990). If literature genially lent its beauty to anaesthetic war, then the aesthetic disparity of literature and war would not be to the credit of literature; but this generosity would be disciplinary suicide. Even in Homer, the disparity is expressed.

Index